D0626810

Due Retui			
Date	Date	Date	Date

German Foreign Policy, 1890-1914, and Colonial Policy to 1914: a Handbook and Annotated Bibliography

by

Andrew R. Carlson

The Scarecrow Press, Inc.

Metuchen, N.J.   1970

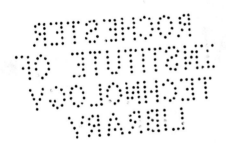

Table of Contents

Introduction

The purpose of this book is to place a convenient guide in the hands of the researcher who is undertaking any type of study in the field of German foreign policy for the period 1890-1914, and German colonial policy for the years prior to 1914. The date 1890 has not been arbitrarily chosen as a starting point: after the dismissal of Bismarck by William II in 1890, it is possible to discern a new course in German foreign policy. The date 1914 requires no explanation.

The handbook is divided into seven sections. The first four sections deal with the type of government in Germany and the formulation of its foreign and colonial policy. Textbooks and special studies do not usually give a very clear picture of how, or by whom, foreign policy was made in Germany. Nor do they go into any detail on how the German Reich and the cities within the Reich were governed. It is necessary to have a good understanding of this subject in order to have a clear idea of foreign policy in the Wilhelmian Reich.

The fifth section is a list in considerable depth of persons who helped to shape the foreign (and colonial) policy of Germany and the sixth, a list, in detail, of events affecting Germany in the years 1888-1914.

The seventh section is an extensive annotated bibliography arranged basically by special subject within German foreign and colonial policy.

Chapter I

German Government, Leadership, and Politics, 1890-1914[1]

The constitution of the German Empire (Reich), adopted in 1871, was designed to unify the country. The federal union was composed of twenty-five states, each enjoying a large measure of local sovereignty, but Prussia was given preeminence. The constitution adopted for the new Reich was the constitution of the North German Confederation as supplemented by agreements with the south German states of Baden, Hesse, Bavaria, and Württemberg. It was submitted to the newly elected Reichstag on March 21, 1871, adopted as submitted on April 14, and promulgated by Bismarck on April 20. Except for a few modifications, brought about more by usage and custom than by official action, this constitution governed the Reich until 1917. Only seven votes were cast against its adoption in the Reichstag in 1871. The constitution was tailored to fit the personal relationship established between Bismarck and William I and while the government was in the hands of these two the constitution showed the least amount of strain. Basic constitutional problems such as federalism versus centralization, the role of Prussia, ministerial responsibility, and extension of democratic rights were all submerged so long as Bismarck remained chancellor.

The head of the state, the German emperor, was also king of Prussia. According to the constitution: "The emperor shall represent the empire in the law of nations, to declare war and conclude peace in the name of the empire, to enter into alliances and other treaties with foreign states, to accredit and receive ambassadors. The consent of the Bundesrat is required for a declaration of war in the name of the empire, with the exception of cases of an attack upon the territory of the empire or its coasts. The emperor sum-

mons, opens, prorogues, and closes the Bundesrat and Reichstag. "
The emperor also served as commander-in-chief of the army and
navy and possessed the right to veto any constitutional amendment.

The emperor appointed the imperial chancellor, who was
usually at the same time minister president of Prussia and foreign
secretary for Prussia.   The chancellor was responsible to no one
other than the emperor.   Even though a chancellor could receive a
vote of censure by the Reichstag, as Bethmann Hollweg did in 1913
following the Zabern Affair (q.v.), only the emperor could dismiss
him.

The legislative power of the empire rested in a parliament
of two parts, the Bundesrat, or upper chamber, and the Reichstag,
or lower.   The Bundesrat, the more powerful of the two, was composed of 58 appointed delegates (61 after 1911 when three votes were
alloted to Alsace-Lorraine).   These delegates, representing the federal states, were appointed by their respective governments.   The
Reichstag consisted of 397 members elected for a term of five
years by universal suffrage of males over twenty-five years of age.
Representation in the Bundesrat and Reichstag was as follows:

States of the Empire	Area (Sq. Mi.)	Population (1910)	No. of votes in Bundesrat	No. of Dep. in Reichstag
Kingdom of Prussia	134,616	40,165,219	17	236
Kingdom of Bavaria	29,292	6,887,291	6	48
Kingdom of Saxony	5,789	4,806,661	4	23
Kingdom of Württemberg	7,534	2,437,574	4	17
Grand-duchy of Baden	5,823	2,142,833	3	14
Grand-duchy of Hesse	2,966	1,282,051	3	9
Grand-duchy of Mecklenburg-Schwerin	5,068	639,958	2	6
Grand-duchy of Saxony (Saxe-Weimar)	1,397	417,149	1	3
Grand-duchy of Mecklenburg-Strelitz	1,131	106,442	1	1
Grand-duchy of Oldenburg	2,482	483,042	1	3
Duchy of Brunswick	1,418	494,339	2	3
Duchy of Saxe-Meiningen	953	278,762	1	2
Duchy of Saxe-Altenburg	511	216,128	1	1
Duchy of Saxe-Coburg-Gotha	764	257,177	1	2
Duchy of Anhalt	888	331,128	1	2

States of the Empire	Area (Sq. Mi.)	Population (1910)	No. of votes in Bundesrat	No. of Dep. in Reichstag
Principality of Schwarz-burg-Sondershausen	333	89,917	1	1
Principality of Schwarz-burg-Rudolstadt	363	100,702	1	1
Principality of Waldeck	433	61,707	1	1
Principality of Reuss (Elder Line)	122	72,769	1	1
Principality of Reuss (Younger Line)	319	152,752	1	1
Principality of Schaumburg-Lippe	131	46,652	1	1
Principality of Lippe	469	150,937	1	1
Free Town of Lübeck	115	116,599	1	1
Free Town of Bremen	99	299,526	1	1
Free Town of Hamburg	160	1,014,664	1	3
Imperial territory of Alsace-Lorraine	5,604	1,874,014	3	15
Total	208,780	64,925,993	61	397

A great difference in population among the various Reichstag election districts contributed to unrepresentativeness in the German parliament. The electoral districts as laid out in 1871 each represented approximately 100,000 inhabitants. However, by the outbreak of the war in 1914 the population had changed so that a Berlin deputy represented an average of 125,000 voters, whereas a rural Prussian deputy represented an average of 24,000. No effort was made to reapportion the seats in the Reichstag to reflect a shift in population from rural areas to the cities. By 1914, the traditionally conservative, rural areas were, on the basis of population, over-represented in the Reichstag.

The chancellor was the chairman of the Bundesrat with no vote. As chairman of the Bundesrat, he represented it in the Reichstag, though other members of the Bundesrat could and did appear in the Reichstag to defend legislation. It was the duty of the chancellor to present to the Bundesrat any legislation which was initiated in the Reichstag. It must be noted that the right of the Reichstag to initiate legislation was very limited, and legislation initiated in the Reichstag could easily be dismissed in the Bundesrat.

The chancellor's position as chairman of the Bundesrat did
not give him great influence in that body. In practice the chancellor nearly always delegated the chairmanship to the secretary of
state for internal affairs. The real power of the Bundesrat resided
in the Präsidium where Prussia, by means of her seventeen votes,
was able to dominate. In the Bundesrat the various states had to
vote as a unit as stated in the constitution. No individual voting
was permitted. Only fourteen votes were needed to prevent any
change in the Imperial Constitution, so Prussia in effect had a built-
in veto with her seventeen votes. The chancellor's power in the
Bundesrat was due to the fact that he was foreign minister of Prussia. The Prussian foreign minister instructed the seventeen Prussian votes in the Bundesrat which were sufficient to block constitutional change.

The chancellor appointed the state secretaries for foreign affairs, home office, admiralty, justice, treasury, and post office and
telegraph, and, after the turn of the century, the state secretary
for the colonial office. He also appointed the following presidents
of imperial bureaus: Railroads, Exchequer, Bank, Debt Commission, and Court-Martial.

The state secretaries were responsible to the emperor but
did not constitute a cabinet in the English, French or American
sense and bore no semblance of ministerial responsibility. The secretaries were individual agents of the chancellor who need not consult each other. They often pursued different policies and were
often openly hostile to each other. The state secretaries also became members of the Prussian ministry, so that they could represent Prussia in the Bundesrat. This enabled them to become chairmen of the different Bundesrat committees where all the important
discussions took place. All committees, except the committee on
foreign affairs, where a Bavarian presided, were chaired by Prussian delegates.

The Reichstag had to vote on the budget, including military
appropriations. Its consent was also required for new taxes. The
Reichstag had little control over the emperor, the chancellor, or
the state secretaries, nor had it much power to initiate legislation.

The Reichstag has often been criticized for these weaknesses, but it was an indispensible link in the legislative process. It reviewed, debated and sometimes amended or defeated proposed legislation. Before a piece of legislation could become law it had to be approved by both the Reichstag and the Bundesrat as well as signed by the emperor and the chancellor. The Reichstag also possessed power of obstruction in regard to the purse.

Prussia, the largest state in the German empire, constituted two-thirds of both the territory and the population of the Empire. Prussia was governed by the constitution granted by the king in 1850. The crown was hereditary in the male line according to primogeniture. In the exercise of the government the king was assisted by a council of ministers appointed by royal decree. The legislative authority was shared by the king with a representative assembly, the Landtag, composed of two chambers, the first being called the Herrenhaus or House of Lords, and the second, the Abgeordnetenhaus, or Chamber of Deputies. The assent of the king and both chambers was required for the making of all laws. Financial projects and estimates had to be submitted first to the Abgeordnetenhaus and had to be accepted or rejected en bloc by the Herrenhaus. The right to propose laws was vested in the executive government and in each of the two chambers.

The Herrenhaus was composed of: (1) the princes of the royal family who were of age, including the scions of formerly sovereign families of Hohenzollern-Hechingen and Hohenzollern-Sigmaringen; (2) the sixteen chiefs of the Prussian houses of mediatized princes, as recognized by the Congress of Vienna; (3) the heads of the territorial nobility formed by the king and numbering some fifty members; (4) a number of life peers chosen by the king from among the rich landowners, great manufacturers, and "national celebrities"; (5) eight titled noblemen elected in the eight older provinces of Prussia by the resident landowners of all degrees; (6) the representatives of the universities, the heads of "chapters," and the Bürgermeisters of towns with more than 50,000 inhabitants; and (7) an unlimited number of members nominated by the king for life or for a more or less restricted period. The Herrenhaus was dominated by the landowning Junkers.

The Abgeordnetenhaus consisted of 433 members: 352 for the old kingdom, to which eighty members were added in 1867 representing the newly-annexed provinces, and one for Lauenburg, added in 1876. The members of this house were elected by any man in Prussia "who has attained his twenty-fifth year and is qualified to vote for the municipal elections of his place of domicile."

For local government, Prussia was divided into provinces, government districts (Regierungsbezirke), urban circles (Stadtkreise), and rural circles (Landkreise). Urban circles consisted of towns of over 25,000 inhabitants; rural circles, of the smaller towns, rural communes (Landgemeinde), and manors (Gutsbezirke). For provinces and rural circles, local authorities of the constituent areas elected deliberative assemblies which appointed executive committees. Each province had a governor (Oberpräsident); each government district had a president, and dealt chiefly with local affairs of state concern. In towns the deliberative authority was the town council (Stadtverordnetenversammlung), elected on the three class system of suffrage. The executive was a magistracy with the Bürgermeister as president. Each rural circle had a Landrat. Local administrative business dealt with, for instance, poor-relief, roads, light, railways, and so forth. In agricultural districts, local government naturally concerned itself with farming matters; in the towns, interest lay in education, sick insurance, valuation, collection of certain taxes, mustering of recruits, and management of gas, water, and electric works. The workings of all the local governments were finally subject to the control of the king of Prussia.

The chancellor of the German empire, as noted above, was nearly always minister president of Prussia. Only twice was this practice not followed, once briefly during Bismarck's tenure and later with Caprivi. The combination of offices was ordinarily a necessity. Without possessing the decisive influence in the Prussian ministry, the chancellor had little basis for power. This influence could be attained only through a constant close contact with the several Prussian ministers. The office of minister president in the hands of another person undermined the position of the chancellor.

This was evident in the crisis which involved Caprivi and Botho von Eulenburg. As minister president the chancellor had to defend the policy of the Prussian minister council in the Prussian Reichstag. The upper house could always be brought into line, by the king's creating new members.

Foreign policy in Wilhelmian Germany was the constitutional responsibility of the emperor but mainly his chancellor directed the conduct of foreign relations. The chancellor, in turn, appointed an imperial secretary for foreign affairs to keep him informed. Foreign policy was often much influenced by the personality, experience, or knowledge of a single advisor in the foreign office, as was true during the service of Baron Friedrich von Holstein (q.v.) in the political department of the foreign office.[2]

German foreign policy was fragmented by this system, which often led to different policy guidance at different levels on the same situation. The emperor, the chancellor, the state secretary for foreign affairs and the senior foreign affairs advisor would each attempt to achieve his own goal in a particular event. Some of the southern states of the Empire retained a ceremonial right to conduct foreign affairs as well.

Other agencies were often more important in the conduct of foreign policy than the foreign office. The general staff had its own foreign policy and operated on its own initiative independent of even the emperor, as in the case of the contingency plans for the invasion of Belgium made, it is believed, without the knowledge of even the emperor. Another example of its initiative is the agreement made by the general staff in 1909 with Austria that changed the defensive character of the Dual Alliance of 1879.

The state secretary for naval affairs played an increasingly important role in foreign affairs after 1897. The powerful influence of Tirpitz on the emperor and his stature as a nationalist in German public opinion were crucial factors in the failure of attempts to relieve Anglo-German tension.[3]

Still another group can be considered influential in the conduct of foreign affairs. Emperor William II, who, a man in his thirties, bungled along no certain course, placed much reliance upon his per-

sonal adjutants, his civil and military cabinets, his traveling com-
panions, and other secret camarillas, and they in turn promoted unusual courses and encouraged him to change policies agreed upon
with his chancellor.   It is impossible to say how much influence
these people, such as Eulenburg (q.v.), had on the emperor, but it
should not be overlooked.   Chancellor Caprivi fell from power in
1894, largely as a result of carefully contrived plots against him,
and the dismissal of Bethmann-Hollweg in 1917 was prepared in
much the same way, as a result of people being able to "get the Kaiser's ear."   In the conduct of foreign affairs, personal machinations
were often more important than official channels.   Intrigue and ruth-
lessness were considered regular means for political survival.
Bribery and stock-exchange speculation were indulged in by all.

   As can be imagined in this set up, vital foreign policy decisions were sometimes taken by totally irresponsible agencies.   Decisions were made by the military that reversed the policy of the
chancellor and the foreign office.   Germany at the outbreak of the
war was still semi-autocratic.   The empire was a state in which
decisions affecting the lives and liberties of its citizens remained in
the hands of persons and agencies not subject to parliamentary or
popular control.

   With the ascension of William II in 1888 and the subsequent
dismissal of Bismarck in 1890, Germany embarked on a new course
in foreign policy (Weltpolitik or "world policy").   A few short se-
lections from some of the emperor's speeches can be used to best
describe Weltpolitik, Germany's aspiration to a "place in the sun":

> Nothing must henceforth be settled in the world without
> the intervention of Germany and the German emperor.
>
> Present events invite us to forget internal discord; let
> us be united in case we should be compelled to intervene
> in the politics of the world.
>
> The ocean proves that upon it and far away beyond it no
> great decision can any longer be taken without Germany.
> I do not agree that our German nation has for thirty
> years conquered and bled under its princes in order to
> be pushed on one side in foreign affairs.   To prevent
> this by suitable and, if necessary, severe measures is

my duty and my highest privilege.

The new concept found its foremost expression in the building of the Baghdad Railroad, the launching of a large navy, and the
quest for colonies. By assuming the role as protector of Turkey,
Germany threatened to thwart the traditional aims of Russia in Asia
Minor and the Balkans. Through their colonial aspirations the Germans posed a threat to the colonial policies of the other great powers. The German navy posed a threat to British domination of the
high seas. When Germany embarked on the new Weltpolitik in 1890,
her international position was strong and her relations with other
powers good. By 1907, all this had changed for the worse and
Germany's "new course" had aroused the gravest suspicions, due in
part to the manner in which it was carried out, including a combination of abrupt forcing plays, attempts at blackmail, and the use
of threats. Coupled with the fragmented German foreign policy, the
irresponsible statements of the emporer, and general blundering, it
spelled disaster for the brilliance and glitter of Wilhelmian Germany.

Notes

1.   For more detailed information on the constitutional development of Germany see: Ernst Rudolf Huber, Deutsche Verfassungs-
geschichte seit 1789 (Stuttgart, 1957 ff.), 4 vols. Huber has supplemented his historical narrative with a multi-volume collection of
documents on German constitutional development. The pertinent
volume for the period under study is Dokumente zur Verfassungs-
geschichte 1851-1918 (Stuttgart, 1964). Another book which is of
interest is Lysbeth W. Muncy, The Junker in the Prussian Administration Under William II (Providence, 1944). Older but still useful
are: William H. Dawson, The German Empire and the Unity Movement (New York, 1919), 2 vols.; Arthur Rosenberg, The Birth of
the German Republic (New York, 1931); Paul Laband, Das Staats-
recht des deutschen Reiches (Tübingen, 1901), 4 vols.; Fritz Konrad Krüger, Government and Politics of the German Empire (New
York, 1915); Burt Estes Howard, The German Empire (New York,
1906) is a detailed study of the structure of imperial Germany;
Herman Gerlach James, Principles of Prussian Administration (New
York, 1913) is a thorough study of the government of Prussia; Konrad Bernhak, "The Local Government of Country Communities in
Prussia, " Annals of the American Academy of Political and Social

Science, III (1893), p. 393-408.

Felix Salomon, ed., Die deutschen Parteiprogramme (Leipzig, 1912), 2 vols., contains the platforms of the German political parties for the years 1845-1912; Oskar Stillich, Die politischen Parteien in Deutschland (Leipzig, 1908, 1911), 2 vols., is a study of pre-war German political parties. More recent studies on the development of German political parties prior to World War I are: Ludwig Bergsträsser, Geschichte der politischen Parteien in Deutschland (Berlin, 1932); Willy Kremer, Der soziale Aufbau der Parteien des deutschen Reichstags 1871-1918 (Emsdetten, 1934); Thomas Nipperdey, Die Organisation der deutschen Parteien vor 1918 (Düsseldorf, 1960); Wolfgang Treue, Deutsche Parteiprogramme 1861-1954 (Göttingen, 1954); Eberhard Pikart, "Die Rolle der Parteien in deutschen Konstitutionellen System vor 1914," Zeitschrift für Politik, IX (1962), p. 12-32; John C. Röhl, Germany Without Bismarck: The Crisis of Government in the Second Reich 1890-1900 (Berkeley, 1967) is an analysis of the shortcomings of the Bismarckian system of government as they became evident in the period after his fall from power.

James J. Sheehan, "Political Leadership in the German Reichstag, 1871-1918," The American Historical Review, LXXIV (Dec., 1968), p. 511-528, is a good introduction to the Reichstag; Louis Rosenbaum, Beruf und Herkunft der Abgeordneten zu den deutschen und preussischen Parlamenten, 1847-1919: ein Beitrag zur Geschichte des deutschen Parlaments (Frankfurt A/M, 1923) describes the composition of the Reichstag; Max Schwarz, MdR: Biographisches Handbuch der Reichstage (Hannover, 1965) is a convenient list of all members of the Reichstag; Walter Gagel, Die Wahlrechts in der Geschichte der deutschen liberalen Parteien, 1848-1918 (Düsseldorf, 1958); and, Richard August, Bismarcks Stellung zum parlamentarischen Wahlrecht (Leipzig, 1917); and Jürgen Bertram, Die Wahlen zum deutschen Reichstag vom Jahre 1912 (Düsseldorf, 1964) all deal with election of Reichstag deputies; Karl Demeter, "Die soziale Schichtung des deutschen Parlaments seit 1848: ein Spiegelbild der Strukturwandlung des Volkes," Viertel jahrschrift für Sozial- und Wirtschaftgeschichte, XXXIX (No. 1, 1952), which points out the decline of the number of bureaucrats in the Reichstag; Hans Jaeger, Unternehmer in der deutschen Politik 1890-1914 (Bonn, 1967), is a statistical analysis of business and politics; Hans Jaeger, "Unternehmer und Politik im wilhelminischen Deutschland," Tradition (January, 1968), points out the relationship between business and politics; John P. Cullity, "The Growth of Government Employment in Germany, 1882-1950," Zeitschrift für d. gesamte Staatswissenschaft (April, 1967).

Hans-Jürgen Puhle, Agrarische Interessenpolitik und Preussischer Konservatismus im wilhelminischen Reich (1893-1914): Ein Beitrag zur Analyse des Nationalismus in Deutschland am Beispiel des Bundes der Landwirte und Deutsch-Konservatien Partei (Hannover, 1967), is an analysis of the relationship between the Agrarian League and the Conservative Party; Hans Rosenberg, "Die Pseudodemokratisierung der Rittergutsbesitzerklasse," in Moderne deutsche Sozialgeschichte, ed. Hans-Ulrich Wehler (Cologne, 1960), p. 287-308, is a discussion of the evolution of the landed elites in the area east of the Elba River; Hartmut Kaelble, Industrielle Interessenpolitik in der wilhelminischen Gesellschaft: Centralverband deutscher Industriellen 1895-1914 (Berlin, 1967), points out the existence of economic elites in many of the state parliaments; Erich Matthian and Eberhard Pikart, Die Reichstagsfraktion der deutschen Sozialdemokratie 1898 bis 1918 (Düsseldorf, 1966), 2 vols., traces the policy followed by the Social Democratic Party. Eugene N. and Pauline R. Anderson, Political Institutions and Social Change in Continental Europe in the Nineteenth Century (Berkeley, 1967), is a valuable starting point in the study of the relationship between German government and German society in the nineteenth century.

2.   Holstein's influence in foreign affairs did not terminate with his leaving the foreign office on April 19, 1906. (After he tried to use the Morocco Crisis to drive a wedge in the recently formed Anglo-French entente; the resulting threat of war had frightened both the Kaiser and Bülow.) After Holstein's fall, Bülow and Kiderlen-Wächter were his constant visitors, also corresponding with him, seeking his advice, until his death on May 9, 1909.

3.   Further bolstering the naval secretary was the alliance of "rye and steel," which backed the increases in the navy after 1897: the great land-owners whose interests were best served by a high tariff supported the program of the industrialists who promoted the building of a large navy. The industrialists, in turn, supported the large land-owners' desire for a high tariff on grain.

Chapter II

Municipal Government[1]

The Prussian municipal code of 1853 applied to those areas of local government which are known as Städte. The distinction between a city (Stadt) and a rural area or township (Gemeinde) was not based on differences in population but on a legal principle which had its roots in the previous century. Originally, no doubt, the term Stadt was restricted to those settlements which had considerable populations, while the term Landgemeinde was applied to sparsely settled areas; but this distinction has been so far lost that in the 1890's one finds Städte with only a few hundred inhabitants and Gemeinden which have grown to populous centers of from ten to fifty thousand. The Gemeinde, no matter its population, was governed differently from the Stadt and had its own plan of administration.

The Prussian municipal code of 1853 was extended to all inhabited places which had at any time obtained the right to rank as Städte, whatever current importance or population. A provision was also made that other places might, by royal decree, be ranked as Städte, though no fixed rule was made to regularize this action. In the years especially after 1870, the country's remarkable industrial development resulted in the rapid growth of Städte. At the outbreak of the war in 1914, there were about twelve hundred Städte, cities, in Prussia. They ranged from little hamlets of a few hundred population to the metropolis, Berlin, with more than two million. All were governed in substantially the same way.

The rapid growth of the Prussian population not only added greatly to the number of Städte, but also necessitated many changes in the boundaries of existing municipalities. For such a change the

20

code made special provision. When a city desired to change its
boundaries, it made application to the higher authorities, usually to
those of the province, who might make an order subject to the approval of the Prussian ministry of the interior. In some cases the
approval of the king was also required.

The Prussian city was a corporation, with all the rights and
privileges ordinarily appertaining thereto. It had the right to sue
and be sued, to hold property and to make contracts. In addition it
had a considerable range of powers not derived from any statutory
enactment, for the German practice had not been to specify word
for word the rights or interests which a municipal corporation may
exercise. The code of 1853 merely empowered the local authorities
to do whatever they might deem necessary or advisable in the interests of the city. In the case of strictly local affairs, they were to
do this on their own initiative and responsibility, but in the case of
affairs not wholly local their action was to be subjected to the approval of the higher authorities. On the face of it, this would appear to have given the cities a large measure of home rule. However, the Prussian municipal code of 1853 did not establish anything
approaching municipal home rule, as Americans understand the term.
For it was the higher authorities, not the city councils, who really
decided (within the broad terms of the code) whether a matter was
strictly local in character or whether it was of more than city-wide
importance. In principle the division of jurisdiction was reasonable
enough, but in its actual operations it left a good deal to be desired.
This practice of giving the city a general grant of powers and then
curtailing its jurisdiction by the requirement of approval from some
higher source has been one of the most salient characteristics of
Prussian policy.

The power of the police of the cities may be used as an illustration. The wording of the municipal code would imply that central supervision was intended to be exercised over municipal police
in the ordinary sense; that is, through the reports of city officials
in reporting their activities in preserving law and order. But the
royal government of Prussia during the interval between 1853 and
1918 did not construe the provision in this way. On the contrary,

it interpreted "supervision of municipal police" as including active
central control over all things related to the public security, health,
morals, and even the public convenience. Authorities higher than
the city level intervened in matters of housing, sanitation, market
regulations, billboards; in some instances they dictated the architecture of municipal buildings, the adornment of streets, and the loca-
tion of public monuments.

Justification for intervention was offered, e.g.: bad housing
is notoriously a cause of crime and to that extent housing is a police
matter; hence housing regulations of city authorities fall within the
central government's police supervision. During the years preceding
the war, therefore, municipal home rule in Prussia became consid-
erably restricted.

Supervisory control over all local governments during these
years was exercised by the national government through the Prussian ministry of the interior. The head of this ministry was appointed by the king of Prussia and was not removable by the Prussian parliament.

As in other departments of the Prussian royal government,
the ministry of the interior maintained a permanent staff of expert
officials who assisted the minister. The amount of work which this
office was called upon to perform was very considerable, despite
the fact that it dealt directly with the towns and cities in very few
cases; it exercised its control, for the most part, through the authorities of the circle, district, and province.

In this connection it should be explained that Prussia before
1914 was divided into twelve provinces. At the head of each was a
provincial president appointed by the Prussian king. This official
corresponded in many respects to the French prefect, for he was
not only the administrative head of his division but the local agent
of the central government as well. In his work of supervising local
government he was assisted by a provincial committee, which was
appointed, usually from among its own members, by a provincial
assembly. This body corresponded roughly to the general council of
a French department. These twelve province presidents executed
ministerial instructions within their jurisdictions and exercised a

general supervision over the district authorities.

Each province, again, was divided into districts and each of these districts had its president and its district board, appointed by the king. The board was composed of permanent officials. It was with these district authorities that the Prussian city officials came mainly into contact. When the exercise of any municipal function required the approval of the higher authorities, it was usually the district board that had to be approached. It was this body, for example, that decided conflicts between the two branches of the city council.

The districts, finally, were divided into circles, but only the smallest cities had anything to do with the authorities of these sections, for any city of more than 25,000 population could be formed by ministerial decree into a circle by itself. That was done in the case of nearly one hundred larger Prussian cities, and in such cases the functions ordinarily performed by the authorities of the circle were taken over by a committee of the municipal administrative board. Berlin did not deal with the central government through the authorities of either circle or district; its administration was supervised, on behalf of the national government, by the president of the province of Brandenburg.

Perhaps the most striking feature of the old municipal system (in Prussia, but not in the other German states) was the three-class system of voting. This electorate, according to the words of the code, was composed of all male German citizens twenty-five years of age or over who had during a period of one year fulfilled these three conditions: (1) resided continuously within the city limits; (2) paid the regular municipal taxes; and (3) owned a dwelling house within the municipality, or pursued some substantial trade or vocation which yielded an income, or had been specially assessed for taxes. Furthermore, non-residents were allowed to vote if they had, within the year, paid a certain sum in direct local taxes; and corporations, if they satisfied the same requirement, were enrolled in the ranks of the municipal electorate and permitted to vote through their officers. There were some disqualifications, chiefly of individuals who were in receipt of aid from the public poor-relief bureaus.

On the face of things, the Prussian cities had manhood suffrage before the war, for virtually every male citizen over twenty-
four years of age had a vote. But every voter did not have an
equal vote. On the contrary the municipal code provided that the whole
body of voters should be divided into three classes, roughly in accordance with the amount of taxes paid by them, and that each class
should elect one third of tho city council. Thus the heaviest taxpayers formed class I, the moderate taxpayers formed class II, and
the rest of the voters came in class III. The first class rarely included more than five percent of the whole electorate and more than
three-fourths of the voters found themselves in the third class. In
view of the fact that each class elected one-third of the councillors,
it was inevitable that the well-to-do voters, under this system,
would always control a majority in council--which is what happened.
Opulence became the measure of influence.

Sometimes this three-class system of voting had ludicrous
results. In Essen, for example, there were only three voters in
the first class, four hundred in the second, and more than 20,000
in the third. Nevertheless the 403 voters out of 21,047 elected two-
thirds of the councillors. A single voter in the first class counted
as the equivalent of nearly 7,000 voters in the third. Even the
chancellor of the empire, Prince Bülow, found himself in the third
class while brewers and sausage-makers climbed into the first. In
Berlin, before the war, there were about two thousand voters of the
first class, while the third class contained more than half a million.[2]

This curious plan, once branded as "the most miserable and
absurd election law ever formulated in any country," remained in
operation through 1918. It was defended on the ground that it provided a safeguard against wastefulness and extravagance in municipal
government. The city is a business concern--so the defenders of
the three-class system argued--a builder of streets and public works,
a purveyor of water and gas, an employer of labor. Its organization ought, therefore, to approximate that of a business corporation,
and in a business corporation all stockholders do not have equal voting power. The big stockholders have control. So, in choosing a

city council which is merely the municipal board of directors, the heavy taxpayers ought to have more weight than those who pay only small sums into the public treasury. It is not fair that the few should provide most of the city's income and the many control the spending of it. That, in general, was the line of argument commonly used.

In effect it disfranchised about three-fourths of the voters, for although they could choose one-third of the city councillors they could never, under any circumstances, hope to control a majority. Knowing this, a considerable proportion of them remained away from the polls. Hence the majority of the councillors, being chosen by men of wealth, became faithful mirrors of the business man's attitude toward public questions. They were keen for efficiency, economy, and business methods. They believed in administration by experts, in a close scrutiny of the budget, in everything that would cut the costs. On the other hand, the humanitarian aspects of municipal administration did not interest them much. Clean streets in the business district seemed to be of more importance than playgrounds down among the tenements. Hence the foreign visitor who praised the "thrifty municipal housekeeping" of the Prussian city usually overlooked the lack of playgrounds for the children of the poor, the meagerness of facilities for public recreation, and the high infant death rate in the crowded sections.

Naturally the three-class system was not popular with the masses of the people, and the Social Democrats always opposed it strongly. But their protests availed nothing in the years preceding the war.[3] They objected also to the system of open voting at city elections--for no printed ballots were used in Prussian municipal elections before the war. The different classes voted at separate polling places and on different days. There were no formal nominations. Every voter, when he came to the poll, was asked to state the name of his candidate. This the law required him to do "orally and in a loud voice" (mündlich und laut). Everybody in the room could hear him. There was no secrecy about it. Hence the door was thrown wide open to intimidation and wrongful pressure of all sorts.[4]

Another objectionable feature of the old municipal system was the requirement that one-half the councillors chosen to represent each of the three classes should be owners of real estate. If, after an election, it was found that this requirement had not been satisfied, the non-propertied councillors who had obtained the smallest number of votes were unseated and another election was held to fill the vacancies. This requirement did not mean much to the two upper classes, but in the case of the third class it meant a great deal, for the third class contained a large number of voters who could have been elected and who would have made good councillors but for their lack of property. In Berlin, for example, less than five percent of the third-class voters were owners of real estate and in the other large cities the proportion was not much larger. To evade the requirement, it became the practice of candidates to acquire small undivided interests in some one piece of property. A dozen of them would combine in purchasing a vacant lot or small house, each paying a few marks for his share and leaving it heavily mortgaged. But the administrative courts soon put an end to this evasion by ruling that sole ownership of some substantial piece of property was required by the spirit of the law. Much dissatisfaction was caused by this provision, especially among members of the great industrial classes.

The organs of city government in Prussia before the war were the council (Stadtverordnetenversammlung), the administrative board (Magistrat), and the burgomaster (Bürgermeister). In the largest cities there were two Bürgermeisters, one assisting the other. The councillors were chosen by the voters under the system just described; the members of the administrative board were chosen by the council. There were two types of members, chosen either for twelve years or for six. In either case they were usually reappointed when their terms expired. Either a paid or an unpaid magistrate was the head of each municipal department, e.g. law, finance, public works, sanitation, and so on. For each department, moreover, there was a joint commission made up of a paid magistrate as chairman, one or more unpaid magistrates, several members of the council, and some citizens appointed by the Bürgermeister. These joint commissions, under the guidance of their respective chairmen, considered questions of departmental policy but had no final powers. The Bürgermeister was chosen by the city council for a term of at least twelve years and sometimes for life. The choice was subject to the approval of the higher authorities. In the smaller cities this confirmation was given by the authorities of the district; in the larger cities, by the king of Prussia. Usually the approval was given as a matter of course, but sometimes it was refused. On one occasion the German emperor, as king of Prussia, delayed the confirmation of a Bürgermeister who had been chosen by the city council of Berlin. After a year's delay, during which the post remained vacant, the council made another choice, which was duly confirmed. This right to refuse confirmation was always a thorn in the flesh of the Social Democrats, for it meant that no avowed member of that party could ever hold the chief executive post in any Prussian city. In a few instances the city councils chose men of this party allegiance but in no case was confirmation granted.

In the rise and fall of the old Prussian municipal system the student of government may find some instructive lessons. A municipal system may be outwardly strong while inwardly weak. It may be highly efficient, yet not win the confidence of the people. Rapid growth and material prosperity may mask, for a time, serious defects in a political system.

The growth of German cities during the era from 1890 to the outbreak of the World War was extraordinarily rapid. We are accustomed to think of the United States as a land of marvellous urban expansion during these years, but city for city the Germans made equal or greater gains. The following table shows in round numbers the increase in population of some typical German and American cities during the period 1890-1910:

City	1890	1910
Hamburg	569,000	953,000
Boston	448,000	671,000
Munich	349,000	595,000

City	1890	1910
Baltimore	434,000	558,000
Leipzig..........................	335,000	586,000
Buffalo	255,000	424,000
Dresden..........................	276,000	547,000
New Orleans	242,000	339,000
Hanover	163,000	302,000
Milwaukee	204,000	374,000
Cologne	281,000	511,000
Cincinnati	296,000	364,000
Breslau	335,000	511,000
Cleveland........................	261,000	561,000
Frankfurt........................	180,000	414,000
Pittsburgh.......................	238,000	534,000

The industrial prosperity of the whole German nation and its great commercial development reflected in the factory and seaport cities, which grew at an amazing rate. When a nation or a city is growing both great and rich its government will claim, and will receive, a good deal of the credit. So the expansion and prosperity of the cities helped to make both Germans and outsiders oblivious to the fundamental weaknesses of the municipal system. If one were bold enough to question the basic soundness of this system, the officials always had a ready reply: "Look at our growth in population and wealth. Look at our streets, our public buildings, our factories and stores, our residential sections, our parks, our schools and technical institutes, our water and sewerage systems, our street railways, our municipal abattoirs, and compare them with those of other countries."

The visitor looked--and usually agreed. The streets were models of cleanliness (especially those usually patronized by tourists); the police were intelligent and courteous; the whole atmosphere was one of business-like and beneficent paternalism. Sometimes an American journalist, after he got back to the United States, would write a magazine article, or even a book, extolling the virtues of German city government and contrasting it with the sordid conditions which existed in the less enlightened municipalities of the United States. One illustration will suffice:

"Important as are the honesty and the efficiency of the German city, it is the bigness of vision, boldness of execution, and far-sighted outlook on the future that are most amazing. Germany is building her cities as Bismarck perfected the army before Sadowa and Sedan; as the empire is building its warships and merchantmen; as she develops her waterways and educational systems. The engineer and the architect, the artist and the expert in hygiene, are alike called upon to contribute to the city's making. The German cities are thinking of tomorrow as well as of today, of the generations to follow as well as the generation that is now upon the stage. Germany almost alone among the civilized nations sees the city as the permanent center of the civilization of the future, and Germany almost alone is building her cities to make them contribute to the happiness, health, and well being of the people. This seems to be the primary consideration with officials and citizens. It is this that distinguishes the cities of this country from the other cities of the world.

"The business men who rule them seem to think in social rather than in individual terms. They have a sense of team-play, of cooperative effort, of being willing to sacrifice their immediate individual interests to the welfare of the community. Cities cooperate with the state, they spend generously for education, they make provision for hospitals, for recreation, for housing the people. The city partakes of the spirit of the empire. It inspires a kind of loyalty I have never seen in any other country of the world. Germany is treating the new behemoth of civilization, the modern industrial city, as a creature to be controlled and made to serve rather than to impair or destroy humanity. She is doing this through city planning, the new art of city building, through education, through sanitation and hygiene, by uniting the expert with the administrator, and by making science the handmaiden of politics. "[5]

There can be no question about the high degree of administrative efficiency attained by Prussian cities during the pre-war era. Their affairs were conducted with scrupulous honesty, and strictly in accordance with the best business methods without waste of the public money. Nowhere in the world did the people get better value

in actual service for the taxes levied upon them. Americans often
marvelled that these cities could keep their streets so well paved
and so clean and yet spend so little money in doing it. They com-
mented on the absence of scandals in Prussian city administration
and on the fact that the German vocabulary contained no equivalent
for "graft"--because the thing itself was virtually unknown. When
American students of municipal government went to Berlin they were
shown over the sewer farms and through the civic abattoirs (from
both of which the city was said to be making a profit) and were
greatly impressed by the efficiency with which everything seemed to
be done. They thought of the Tweed rings and gas rings and trac-
tion rings, the boodle aldermen and the forty thieves, the Ruefs and
Crokers and Coxes, the heelers and the hinky-dinks who dominated
the affairs of their own large cities--and told the German that he
had reason to be thankful. Here were cities with the sort of government which the American municipal reformer was hoping that his
own country might someday be able to obtain!

     But efficiency is not the only desideratum in city govern-
ment. It is not enough that government shall be "for the people."
It must be of the people and by the people as well. It matters not
how honest a government may be, or how economical its operations,
or how expert its personnel, or how high-minded its appointive officers; these will not ensure the permanence of a municipal system if
it is carried on without responsiveness to the desires of the people
as a whole. It is human nature that people will even prefer misgovernment of their own manufacture to efficient government imposed
upon them; a trait perhaps unfortunate, but one that cannot safely be
disregarded.

                              Notes

1.   For a more extensive treatment of this subject see William
Bennett Munro, The Government of European Cities (New York,
1909). The revised edition of this work published in 1927 contains
an excellent bibliography of older but still useful works on the subject of German municipal government. In the present section I have,

to a great extent, followed Munro's presentation. Munro's book, however, contains much more material than was needed for the present essay.

2.   In 1908, in all of Prussia, there were 293,000 voters in the first class, 1,065,240 in the second, and 6,324,079 in the third. The first class represented 4% of the male population over-25, the second, 14%, and the third, 82%. In the city of Cologne, the first category of electors numbered 370, the second, 2,584, while the third group had 22,324. In Saarbrücken a single baron formed the first class by himself and announced complacently that he did not suffer from his isolation. Also, in one of the Berlin districts, Herr Heffte, a sausage manufacturer, found himself alone in the first class.

3.   By 1914 the Social Democrats were the largest single party in the Reichstag. Of their power to alter the course of events in Germany, Jean Jaurès, the French socialist, said: "You were granted universal suffrage from above, and your parliament is but a half-parliament.... Yours will be the only country in which the Socialists would not be masters even if they were to obtain the majority in the parliament..."

4.   A large number of voters, preferring to forego their privilege, stayed home rather than let officials know for whom they were casting their votes. In 1903, over twenty-three percent of the eligible voters voted in Prussia for the representation to the lower chamber of the Landtag, while seventy-five percent voted for Reichstag deputies in a secret ballot election.

5.   Frederic C. Howe, European Cities at Work (New York, 1913), p. 4, 7.

Chapter III

The German Foreign Ministry[1]

During the period 1867-1920 the foreign office was succes-
sively that of Prussia, of the North German Federation, and of Germany, and it continued until 1919 to be the foreign office of Prussia as well.

The foreign ministry of Prussia (das preussische Ministerium
der auswärtigen Angelegenheiten) immediately prior to 1867 consisted
of two departments (Abteilungen): a political department (I) and a
legal-commercial department (II). At its head was the Prussian
foreign minister, under him was an under state secretary, who also
had direct responsibility for the political department. The legal-
commercial department was under the immediate supervision of a
director.

The creation of the North German Federation in 1867 brought
no immediate change, the external representation of the Federation
being at first effected through the king of Prussia. In 1870, however, the foreign office of the North German Federation (das auswärtige Amt des norddeutschen Bundes) was set up and placed under
the direct control of the federal chancellor and the title of the under
state secretary was changed to state secretary.

The German foreign ministry (das auswärtige Amt des deutschen Reiches) came into being on April 16, 1871, when the constitution of the German empire came into force. In fact both it and
its immediate forerunner were merely extensions of the Prussian
foreign ministry, and there was no organic division between the two.
Consequently the foreign office was responsible for the relations between Germany and foreign countries as well as for those between
Prussia and the other German states and the Holy See, and in prac-

tice, for the relations between the central government and the federal states. A single central bureau dealt with dispatches to and from Paris or Stuttgart and diplomats could be transferred between an imperial German post like Washington and a royal Prussian post like Munich.

German foreign policy was directed by the imperial chancellor, who was appointed by the emperor and responsible only to him. Until 1918, the chancellor was nearly always at the same time Prussian foreign minister. The state secretary, a civil servant responsible to the chancellor, was head of the foreign office. The organization was at the outset the same as that of the earlier Prussian foreign ministry; it also was divided into a political department (department I, later IA, and often by common usage just A), and a legal-commercial department (department II) which dealt also with personnel, budget, cipher and communications, and protocol matters. Subsequently these departments were further subdivided as follows:

1879:   the personnel section (personnel, budget, cipher and communications, and protocol), except for the personnel of the consular service, was separated from department II and established as an independent personnel department (IB);

1885:   department II was divided into department II (commercial policy, including the consular service) and department III (legal);

1890:   colonial matters were separated from the work of the political department and an independent colonial department (K.A.) was set up;

1895:   the personnel section for the diplomatic service was separated from the personnel department and placed under the political department as a special section (Ap.);

1903:   the consular service was separated from department II and placed under the personnel department (with the designation IC);

1907:   the colonial department was separated from the foreign ministry and established as an independent ministry (Reichskolonialamt);

1915:   the news and information section was separated from the po-

litical department and established as an independent department (AN, later P).

The chancellor, being directly responsible for foreign policy,
inevitably maintained a close supervision over the work of the foreign office and all important instructions went out in his name. Under him the state secretary, besides having supervision over the
daily work of the foreign office, was directly responsible for the
work of the political department, which had no departmental head of
its own. In 1881 an office of under state secretary was established
with the intention of providing a regular deputy for the state secretary and of releasing him from his non-political work. In practice,
however, it was found that the decision of the state secretary was
still needed for important non-political matters and that the under
state secretary tended to become almost totally involved in the work
of the political department. The other, non-political, departments
were under the immediate supervision of a "Dirigent" (director),
each of whom, with the exception of the head of the colonial department, was responsible to the state secretary. The colonial department came under the state secretary only in as far as relations to
foreign states and general policy were concerned; for the administration of the colonies the department was responsible directly to the
chancellor. Each department was staffed by a number of "vortragende Räte" (counsellors) and "Hilfsarbeiter" (assistants). These
terms are designations of appointments and not titles or ranks.

In 1910 the post of Dirigent was established for the political
department. In 1916 a second under state secretary post was created, nominally for economic affairs. In February, 1919, the office
of state secretary was changed to that of foreign minister (Reichs-
minister des Auswärtigen). In April of the same year the foreign
office officially ceased to be also the foreign office of Prussia, although it continued for some time to act as the agent of the central
government in relations with the states, especially Bavaria. Finally,
towards the end of 1919 there began a major reorganization of the
foreign office. The political and commercial departments in existence until then were merged and subdivided into a number of region-

al departments (Länderabteilungen) and other changes were also
made. This reorganization was completed in March, 1920.

From a small ministry composed, in 1871, of two departments and staffed by a state secretary, a director, ten counsellors
and four assistants, the foreign office had grown by 1918 to comprise five departments--political, personnel, commercial, legal and
press--with a state secretary, two under state secretaries, four directors, five Dirigente, and numerous other senior personnel, all
of whom took part in the various armistice and peace negotiations
of 1918 and 1919.

The political department of the foreign office was in charge
of general problems of foreign policy, of colonial affairs (until 1890),
and of press affairs (until 1915), and exercised some control over
the work of the other departments, which were obliged to submit all
matters of political implication to the political department for coun-
ter-signature. Moreover the political department often took over
such questions as railway construction and foreign loans, which
would normally have been handled by other departments, when the
political considerations involved preponderated. Within the political
department work among the vortragende Räte was normally divided
on a regional basis, but the system was fairly flexible.

The total volume of work handled by the foreign ministry increased gradually between 1871 and 1914 and so did the amount of
work handled by the political department. Partly due to the increase
in the volume of business handled by the department and partly owing
to the change in the type of control exercised by the chancellor over
the foreign office, the functions of the vortragende Räte underwent a
considerable change during the period of the First World War. In-
coming documents were normally first submitted to the responsible
vortragender Rat and were then personally submitted by him to the
state secretary of the chancellor. Under Bismarck, the vortragender
Rat was then normally told how to reply. Subsequently however it
was the vortragender Rat, as the expert on a particular subject, who
drafted instructions and replies before these were submitted to the
state secretary or chancellor for approval and signature. In practice this meant that the relationship between the vortragende Räte

and their superiors, and the amount of power and influence wielded
by them, tended to depend on personal characteristics.

Something should be said of the method used to recruit personnel for the foreign office.   Rules for entry into the consular and
diplomatic service were laid down in the 1867 law on federal consulates which stated that apart from the normal civil service examinations there should be another method of entry designed "to attract
good men from other professions into the consular service." A
special examination could be taken by men who had not qualified in
the usual way.   An official handbook published in 1896 pointed out
that in the consular service "practical experience is more important
than in any other branch of the Reich service," since its function
was "to encourage trade, commerce and shipping abroad." It ad-
vised aspirants to learn Turkish, Arabic, and other oriental languages, in addition to the European languages which were an entrance requirement.   In the final examination jurisprudence carried
little weight and was not required for entry into the diplomatic corps.
This was the opposite of most civil service examinations in Germany where a knowledge of jurisprudence was essential.   Candidates
had to demonstrate their knowledge of history "with special reference to Germany" and of the geography of "the main countries and
peoples of the earth, their forms of government, population, produce
trade, industry, financial position and colonies."   A good grounding
in economics, with a knowledge of the development of the discipline
since Adam Smith, was also essential.[2]   A memorandum of 1908 on
recruitment to the foreign office said that "a sound education" was
necessary; those who did not have a degree would be required to
spend five years on probation instead of the usual four, and to at-
tend lectures in history, economics, international law, finance, and
commerce.   In the final examination there were papers in English
and French and some of the essays written in the examination room
had to be written in these two languages.   The oral examination in
history and geography was likewise conducted in French and English.
The main requirement, however, was "the possession of qualities
essential in diplomacy," and the chancellor was entirely free to decide what these qualities were, and who did or did not possess

them. [3]

Noble birth was almost essential for service in the embassies: at one point the only ambassadors of bourgeois origin were
those in Peru, Venezuela, Colombia, and Siam. In 1914, the German foreign service consisted of eight princes, twenty-nine counts,
twenty barons, fifty-four untitled nobles and only eleven commoners.[4]
Alexander von Hohenlohe justified the predominance of the aristoc-
racy in the diplomatic corps on the grounds that the noblemen were
acquainted with the outside world to a greater degree than were the
commoners. It was certainly true that young aristocrats who aspired to serve in the diplomatic corps were often more widely
traveled than their middle-class rivals. Most of them, furthermore,
had foreign wives: in 1891 only one of Germany's ambassadors--
Prince Reuss in Vienna--was married to a German, and the proportion among the younger diplomats was similar.[5]

Those commoners who entered the service were mainly the
sons of great industrialists or rich traders, many of whom had in
fact acquired a title through their wealth and influence. Membership in one of the "feudal" student societies--especially the Borussen
in Bonn, the Saxo-Borussen in Heidelberg, and the Sachsen in Göt-
tingen--was as important a precondition of entry in the diplomatic
service as having a commission in one of the Guards regiments.
The consular service, on the other hand, was wholly middle class,
though even here it was useful to have gone to the right university,
joined the right student society, and to have a sizable income.[6]

At least in theory, according to the 1869 law, selection of
personnel for the foreign office should not be influenced by the candidate's religion. However, Catholics and Jews (as well as Social
Democrats) were almost wholly excluded from holding high office in
the German Reich or in the Prussian bureaucracy. Almost one-
third of Germany's population was Catholic. In 1900 there were
four directors, twenty-five vortragende Räte and twenty Hilfsarbeiter
in the foreign office; of these, two vortragende Räte and three Hilfsarbeiter were members of the Roman Catholic Church. The situation was even worse for the Jews who were the best educated class
in Germany (for every 100,000 males of each denomination in Prus-

sia, 33 Catholics, 58 Protestants, and 516 Jews became university students).[7] It was difficult for Jews or Christians of Jewish origin to enter the higher civil service. Social Democrats and even the sons of known Social Democrats were excluded from the bureaucracy automatically. In view of the long training period and the expensive education necessary for entry into the higher civil service, there was in any case little opportunity for factory workers and others without private means to become contenders for a place. Most of the internal memoranda on entrance to the civil service stressed that "throughout the four year probationary period there must be neither payment of any kind (not even expenses) nor a promise of eventual appointment." To embark on a public career without adequate financial support was foolhardy. A civil servant's salary was not commensurate with his social obligations. A vortragender Rat generally earned under 10,000 marks, a director 15,000 and a state secretary 24,000. The chancellor himself received only 54,000 marks, which was less than half the amount earned by a top ambassador. Capable men nevertheless were attracted to a career in the foreign office, often for reasons of prestige and social advancement of family. After the army officer, no one was more respected in Wilhelmian Germany than the higher civil servant. To the educated middle class a career in the bureaucracy could bring rank, decorations, perhaps enoblement, and, in exceptional cases, political power.

Notes

1.   For a more detailed account of the historical development of the German Foreign Office see Heinz Sasse, "Die Entstehung der Bezeichnung Auswärtiges Amts," Nachrichtenblatt Vereinigung Deutscher Auslandsbeamten, Hefte 10 (1956). The introduction by F. G. Stambrook to A Catalogue of Files and Microfilms of the German Foreign Ministry Archives, 1867-1920 (Washington, 1959), contains a great deal of useful information on the organization of the German foreign office. Stambrook presents a detailed analysis of the filing methods used in the foreign office. The present account of the historical development and organization of the German Foreign Office is based, in part, on a section of Stambrook's splended introduction.

2.   B. W. von König, Handbuch des Deutschen Konsularwesens
(Berlin, 1896), p. 45 ff.

3.   J. C. G. Röhl, "Higher Civil Servants in Germany, 1890-
1900, " Journal of Contemporary History, III (1967), p. 106.

4.   Rudolf Morsey, Die Oberste Reichverwaltung unter Bismarck
1867-1890 (Münster, 1957), p. 246.

5.   J. C. G. Röhl, "Higher Civil Servants in Germany, 1890-
1900, " p. 106-107.

6.   Ibid.

7.   P. G. J. Pulzer, The Rise of Political Anti-Semitism in
Germany and Austria (London, 1964), p. 12.

Chapter IV

German Colonial Policy[1]

The study of Germany as a colonial power can be undertaken from a number of different points of view. The acquisition of overseas possessions by the Reich was an important aspect of Bismarck's work and no examination of his policy would be complete without considering his achievements in the field of colonial expansion. The establishment of German authority in the interior of the overseas territories, the setting up of organs of administration, the "colonial scandals," and the "new era" of colonial policy in which Dr. Dernburg played a leading role are all significant aspects of German history in the reign of William II. The desire of the Pan-Germans to expand their overseas empire at the expense of other countries (such as Portugal) and the economic penetration of the Ottoman Empire (the Berlin-Baghdad railway project) contributed to the distrust of Germany which was a factor in the arms race in the early twentieth century. The campaigns in the First World War which led to the conquest of German colonies were no mere "sideshows," for they contributed significantly to the defeat of the Reich.

The overseas possessions were also significant in Germany's domestic affairs. On the one hand the colonies were a unifying factor in the new Reich since they were, like Alsace and Lorraine, truly "national" territories which were a part of all the empire and did not belong to any one of the federal states into which Germany was divided. On the other hand the colonies were a cause of internal strife in Germany. The political parties were sharply divided on questions concerning colonial policy and the future of the overseas possessions was a vital issue in the hotly contested Reichstag general election of 1907.

Again, it is possible to consider the German colonial empire
from an African or Pacific, rather than from a European, point of
view. An examination of such aspects of Germany's work in her
colonies as exploration, missionary activities, land policy, planta-
tions, railways, and native welfare shows the profound effect of the
German impact upon Africa, Shantung, and the Pacific islands.

No European country has held overseas possessions for so
short a period as Germany. The colonial empire began in 1884
when Bismarck placed under imperial protection the establishments
set up by Lüderitz at Angra Pequeña. It ended in 1919 when the
Treaty of Versailles deprived Germany of all her colonies. That
Germany was a colonial power for only thirty-five years simplifies
the task of the colonial historian: there is much less material to
deal with than that found by scholars interested in the development
of British, French, Dutch, or Spanish expansion overseas.

The Germans were late-comers and made some mistakes.
But they learned quickly. Between 1884 and 1914, German colonial
policy passed rapidly through the several distinct phases, which in
the colonial history of other countries were a matter of gradual evolution. The first six years (1884-1890) when Bismarck was still
chancellor, saw the establishment of the colonial empire and the attempt to administer it through chartered companies. This method
failed and the Reich learned it had to shoulder the full responsibility
for governing the colonies itself.

The next phase in the history of Germany as a colonial pow-
er--the years between Bismarck's fall in 1890 and the crisis caused
by the "colonial scandals" in 1906--saw the establishment of the
authority of the Reich in most of the interior of the overseas possessions. The leading figure in this period was Dr. Kayser, the director of the colonial section of the foreign office in the Nineties.
It was an era of "little wars" against the natives. But it was a
period that ended in disaster and disillusionment. There were serious revolts both in South West Africa and in East Africa and grave
scandals in colonial administration were brought to light. The economic results of colonization were disappointing. Bitter controversy
heralded a "new era" in the administration of the overseas terri-

tories. Between 1907 and 1914, the third phase, a more enlightened policy of reform and economic progress was pursued under the influence of Dr. Dernburg, in charge of the newly established colonial office. By the eve of the First World War there was much less to criticize in Germany's colonial rule than there had been only a few years before. Administrators such as Dernburg, Rechenberg, Solf, and Schnee were men of ability, courage, and integrity. The loyalty of the natives to the Germans during the colonial campaigns of the First World War suggests that there was no longer any serious discontent with German rule.

The study of Germany's colonial empire is, however, beset with certain difficulties. Few historical events can have bequeathed to posterity such a legacy of controversial literature. There were sharp differences of opinion in Germany itself about the acquisition and the administration of the overseas possessions. And there were controversies between foreigners who denounced the colonial record of the Reich and Germans who defended it. Even before the German flag had been hoisted over a single overseas territory there were lively arguments concerning the desirability of founding an overseas empire. In the 1870's some German writers took the view that it would be a mistake for the Reich to enter the ranks of the Colonial Powers. They considered that overseas possessions cost men and money to acquire and would be a constant burden on the taxpayer. Bismarck to the end of his life doubted the wisdom of acquiring colonies. He believed that it was to great advantage that Germany remain a purely Continental state with no overseas commitments. He saw that the establishment of an overseas empire might involve Germany in serious disputes with Britain upon whose neutrality in continental conflicts he had thus far been able to rely. But there were early "colonial enthusiasts" who demanded the establishment of an overseas empire so that Germany might control much needed raw materials and foodstuffs and might find new outlets for her manufactured goods. The desirability of settling Germans under their own flag--instead of allowing them to emigrate to the United States-- was another argument in favor of founding colonies.

When Bismarck established German colonies in the 1880's,

the controversy took a new turn.   Many of those who had once criticized the founding of territories overseas now became critics of the
newly established colonial administrations.   Every blunder in the
handling of the natives and every failure of a colonial company enabled the critics to say that their worst fears had proved correct.

This controversy reached its climax in the early years of the
twentieth century when Socialists and Catholics joined to denounce
those responsible for "colonial scandals." Erzberger claimed that
millions of marks had been squandered in the overseas territories.
Officials and planters were accused of gross cruelty to the natives.
Eventually the government was unable to resist the demand that the
courts should consider charges of this kind.   The trial of Carl
Peters and his dismissal from the colonial service showed that even
the popular founder of German East Africa could be brought to book
for his misdeeds.   The revolt of the Herero in South West Africa
and the Majimaji rising in German East Africa showed that the Germans had failed to establish themselves firmly in two of their most
important overseas territories.

In 1907, however, a "new era" dawned in the German colonies.   Dr. Dernburg, the first colonial minister, made strenuous efforts to reform the administration of the colonial empire.   But the
controversies continued.   On the one hand Dernburg's right-wing
critics denounced the reformers as men who were ruining the colonies by slackening the strict discipline which was necessary to maintain order among the natives.   On the other hand the Socialists eag-
erly watched for sign of a lapse into the old discredited methods.

During the First World War a new controversy arose.   In
order to blacken Germany's name in neutral countries, English pub-
licists (such as Northcliffe) and eventually the British government
embarked upon a campaign to brand the Germans as inhuman mon-
sters who maltreated the natives in their colonies in the vilest fashion.   Some of the evidence assembled to support these allegations
was derived from criticisms made by Germans themselves of the
colonial administration of the Reich particularly before the "new era"
of 1907-1914.   But some of the allegations concerning Germany's
colonial record which were made at this time were either sheer in-

ventions or were garbled versions of accusations which had long before been shown to have little foundation in fact.

When Germany had to surrender her colonies in 1919 the Allies explained that they were not doing anything so vulgar as to annex somebody else's territories. Such an action would be contrary
to the letter and to the spirit of Wilson's fourteen points. They
claimed that they were acting from the highest motives and that they
were rescuing millions of downtrodden natives from a cruel and des-
potic rule. The Germans repudiated this accusation and denounced
what they called the "colonial guilt lie." They admitted that unfortunate mistakes had been made in the early days of colonization but
they claimed that the worst abuses had been eradicated long before
1914. They argued that all colonial powers had, at one time or another, been guilty of actions which they had later wished to forget.
The "red rubber" scandals in the Congo had not been forgotten and
the Germans claimed that it was pure impudence on the part of the
French, the Belgians, and the Portuguese to set themselves up as
judges of German colonial administration. The controversy continued throughout the twenty years between the two World Wars and
when Hitler came into power he demanded the return to Germany of
her former overseas possessions.

The historian of the German colonies has to scrutinize with
the greatest care any document, book, pamphlet, article, or report
that he believes valuable or which purports to be a history of Germany as a colonial empire, as much of what has been written on
Germany's overseas possessions is tainted by propaganda. The effects on her foreign policy of Germany's acquisitions overseas are
generally recognized and impartially recounted, but the development
of the colonies themselves, and their administration, are frequently
neglected or misrepresented.

Although Germany held no colonies before 1884 her people
lacked neither colonial traditions nor experience in exploration and
settlement. In the Middle Ages traders and settlers extended German influence both by land and sea. They moved down the Danube
valley and along the Baltic coast. The Hanseatic League established
trading posts in Baltic and North Sea ports. In the great Age of

Discovery Germany was distracted by internal struggles and was not
situated near the new trade routes of the world, so that she did not
play an important part in exploration or trade in the East Indies or
America. Her rôle in opening up new countries at this time was
not, however, entirely insignificant. In the first half of the six-
teenth century the Welsers, a German banking house, governed part
of Venezuela for some thirty years, and Federmann, one of the settlers, explored Colombia. In the seventeenth century, Brandenburg-
Prussia secured a few possessions overseas. The Great Elector
bought two trading stations on the southeast coast of India, and
founded the African Commercial Company which established itself on
the Gold Coast. His successor purchased part of the island of To-
bago. Prussia, however, was not strong enough to develop a colonial empire, and these possessions were given up early in the eighteenth century.

The need for colonies began to be felt in Germany after 1815.
Many Germans were emigrating owing to political discontent and economic distress. Over a million Germans went to the United States
of America between 1830 and 1860, most of them settling in the Old
North-West--north of the Ohio and east of the Mississippi--and in
Texas. Others went to the Province of Rio Grande do Sul in Brazil
and to Valdivia in Chile. As the Germans settled under foreign
flags they were often lost to their native country. On the other
hand, the establishment of a colonial empire in temperate regions
would enable settlers to retain their nationality and culture and would
increase Germany's importance as a world power. Unfortunately
most of the temperate regions suitable for white settlement had already been secured by other powers. In America, expansion was
barred by the Monroe Doctrine. Further, as Germany became in-
dustrialized, it was felt that she should secure control over tropical
regions which could supply her with raw materials and food in return for manufactured articles. There were still rich tropical areas
in Africa and the Pacific which had not been annexed by European
states. But owing to pressing problems at home, the lack of naval
forces, and the fear of antagonizing other powers neither individual
German states nor the Germanic confederation made any attempt to

obtain territory overseas. Meantime German explorers, missionaries, and traders were in effect laying the foundations of future
colonial expansion.

Of the work of German explorers in the nineteenth century,
much of which was done for foreign governments and associations,
only a few outstanding examples can be mentioned here. In Africa,
Barth carefully investigated Lake Chad and neighbouring regions in
the early 1850's. Von der Decken surveyed the southern slopes of
Mount Kilimanjaro in 1861-62. Schweinfurth's expedition of 1868-72
explored the upper Nile. At the same time Nachtigal was exploring
the River Shari which runs into Lake Chad. Between 1879 and 1886
Junker traveled in the region between this lake and the Nile. Von
Wissmann twice crossed central Africa in the eighties. In South
America, Alexander von Humboldt made an important journey to
Venezuela, Peru, and Mexico at the beginning of the century. Some
twenty years later von Spix and von Martius were sent by the king
of Bavaria to South America and there they explored the River Ama-
zon. Valuable information about the physical features of China was
secured by von Richtofen in seven expeditions undertaken between
1868 and 1872. In Australia, Leichhardt crossed Queensland from
Sydney to the Gulf of Carpentaria in the forties and (wrote Lang)
"virtually added a vast and valuable province to the British Empire."
In New Zealand, von Hochstetter and von Haast undertook a geologi-
cal survey of Auckland Province in 1858. Von Haast also traveled
in Nelson Province. German missionaries, too, were active in
many parts of the world, particularly in Africa. The Barmen Rhine
Mission, for example, worked in Namaqualand, and the Basel Mis-
sion--a Swiss body run by Germans--worked in Togoland.

The development of her commerce and shipping was another
factor in the extension of Germany's influence overseas. Recovery
from the paralysis produced by Napoleon's continental system was
slow. Germany's sea-borne trade was to a great extent in the hands
of the English and Dutch. The stringent navigation laws and the
petty rivalries and differential harbor dues among the German
coastal states hampered the development of a merchant marine. The
lack of a fleet was felt particularly in the Mediterranean, where the

activities of the Barbary pirates menaced commerce. In the 1830's
and 40's the Prussian merchant marine expanded with the revival of
the Baltic corn trade. More important was the rise of the shipping
of Hamburg and Bremen in the great Atlantic trades. Between 1820
and 1830 German vessels began bringing sugar and coffee from Brazil. Although Hamburg's prosperity was temporarily checked by the
disastrous fire of May, 1842, the founding of the Hamburg-America
Company in 1847 and of the North German Lloyd Company in Brem-
en ten years later mark the beginning of a new era of prosperity
for these Hanse towns. The activities of three great Hamburg companies in regions which subsequently became German colonies deserve mention. The firm of O'Swald controlled much of the trade
of the east coast of Africa in the 1860's, Woermann held a powerful
position on the Cameroons coast in West Africa, and the house of
Godeffroy virtually monopolized the trade of Samoa.

The establishment of the North German Confederation in
1867, and its expansion into the German Empire four years later,
led to a new interest in the acquisition of territory overseas. Colonial enthusiasts claimed that a great power which aspired to play
a leading part in world affairs should have possessions abroad.
They considered that Germany needed homes for emigrants, fresh
sources of raw materials and tropical foods, and new markets for
manufactured articles. The vast bulk of the nation, however, felt
that to acquire colonies might be costly in men and money and might
lead to serious disputes with other powers. It would above all be
foolish to quarrel with Britain at a time when Germany was anxious
to keep France completely isolated. Bismarck declared that "for
Germany to acquire colonies would be like a poverty-stricken Polish
nobleman providing himself with silks and sables when he needed
shirts." Gradually, however, the importunities of traders, finan-
ciers, and others interested in expansion overseas began to have
their effect upon the Chancellor. In 1876 a group of merchants suggested to Bismarck the establishment of a protectorate over the
Transvaal. He had rejected such a proposal before and he rejected
it again. But on this occasion he admitted that Germany could not
dispense permanently with colonies. The foreign situation was not

favorable for any action at the moment.

Between 1876 and 1884 Bismarck frequently stated that he did
not wish to acquire colonies and there seems no reason to doubt his
sincerity.   But he felt that Germany's prestige as a great power
must be maintained and consequently he supported Germans abroad
in their disputes with foreign countries.   He also concluded commercial treaties with native rulers in the Pacific.   When the house
of Godeffroy failed in 1878 he endeavoured to maintain Germany's
position in the Samoan Islands by submitting a bill to the Reichstag
for the underwriting of a new company to take over Godeffroy's
rights from their creditors, the London firm of Baring Brothers.
The National Liberals, whose support Bismarck still needed, rejected the proposal and Bismarck recognized that the time was not yet
ripe for the founding of colonies.

In the early Eighties, German expansionists could point to
renewed colonial activity by foreign countries.   England's purchase
of some of the Suez Canal shares in 1875 and her bombardment of
the forts of Alexandria in July 1882 were the prelude to intervention
in Egypt.   At the same time she was active in East Africa, West
Africa, and New Guinea.   The French established a virtual protectorate over Tunis in 1881 and the Italians were taking the first steps
towards the founding of colonies on the shores of the Red Sea.
Clearly if Germany did not act promptly the few remaining regions
of the world suitable for exploitation would be appropriated by other
powers.

German public opinion was becoming more favorable to the
establishment of colonies.   The rise of economic nationalism may
be seen in the adoption of a policy of protection in 1879.   The old
arguments on the need for raw materials and new markets, which
were put forward by Fabri in his Does Germany need Colonies?, appeared to have a greater force.   Moreover, the new wave of emigration which followed the industrial depression of the Seventies
caused some alarm.   The support given to two societies formed in
the early 1880's to foster colonization indicates the new interest in
the question.   The Kolonialverein (colonial society) was founded in
1882 and had over 10,000 members within three years.   Carl

Peters' Gesellschaft für deutsche Kolonisation (society for German colonization) of 1884 hoped to raise money to finance colonial enterprise in East Africa. Rivalry between these two bodies ended in their amalgamation in 1887 when the Deutsche Kolonialgesellschaft (German colonial society) was set up.

In 1884, Bismarck was ready to act. The conclusion of the Dual Alliance (Germany and Austria-Hungary, 1879), the League of the Three Emperors (Germany, Austria-Hungary, and Russia, 1881) and the Triple Alliance (Germany, Austria-Hungary, and Italy, 1882) initiated a brief period of diplomatic calm before the storms caused principally by Boulangism and the Bulgarian problem of 1885-87. Bismarck felt able to face British opposition in colonial affairs. Early in 1883 he asked what claims Britain had to territories in the Angra Pequeña district in South West Africa. Britain answered that she held Walfish Bay and the Guano Islands and that her rights would be infringed by any claims to lands between Cape Colony and Angola. Bismarck thereupon inquired on what grounds Britain took up this attitude. No reply was forthcoming. On April 24, 1884, Bismarck placed under Imperial protection the "establishments" of the German merchant Lüderitz at Angra Pequeña (Lüderitz Bay).

This was followed by the founding of a German colonial empire in Africa and the Pacific, some features of which deserve notice. It was accomplished in the astonishingly short period of six years, few new acquisitions being made after 1890. It was marked by sharp practice on the part of adventurers who went to Africa ostensibly as traders or explorers and then suddenly produced authority from the Government to conclude treaties with native chiefs for placing their territories under German protection. Yet the speed and the unusual manner of German representatives, although there were serious disputes, particularly with Britain, did not involve Germany in war with any European power. Further, except for von Wissmann's suppression of the Arab revolt in East Africa, there were no military expeditions against the natives in the German colonies in the Eighties. This is in strong contrast with the difficulties that other European countries were having in Africa at this time. Another interesting feature is Germany's attempt to govern some of

the colonies by chartered companies. Bismarck desired to reduce
to a minimum the responsibilities of the home government.

The German colonial empire eventually had an area of a million square miles and an estimated native population of about fifteen
million. Most of the colonies were in Africa. The largest and
most promising was German East Africa (Tanganyika) with an area
of 384,000 square miles. Valuable tropical products such as cotton,
rubber, tobacco, and coffee could be raised. Some of the highlands
were suitable for white settlement and there were adequate ports.
The first task of the Germans was to break the power of the Arab
slave traders and this was done in 1888. Carl Peters, who had
done so much to stake out Germany's claims to this region, was
bitterly disappointed at the Anglo-German Treaty of 1890 by which
Germany recognized Britain's rights over Witu, Uganda, Nyasaland
and Zanzibar in return for Heligoland. He complained that "two
kingdoms, Witu and Uganda, had been sacrificed for a bath-tub in
the North Sea." On the west coast of Africa, Germany secured
three colonies--South West Africa (322,450 square miles), the Cameroons (Old Cameroons 192,000 square miles, and New Cameroons,
100,000 square miles) and Togoland (33,000 square miles). South
West Africa included much desert but diamonds were found in 1908
and some districts were suitable for white settlement. Many difficulties had to be overcome before the country could be developed.
Expensive public works had to be constructed and native hostility
overcome. The Cameroons and Togoland were useful sources of
tropical products, but their climate was unsuitable for white settlement.

In the Pacific, Germany obtained the north-east of the island
of New Guinea (Kaiser Wilhelmsland), some of the Solomon Islands,
New Britain (Neu Pommern), New Ireland (Neu Mecklenburg), the
Duke of York Islands (Neu Lauenburg) and some smaller islands.
These islands produced copra, phosphates, rubber, coffee, and so
forth. They were regarded as useful for the construction of naval
and trading harbors and coaling and cable stations.

Regarded as a whole, the German possessions overseas had
two weaknesses. First, the colonial empire was a series of scat-

tered territories that had been seized because they were the only
areas available.   It had no geographical unity such as that possessed
by the empires of Britain and France.   The British Empire was
linked by the great sea routes of the North Atlantic and the Indian
Ocean.   An important part of the French Empire could be regarded
as a natural expansion of the mother country across the Mediterranean.   Secondly, the German possessions lacked some of their natural harbors and were difficult to defend.   Thus the chief port of
German South West Africa (Walfish Bay) was in British hands.   Sim-
ilarly, Britain held the strategically important islands of Zanzibar
and Pemba off the coast of German East Africa.   The development
of New Guinea was jealously watched by Australia.

     Although there had been much expansionist propaganda, Bis-
marck had to deal with serious opposition to his colonial policy.
The Social Democrats argued that the seizure of colonies might benefit capitalists but would lead to the exploitation of natives.   The Radicals held that most of the colonies were useless for immigration,
that their exploitation would be expensive, and that tropical products
could be obtained from the colonies of other countries.   Critics
were able to point to abuses.   It was soon seen that most of the
chartered companies were not governing the colonies properly.   They
were interested in securing quick profits and not in tackling problems of administration.   The German South West Africa Company
gave up its political rights in 1888, The German East Africa Company in 1891, the New Guinea Company in 1899, surviving purely as
commercial concerns.   In the Cameroons and Togoland there were
no chartered companies from the beginning.

     After 1891, the principal German colonies were ruled by gov-
ernors responsible to the emperor.   In Berlin, colonial affairs were
in the hands of the colonial section of the foreign office.   There was
also an advisory colonial council appointed by the chancellor.   Dr.
Kayser, who was director of the department from 1890 to 1896, was
only partially successful and he made two serious mistakes.   First,
unduly large concessions were made to companies.   Thus nearly a
third of German South West Africa was controlled by only nine companies in 1903.   Secondly, colonial administration was too central-

ized and bureaucratic and was in the hands of unsuitable persons--
for example, army officers with no experience of tropical countries
and their inhabitants. Misgovernment led to native uprisings in the
1890's and later which had to be suppressed by costly military expeditions. The Social Democrats kept the question of colonial scandals before the Reichstag and some action was taken against the
worst offenders. Thus Carl Peters, Leist (Governor of the Cameroons), Wehland (a judge in the Cameroons) and von Horn (Governor
of Togoland) had to leave the colonial service. There was, however, a brighter side to German colonial administration in the
troubled years 1890 to 1906. Much exploration was undertaken.
Some economic progress was made. Public works were constructed,
a certain interest was taken in the welfare of natives, and mission
schools and hospitals were set up. Also, valuable scientific work
was done, particularly in the study of tropical medicine and tropical
agriculture.

Opportunities for extending Germany's colonial empire were
scant between 1890 and 1896. The young Emperor William II, who
wanted Germany to have a "place in the sun," cast envious eyes
upon the vast African possessions of Belgium and Portugal and hoped
to benefit from the weakness of Spain, Turkey, and China to secure
new territories and spheres of influence. In 1898 Germany obtained
a naval base at Kiao Chow and in the same year the Spanish-American war enabled her to put pressure upon Spain to give up some of
her islands in the Pacific. Eventually she bought three groups of
islands--the Carolines, the Pelews and the Mariannes (except Guam).
The Samoan Islands, which had been jointly governed by Britain,
Germany, and the United States for twenty years, were divided
among these powers in 1899, Germany obtaining Opolu and Sawai.
The Anglo-German Treaty of 1898 delimited spheres of influence in
the Portuguese colonies in Africa in the event Portugal obtained a
loan from the two signatories on the security of her colonial customs receipts. Germany hoped for a speedy partition of the Portuguese colonies but Britain did not. In 1899 Britain virtually de-
stroyed the Treaty of 1898 by making an agreement with Portugal
for the mutual protection of colonies. The Portuguese colonies

never came on to the market. The emperor's hopes for establishing a protectorate over the Transvaal were also disappointed. In
the Near East, however, he was more successful. Germany pursued a policy of "peaceful penetration" in Turkey in the Eighties and
Nineties, and in 1902 a German firm secured a concession to build
the Baghdad Railway, linking that city with Constantinople, on the
European side of the Bosporus.

Criticism of abuses in Germany's colonial administration
came to a head in 1906. Loss of lands, forced labor, and harsh
punishments had driven the natives to revolt in Germany's three
principal African colonies. Von Puttkamer's inhuman treatment of
natives in the Cameroons and General Trotha's savage suppression
of the Herero revolt in South West Africa in 1905-6, were the culmination of years of misgovernment on the part of some of the colonial officials. Public opinion in Germany was aroused, and in
1906 the Reichstag rejected a supplementary colonial estimate. A
general election followed and von Bülow triumphed over his Social
Democrat and Centre (Roman Catholic) opponents. But the government had had a lesson and thorough reforms of the colonial administration were undertaken.

The colonial section of the foreign office was raised to an
independent department in 1907. Dr. Dernburg was appointed colonial secretary and remained in office until 1910. He went to London
and to Africa to see how Britain administered her colonies and then
visited the United States to study methods of cotton culture. Careful attention was paid to the training of officials and a colonial institute was set up at Hamburg for this purpose. In the colonies,
German settlers and even some of the natives received a limited
share in the management of local affairs. The colonial land policy
was changed and the Government tried to buy land back from the
companies. Public works were pushed forward. The important
railway from Dar-es-Salaam across East Africa to Kigoma, for example, was opened in 1914.

Serious attention was paid to native welfare under Dr. Dernburg and plans were made for the gradual abolition of domestic
slavery: compulsory labor might be used only on public works and

it had to be paid for. Important research in tropical medicine was
undertaken; for example, Dr. Koch, working in East Africa, dis-
covered a remedy for sleeping sickness. The new colonial policy
had been in force for only seven years when the First World War
broke out. Even in this short period some of its beneficent results
were seen. The natives appeared to be reasonably contented.
There were no uprisings and on the whole during the war the natives were faithful to Germany.

Just before the war, the emperor was as anxious as ever to
extend Germany's territory overseas, but the opposition of Britain,
France and Russia made this difficult. In 1911 Germany obtained a
strip of French Equatorial Africa (the New Cameroons) in return for
giving up all claims to Morocco. A year later a new Anglo-German
agreement on the possible partition of the Portuguese colonies in
Africa was reached. A different cause for intervention was envisaged this time: if the lives, property, or vital interests of British
or German citizens were threatened by disturbances in Mozambique
or Angola and the Portuguese government could not provide adequate
protection, the two powers would cooperate to safeguard their interests. The Baghdad railway project was held up by the Young Turk
revolution (1908) and by opposition from Britain, Russia, and France.
In June, 1914, an Anglo-German agreement on the railway was in-
itialled but it was never signed. By the outbreak of war the line
had been built from Scutari across Anatolia to Adana (near Tarsus).

In some respects Germany was disappointed with her colonies. They attracted few settlers and they supplied German industry
with only a small part of the raw materials it needed. With the exception of Togoland they failed to become self-supporting and involved
Germany in serious disputes with foreign powers.

During the First World War all Germany's possessions overseas were conquered by the Allies. Most of them were overrun
without difficulty. In East Africa, however, von Lettow Vorbeck
made a long and gallant resistance against superior numbers. After
the war the colonial empire was partitioned among the victors, the
territories being held as mandates for the League of Nations. The
mandatory powers tried to assimilate the former German colonies to

their own colonies as much as possible. Thus, for instance, South
West Africa was administered as an integral part of the Union of
South Africa.

Notes

1.   The text, tables and maps in this section are taken from:
W. O. Henderson, Studies in German Colonial History (Chicago,
1962), p. ix-xiii, 1-10, 131-141. Henderson's book is the only
book in English that presents a complete overview of the German
colonial situation. More detailed information is available primarily
in pre-1914 studies published in Germany. A few well-balanced
studies have appeared in recent years as noted in the bibliography
at the end of this book. The most recent addition to this literature
is Helmut Bley, Kolonialherrschaft und Sozialstruktur in Deutsch
Südwestafrika 1894-1914 (Hamburg, 1968), 390p., which is a complete and competent study. A good bibliography is presented on
pages 377 to 386.

Table 1

German Colonies	Area (sq. miles)	Administration after 1919
AFRICA		
East Africa	384,000	1. Tanganyika Territory: British mandate 2. Ruanda and Urundi districts: Belgian mandate 3. Kionga district (mouth of River Rovuma): Portuguese mandate
South West Africa	322,000	1. Union of South Africa mandate 2. Caprivizipfel (the 'corridor' to the Zambezi) administered under Bechuanaland Protectorate
Cameroons (Kamerun)	305,000	1. New Cameroons ('corridors' to River Congo and Ubangi ceded by France to Germany in 1911) returned to France: no mandate 2. Remainder held as mandates by France (166,000 sq. miles) and Britain (34,2000 sq. miles)
Togoland	34,000	Divided between Britain and France (mandates)
PACIFIC OCEAN AND CHINA		
Caroline, Marianne and Marshall Islands	1,000	Japanese mandate
New Guinea and Bismarck Archipelago	93,000	Commonwealth of Australia mandate. Nauru Island was a British Empire mandate: governed by Britain, Australia and New Zealand: administration changed every five years
Samoa (Opolu and Sawaii)	1,000	New Zealand mandate
Kiao Chow	200	Conquered from Germany by Japan and ceded to China.

Table 2

Distribution of the White Population in Germany's Colonies in Africa and the Pacific (excluding Kiao Chow), 1911

	Civil Servants	Army and Police	Mission-aries and Clergy	Mer-chants, Shop-keepers, Innkeepers	Artisans, Laborers Miners	Planters and Farmers	Other Male Inhabi-tants	Women and Children	Total White Popu-lation	Total German Popu-lation
South West Africa	881	2,072	70	1,035	2,572	1,390	895	5,047	13,962	11,140
East Africa	401	195	428	311	293	683	538	1,378	4,227	3,113
Cameroons	244	119	117	436	84	111	122	222	1,455	1,311
Togoland	87	-	66	64	29	5	50	62	363	327
Pacific colonies	121	-	266	288	98	208	140	539	1,660	1,056
Totals	1,734	2,386	947	2,134	3,076	2,397	1,745	7,248	21,667	16,947

Table 3

Foreign Trade of the German Colonies, 1901-1912 (in thousands of Marks)*

	Four African Colonies		Colonies in the Pacific		Kiao Chow		Total Trade		Excess of Imports over Exports
	Imports	Exports	Imports	Exports	Imports	Exports	Imports	Exports	
1901	33,406	15,820	4,450	3,568	13,459	5,289	51,615	24,677	26,938
1902	37,024	18,342	5,879	3,776	25,645	8,909	68,548	31,027	37,558
1903	34,862	21,678	6,946	3,885	34,974	14,749	76,782	40,312	36,470
1904	40,672	20,821	5,796	4,002	44,870	19,983	91,338	44,806	46,532
1905	62,514	23,438	8,858	4,398	69,176	24,717	140,548	52,553	87,995
1906	113,517	25,523	8,381	5,641	82,374	34,225	204,272	65,389	138,883
1907	80,199	35,923	8,546	5,240	55,380	32,597	144,125	73,760	70,365
1908	84,264	37,726	7,593	8,724	69,041	47,344	160,898	93,794	67,104
1909	97,613	58,264	9,799	11,350	65,464	54,732	172,876	124,346	48,530
1910	119,949	82,643	9,708	18,199	69,375	60,561	199,032	161,403	37,629
1911	130,131	81,579	12,081	16,416	114,938	80,295	257,150	178,290	78,860
1912	128,478	103,748	14,201	17,132	121,254	79,640	263,933	200,520	63,415

*This table is based on tables in the Deutsches Kolonial-Lexikon, II, p. 34, and André Touzet, Le Problème Colonial et la Paix du Monde. Les Revendications Coloniales Allemandes (1937), p. 228. The figures include the import and export of money except for Samoa. The sharp rise in the imports of the African colonies in 1906 is due to the fact that Government goods sent to South West Africa were included in that year, but were excluded in 1904-5 (Herero rebellion). The Togoland statistics include the value of the duties levied upon imports before 1905 but not afterwards. The Kiao Chow figures are reckoned from 1 October to 30 September. Until the end of 1905 they represent the transit trade of the free port. They include that part of the trade of the Chinese province of Shantung which passed through Kiao Chow.

Table 4

Germany's Commercial Relations with her Colonies from 1891
to 1910 in Relation to her Total Trade (in million marks)

	Imports			Exports		
	Total Imports to Germany	Imports from the Colonies	Percentage of Colonial Imports	Total Exports from Germany	Exports to the Colonies	Percentage of Exports to Colonies
1891	4,656,0	5,9	0·13	3,503,9	6,0	0·17
1892	4,435,5	4,4	0·10	3,346,1	5,3	0·16
1893	4,306,4	4,2	0·10	3,397,2	4,8	0·14
1894	4,632,8	3,8	0·08	3,141,5	4,6	0·15
1895	4,371,5	3,3	0·08	3,530,3	4,5	0·13
1896	4,808,8	4,3	0·09	3,982,5	5,5	0·14
1897	5,048,5	4,6	0·09	3,937,5	8,6	0·22
1898	5,798,7	4,6	0·07	4,264,6	10,9	0·25
1899	6,084,1	4,8	0·07	4,529,8	14,7	0·32
1900	6,320,4	6,5	0·10	4,893,8	23,3	0·48
1901	5,710,3	5,8	0·10	4,512,6	20,7	0·46
1902	5,805,8	6,9	0·12	4,812,8	21,1	0·44
1903	6,321,1	7,3	0·12	5,130,3	23,5	0·46
1904	6,854,5	11,1	0·16	5,315,6	33,1	0·62
1905	7,436,3	17,7	0·24	5,841,8	43,6	0·74
1906	8,438,6	20,3	0·24	6,475,6	43,0	0·67
1907	9,003,3	22,9	0·25	7,094,9	37,9	0·53
1908	8,077,1	21,9	0·27	6,481,5	36,5	0·56
1909	8,860,4	29,4	0·33	6,858,7	41,8	0·61
1910	9,310,0	50,1	0·54	7,644,2	55,6	0·73

See last table in Otto Mayer, Die Entwicklung der Handelsbeziehungen Deutschlands zu seinen Kolonien (1913).

Table 5

Table illustrating the extent to which the Colonies supplied Germany with raw materials and other products (as percentage of Germany's total consumption in 1910)

	Quantity (per cent.)	Value (per cent.)
Cotton	0·25	0·25
Rubber	13·62	12·33
Oils and fats	2·12	2·66
Tropical timber	4·07	3·43
Wool	0·03	0·02
Hides and skins	0·15	0·17
Wax	8·09	8·14
Ivory	6·06	6·09
Mica	6·21	6·31
Precious stones	0·30	37·35

See Otto Mayer, Die Entwicklung der Handelsbeziehungen Deutschlands zu seinen Kolonien (1913), p. 178.

Table 6

German Trade with the Middle East, 1908-13

In million marks

	1908	1909	1910	1911	1912	1913
Imports from:						
Turkey	47·56	57·29	67·45	70·09	77·65	73·93
Egypt	38·37	51·50	64·10	64·70	80·63	-
Persia	0·20	0·32	0·79	1·11	-	-
Exports to:						
Turkey	64·07	78·92	104·87	112·88	112·84	98·42
Egypt	23·22	23·43	26·19	31·15	27·29	-
Persia	-	0·12	0·46	0·22	0·14	0·15

German Colonies in the Pacific

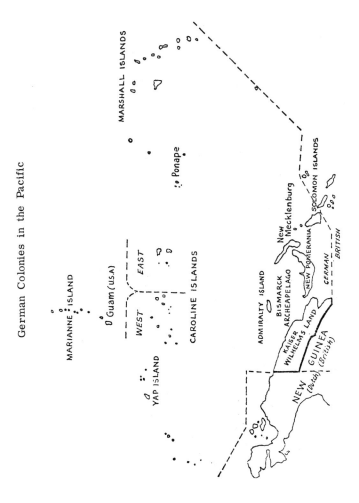

Railways in the Near East, 1918

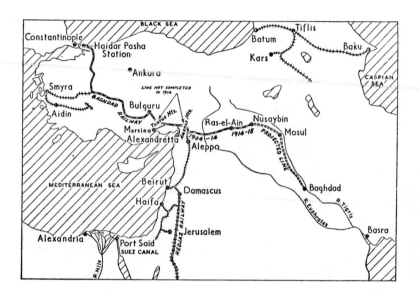

German East Africa

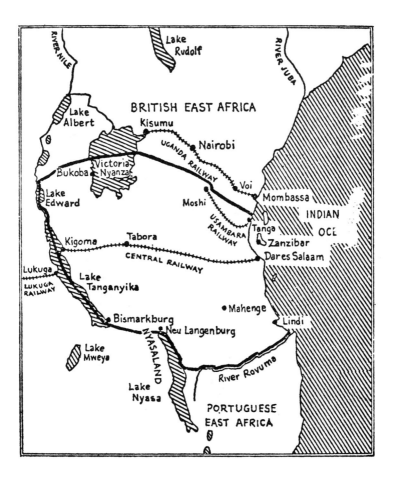

German Colonies in Africa

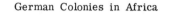

······ Frontiers of the Cameroons to 1911

Chapter V

Personalities in German Foreign Policy, 1890-1914

1888-1918   William II (1859-1941). Emperor of Germany, King
             of Prussia.

Chancellors:

1871-1890   Bismarck-Schönhausen, Otto, Prince von (1815-1898)
             Count in 1865, prince in 1871. Prussian minister to
             the Federal Diet in Frankfurt, August 1851-1859;
             minister in St. Petersburg, April 1859-1862, in Paris,
             May-September 1862; Prussian minister-president,
             1862-1872, 1873-1890; Prussian foreign minister, 1862-
             1890; chancellor of North German Confederation, 1867-
             1871.

1890-1894   Caprivi, Georg Leo von (1831-1899). Prussian general;
             head of the admiralty, 1883-1888; commanding general,
             10th Army Corps, Hannover, 1889-1890; Prussian
             minister-president, 1890-1892.

1894-1900   Hohenlohe-Schillingsfürst, Chlodwig, Prince zu (1819-
             1901). ambassador in Paris, 1874-1885; governor of
             Alsace-Lorraine, 1885-1894; Prussian minister-
             president, 1894-1900.

1900-1909   Bülow, Bernhard, Prince von (1849-1929). First secre-
             tary in Paris, 1878-1884, in St. Petersburg, 1884-
             1888; minister in Bucharest, 1888-1894; ambassador in
             Rome (Quirinal), 1894-1897; state secretary for foreign
             affairs, 1897-1900; Prussian minister-president, 1900-
             1909.

1909-1917	Bethmann-Hollweg, Theobald von (1856-1921). Head of administration in Brandenburg, 1899-1905; Prussian minister of interior, 1905-1907; state secretary of the interior, 1907-1909; Prussian minister-president, 1909-1917.
1917	Michaelis, Dr. Georg (1857-1936). Prussian civil servant; food controller, 1915-1917; chancellor, July 14 - Oct. 30, 1917.
1917-1918	Hertling, Georg, Count von (1843-1919). Minister-president of Bavaria, 1912; chancellor, Oct. 30, 1917 - Sept. 30, 1918.
1918	Max, Prince of Baden (1867-1927). Nephew of Grand Duke Friedrich; chancellor, Oct. 4 - Nov., 1918.

Ambassadors--London (minister to 1862):

1827-1842	Bülow, Heinrich von. Prussian minister in London.
1842-1854	Bunsen, Josias von. Prussian minister-resident in Rome, 1827-1838, in Bern, 1839-1841.
1854-1873	Bernstorff, Albrecht, Count von (1809-1873). Prussian foreign minister, 1861-1862.
1873-1885	Münster, Georg Herbert, Count zu, Baron von Grothaus, from 1899 Prince Münster von Derneburg (1820-1902). Hannoverian minister in St. Petersburg, 1856-1864; ambassador in Paris, 1886-1900.
1885-1901	Hatzfeldt-Wildenburg, Paul, Count von. See under: State Secretaries for Foreign Affairs.
1901-1912	Metternich zur Gracht, Paul, Count von Wolff (1853-1934). First secretary in London, 1890-1895; consul-general in Cairo, 1895-1897; Prussian minister in Hannover, 1897-1900.
1912	Marschall von Bieberstein, Adolf Hermann, Baron (1842-1912). See under: State Secretaries for Foreign Affairs.

1912-1914 Lichnowsky, Karl Max, Prince von (1860-1928). First
secretary in Vienna, 1894-1899; vortragender Rat in
foreign office, 1899-1904.

Ambassadors--Vienna:

1859-1866⌉ Werther, Karl, Baron von. See under: Ambassadors--
1866-1869⌋ Paris.

1869-1876 Schweinitz, Hans Lothar, General von. See under:
Ambassadors--St. Petersburg.

1876-1878 Stolberg-Wernigerode, Otto, Prince zu. Vice-President
of Prussian ministry of state, 1878-1881; lord high
chamberlain, 1884-1894; member of Reichstag (Independent Conservative), 1871-1878; president of Prussian
house of lords, 1872-1876, 1893-1896.

1878-1894 Reuss, Heinrich VII, Prince von (1825-1906). Ambassador in St. Petersburg, 1867-1876, in Constantinople,
1877-1878.

1894-1902 Eulenburg-Hertefeld, Philipp, Count zu, after 1900
Prince (1847-1921). Secretary of legation in Munich,
1881-1887; minister in Oldenburg, 1888-1890, in Stuttgart, 1890-1891, in Munich, 1891-1894; frequently the
foreign office representative in Kaiser's retinue.

1902-1907 Wedel, Karl, Count von, later Prince, General (1842-
1919). Military attaché in Vienna, 1877-1887; military
aide-de-camp to the Kaiser, 1889-1894; minister in
Stockholm, 1892-1894; ambassador in Rome, 1899-1902;
governor of Alsace-Lorraine, 1907-1914; also held several military commands.

1907-1916 Tschirschky und Bögendorff, Heinrich von. See under:
State Secretaries for Foreign Affairs.

Ambassadors--Paris:

1863-1869	Goltz, Robert, Count von der. Prussian minister in Athens, 1857-1859; in Constantinople, 1859-1862, in St. Petersburg, 1862-1863; Prussian minister, then ambassador in Paris, 1863-1869.
1869-1870	Werther, Karl, Baron von (1809-1894). Prussian minister in St. Petersburg, 1854-1859, in Vienna, 1859-1866, 1866-1869; ambassador of North German Federation in Paris, 1869-1870, German ambassador in Constantinople, 1874-1877.
1871-1874	Arnim-Suckow, Harry, Count von. German minister, then ambassador to Paris.
1874-1885	Hohenlohe-Schillingsfürst, Chlodwig, Prince zu. See under: Chancellors.
1886-1900	Münster, Georg Herbert, Count zu, Baron von Grothaus, from 1900 Prince Münster von Derneburg. See under: Ambassadors--London.
1900-1910	Radolin-Radolinski, Hugo Leszczyc, Count, from 1888 Prince von (1847-1917). Prussian minister in Weimar, 1882-1884; ambassador in Constantinople, 1892-1895, in St. Petersburg, 1895-1900.
1910-1914	Schoen, Wilhelm, Baron von. See under: State Secretaries for Foreign Affairs.

Ambassadors--St. Petersburg (Reuss was first ambassador; those preceding him were Prussian ministers):

1854-1859	Werther, Karl, Baron von. See under: Ambassadors--Paris.
1859-1862	Bismarck-Schönhausen, Otto, Prince von. See under: Chancellors.
1862-1863	Goltz, Robert, Count von der. See under: Ambassadors--Paris.
1863-1867	Redern, Heinrich, Count von.

1867-1876   Reuss, Heinrich VII, Prince von. See under: Ambas-
             sadors--Vienna.

1876-1892   Schweinitz, Hans Lothar, General von (1822-1901).
             Ambassador in Vienna, 1869-1876.

1892-1895   Werder, Bernhard, General von. Military plenipotenti-
             ary in St. Petersburg, 1869-1886, governor of Berlin,
             1886-1888.

1895-1900   Radolin-Radolinski, Hugo Leszczyc, Count, from 1888
             Prince von. See under: Ambassadors--Paris.

1901-1905   Alvensleben, Friedrich Johann, Count von (1836-1913).
             Minister at The Hague, 1882-1884, in Washington, 1884-
             1886, in Brussels, 1886-1901.

1905-1907   Schoen, Wilhelm, Baron von. See under: State Secre-
             taries for Foreign Affairs.

1907-1914   Pourtalès, Friedrich, Count von. Temporary assistant
             in the foreign office, 1886-1888; first secretary in St.
             Petersburg, 1888-1890; vortragender Rat in foreign of-
             fice, 1890-1899; minister at The Hague, 1899-1902;
             Prussian minister in Munich, 1903-1907.

Ambassadors--Constantinople:

1869-1872   Keyserling-Rautenburg, Heinrich, Count von (1831-1874).

1872-1873   Keudell, Robert, Baron von. See under: Ambassadors
             --Rome.

1874-1877   Werther, Karl, Baron von. See under: Ambassadors--
             Paris.

1877-1878   Reuss, Heinrich VII, Prince von. See under: Ambas-
             sadors--Vienna.

1879-1881   Hatzfeldt-Wildenburg, Paul, Count von. See under:
             State Secretaries for Foreign Affairs.

1882-1892   Radowitz, Joseph Maria von (1839-1912). Minister in
             Athens, 1874-1882; ambassador in Madrid, 1892-1908.

1892-1895   Radolin-Radolinski, Hugo Leszczyc, Count, from 1888
             Prince von. See under: Ambassadors--Paris.

1895-1897   Saurma v.d. Jeltsch, Anton von.   Consul-general in
            Alexandria, 1876-1882; minister in Bucharest, 1882-
            1885, at The Hague, 1885-1891; Prussian minister in
            Stuttgart, 1891-1893; ambassador in Washington, 1893-
            1895, in Rome (Quirinal), 1897-1899.
1897-1912   Marschall von Bieberstein, Alfred, Baron von.   See
            under: State Secretaries for Foreign Affairs.
1912-1915   Wagenheim, Hans, Baron von.   Consul-general in Sofia,
            1888-1892; first secretary in Constantinople, 1899-1904;
            minister to Mexico, 1904-1908; chargé d'affaires in
            Tangier, 1908; minister in Athens, 1909-1912.

Ambassadors--Rome (minister to 1875, Quirinal):

1873-1887   Keudell, Robert, Baron von (1824-1903).   In charge of
            personnel division of foreign office, 1863-1872; minister
            in Constantinople, 1872-73.
1887-1893   Solms-Sonnenwalde, Eberhard, Count zu (1825-1912).
            Minister in Madrid, 1878-1887.
1893-1897   Bülow, Bernhard, Prince von.   See under: Chancellors.
1897-1899   Saurma v.d. Jeltsch, Anton von.   See under: Ambas-
            sadors--Constantinople.
1899-1902   Wedel, Karl, Prince von.   See under: Ambassadors--
            Vienna.
1902-1909   Monts, Anton, Count von.   Secretary of Prussian lega-
            tion to the Holy See, 1884-1886; first secretary in Vien-
            na, 1886-1890; Consul-general in Budapest, 1890-1894;
            Prussian minister in Oldenburg, 1894-1895, in Munich,
            1895-1902.
1909-1912   Jagow, Gottlieb von.   Secretary in Rome, 1901-1907.
1913-1915   Flotow, Johannes von.   Counsellor in Paris, 1904-1907;
            vortragender Rat in foreign office, 1907-1910; minister
            in Brussels, 1910-1913.   (Prince Bernhard von Bülow
            was on a special diplomatic mission to Rome from De-
            cember 14, 1914 to May 25, 1915.)

Ambassadors--Madrid (minister to 1887):

1874-1878   Hatzfeldt-Wildenburg, Paul, Count von.   See under:
             State Secretaries for Foreign Affairs.
1878-1887   Solms-Sonnenwalde, Eberhardt, Count zu.   See under:
             Ambassadors--Rome.
1887-1892   Stumm, Ferdinand, Baron von.   First secretary in St.
             Petersburg, 1878-1881, in London, 1881-1883; Prussian
             minister in Darmstadt, 1883-1885; minister in Copen-
             hagen, 1885-1887.
1892-1908   Radowitz, Joseph Maria von.   See under: Ambassa-
             dors--Constantinople.
1908-1910   Tattenbach, Christian, Count von.   Minister in Tangier,
             1889-1895, in Lisbon, 1897-1908.
1910-1918   Ratibor und Corvey, Max, Prince von.   First secretary
             in Vienna, 1890-1894; minister in Athens, 1902-1906, in
             Belgrade, 1906-1908, in Lisbon, 1908-1910.

Ambassadors--Washington (minister to 1893):

1871-1882   Schlözer, Kurd von.   Secretary of legation in St. Peters-
             burg, 1857-1862; temporary chargé d'affaires in Copen-
             hagen, 1863; secretary of legation to the Holy See, 1864-
             1869; consul-general of North German Federation in
             Mexico, 1869-1871; minister to the Holy See, 1882-
             1892.
1882-1884   Eisendicher, Karl von.
1884-1886   Alvensleben, Friedrich Johann, Count von.   See under:
             Ambassadors--St. Petersburg.
1886-1891   Arco-Valley, Emmerich, Count von und zu.   Minister
             in Tokyo, 1901-1906.
1891-1893   Holleben, Theodor von.   Minister in Tokyo, 1885-1891;
             minister-resident in Argentina and Uruguay, 1875-1885.
1893-1895   Saurma v.d. Jeltsch, Anton von.   See under: Ambas-
             sadors--Constantinople.

1895-1897   Thielmann, Max, Baron von.   First secretary in Paris,
            1880-1882, in Constantinople, 1882-1886; consul-general
            in Sofia, 1886-1887; Prussian minister in Darmstadt,
            1887-1890, in Hamburg, 1890-1894; state secretary of
            Reich treasury, 1897-1908.
1897-1903   Holleben, Theodor von.
1903-1908   Speck von Sternberg, Hermann, Baron von.   First sec-
            retary in Washington, 1898-1900; German representative
            on Samoa Commission; consul-general in Calcutta, 1900
            1903; minister on special mission to Washington, 1903.
1908-1917   Bernstorff, Johann Heinrich, Count von (1862-1939).
            First secretary in London, 1902-1906; consul-general
            in Cairo, 1906-1908.

Ministers--Brussels:

1886-1901   Alvensleben, Friedrich Johann, Count von.   See under:
            Ambassadors--St. Petersburg.
1901-1910   Wallwitz, Nikolaus, Count von.
1910-1913   Flotow, Johannes von.   See under: Ambassadors--
            Rome.
1913-1914   von Below-Saleske.   Minister in Sofia, 1910-1913.

Ministers--Belgrade:

1876-1892   Bray-Steinburg, Hippolyt, Count von.   Consul-general
            in Belgrade, 1876-1878, post became a ministry in
            1879; minister in Bucharest, 1897-1899, in Lisbon,
            1892-1894.
1892-1903   Waecker-Gotter, Baron von.   Minister in Lisbon, 1888-
            1892.
1904-1906   Heyking, Edmund, Baron von.   Consul-general in Cal-
            cutta, 1889-1893; minister in Tangier, 1895-1896, in
            Peking, 1896-1899.

1890-1908   Ratibor und Corvey, Max, Prince von. See under:
             Ambassadors--Madrid.

1908-1911   Reichenau, F. von. Minister to Stockholm at the out-
             break of war.

1911-1914   Griesinger, Julius A., Baron von.

Ministers--Bucharest:

1882-1885   Saurma v.d. Jeltsch, Anton von. See under: Ambas-
             sadors--Constantinople.

1885-1888   Busch, Dr. Klemens August. See under Under State
             Secretaries for Foreign Affairs.

1888-1893   Bülow, Bernhard, Prince von. See under: Chancellors.

1893-1897   Leyden, Casimir, Count von. First secretary in Lon-
             don, 1888-1890; consul-general in Cairo, 1890-1893;
             minister in Tokyo, 1898-1901, in Stockholm, 1901-1905.

1897-1899   Bray-Steinburg, Hippolyt, Count von. See under:
             Ministers--Belgrade.

1899-1910   Kiderlen-Wächter, Alfred von. See under: State Sec-
             retaries for Foreign Affairs.

1910-1912   Rosen, Dr. Friedrich. Vortragender Rat in the foreign
             office, 1901-1905; minister in Tangier, 1905-1910, in
             Lisbon, 1912-1916.

1912-1914   Waldthausen, Dr. von.

1915-1916   Bussche-Haddenhausen, Dr. Hilmar, Baron von dem.
             First secretary in Washington, 1903-1906; vortragender
             Rat in foreign office, 1907-1910; under state secretary
             for foreign affairs, 1916-1918.

Ministers--Lisbon:

1888-1892   Waecker-Gotter, Baron von. See under: Ministers--
             Belgrade.

1892-1894   Bray-Steinburg, Hippolyt, Count von. See under:

Ministers--Belgrade.

1894-1898   Derenthall, Eduard von. Consul-general in Cairo, 1883-1884, in Alexandria, 1884-1887; minister in Weimar, 1887-1894, in Stuttgart, 1898-1903.

1898-1908   Tattenbach, Christian, Count von. See under: Ambassadors--Madrid.

1908-1910   Ratibor und Corvey, Max, Prince von. See under: Ambassadors--Madrid.

1910-1912   Bodmann, Baron von und zu.

1912-1916   Rosen, Dr. Friedrich. See under: Ministers--Bucharest.

Ministers--Tangier:

1889-1895   Tattenbach, Christian, Count von. See under: Ambassadors--Madrid.

1896-1899   Schenck zu Schweinsburg, Baron. Minister in Peking, 1893-1896.

1899-1905   Mentsingen, Friedrich, Baron von.

1905-1910   Rosen, Dr. Friedrich. See under: Ministers--Bucharest.

1910-1914   Seckendorff, Baron von.

Ministers--Peking:

1874-1893   Brandt, Maximillian August Scipio von.

1893-1896   Schenck zu Schweinsburg, Baron. See under: Ministers--Tangier.

1896-1899   Heyking, Edmund, Baron von. See under: Ministers--Belgrade.

1899-1900   Ketteler, Klemens, Baron von.

1900-1906   Mumm von Schwarzenstein, Alfons, Baron. Vortragender Rat in foreign office, 1894-1898; chargé d'affaires in Washington, 1899; Ambassador in Tokyo, 1906-1911.

1906-1911 Rex, Count von. Minister in Teheran, 1898-1906, in Tokyo, 1911-1914.

1911-1914 von Haxthausen.

1914-1917 von Hintze.

Ministers--Tokyo:

1886-1892 Holleben, Theodor von. See under: Ambassadors-- Washington.

1892-1897 Gutschmidt, Felix, Baron von.

1897-1898 Treutler, Baron von.

1898-1901 Leyden, Casimir, Count von. See under: Ministers-- Bucharest.

1901-1906 Arco-Valley, Emmerich, Count von und zu. See under: Ambassadors--Washington.

1906-1911 Mumm von Schwarzstein, Baron. See under: Ministers--Peking.

1911-1914 Rex, Count von. See under: Ministers--Peking.

Ministers--Sofia (consul-general to 1909):

1886-1887 Thielmann, Max, Baron von. See under: Ambassa- dors--Washington.

1888-1892 Wagenheim, Hans, Baron von. See under: Ambassa- dors--Constantinople.

1893-1898 Voigts-Rhetz, Konstantin Bernhard von.

1898-1900 Reichenau, F. von. See under: Ministers--Belgrade.

1900-1905 Below-Rutzau, Gustav von.

1905-1910 Romberg, Gisber, Baron von.

1910-1913 von Below-Saleske. See under: Ministers--Brussels.

1913-1916 Michahelles.

1916-1918 Oberndorff, Count von.

State Secretaries for Foreign Affairs:

Jan. 1870-Sept. 1872   Thile, Karl Hermann von (1812-1889). Prus-
                        sian minister to the Holy See, 1855-1857, in
                        Vienna, 1857-1859; head of Prussian/German
                        foreign office, 1862-1872.

Dec. 1872-Oct. 1873   Balan, Hermann von (acting). Minister in
                        Brussels, 1868-1874.

Oct. 1873-1879   Bülow, Bernhard Ernst von (1815-1879).
                        Father of the chancellor.

Nov. 1879-April 1880   Limburg-Stirum, Friedrich Wilhelm, Count zu
                        (acting). Prussian minister in Weimar, 1875-
                        1880; member of Prussian chamber of depu-
                        ties, 1871-1905 (from 1893 leader of German
                        Conservative Party); member of Reichstag,
                        1893-1906. In 1881, given indefinite leave of
                        absence from foreign office.

April 1880-Oct. 1880   Hohenlohe-Schillingsfürst, Chlodwig, Prince zu
                        (acting). See under: Chancellors.

Oct. 1880-June 1881   Limburg-Stirum, Friedrich Wilhelm, Count
                        zu (acting).

July 1881-Oct. 1885   Hatzfeldt-Wildenburg, Paul, Count von (1831-
                        1901). Provisionally admitted to Prussian
                        diplomatic service on June 3, 1859, and sent
                        as an attaché to Paris. As result of his out-
                        standing work he was admitted to regular dip-
                        lomatic service in Nov. 1860 without first
                        having to take customary examinations, and ap-
                        pointed second (supernumerary) secretary in
                        Paris. Secretary in Paris, 1860-1866; sec-
                        retary of legation at The Hague, 1866-1868;
                        vortragender Rat in foreign office from 1868;
                        on Bismarck's personal foreign office staff,
                        1870-1871; head of the French section in the
                        foreign office, 1872-1874; minister in Madrid,
                        1874-1878; ambassador in Constantinople,

1879-1881, in London, 1885-1901. Served as acting state secretary from July 1881-Oct. 1882, before being appointed.

Oct. 1885-March 1890 Bismarck, Herbert, Count von (1849-1904). Acting, Oct. 1885-April 30, 1886. Eldest son of Bismarck. From Jan. 15, 1874, in foreign office; attached to several legations, but principally employed as private secretary to his father; first secretary in London, Nov. 1882-1884; acting first secretary in St. Petersburg, Jan. 1884; minister at The Hague, May 11, 1884-1885; under state secretary in foreign office, May 10, 1885-1886; Prussian minister of state, 1888-1890.

March 1890-Aug. 1897 Marschall von Bieberstein, Adolf, Hermann, Baron (1842-1912). Minister representing Baden in Berlin, 1883-1890; ambassador in Constantinople, 1897-1912, in London, 1912; first German delegate to The Hague Second Peace Conference.

Aug. 1897-Oct. 1900 Bülow, Bernhard, Prince von (acting, Aug. 1897-Oct. 1897). See under: Chancellors.

Oct. 1900-Jan. 1906 Richthofen, Oswald, Baron von (1847-1906). Director of colonial department of foreign office, 1896-1897; under state secretary for foreign affairs, 1897-1900.

Jan. 1906-Nov. 1907 Tschirschky und Bögendorff, Heinrich von (1858-1916). Temporarily employed in foreign office, 1885-1887; secretary of legation in Athens, 1888-1890, in Bern, 1890-1892; first secretary in Constantinople, 1893, in St. Petersburg, 1894-1900; minister in Luxembourg, 1900-1902; ambassador in Vienna, 1907-1916 (his chargé d'affaires for 1912-1915 was Prince Stolberg); several times foreign office representative in Kaiser's retinue.

Nov. 1907-June 1910   Schoen, Wilhelm, Baron von (1851-1933).
                       Minister in Copenhagen, 1900-1905; ambassa-
                       dor in St. Petersburg, 1905-1907, in Paris,
                       1910-1914; frequent representative of foreign
                       office in Kaiser's retinue.

June 1910-Dec. 1912   Kiderlen-Wächter, Alfred von (1852-1912).
                       Secretary in St. Petersburg, 1881-1885, in
                       Paris, 1885-1886, in Constantinople, 1886-
                       1888; vortragender Rat in charge of Balkan
                       and Near East affairs in foreign office, 1888-
                       1894; Prussian minister in Hamburg, 1894-
                       1895; minister in Copenhagen, 1895-1899, in
                       Bucharest, 1899-1910; temporary state secre-
                       tary for foreign affairs, Nov. 1908-March
                       1909.

Dec. 1912-Nov. 1916   Jagow, Gottlieb von (1863-1935). First sec-
                       retary in Rome, 1901-1906; vortragender Rat
                       in foreign office, 1906-1907; ambassador in
                       Rome (Quirinal), 1909-1912.

Nov. 1916-Aug. 1917   Zimmermann, Alfred. Assistant in foreign
                       office; vortragender Rat in foreign office,
                       1905-1910; under state secretary for foreign
                       affairs, 1911-1916.

Aug. 1917-July 1918   Kühlmann, Richard von (1873-1948). First
                       secretary of legation in Teheran, 1901-1903,
                       in Tangier, 1904-1905, in The Hague, 1907;
                       first secretary in London, 1908-1914.

July 1918-Oct. 1918   Hintze, Paul von, Admiral (1864-1941). Mil-
                       itary plenipotentiary at Russian Court, 1908-
                       1911, foreign office representative with high
                       command, Oct.-Nov. 1918; ambassador to
                       Norway, 1917-1918.

Oct. 1918-Dec. 1918   Solf, Dr. Wilhelm Heinrich (1862-1936).
                       Governor of Samoa, 1900; state secretary of
                       Reich colonial office, 1911-1918.

Dec. 1918-April 1919   Brockdorff-Rantzau, Ulrich, Count von.

Under State Secretaries for Foreign Affairs (post created in 1881, two positions from 1916):

1881-1885	Busch, Dr. Klemens. Dragoman in Constantinople, 1861-1872; consul in St. Petersburg, 1872-1874; temporarily attached to political division of foreign office, 1874-1879; temporary head of political division of foreign office, 1880-1881; minister in Bucharest, 1885-1888, in Stockholm, 1888-1892, in Bern, 1892-1895.
1885-1886	Bismarck, Herbert, Count von. See under: State Secretaries for Foreign Affairs.
1886-1890	Berchem, Max, Count von. First secretary in St. Petersburg, 1875-1878, in Vienna, 1878-1883; chargé d'affaires in Stockholm, 1884; director of economic policy division of foreign office, 1885-1886.
1890-1897	Rotenhan, Wolfram, Baron von. First secretary in Paris, 1884-1885; minister in Bern, 1897, to the Holy See, 1897-1908.
1897-1900	Richthofen Oswald, Baron von. See under: State Secretaries for Foreign Affairs.
1900-1907	Mühlberg, Otto von. Vortragender Rat in foreign office, 1885-1900; Prussian minister to the Holy See, 1907-1918.
1907-1911	Stemrich, Wilhelm.
1911-1916	Zimmermann, Alfred. Assistant in foreign office, vortragender Rat in foreign office, 1905-1910.
1916-1918	Bussche-Haddenhausen, Dr. Hilmar, Baron von dem. See under: Ministers--Bucharest.
1916-1918	Stumm, Wilhelm von. Vortragender Rat in foreign office, 1909-1911; director of political division of foreign office, 1911-1916.

Directors of the Political Division IA (post created in 1910):

| 1910-1911 | Zimmermann, Alfred. See under: Under State Secretaries for Foreign Affairs. |
| 1911-1916 | Stumm, Wilhelm von. See under: Under State Secretaries for Foreign Affairs. |

Directors of the Personnel Division IB:

1879-1881	Bülow, Otto von (Dirigent).
1881-1890	Post vacant.
1890-1895	Humbert, Georg Paul Andreas (Dirigent).
1895-1902	von Eichorn (Dirigent).
1903-1907	von Schwarzkoppen (Dirigent).
1907-1912	von Schwarzkoppen.
1913-1918	Mathieu.

Directors of Division II (Legal and Commercial):

1863-1881	von Philipsborn.
1881-1882	von Jordan.
1882-1885	von Boganowski.

Directors of Division II (Commercial):

1885-1886	Berchem, Max, Count von. See under: Under State Secretaries for Foreign Affairs.
1886-1899	Richardt.
1899-1913	von Koerner.
1913-1919	Johannes, Hermann.

Directors of Division III (Legal):

1885-1902   Hellwig.

1902-1911   von Franzius.

1911-1918   Kriege, Johannes.

Directors of Division IV (Colonial Affairs):

1890   Krauel, Dr. Friedrich (Dirigent April-June 1890).
             Temporarily attached to foreign office, 1884-1885; offi-
             cial in charge of colonial affairs, May, 1885-1890; min-
             ister in Buenos Aires, 1890-1904, in Rio de Janeiro,
             1894-1898.

1890-1896   Kayser, Dr. Paul. As Dirigent, from 1890-1894.
             Vortragender Rat in foreign office, 1886-1890.

1896-1897   Richthofen, Oswald, Baron von. See under: State Sec-
             retaries for Foreign Affairs.

1898-1900   Buchka, Dr. von.

1900-1905   Stübel, Dr. Oskar Wilhelm.

1905-1907   Hohenlohe-Langenburg, Ernst, Prince zu (acting).

1906-1907   Dernburg, Dr. Bernhard (1865-1937) (acting). Director
             of Bank of Darmstadt; state secretary of the Reichs
             colonial office, 1907-1910. For state secretaries of
             the Reichs colonial office who followed Dernburg see
             below: Other Important Foreign Office and Colonial Of-
             fice Administrators. This division was removed from
             the foreign office in 1907.

Vortragende Räte of the Political Division IA:

1853-1871   Abeken, Heinrich (1809-1872). In Prussian foreign min-
             istry from 1848.

1863-1872   Keudell, Robert, Baron von. In charge of Personnel
             Division. See under: Ambassadors--Rome.

1864-1886	Bucher, Lothar (1817-1892).
1868-1874	Hatzfeldt-Wildenburg, Paul, Count von. See under: State Secretaries for Foreign Affairs.
1872-1874	Radowitz, Joseph Maria von. See under: Ambassadors--Constantinople.
1874-1879 1880-1881	Busch, Dr. Klemens August. Temporarily attached to political division of foreign office, 1874-1879; temporary head of political division of foreign office, 1880-1881. See under: Under State Secretaries for Foreign Affairs.
1874-1879	Jasmund, von. Consul-general in Alexandria before working in political division; appointed minister in Bucharest in 1879 but died shortly after obtaining post.
1874-1884	Kusserow, Heinrich von. Specialist for colonial affairs.
1878-1908	Holstein, Friedrich, Baron, von (1837-1909).
1878-1892	Lindau, Dr. Rudolf. Attached to Paris Embassy for press and commercial affairs, 1871-1878; from 1878 Legationsrat in foreign office.
1880-1888	Rantzau, Kuno, Count zu. Prussian minister in Munich, 1888-1891. Married Marie, only daughter of Otto von Bismarck, in Nov. 1878.
1881-1888	Brauer, Arthur von.
1885-1890	Krauel, Dr. Friedrich. Specialist for colonial affairs. See under: directors of Division IV (Colonial Affairs).
1886-1890	Kayser, Paul. Specialist in colonial affairs. See under: Directors of Division IV (Colonial Affairs).
1888-1890	Kiderlen-Wächter, Alfred von. In charge of Balkan and Near East affairs. See under: State Secretaries for Foreign Affairs.
1890-1899	Pourtalès, Friedrich, Count von. See under: Ambassadors--St. Petersburg.
1892-1893	Rössler, Konstantin.
1894-1906	Lindenau, Karl von. Temporary assistant in foreign office, 1891-1894; Legationsrat, 1894-1906; from 1895 also attached to chancellor's staff.
1894-1916	Hammann, Otto. In charge of press division.
1894-1898	Mumm von Schwarzstein, Alfons, Baron. See under:

Ministers--Peking.

1896-1908	Klehmet, Reinhold. Temporary assistant in foreign office, 1894-1895; consul in Athens, 1908-1911.

1898-1900   Mühlberg, Otto von. See under: Under State Secretaries for Foreign Affairs.

1899-1904   Lichnowsky, Karl Max, Prince von. See under: Ambassadors--London.

1900-1904   Rosen, Dr. Friedrich. See under: Ministers--Bucharest.

1900-1911   Kriege, Johannes. Second German delegate to The Hague Second Peace Conference.

1901-1902   Rücker-Jenisch, Martin, Baron von. Prussian minister to Darmstadt, 1906-1913; on several occasions foreign office representative in Kaiser's retinue; Bülow's cousin.

1902-1907   von Kriess.

1904-1907   Below-Schlatau, Paul von. Temporarily employed in foreign office, 1888-1890; first secretary in Paris, 1897-1899.

1905-1910   Zimmermann, Alfred. See under: Under State Secretaries for Foreign Affairs.

1906-1907   Jagow, Gottlieb von. See under: State Secretaries for Foreign Affairs.

1907-1910   Bussche-Haddenhausen, Dr. Hilmar, Baron von. See under: Ministers--Bucharest.

1907-1910   von Eckert.

1907-1910   Flotow, Johannes von. See under: Ambassadors--Rome.

1908-1911   Griesinger, Julius, A., Baron von.

1909-1911   Stumm, Wilhelm von. See under: Under State Secretaries for Foreign Affairs.

1910-1917   Wedel, Botho, Count von.

1910-1912   Romberg, Gisber, Baron von. See under: Ministers--Sofia.

1910-1916   Langwerth von Simmern.

1911-1919   Montgelas, Max, Count von.

1911-1913   Mirbach-Harff, Wilhelm, Count von.

1912-1919   von Rosenburg.

Other Important Foreign Office Officials:

Bülow, Hans Adolf von.   First secretary at legation in Brussels,
     1905-1907.
Derenthall, Eduard von.   First secretary in Rome, 1876-1883; con-
     sul-general in Cairo, 1883-1884, in Alexandria, 1884-
     1887; Prussian minister in Weimar, 1887-1894.
Eckardstein, Hermann, Baron von (1864-1933).   Diplomatically with
     German embassy in London, although not in government
     service; granted title counsellor of legation 1898; first
     secretary in London, December, 1899-1902.
Eulenburg, Botho, Count zu (1831-1912).   Prussian minister-presi-
     dent, 1892-1894; Prussian minister of interior, 1878-
     1881.
Goltz, Karl August, Count von der.   First secretary in Vienna,
     1884-1886; in Rome, 1886-1890.
Hutten-Czapski, Bogdan, Count von.   Attached to German embassy
     in Paris, 1882-1883; aide-de-camp to governor of
     Alsace-Lorraine, 1884-1885; squadron leader in Kassel,
     1886-1896; castellan of Posen; member of Prussian up-
     per house; unofficial aide and advisor of Prince Hohen-
     lohe.
Köller, Ernst Matthias.   Under secretary of state for Alsace-Lor-
     raine, 1889-1894; Prussian minister of interior, Octo-
     ber, 1894-December, 1895; head of administration of
     Schleswig-Holstein, 1897-1901; state secretary for Al-
     sace-Lorraine, 1901-1908.
Kühlmann, Richard von.   See under: State Secretaries for Foreign
     Affairs.
Lancken-Wakenitz, Baron von der.   Counsellor at Paris embassy,
     1907-1913.
Lerchenfeld-Koefering, Hugo, Count von und zu (1843-1925).   Bavar-
     ian minister in Berlin, 1880-1919.

Lindenfels, Gustav von. Vortragender Rat in economic policy divi-
    sion of foreign office, 1885-1897.

Miquel, Hans von. Second secretary in Paris, 1902-May, 1905;
    first secretary in St. Petersburg, 1905-1908; in Con-
    stantinople, 1908-1912.

Mutius, G. von. Secretary in Paris embassy, 1909-1911, in Con-
    stantinople, 1912-1914.

Müller, Felix von. Minister to The Hague, 1908-1915.

Pückler, Karl, Count von. First secretary in Rome, Dec. 1895-
    1898, in London, Jan.-Dec. 1899, in Vienna, 1899-
    1900, in St. Petersburg, Aug. 1900-Nov. 1901.

Reischach, Hugo, Baron von (1854-1934). Court-marshal to Kaiserin
    Friedrich; master of the horse to William II from 1905.

Rottenburg, Dr. Franz Johannes (1845-1907). Employed by Bis-
    marck in foreign office from 1876; Bismarck's assist-
    ant in Reich chancellery, 1881-1890; under state secre-
    tary in ministry of interior, 1891-1896.

Rücker-Jenisch, Martin von, from Jan. 27, 1906, Baron von Jenisch.
    Minister, consul-general, and diplomatic agent in Cairo,
    1903-1906; minister in Darmstadt, 1906-1913; on sever-
    al occasions foreign office representative in Kaiser's
    retinue.

Rüdenhausen, Castell. First secretary in Rome, 1899-1901.

Scheel-Plessen, Ludwig, Baron von, from 1898 Count von Plessen-
    Cronstern. First secretary in Constantinople from
    June, 1883, in St. Petersburg from Aug. 1883, in Lon-
    don, 1884-1888; minister in Athens, 1894-1902.

Stengel, Karl, Baron von. Professor of international law at Univer-
    sity of Munich; second delegate to The Hague First
    Peace Conference, 1899.

Zorn, Philipp. Professor of International Law at University of
    Königsberg; member of German delegation to The Hague
    First Peace Conference, 1899.

Other Important Colonial Officials:

Lindequist, Dr. Friedrich von (1862-1945).   Governor of German
        Southwest Africa, 1905-1907; under state secretary of
        Reichs colonial office, 1907-1910; state secretary of
        Reichs colonial office, 1910-1911, resigned over Agadir
        Agreement.

Solf, Dr. Wilhelm Heinrich (1862-1936).   State secretary of Reichs
        colonial office, 1911-1918. See under: State Secre-
        taries for Foreign Affairs.

Bell, Dr. Johannes.   State secretary of Reichs colonial office, 1918;
        Centerist; signed Versailles Treaty on behalf of German
        nation on June 28, 1919, along with Majority Socialist
        and future German foreign minister (1919-1920) Her-
        mann Müller.

Leutwein, Theodor, Major.   Commander of forces in German South-
        west Africa, 1894-1895; governor of Southwest Africa,
        1895-1904.

Mechler, Gustav Emil.   In foreign office, 1870-1886; temporary
        head of chancellor's secretariat, 1886-1889; head of
        central bureau of foreign office, 1889-1920.

Nachtigall, Gustav.   Consul-general at Tunis, 1883-1885; commis-
        sioner for West Africa, 1884.

Schele, Friedrich Rabod, Baron von.   Governor of German East
        Africa, 1893-1906.

Chiefs of Staff of the Army:

1857-1888   Moltke, Helmuth, Count von, Field Marshal (1800-
             1891).
1888-1891   Waldersee, Alfred L. H. K., Count von, General (1832-
             1904).
1891-1906   Schlieffen, Alfred, Count von, General (1833-1913).
1906-1914   Moltke, Helmuth J. L., Count von, General (1848-
             1916).

1914-1916 Falkenhayn, Erich von, General (1861-1922). Also
served as Prussian minister of war, 1913-1916; commander in Rumania and Caucasus, 1916-1918.

1916-1918 Hindenburg und Benckendorff, Paul von, Field Marshal
(1847-1934). Recalled from retirement in Sept. 1914,
to take command on eastern front; president of the
German republic, 1925-1934.

Chiefs of the Imperial Military Cabinet:

1888-1901 Hahnke, Wilhelm.
1901-1908 Hülsen-Häseler, Dietrich, Count von (1852-1908).
1908-1918 Lyncker, Moritz, Baron von (1845-1923).

Other Important Army Figures:

Plessen, Hans Georg Hermann von. General commander of imperial
headquarters, 1892-1918. Chief aide-de-camp to Kaiser, 1888-1918; German Army adjutant-general, 1914.

Chelius, Oskar von. Military plenipotentiary at Russian Court under Pourtalès; aide-de-camp and friend of Kaiser.

Kageneck, Karl, Count von. Military attaché in Vienna under
Tschirschky und Bögendorff, 1908-1914.

Goltz, Kolmar, Baron von der, General (1843-1916). Head of German military mission to Turkey, 1909-1911; officer assisting the Turkish army, 1882-1895.

Liman von Sanders, Otto, General. Head of military mission to
Turkey, 1913-1914.

Ludendorff, Erich F. W., General (1865-1937). Head of mobilization section of general staff, 1911-1914.

Gröner, Wilhelm, General (1867-1939). Head of railway section of
general staff, 1914-1916.

Schwarzhoff, Gross von, Colonel. German delegate to The Hague
First Peace Conference; Chief of Staff of China Expedi-

tionary Corps, 1900-1901.

Schulenburg, Friedrich, Count von der.   Military attaché in London, 1902-1906.

Chiefs of the Admiralty:

1872-1883   Stosch, Albrecht von, General and Admiral (1818-1896). Also, minister of state for same period.

1883-1888   Caprivi, Georg Leo, Count von.   See under: Chancellors.

1888-1889   Monts, Alexander, Count von, Admiral (1832-1889).

On March 30, 1889, the solitary chief of the admiralty was replaced by a chief of high command of the navy (with the rank and privileges of a commanding general in the army), a chief of the imperial naval cabinet, and a state secretary of the imperial naval office serving under the Reich chancellor.

State Secretaries for the Navy:

1888-1889   Häusner, Rear-Admiral von.

1890-1897   Hollmann, Friedrich von, Admiral (1842-1913).

1897-1916   Tirpitz, Alfred von, Admiral (1842-1913).   Commander of cruiser squadron in Far East, 1896-1897.   Resigned in March, 1916, as protest against emperor's unwillingness to make full use of German sea power.

1916-1918   Capelle, Eduard von, Admiral (1855-1931).   Under state secretary for the navy under Tirpitz.

Chiefs of the Imperial Naval Cabinet:

1889-1908   Senden und Bibran, Gustav, Baron von, Admiral (1847-1909).

1908-1918 Müller, Georg Alexander von, Admiral (1854-1940).

Took over the duties of Chief on March 8, 1906, from

the ailing Senden, but not formally until April 1908.

Other Important Naval Figures:

Goltz, Admiral von der. First chief of high command, 1889.

Knorr, Eduard von, Admiral (1840-1920). Chief of high command,
1895-1899.

Diederichs, Otto von, Rear-Admiral (1843-1919). Commander of
the cruiser division in Far East, 1897-1898; chief of
admiralty staff, 1900-1902.

Pohl, Hugo von, Admiral (1855-1916). Chief of admiralty staff.

Behncke, Paul, Acting Chief of the admiralty staff when von Pohl
was absent.

Widenmann, Wilhelm, Captain (1871-195?). Naval attaché in London, 1907-1912.

Müller, Erich von (1877-??). Naval attaché in London, 1912-1914.

Keim, August. Presiding officer of German navy league, 1900-
1908.

Salm-Horstmar, Otto, Prince und Rheingraf zu. President of Navy
league to June 14, 1908.

Chapter VI

Events in German Foreign and Colonial Policy 1888-1914

June 15, 1888   William II 1888-1918 (1859-1941) crownod as
Emperor of Germany.

Jan. 28, 1888   Military agreement between Italy and Germany providing for the use of Italian troops against France in the event of a
Franco-German war.

Feb. 3, 1888   Publication of the German-Austro-Hungarian Alliance of Oct. 7, 1879. It was published at this time as a warning
to Russia where nationalist agitation against Germany and Austria
was at a high point. There was some talk in Germany of a preventive war against Russia; however, this plan was vetoed by
Bismarck.

Feb. 6, 1888   Bismarck's Reichstag speech dealing with the Russian situation and ending with, "We Germans fear God and nothing
else in the world." The main terms of the Triple Alliance and the
Mediterranean Agreements were allowed to leak out at this time.
The terms of these agreements helped to diminish the aspirations
of both France and Russia.

    Background of the Triple Alliance.
    This pact grew out of the 1879 treaty between Germany
and Austria-Hungary, which remained in force until 1918.
The provisions of the latter agreement were: (1) if either
party were attacked by Russia, the other party should come
to its assistance with all forces at its disposal; (2) if either should be attacked by some other power, the other
should preserve at least neutrality; and (3) if another power
should be supported by Russia, then each ally was obliged
to aid the other ally.

The Austro-German alliance was the result of a period of
tension between Russia and Germany following the Congress
of Berlin of June 13 to July 13, 1878. The Russian national-
ists blamed Bismarck for Russia's diplomatic defeat at this
congress as to acquisitions allowed Russia. For months following the Congress of Berlin there were recriminations in
the newspapers between Germany and Russia. This culminated
in a threatening letter to William I from the Tsar, Alexander
II. Bismarck had always been fearful of a coalition being
set up by Russia against Germany. He now suspected that
Andrassy would soon be replaced by the pro-Russian party
in Vienna. Therefore Bismarck decided on the Austro-
German alliance which was welcomed by Andrassy although
Emperor William I was opposed to it and resisted attempts
to complete it. In the end he yielded only when Bismarck
threatened to resign if the emperor did not approve the
alliance.

There was some thought of bringing England in on the
agreement. Disraeli was amenable to this suggestion but
the German ambassador, Count Münster, misrepresented
the alliance as one directed mainly against France. Bismarck then allowed the idea to be dropped.

The immediate result of the negotiations for the Austro-
German alliance was the mission of Saburov to Berlin in Sept.
and Oct. 1879 in an effort to effect a Russian-German alliance by reviving the Three Emperors' League. Bismarck,
however, evaded the advances made by Saburov and it was
not until June 18, 1881 the pact was concluded between
Russia, Austria, and Germany for a period of three years.
It was renewed in 1884 for another three years. The provisions of the agreement were: (1) if one of the contracting
powers found itself at war with a fourth power, except
Turkey, the other two were to maintain friendly neutrality;
(2) modifications of the territorial "status quo" in Turkey
should take place only after agreement between the three
powers; (3) if one of the three powers felt compelled to go
to War with Turkey, it should consult the other two powers
in advance as to the eventual results; (4) the principle of
the closure of the Straits was recognized. If this principle
were infringed by Turkey the three powers should warn
Turkey that they would regard her as having put herself in
a state of war with the aggrieved power; (5) Austria reserved
the right to annex Bosnia and Herzegovina when she saw fit;
and (6) the three powers agreed not to oppose the eventual
union of Bulgaria and Eastern Rumania.

This treaty was kept secret. Russia was anxious for an
alliance with Germany as protection against Austrian policy
in the Balkans. Russia was equally anxious for recognition
of the closure of the Straits in the event of possible attack

by England. Bismarck refused to make an agreement with
Russia unless Austria was included. The Austrians, them-
selves, were hostile to the idea until the advent of the
Gladstone government in England, which was unfriendly to
Austria.

Italy became the third member of the Triple Alliance on
May 20, 1882. The Agreement with Austria and Germany
was concluded for five years and renewed at intervals until
1915. The terms of the alliance were: (1) if Italy were attacked by France without provocation, Germany and Austria
were to come to Italy's aid; (2) if Germany were attacked
by France, Italy would come to Germany's aid; and (3) if
one or two of the contracting parties were attacked or involved in war with two or more great powers, the others
were to preserve benevolent neutrality. The treaty was the
result of Italy's isolation after the French occupation of
Tunis and was also a reflection of the popular demand for
security against radicalism and the prospect of intervention
by other powers in behalf of the Pope. The Italians wanted
a treaty of guaranty, assuring them of possession of Rome.
Neither Austria nor Germany was willing to consider this
proposition, even though Austria was eager for an agreement to put an end to the irredentist agitation which had
been very active since 1876. Germany was uneasy about
renewed Pan-Slav agitation and the possibility of a Franco-
Russian alliance. The Italians received no guaranty of
Rome but received assurances against attack by France.

Feb. 20, 1887   Renewal of the Triple Alliance for five years. Ne-

gotiations had been carried on since Nov. 1886. The Italians de-

manded more far reaching support of their interests in North

Africa. This Bismarck was willing to concede in return for Italy's

friendship in the event of a war with France. Austria, whose at-

tention was focused on the Balkans, objected to this Italian demand.

In the end the alliance was renewed and special German-Italian and

Austro-Italian agreements were made. Germany promised Italy

that if France tried to expand in North Africa, and if Italy were

obliged to take action or even declare war on France, Germany

would come to the aid of Italy. If France were defeated, Germany

would not object to Italy's taking "territorial guaranties for the

security of the frontiers and of her maritime position." The

Austro-Italian agreement provided for the maintenance of the

"status quo" in the Orient. If this became impossible, neither

party should occupy territory except in agreement with the other

on the principle of reciprocal compensation. This agreement was
not to apply to the eventual Austrian annexation of Bosnia and
Herzegovina.

Sub Triple Alliance Agreement: Oct. 30, 1883.
    An Alliance of Rumania and Austria to which Germany ad-
hered. Rumania was dissatisfied with the settlement made
at the Congress of Berlin in 1878. They were fearful that
the Russians would try to make further advances into the
Balkans and violate Rumanian territory. Terms of agreement were: (1) Austria was to come to the aid of Rumania
if she were attacked without provocation; and (2) Rumania
was to come to Austria's aid if Austria were attacked in a
portion of its states bordering on Rumania. Such an attack
would most likely come from Russia. The treaty was concluded for five years and renewed at periodic intervals until
1916. On May 15, 1888 Italy adhered to this alliance of Rumania and Austria, of which Germany was a secret partner.
This alliance can be thought of as an appendage of the Triple
Alliance.

Background of the Mediterranean Agreements.
    First agreement: Feb. 12, 1887. This agreement was be-
tween England and Italy and was adhered to by Austria on
March 24, 1887, and by Spain on May 4, 1887. The agreement took the form of an exchange of notes; Anglo-Italian,
Anglo-Austrian, Italian-Spanish. It was acceded to by
Germany and Austria on May 21, 1887. Bismarck, ex-
ploiting the acute Anglo-French tension over Egypt and the
Italian-French tension over the tariff war, encouraged the
agreement. Its provisions were: (1) maintenance of the
"status quo" in the Mediterranean, including the Adriatic,
Aegean, and Black Seas; (2) advance agreement among
contracting parties necessary if "status quo" becomes impossible to maintain; (3) Italy was to support English policy
in Egypt; (4) England was to support Italian policy in North
Africa; (5) The Anglo-Austrian note stressed the community
of interest of the two powers in the Near East; and (6)
Spain promised not to make any arrangements with France
regarding North Africa which would be aimed at Italy,
Austria, or Germany. England refused to bind herself to
specific action, but the effect of the agreement was to
provide a basis for common action in the event of a
disturbance in the Mediterranean by France or Russia.

    Second Mediterranean Agreement (or Middle-Eastern
Entente: Dec. 12, 1887. This agreement was between
Austria, Italy, and England (Bismarck refused to participate) and contained the following parts: (1) a restatement of
the principle of maintaining the "status quo" in the Near East;
(2) a resolution concerning the importance of keeping Turkey
free of all foreign domination; (3) a prohibition against Turkey's
ceding her rights in Bulgaria to any other power or allowing

the occupation of Bulgaria by any other power; (4) a prohibition
against Turkey's giving up any right in the Straits or in Asia
Minor; and (5) an agreement by Austria, Italy, and England to
support Turkey in any effort by her to resist border encroachment, and if Turkey took no measures to resist encroachment,
an agreement that Austria, Italy, and England could consider
themselves justified to act, jointly or separately, in the provisional occupation of any Turkish territory deemed necessary
to secure enforcement of the treaty.

March 18, 1890 Dismissal of Bismarck. William II decided, after
two readings of a bill to prolong the Anti-Socialist Law, to let the law
expire. The Anti-Socialist Law was enacted on Oct. 19, 1878 and renewed at various intervals until 1890. The assassination attempts by
Hödel and Nobling, neither of whom was a socialist, nevertheless
prompted the passage of the bill. Bismarck had been behind the measure, wanting for a long time to supress Socialist activity in Germany.
When the Emperor came out against the renewal of the bill in 1890 he
widened the gap between himself and Bismarck. Behind this difference of opinion was the fundamental question: Who should rule Germany, Bismarck or the Emperor? William II wished to limit Bismarck's power further by setting aside the right of the Chancellor
to be present at the interviews of the Emperor and the ministers.
In addition to these differences Bismarck and William II differed
basically on policy toward Russia. Further, William II did not
agree with Bismarck's desire for closer relations with Austria and
England. Bismarck was ordered to ask permission to resign, but
he refused. Bismarck was finally forced to resign and was made
Duke of Lauenburg.

1890-1894 Chancellorship of General Georg Leo von Caprivi (1831-
1899). Caprivi was an able soldier and a capable administrator but
was without political experience. Caprivi descended from an Italian
family of Carniola which had settled in Prussia in the eighteenth
century. Caprivi was a member of the upper house in Prussia and
had served as an army officer during the wars of 1866 and 1870-
1871.

March 23, 1890   A German ministerial conference, on the advice
of Baron Fritz von Holstein, decided not to renew the Reinsurance
Treaty with Russia.   Holstein had for a long time been a close col-
laborator of Bismarck, but had in recent years drifted away from
him.   The treaty was allowed to lapse on June 18, 1890 despite numerous attempts on the part of Russia to re-open the question of
renewal.

Background of the Reinsurance Treaty.
On June 18, 1887, this secret treaty between Russia and
Germany was signed.   This treaty replaced the Three Emperors' Alliance, which Russia refused to renew.   The terms of
the treaty were: (1) the two powers promised each other neutrality in the event of either becoming involved in a war with
a third power.   However, this was not to apply in the case of
an aggressive war by Germany against France, of an agressive war by Russia against Austria; (2) both powers were to
work for the maintenance of the "status quo" in the Balkans,
but Germany was to recognize Russia's proponderent influence
in Bulgaria; (3) the principle of closure of the Straits was af-
firmed; (4) an additional and very secret protocol promised
German assistance in re-establishing a regular government in
Bulgaria--Germany was to oppose the restoration of the Batten-
berg in Bulgaria; and (5) a secret protocol also promised moral
and diplomatic support to the "measures which His Majesty (the
Tsar) may deem it necessary to take to control the key of his
empire" meaning the entrance to the Black Sea.   The Reinsurance Treaty represented Bismarck's effort to keep Russia from
forming an alliance with France.   Bismarck thought that it was
good business to buy Russian friendship by signing away things
which he knew Russia could never get on account of English
and Austrian opposition.

March 1890   Karl Peters entered Uganda by way of the Tana River
country.   He induced Mwangge to sign a treaty, by which it was
hoped that a German influence in Uganda might be established.

Background on German East Africa.
1860-1865: explorations of the German discoverer, von der
Decken, in East Africa.   He first outlined schemes for a German domination in this region.
1878: the German African Society, as a branch of the International African Association, established a number of posts in
the region between Bagamoyo and Lake Tanganyika.
Nov. 19, 1884: Karl Peters, moving spirit of the German
colonial movement, signed the first of a long series of treaties
with the native chiefs of the regions behind Bagamoyo.
Feb. 12, 1885: the German East Africa Company was
chartered to take over the claims established by Karl Peters.

Feb. 17, 1885: the German government established a protectorate over East Africa from the Umba River in the south
to the Rovuma in the north.
April 8, 1885: the Denhardt brothers secured the Witu region from the local sultan for the newly founded Witu Company.
May 27, 1885: the German government established a protectorate over Witu.
Aug. 14, 1885: the Sultan of Zanzibar was convinced, partly
because of a naval demonstration and an ultimatum, to recognize
the German protectorate over Witu.
May 12, 1886: Germany recognized Portuguese claims to
all the territory between Angola in West Africa and Mozambique
in East Africa.
Oct. 29-Nov. 1, 1886: investigation by a British-German-
French commission of claims in East Africa yielded an agreement defining the possessions of the Sultan of Zanzibar. The
German and British spheres of interest were defined by a line
from the mouth of the Umba River, northwest around the northern base of Mt. Kilimanjaro and thence northwest to the point
where the first parallel south latitude strikes the east coast of
Lake Victoria. In the north the British sphere extended to the
Tana River, leaving Witu to the Germans.
April 28, 1888: the Germans secured from the Sultan a 50
year lease of that part of the coast between the Rovuma and
the Umba Rivers.
1888-1890: an insurrection of the coast Arabs under Bushiri
led, in Dec. 1888, to the British joining the Germans in a
blockade of the coast. The uprising was ultimately put down
by Hermann von Wissmann.

July 1, 1890 Heligoland Treaty between Germany and England. Ger-

many relinquished large claims to Uganda and Witu, in East Africa

and received in return the island of Heligoland, which England had

obtained from Denmark in 1815. By 1890 the island was regarded

as practically useless, and the treaty was therefore looked upon as

a demonstration of German readiness to purchase English friendship.

The frontier of British East Africa was extended on the west side

of Lake Victoria as far as the frontier of the Congo State.

Background of the German colonial policy.
Feb.-April 24, 1883: establishment of the Germans, under
F. A. E. Lüderitz, a German merchant, at Angra Pequeña in
Southwest Africa. This move marked the beginning of German
colonialism. Behind this move was the German colonial society
(Deutsche Kolonial Gesellschaft), founded in 1882, and a fundamental change in Bismarck's policy to one of imperialism in
spite of opposition by the British to German influence in Southwest Africa. In August 1883, Lüderitz purchased from the natives a large tract of land north of the Orange River. In Feb-

ruary of the same year the German government had inquired in London whether the British government exercised any authority in this region. England gave Germany an evasive reply, but when Lüderitz hoisted the German flag at Angra Pequeña there was much excitement in London and in South Africa. The British Government announced that it regarded any claim in this region as a infringement of Britain's legitimate rights. An acrimonious discussion between London and Berlin followed. The British government in South Africa urged that England annex all territory to the north as far as White Fish Bay. This plan was frustrated when on April 24, 1884 the Germans proclaimed a protectorate over the region, which extended over all Damaraland. Sovereignty was vested in the Deutsche Kolonial Gesellschaft until it was assumed by the German government in 1892. The British under Cecil Rhodes moved in Feb. 1884 to make treaties with the native chiefs of Bechuanaland. This move was made because of fear of German expansion as far as the Transvaal region, which would cut the British route to the north. There followed two years of growing tension between England and Germany. The dispute extended to West African territories such as the Cameroons. Bismarck was able finally to establish a loose entente with Jules Ferry and the French in regard to Egypt. This was accomplished at a financial conference held in London during the months of June, July, & Aug. 1884. This agreement with the French forced the British to accept Germany as a colonial power.

Feb. 26, 1884: a British agreement was concluded with Portugal recognizing that nation's rights to territory at the mouth of the Congo River. This move was intended to frustrate the designs of King Leopold of Belgium who was head of the Congo Association. France and Germany protested and England was forced to abandon the treaty on June 26, 1884.

Nov. 15, 1884-Feb. 26, 1885: the Berlin conference on African affairs was arranged through the joint efforts of Bismarck and Jules Ferry. Fourteen nations, including the United States, agreed: (1) to work for the supression of slavery and the slave trade; (2) complete liberty of commerce should prevail in the Congo Basin and its affluents on the adjacent coasts; (3) freedom of navigation on the Congo and Niger Rivers and their affluents was to be maintained; (4) the Congo Basin was to be declared neutral; (5) the principle of effective occupation to establish a claim on the coasts was to be set up; and (6) to recognize the Congo Free State, which had developed under Leopold of Belgium from the International Association for the Exploration and Civilization of Central Africa, founded in 1876. In 1878 this organization became known as the International Association of the Congo.

March 31, 1885: Jules Ferry slipped from power in France after a minor reverse at Langson in the course of the war with China over Annam and Tonkin which lasted from July 12, 1884 to June 9, 1885. His fall marked the end of the German-French entente in colonial affairs which had been established in London in June, July & Aug. 1884. There followed a period of gradual

Anglo-German reconciliation with recognition of the German ac-
quisitions in Africa and the Pacific. In the years immediately
following the fall of Ferry there was a rapid development in
France of nationalist and revanchist agitation in reaction to
Ferry's policy of entente with Germany in colonial affairs.
General Georges Boulanger became minister of war in January
1886 and quickly became the symbol for a policy of revenge on
Germany.

Dec. 24, 1885: an agreement between France and Germany
was signed defining the frontier between the French Congo and
the Cameroons. German traders under Woermann and his company had opened a factory on the Cameroons coast in 1860.

July 14, 1886: an Anglo-German agreement delimiting the
frontier between the Gold Coast and Togoland was signed.

July 27, 1886: an Anglo-German agreement delimited the
Nigeria-Cameroons frontier.

Dec. 30, 1886: a German-Portuguese agreement fixed the
boundary of the Kabinda enclave between German Southwest Africa and Angola.

Aug. 17, 1890   Visit of Emperor William II to Tsar Alexander III,
of Russia, at Narva. This marked the last attempt by the Russians
to seek some agreement with Germany; however, William II evaded
Russian attempts promoting accord.

Oct. 28, 1890   Following the supression of the Coastal Arab uprising under Bushiri, the German East Africa Company gave over all
its territorial rights to the German government.

1891   The "German General League" (Allgemeiner Deutscher Verband), with Dr. Karl Peters, the explorer, as its first president,
was formed for the encouragement of Germanism abroad.

History of Pan-German League.
Under the direction of a Leipzig publicist, Professor Ernst
Hasse, the aims of this society had gradually taken on a more
agressive and chauvinistic form. In 1902 its name and constitution were changed in sympathy with its larger scheme of propaganda. The society became known as the "Pan-German League"
(All-Deutscher Verband). Covering the whole of Germany with
a network of branches, each one a center of organization and
agitation, the reconstructed League appealed to the nation with
a program of territorial aggrandizement which sought to give
concrete expression to the vague aspirations of the more ideal-
istic fore-runners of the Pan-German movement, the poets and
philosophers of a century before. Its object now became the
creation of a Greater Germany which should include all the German speaking peoples, irrespective of geographical areas. It

was the contention of the Pan-German movement that to the
Greater Germany must belong the German parts of Austria,
Switzerland, Holland, Luxembourg, and Belgium. None of the
non-German speaking peoples in the German Empire was to be
put out, but the Germans outside were to come in. Serious
politicians smiled at the idea as irresponsible and fatuous; it
was both, yet it took root and made quick growth, with the result of creating in the countries whose integrity was threatened
great unrest and justifiable resentment. The Pan-German
movement exercised a considerable influence on the mind of
the German nation. The doctrines of the League implied the
repudiation of international faith and the negation of public right.
Otto Hammann, in Der Neue Kurs (1918), p. 104, describes the
effect of the League abroad: "Well as it may have acted as a
national leaven amongst the Germans at home and abroad, it
has greatly injured the reputation of Germany abroad by its ful-
some boasting of the power of the empire and its naive depre-
ciation of foreign nationalities."
     The following two documents give some indication of the over-
all aims of the Pan-German League:

The Constitution

1. The Pan-German League strives to quicken the national
    sentiment of all Germans and in particular to awaken and
    foster the sense of racial and cultural kinship of all sec-
    tions of the German people.
2. These aims imply that the Pan-German League works for:
    1. preservation of the German people in Europe and over-
        seas and its support wherever threatened;
    2. settlement of all cultural, educational, and school prob-
        lems in ways that shall aid the German people;
    3. the combating of all forces which check the German na-
        tional development; and
    4. an active policy of furthering German interest in the
        entire world. The League is particularly interested in
        working for practical results in the German colonial
        movement.

The Policies of the League
(adopted in convention, 1898)

1. Adoption of bill for reorganization of the navy.
2. Laying of a cable from Kiaochow (China) to Port Arthur,
    with connection with the Russian-Siberian cable.
3. Strengthening of the German foothold in Kiaochow.
4. German coaling and cable stations in the Red Sea, the West
    Indies, and near Singapore.
5. Complete possession of Samoa.
6. More subsidized German steamship lines to Kiaochow and
    Korea.
7. Understanding with France, Spain, Portugal, and the Nether-

lands about the laying of an independent cable from West Africa through the Congo to German East Africa, Madagascar, Batavia, and from Tonkin to Kiaochow.

8. Development of harbor of Swakopmund (German Southwest Africa) and railroads to Windhoek (German Southwest Africa).
9. Securing of concessions for commerce and industry in Asia Minor.
10. Raising of the fund for German schools in foreign countries to 500,000 marks (was 150,000 marks), division in foreign office to be created to deal with these schools; creation of pension fund for their teachers; standard German textbooks to be supplied to these schools.
11. Further endowment of the colonization commission by 100 million marks, the Polish commission to be under the general commission.
12. Transference to the West of all officials (local, etc.) and military men of the Polish race.
13. Guarantee of increase in pay to the German officials in Polish parts of the East Province.
14. Acquisition of imperial holdings on the French border at Alsace-Lorraine and of Prussian royal holdings on the Danish border in Schleswig.
15. Employment of only German labor in imperial and state possessions and domains.
16. Prohibition of the immigration of less worthy elements into the German empire.
17. Possession of German citizenship by all Germans from the empire in foreign countries.
18. Taxation of foreign language-speaking firms, projects, and advertisements.
19. Prohibition of the use of foreign languages in clubs and meetings.
20. Germanization of all foreign place names in the German empire.
21. Establishment of a German consulate general for Bohemia in a German town in Bohemia.
22. Increase in the number of German commercial consuls in the Levant, Far East, South Africa, and Central and South America.
23. Increase in the number of German public libraries in the Eastern provinces, in Schleswig and in Alsace-Lorraine. State and imperial subsidies ought to support them.
24. Setting aside of a sum of money in the colonial office treasury to be used to pay for the attendance of sons of Germans living in foreign countries at German schools in the fatherland.
25. A lessening of the obligation to military service of Germans living in foreign lands.
26. Germanization of foreign words in official language:
    Gouverneur to Landeshauptmann.
    Gouvernement to Landesregierung.
    Kommandant to Befehlshaber.

Feb. 18-27, 1891 Visit of the Empress Frederich, mother of William II to Paris. This visit was marred by anti-German demonstrations, which resulted in increased tensions between France and Germany.

May 6, 1891 Premature renewal of the Triple Alliance. The original three documents which constituted the basis of the Triple Alliance were revised and merged into one, with Germany assuming increased obligations to support the Italian claims in North Africa. The premature renewal of the treaty was prompted by German fears that France might be in the process of bringing pressure to bear on Italy which would force Italy out of the Triple Alliance and into the French camp. The three contracting parties to the Triple Alliance were to do all in their power to achieve English support of Italian aspirations.

July 4, 1891 State visit of Emperor William II to England. The Kaiser visited with Queen Victoria who was his maternal grandmother. There were rumors that England would associate itself with the Triple Alliance.

1892-1894 The Caprivi commercial treaties with Austria, Italy, Switzerland, Spain, Serbia, Rumania, Belgium, and Russia. The treaties reduced agricultural duties, which helped to revive the high prices on food. The treaties also laid the base for the expansion of German trade in industrial products in the treaty countries, in effect recognizing the preponderence of German industry over agriculture. This brought the wrath of the Bund der Landwirte (Agrarian League) which amalgamated with the older Deutscher Bauernbund (German Peasants' League). The Bund der Landwirte was able to obtain a number of concessions from the government and ultimately came to serve as a spearhead for conservatism in the political sense.

July 13, 1893 French ultimatum to Siam. This caused a short, severe crisis in Anglo-French relations. The French stood their ground against England thus making a good impression on Russia. The Germans were half prepared to back England, but became disgusted when that country backed down.

July 15, 1893   Passage of the German military bill. This bill reduced the term of service in the infantry to two years, but it increased the size of the German army. This bill created a great deal of uneasiness in France and Russia.

Nov. 15, 1893   An Anglo-German agreement defining the Nigerian-Cameroons boundary. According to this agreement the region to the east of Lake Chad to within 100 miles of the Nile was assigned to Germany.

March 15, 1894   Franco-German agreement on the boundary between the Cameroons and the French Congo. The French were given the basin of the Shari River and the Bagirmi region. This agreement left the French free to advance through the Sudan to the Nile River.

March 16, 1894   Conclusion of Russian-German tariff treaty. It took years of negotiations and tariff wars before this treaty was concluded. This agreement demonstrated Russia's desire not to be drawn into hostilities with Germany.

May 12, 1894   Treaty between Britain and the Congo Free State. Britain leased to King Leopold of Belgium a large tract on the left bank of the Upper Nile, the lease to be good for the remainder of his life. Included in the treaty was the leasing by Leopold, for him and his successors, of a large tract of land lying to the west of the first tract. In return Leopold leased to Britain a corridor twenty-five kilometers wide between Lakes Tanganyika and Albert Edward, which was to serve as a connecting link for the Cape-to-Cairo telegraph and railway system, a project which had been in the discussion stage since 1888. The British were as aware of the importance of the Sudan for the assurance of Egypt's water supply as were other powers who were trying to penetrate this area. England was able to check the German move into Uganda (see above, Heligoland Treaty of July 1, 1890). However the Belgians and the French were attempting to move into the Sudan and the region of the Upper Nile. The British initially had tried to block the French advance by assigning the area in question to Germany. This agreement of November 1893 soured when the Germans on March 15, 1894 signed away the region to France. It was following this action that the British leased the territory of the Upper Nile to Leopold, the man the British considered their least dangerous competitor. The French protested as did the Germans. The German protest was on account of the corridor which ran along German East Africa. In June 1894, the English abandoned this corridor to conciliate the Germans. Pressure from France finally forced Britain to allow the treaty with the Congo Free State to lapse. This action demonstrated the rift between England and Germany in colonial affairs. It also pointed out the tendency of Germany and France to collaborate in colonial affairs against England.

June 1894 Breakdown of the efforts of Rosebery and Kalnoky to establish a connection between England and the Triple Alliance. The negotiations had been going on for six months and finally broke down because Germany was not willing to assume responsibility for any English interest. This breakdown marks the beginning of Anglo-German estrangement.

Sept. 1, 1894 A German-Portuguese agreement defining the boundaries between German East Africa and Mozambique.

Oct. 6, 1894 Britain invited Germany, France, Russia, and the United States to join in intervention in the Far East. The projected intervention failed to mature because of the unwillingness of the United States and Germany to participate.

Oct. 26, 1894 Resignation of Caprivi who had estranged the following groups in Germany: (1) the agrarians by his tariff policies,

(2) the center party through his failure to carry the Prussian School Bill in 1890, (3) the colonialists by the East Africa Agreement with England in 1890, (4) the militarists through the reduction of the term of service in the infantry from three to two years in 1893. The independence and unexpected initiatives of William II in both domestic and foreign policy continued to plague Caprivi. It became increasingly difficult for the chancellor to work with the emperor and the only recourse left him was resignation.

1894-1900 Chancellorship of Prince Chlodwig zu Hohenlohe-Schillingsfürst (1819-1901). Hohenlohe was an old man, a Catholic, and a liberal, and was not inclined to oppose openly the will of the youthful Emperor. He was a member of the Bavarian parliament from 1846-1866, and was prime minister of Bavaria from 1866-1870, pursuing a nationalistic and anti-clerical policy. During the years 1873-1885 he was the German ambassador in Paris. He was governor of Alsace-Lorraine from 1885-1894.

April 17, 1895 Treaty of Shimonoseki between China and Japan. Japan was prepared to make a territorial deal with Russia but was rejected because of the readiness of the Germans to join with Russia in any action that would check Japanese expansion. This was due to the growing German commercial interest in the Far East as well as a German desire to re-establish close relations with Russia. The thinking behind this move was to divert Russia to the Far East, thus emasculating the Franco-Russian alliance.

April 23, 1895 Intervention of Russia, Germany, and France in Tokyo. England refused to join in this action in which the Japanese were obliged to return the Liaotung Peninsula to China in consideration for an indemnity of thirty million taels. All of the intervening powers thought that they would benefit from this maneuveur. This marks the start of acute antagonism between Russia and Japan in the Far East. It also marks the formation of the Far Eastern Triplice of Russia, France, and Germany which in the following years exploited the weakness of China.

June 1895   Opening of the Kiel Canal from the North Sea to the Baltic.

June 25, 1895   Formation of the Salisbury cabinet in England, with Joseph Chamberlain in the colonial office.   There is an increase in English imperialism.   Because of English isolation and the situation in North Africa and the Far East Salisbury tried to throw off the danger of French and Russian advances by reconstituting closer relations with Germany and the Triple Alliance.

Aug. 5, 1895   Interview between William II and Salisbury at the Cowes yacht races.   Salisbury hinted at the advisability of partitioning the Ottoman Empire as the best solution to the chronic Middle East troubles.   Salisbury suggested that the Russians should be allowed to take Constantinople.   The Germans misunderstood Salisbury's plan and instead interpreted it as a move to involve the continental powers in the Middle East thus putting to an early end the friendship of Russia and Germany then being revived.   William II rejected all of Salisbury's suggestions.   When he became aware of the mistake he had made he attempted unsuccessfully to arrange a further interview with Salisbury.   The profound distrust which developed between Salisbury and William II tended to agravate relations between England and Germany.   Baron von Holstein encouraged this distrust.

Jan. 3, 1896   The Kruger Telegram Incident.   William II sent a telegram to President Kruger of the South African Republic (Transvaal) congratulating him on the defeat of the raiders led by Dr. Jameson.   The raid was the culmination of a long development of acute tension in the relations between England and the Transvaal. German interests in the Transvaal were considerable but not decisive.   They made themselves advocates of the Transvaal because they hoped to forcibly demonstrate the value of German friendship to England by threatening continuing annoyance.   This plan was proposed by Baron von Holstein.   When William II heard of the Jameson raid he assumed that the British government was behind it.   The

Kaiser demanded strong repressive measures, including German
military intervention on behalf of Kruger and the Transvaal government, against the raiders. William's advisors managed to cool his
ardor somewhat, but in the end they agreed to the telegram of con-
gratulations to Kruger. The telegram caused a storm of indignation
and recrimination in England, especially when it became known that
the real purpose of the German government was to beat the British
into friendship. The governments in both England and Germany remained calm, but public opinion in the two countries was stirred up
to such an extent that a policy of friendship between England and
Germany became impossible. Loud demands in Britain were voiced
for a pact with Russia and France. An agreement was concluded
between England and France on Jan. 15, 1896. The Kruger telegram marked the first violent outbreak of popular hostility between
England and Germany.

May 23, 1896 An Anglo-German loan of sixteen million pounds
sterling to China. The loan was for a period of 36 years at an interest rate of 5 percent, secured by the customs revenues, the administration of which was meanwhile to continue as constituted.

July 23, 1897 A Franco-German agreement defined the boundary
between Dahomey and Togoland.

July-Aug. 1897 Outbreak of new troubles in Uganda provoked by
King Mwanga. He was forced to flee and surrender to the Germans.

Nov. 14, 1897 Landing of German forces at Kiaochow Bay and occupation of Tsingtao following the murder of two German missionaries on Nov. 1. The Germans had been determined since 1895 to
secure a port on the Chinese coast as a reward for their intervention against Japan but were unable until 1897 to decide which port
was most desirable. Kaiochow was finally settled on. Despite the
fact that during a visit of William II to St. Petersburg in August
1897 Tsar Alexander III had given his approval, the Russian foreign
minister raised objections and claimed prior rights. A period of

tension between Russia and Germany followed but Russia finally gave
up their opposition to the German claim to Kaiochow.

March 6, 1898 Germany finally extracted from China a 99 year
lease on Kiaochow Bay, with exclusive right to build two railways
and develop the mines in Shantung Province (the Tsingtao-Tsinan
Railway opened in 1904). A second Anglo-German loan of sixteen
million pounds sterling for 45 years at 4 1/2 percent was secured
by certain likin and salt revenues, as well as the customs.

March 28, 1898 Passage of the first naval law by the German
Reichstag. This bill was the work of Admiral Alfred von Tirpitz,
Minister of Marine. It laid the basis for the future naval expansion
of Germany. It was argued by the proponents of the bill that a
larger navy was needed to protect German colonials, and German
commerce on the high seas. It was also argued that it was necessary for Germany to have a larger fleet if Germany was going to
make her weight felt in international affairs. The Germans were of
the opinion that if they possessed a large navy, even the strongest
naval power would hesitate before attacking. Admiral Tirpitz hoped
that the possession of a fleet would heighten Germany's alliance value in the eyes of Russia and France. This bill marking the beginning of German naval expansion, was especially distasteful to England, the foremost naval power in the world.

March 29, 1898 Beginning of the discussions between Joseph Chamberlain and the German ambassador. England was attempting to en-
list German support against further Russian encroachments in the
Far East. Bülow, who had been the German foreign minister since
June 1897, treated the matter evasively, being unwilling to antago-
nize Russia. In England there was little official or public enthusi-
asm for Chamberlain's proposal. The over-eagerness of Baron von
Eckardstein, "Counsellor of Legation" in London, complicated the
discussions. Von Eckardstein misled his own government as well
as that of England. Salisbury had visited the Far East on his recent vacation and took the situation there less seriously than Cham-

berlain.

<u>May 13, 1898</u> Chamberlain's speech at Birmingham. This speech
was extremely anti-Russian and in it Chamberlain made a bid for
friendship with Germany and the United States. The speech made
an unfavorable impression both in England and in the world at large.
Neither the United States nor Germany did anything to encourage
Chamberlain.

<u>1898</u> During the Spanish-American War the German fleet appeared
at Manila Bay, which was being blockaded by Admiral Dewey. Germany favored Spain in this conflict. Dewey had to threaten that the
American fleet would fire on the Germans before they could be persuaded to leave.

<u>Aug. 30, 1898</u> Anglo-German agreement regarding the future of the
Portuguese colonies. The government of Portugal was bankrupt and
in urgent need of a loan. The British government was willing to
grant the loan in return for the cession or lease of Delagoa Bay by
Portugal. England wanted this area because it was the key to the
Transvaal and at that time was of prime importance because of the
growing tension in the relations between England and the Transvaal.
Germany demanded a hand in the matter and England reluctantly
agreed out of fear of German collaboration with France, (for which
evidence existed in June of 1898). Germany and England agreed to
share in a loan to Portugal, the security for which was the Portuguese colonies. The northern half of Mozambique and all but a central strip of Angola was assigned to Germany. This area was intended to produce the revenues that would serve as the German
share of the loan repayment. The southern half of Mozambique and
the rest of Angola were assigned to Britain. If the Portuguese government were not able to repay the loan then these territories would
become the permanent possessions of the contracting powers. Germany was of the opinion that Portugal would default in the repayment
of the loan. England was throughout very strongly opposed to the
agreement with Germany, regarding it as a piece of blackmail.

<u>May 18-July 29, 1899</u> First Peace Conference at The Hague.
Nothing was done about disarmament or the limitation of armaments
at this conference. A proposal of compulsory arbitration was rejected, but a permanent court of arbitration was provided for.

<u>1899</u> Germany purchased from Spain, after the Spanish-American
War, the Caroline Islands, Marianne (Ladrone) Islands, and the
Palau (Pelew) Islands, for the sum of 800,000 pounds. Spain sold
these islands to Germany for the following reasons: (1) Spain needed the money, (2) Germany had given Spain moral support in her
war against the United States, and (3) Germany had wanted the islands for some time. In 1885 Germany claimed the Caroline Islands
as no-mans-land, but Spain protested on the ground of prior possession. The question of title was referred to Pope Leo XIII, who decided in favor of Spain but he granted Germany certain trading
rights.

<u>Oct. 9, 1899</u> Outbreak of the Boer War. Rumors of intervention
by Germany, Russia, and France against England. Count Muraviev
made some efforts on behalf of Russia to bring the three powers
against England but neither the Germans nor the French had much
desire to become embroiled in the war.

<u>Oct. 14, 1899</u> The Windsor Treaty between England and Portugal.
The secret agreement renewed older treaties of 1642 and 1661. A
guaranty of Portuguese territory was included as well as a promise
by Portugal not to let munitions pass through Delagoa Bay to the
Transvaal, or to declare neutrality. The agreement was a negation
of the spirit of the agreement made between Germany and England
in Aug. of 1898.

<u>Nov. 14, 1899</u> An Anglo-German agreement settled the Togoland-
Gold Coast frontier and abolished the neutral zone previously established on the upper Volta River.

<u>Nov. 25, 1899</u> Baghdad Railway preliminary concession granted to

the German syndicate, Deutsche Bank, for construction of a line
from Konia to Baghdad.

Background on the Baghdad Railway.

Since the 1850's and 60's, German missionaries and teachers had been active in Anatolia and Mesopotamia and since the
70's, German banking and commercial interests also had agents
within the Turkish Empire, all the latter attempting to drain
away the wealth of that country. The Deutsche Bank and the
Württembergische Vereinsbank of Stuttgart were extending loans
to the Sultan in the 1880's. During this decade a syndicate
was formed by the Siemens banking group to construct railroads
for the more efficient exploitation of the area. This group
envisioned the possible linkage of these lines with the Austro-
German system across the Bosporus, so that eventually something in the nature of a Berlin-Constantinople-Baghdad system
could be established, with branches running to Aleppo, Damas-
cus, Smyrna, and eventually to Persia, Arabia, and Egypt.

There had been innumerable schemes for railways in Anatolia, expecially from the Syrian coast to Baghdad and the
Persian Gulf. It was not originally believed that this penetration should be exclusively German and the railroad planners in
Germany seemed to have hoped to invite the bankers of other
countries to participate. The Turkish Sultan was eager for a
railroad to increase the income from his remote provinces and
to bind his empire together strategically.

On Oct. 4, 1888, the Sultan gave a German company a
concession to build a railroad from opposite Constantinople to
Angora (Ankara) with the idea of going through northern Anatolia to Baghdad. This line was completed in 1892, after which
there was a scramble for a new concession. The British were
highly interested in such a venture but were obliged to withdraw
when the Germans threatened to discontinue support of British
policy in Egypt. On Feb. 15, 1893, the German company received a further concession to extend the line from Angora to
Kaisarieh (this was not built) and for another line, through the
more promising southern districts, from Eskishehr to Konia.
This latter was completed in 1896 and once again the question
arose of continuing the line to Baghdad. All the major powers
put forth projects and applications for the extension of the railroad to Baghdad, but Germany remained in the favored position,
especially after the visit of William II to Constantinople and the
Holy Land in Oct. 1898. William II let it be known in a public
proclamation of his friendship for the 300 million Moslems in
the world.

While in Constantinople the German emperor made several
speeches which indicated that he believed Germany particularly
suited to take the Moslem peoples under its protection. There
was still some feeling in Germany, before the emperor's visit,
that other countries should have a share in the Baghdad railway

project. In the period that followed the visit, the German government urged its bankers to go on with their railroad planning
but to drop their ideas of an international consortium. William
II took to refering to the projected system as "my railroad"
and one of his advisors was reported to have said, "With a
bow to the British lion and a curtsey to the Russian bear, we
will worm our way, little by little, down to the Persian Gulf. "
To the British and the Russians, who were rivals for a pre-
ferred position in Persia, such an avowed intention was disturb-
ing. So was the rapidity with which the Germans ingratiated
themselves with the Turkish government and won a commanding
position in Turkish finance, economic life, and even in the development and training of the Turkish military establishment.

   German designs in the Middle East had profound effects on
the diplomatic allignment of Europe. The three other major
European powers reacted in the following ways to the news that
the concession to build the Baghdad railroad line had been
granted to Germany: (1) France ultimately gave up their opposition and agreed to cooperate with German interests; (2) England's attention was focused on other matters: they had pro-
tected their interests in the Persian Gulf by an agreement on
Nov. 25, 1899 with the Sheik of Kuwait, who promised to concede no territory without British consent; (3) Russia remained
very hostile to the German project. The Baghdad railway project was primarily an economic enterprise but it quickly became a vital factor in the political relations of Germany with
England and Russia.

Nov. 20-28, 1899 Visit of William II and Bülow to England. This
was the first such visit since 1895. In the conversations which took
place between Bülow, Chamberlain, and Balfour a possible Anglo-
German-American agreement was discussed. Bülow suggested to
Chamberlain that he say something publicly of the common interests
which should bind England and Germany together. Chamberlain in
his Leicester speech on Nov. 30 went much further and thereby
raised a storm of ill will in both England and Germany, where pro-
Boer sentiments were very pronounced. Bülow in a speech in the
Reichstag on Dec. 11 rejected the advances and even stressed the
need for a stronger German fleet. The whole affair tended to put
on ice the already cool relations that existed between England and
Germany.

Dec. 2, 1899 British-German-U.S. treaty regarding the Samoan
Islands signed (and ratified Feb. 16, 1900). There had been bitter

relations between England and Germany for the past two years in regard to the Samoan question. Germany wanted to acquire the British share of the group of islands. Because of the Boer War in South Africa the British government finally gave in and Germany got the islands of Upolu and Savaii, the British taking in return the Tonga Islands, Savage Islands, and the lesser islands of the Solomon group, as well as a disputed strip of Togoland. The United States received rights to the Tutuila and other islands. Tutuila was put under the control of the Navy Department and Pago Pago became a U.S. naval base.

Background of German involvement in Samoa.

Jan. 24, 1879: treaty of friendship and commerce between Germany and Samoa which secured the harbor of Apia.

March 24, 1880: agreement between Germany, Britain, and the United States recognizing Malietoa Talavou as king and providing for an executive council consisting of one American, one German, and one Englishman.

June 25-July 26, 1887: conference on the affairs of Samoa held at Washington with England, Germany, and the United States taking part.

July 24, 1887: demanding satisfaction of claims, the Germans landed troops and proclaimed Tamassese king. Malietoa surrendered and was exiled.

Sept. 4, 1888: native revolt under Mataafa directed against Germany.

May 15-16, 1889: terrific hurricane in Apia harbor. Three American and three German warships were driven ashore.

April 29-June 14, 1889: new Samoan conference of the three powers, Great Britain, United States, and Germany, held in Berlin.

June 14, 1889: the Samoa Act. The three powers recognized Malietoa as king and made provisions for joint supervision of the administration.

Aug. 22, 1898: death of King Malietoa. Mataafa and other chiefs were landed by a German warship. On Nov. 12, 1898, Mataafa was elected king but was rejected by both the British and American councils. Civil war broke out between Mataafa and Malietoa Tana, son of the dead king. Mataafa won in Jan. 1899 and set up a provisional government.

March 15, 1899: British and American warships bombarded Apia as a protest against Mataafa and his German supporters.

May 13, 1899: arrival of a joint American-British-German commission which declared that the monarchy was abolished.

Jan. 1900 Acute tensions in Anglo-German relations over the stopping of the German ship Bundesrath on the very inadequate suspicion that she was carrying contraband. The British government was obliged to drop the charges against the ship on Jan. 15.

Feb. 28-March 3, 1900   Muraviev suggested to the French and German governments the possibility of joint "amicable" pressure on England to bring about peace in South Africa. The Germans rejected the suggestion unless action were preceded by a mutual guarantee of acquisition of territory among the three intervening powers. There was no serious attempt made to intervene against England, though the Russians took advantage of England's plight to advance their interests in Persia, Afghanistan, and Tibet and the French, their interest in Morocco.

June 12, 1900   Passage of the second German naval law, providing for a fleet of 38 battleships, to be built within 20 years. This program was carried through the Reichstag by a wave of ill feeling toward England, which the government exploited through the Navy League and other organized propaganda. The German high seas fleet would be second only to that of England. Admiral Tirpitz's idea was that if Germany had a strong navy even the strongest naval power would hesitate before attacking her.

June 13-Aug. 14, 1900   Boxer Rebellion and the seige of Peking legations. This rebellion was the result of the division of China into spheres of influence by European powers. The German minister Baron von Ketteler was murdered on June 20 and German troops carried out thirty-five punitive missions against the Boxers during the period Dec. 12, 1900-April 30, 1901. After months of haggling between the allies the Boxer Protocol was signed on Sept. 7, 1901.

Oct. 16, 1900   Anglo-German Yangtze agreement. This agreement, acceded to by the other major powers, was the result of British anxiety over the designs of the Russians. It provided for the maintenance of the "open door" in "all Chinese territory as far as they (the contracting powers) can exercise their influence" and disallowed all territorial claims by European nations.

Oct. 16, 1900   Resignation of Hohenlohe.

1900-1909   Chancellorship of Count (later Prince, 1905) Bernhard
von Bülow.   Bülow had served in the Franco-Prussian War of 1870-
1871 and was in the diplomatic service from 1876-1897.   From 1897-
1900 he had served as state foreign secretary under Hohenlohe and
as the intimate advisor to the emperor.   Bülow was a brilliant man,
an accomplished orator and a skilled manipulator of men, but he
lacked Bismarck's seriousness, his strength of character, and his
breadth of view.   Bülow's tenure was marked primarily by issues
in foreign and colonial policy.   In domestic policy the main development was the extension of social insurance.

Feb. 23, 1901   An Anglo-German agreement signed regulating the
boundary between German East Africa and Nyasaland.

March 15, 1901   Bülow's speech in the Reichstag, declaring the
Yangtze Agreement did not apply to Manchuria.   This brought an end
to the discussions being held in London on the possibility of an An-
glo-German-Japanese bloc against Russia.   The Germans were not
willing to commit themselves beyond a promise of neutrality in the
event of a Russian-Japanese or Anglo-Russian war.

May 29, 1901   Lord Salisbury's memorandum on British policy defending a policy of isolation.   This memorandum ended the Anglo-
German alliance discussions which had been carried on since March
by Baron von Eckardstein, first secretary in the German Embassy
in London.   Eckardstein had reported that the British were much
more eager for an alliance than was Germany.   This information
induced the German government to insist that the British make an
alliance with the whole Triple Alliance, which England refused to do.

June 1901   Moroccan missions to Paris, London, and Berlin.   Discussions of an Anglo-German pact on Morocco were rejected by
Germans as it was not part of a larger Anglo-German alliance.

Jan. 20, 1902 Anglo-Japanese Alliance marking the end of British
isolation. At first it was considered that Germany might be included in the alliance; however, in the later negotiations this idea was
dropped.

Feb. 1902 Visit of Prince Henry, brother of William II, to the
United States on a special mission of friendship to President Roosevelt. The Manila incident of 1898 had created a coolness between
Germany and the United States which William II thought now would
be a good idea to admit was the fault of Germany. The emperor's
new campaign to win American friendship started as soon as the
Spanish-American War ended. Attentions of many kinds were show-
ered upon the United States. In May, Prince Henry presented to
the United States, for erection in Washington, D. C., a statue of
Frederick the Great. To Harvard University he gave a unique collection of casts of the finest examples of medieval German sculpture
and architecture. He also waived, in favor of the United States, the
rule established in Bismarck's time that German diplomatic representatives should not marry foreigners. In the late summer of
1903 the friendly relationship with the United States was so far restored that an American naval squadron visited Kiel, where a cordial
official welcome awaited it.

June 28, 1902 Renewal of the Triple Alliance for six years. Italy
made demands for greater concessions, but Austria and Germany
were able to evade these requests. Italy was, however, given assurances with regard to Tripoli.

Dec. 14, 1902 A new tariff law enacted upon expiration of the Caprivi treaties. The new law restored the higher duty on agricultural
products and reflected the power of the Agrarian League. The rural
and farming conservatives, in return for protection of their interests,
supported naval policy, which was advocated especially by big business.

Dec. 1902 The Venezuelan government refused to recognize liability

for loans and stores forcibly requisitioned from Germany and other
foreign merchants during the civil war of 1898-1900.   When all rep-
resentations made by the countries involved were disregarded, a
combined German, British, and Italian fleet blockaded the Venezuelan coast, but landed no troops.   Pressure upon the European powers by the United States resulted in their claims being referred to
the Court of Arbitration at The Hague, which decided against the
Venezuelan government.   In the United States the naval demonstration was unnecessarily interpreted by a nervous public as a challenge
to the Monroe Doctrine, but few reasonable men in public office took
that view.

April 1903   Baghdad Railway crisis.   The German company Deutsche
Bank had obtained a definitive concession on Jan. 17, 1902 for the
road from Konia to Basra.   Germany had done its utmost to secure
the cooperation of the British and French governments in arranging
the financing of this project.   Initially, the British government
reacted favorably, but after British bankers were scared off by an
organized press campaign against British participation, both the
British and French governments refused to become associated with
the project.   The Russians remained as before irreconcilably opposed to the whole Baghdad railroad scheme.

Oct. 27-Nov. 23, 1904   German-Russian negotiations for an alliance.
Tension had arisen between England and Russia because a German
company had contracted to re-coal the Russian fleet.   The tsar accepted, on Oct. 30, a German draft of a treaty providing for mutual
aid in the event of an attack by another European power.   The tsar
was not willing to sign until he had consulted with France.   This
proved to be the breakup of the negotiations.   Russia and Germany
did agree on Dec. 12 to aid each other in the event of complications
arising from the coaling of the fleet.

Jan. 1904-1908   The Herrero insurrection in German Southwest Africa.   This uprising was suppressed only after many systematic
campaigns by a force of 20 thousand men.

Feb. 3, 1905   Speech of Mr. Lee, First Lord of the Admiralty.
This speech was directed against the German build-up in naval arm-
aments and demonstrated the growing British concern regarding
German naval plans.

1905   The friendship which developed between William II and President Roosevelt led to the inauguration of a program for a yearly exchange of visiting professors between Germany and the United States,
the American professors lecturing at Berlin and the German, at
Harvard University.   The idea originated with Dr. Althoff, the minister of education for Prussia.   The original exchange professors
visited for one term; but this official system was supplemented by
another, after the formation in America of a fund in connection with
Columbia University, enabling the exchange professors to teach for
two successive terms.

March 31, 1905   Visit of William II to Tangier.   This visit initiated
the first Moroccan crisis.   Delcassé had excluded the Germans from
the Moroccan negotiations and had not officially communicated the
agreement with England.   The Germans were uncertain about the
Anglo-French Entente.   The Germans had declared that they had no
interest in Morocco except for the "open door" policy there.   Delcassé had given Germany assurance that the "open door" would be
maintained in Morocco.   The French then proceeded to make agreements, regarding Morocco, with Spain, Italy, and England.   After
the failure of the German-Russian negotiations in the fall of 1904,
Bülow and Holstein decided to use the Moroccan affair to test the
strength of the Anglo-French Entente.   They were able to persuade
the unwilling Emperor that this was the proper course to follow.
At Tangier, William II proclaimed Germany's adherence to the principles of independence and integrity and declared in favor of the
policy of equal opportunity for all.   His visit created a panic in
Paris and led to a loud outcry against the policy of Delcassé.   Delcassé offered to make good his mistake and tried to buy off the German opposition, but the Germans refused him.

April 6, 1905   The Germans accept the invitation of the sultan of Morocco to an international conference.

May 17 & 25, 1905   British correspondence with France in apprehension about German designs on the Moroccan coast.

June 6, 1905   Fall of Delcassé. He was in favor of accepting British offers, believing that the Germans were only bluffing. He also thought that a Franco-British combination would be invincible. The cabinet voted unanimously against him, fearing that France was not prepared for war and that an agreement with England would precipitate a war at a time when Russia was nearly helpless because of her recent defeats by Japan in the Far East. Delcassé's opponents thought that France would in the event of war be forced to bear the brunt of any German attack. Reuvier took over the foreign office and renewed his efforts to strike a bargain, but the Germans stood by their previous position.

July 24, 1905   Björkö Treaty signed by William II and Tsar Nicholas II during a visit to each other's yachts. The treaty was, for the most part, a return to the draft of Oct. 1904, excepting that it was to be confined to Europe and was to take effect only after the conclusion of peace between Russia and Japan. Bülow objected to restricting the treaty to Europe and threatened to resign, but was persuaded by the Russian foreign office. It was ultimately wrecked by the French government, which refused to even consider joining in such a pact.

Sept. 28, 1905   France and Germany reached an agreement on the agenda for the Moroccan Conference, which was to meet in January of 1906. Germany agreed to nearly all of the French demands, hoping that France would accede to the Björkö Treaty. (As noted above, they did not.)

Jan. 15-April 7, 1906   Algeciras Conference on Morocco. France was supported by all powers except Austria and Germany.

Feb. 10, 1906 The German government decided to increase the ton-
nage of battleships.   It was also decided to add six cruisers and to
widen the Kiel Canal to allow the passage of projected ships of the
Dreadnought type.

Aug. 15, 1906 Visit of King Edward VII of England to William II
at Cronberg.   There was a futile discussion between the two heads
of state on the growing Anglo-German naval rivalry.

Dec. 1906 Parliamentary crisis in Germany.   The Center Party
turned against the administration and defeated a bill for the reorganization of the colonial office and refused funds for military operations against Herrero in Southwest Africa, which had been in revolt since 1904.   Bülow dissolved the Reichstag and called on the
Conservative, National Liberal, and Progressive parties to subordinate partisan interests to the national good and combat the Center
Party and the Socialists.

1906-1910 Tenure of Dr. Bernhard Dernburg as minister for the
colonies.   He patterened colonial administration in Africa after methods employed by the British.   The result involved numerous sweep-
ing changes in the German system of administration, many in favor
of the natives of German colonies.

May 16, 1907 Pact of Cartagena between England, France, and
Spain.   It provided for the maintenance of the status quo in the Mediterranean and that part of the Atlantic Ocean which washes the
shores of Europe and Africa.   The agreement was directed against
supposed German designs on the Balearic Islands and the Canaries.

June 15-Oct. 18, 1907 Second Peace Conference at The Hague.
All efforts of the British to secure some limitation of armaments
were wrecked by the other powers, for which Germany, fearing a
British attempt to check the growth of the German navy, acted as
spokesman.   Germany also rejected all proposals for compulsory
arbitration.   The conference enlarged the machinery for voluntary

arbitration and concluded conventions regulating action to collect
debts, rules of war, rights and obligations of neutrals, and so forth.

July 1907 Renewal of the Triple Alliance for six years, despite the
complete lack of faith on the part of Germany and Austria in Italy's
loyalty.

Aug. 3-5, 1907 Meeting of William II and Nicholas II and their foreign ministers at Swinemünde. In the discussions on the Baghdad
Railway the Russians assured the Germans that any agreement they
made with England would not be directed against Germany.

March-April 1908 Dr. David Jayne Hill, United States Minister to
the Netherlands, appointed to fill the vacancy in Berlin created by
the resignation of Charlemagne Towner, U.S. Ambassador there.
Hill's appointment was approved by the German foreign office and
accepted by the German government. Before Hill assumed the duties of his new post a crisis was created in German-American relations when it became known that the Kaiser did not approve of Hill.
The emperor referred to Hill as "ein ganz kleiner Mann" and Holstein let the story leak out on purpose to the press. The Americans were outraged by William II's attitude and to calm their anger,
the German government was obliged to announce officially that there
never had been any change in the emperor's attitude toward Hill or
in his willingness to receive him in Berlin. This, however, was
an outright lie.

April 23, 1908 The Baltic and North Sea Conventions: the first between Germany, Sweden, Denmark, and Russia; the second between
Great Britain, Germany, France, Denmark, the Netherlands, and
Sweden. They provided for the maintenance of the status quo on
the shores of the Baltic and North Seas and for consulation between
the signatories in case the status quo was threatened.

June 9, 1908 Meeting at Raval between King Edward VII and Sir
Charles Hardinge with Tsar Nicholas II and Isvolski. At this meet-

ing one of the topics discussed was the problem presented by the growth of German armaments.

July 1908 Mulay Hafid took Fez, after having defeated his brother, Abdul Aziz, Sultan of Morocco, in a long civil war. The Germans had supported Mulay Hafid in the affair. Morocco now drifted toward another crisis.

July 24, 1908 Victory of the Young Turk Revolution which had begun on July 6 in Macedonia. The Sultan was forced to restore the constitution of 1876. The whole movement was a reflection of Turkish excitement about the Raval meeting of June 9, 1908. The result was the collapse of German influence in Turkey and a period of frantic Anglophilism.

Aug. 11, 1908 Meeting of King Edward VII and Sir Charles Hardinge with Emperor William II at Friedrichshof. There were discussions of the naval situation, marked by extreme bitterness. The Emperor refused all British suggestions that Germany should reduce her naval program. The German navy's faster gain than anticipated on the British was due to the British reduction in the term of service for their warships. In addition there had been an acceleration in the German building operations.

Aug. 13, 1908 Meeting of Edward VII with Francis Joseph at Ischl. Efforts were made by England to gain Austrian assistance in bringing pressure to bear on Germany.

Sept. 25, 1908 Casablanca affair. Three German deserters from the French Foreign Legion were taken by force from a German consular official. This action led to acute tension in Franco-German relations.

Sept. 26, 1908 Meeting of Izvolski, the Russian foreign minister, and Baron Schoen, the German foreign minister at Berchtesgaden. Schoen agreed to the Russian Straits program on the understanding

that Germany should receive compensation, probably in the form of
Russian acquiescence in the Baghdad Railway question.

Oct. 6, 1908 Proclamation of the Annexation of Bosnia and Herzegovina by Austria. The Germans were outraged by the failure of
Austria to give them advance notice, but supported Austria out of
deference for the Triple Alliance.

Oct. 27, 1908 Izvolski back in Berlin. The Germans once again
made no objections to the Russian Straits program, provided they
were given compensation.

Oct. 28, 1908 The Daily Telegraph Affair. This English newspaper
published an interview with the emperor on the question of Anglo-
German relations. The emperor related that he was friendly to
England but the German people were hostile to England. The publication of the interview created a furor in the Reichstag, resulting
in a widespread demand for some check on the emperor's power.
Bülow, who was responsible, directly or indirectly, defended the
emperor as best he could. The interview served to accentuate the
Anglo-German antagonism.

Nov. 1908 The Kaiser had given an interview to the American journalist, Dr. William Bayard Hale, during July on board the Kaiser's
ship the Hohenzollern docked off Bergen, Norway. The interview
was much more sensational than the one that appeared in The Daily
Telegraph. Hale submitted a copy of the interview to the foreign
office for their approval to print it. Permission was denied. The
New York Times, for whom the interview was secured, refused to
print it because of the sensationalistic nature of it. A much water-
ed down version of the interview was to appear in the December issue of The Century magazine; however, when the Daily Telegraph
incident erupted the German foreign office insisted that the article
must be suppressed. Hale and The Century editors were gracious
enough to see that the printed sheets for the article were handed
over to the Germans for disposal. The suppression, however, led

to much speculation as to what the article contained. The New
York World went so far as to print a facsimile of the Hale interview which was supposed to have been written in Hale's own hand-
writing. Later though the World in a telegram to Bülow admitted
that the whole thing had been faked. The New York American also
claimed to have an authentic copy of the interview as did many of
the English newspapers. The Hale interview served to heighten the
crisis started by the Daily Telegraph interview. If an unexpurgated
copy of the Hale interview had been printed on the heels of the
Daily Telegraph interview it would probably have caused a much
more serious crisis in Germany where people were already demanding that the chancellor be made responsible to the Reichstag, while
others were calling for the abdication of William II. If the Hale
interview had been published war could easily have started in 1908
between England and Germany, because of the nature of the statements made by the Kaiser about England and Edward VII.

Nov. 10, 1908 Germany and France agreed to submit the Casablanca affair to an arbitral board which rendered a report on May 22,
1909.

Feb. 8, 1909 German-French agreement on Morocco. It reaffirmed
the independence and integrity of Morocco, but Germany recognized
France's "special political interest" there in return for recognition
of Germany's economic interests and a promise to associate German nationals in future concessions.

May 21, 1909 German note to Russia, calling upon her to abandon
support of the Serbs and to recognize the annexation of Bosnia and
Herzegovina. The Germans asked for a definite reply. If Russia
did not yield, Germany said that they would allow events to take
their course. Russia was not prepared to support the Serbs, and
Izvolski saw an opportunity to get off the hook. Russia yielded to
Germany but Izvolski started the legend of a German ultimatum to
Russia. The British were angry with Russia for having backed
down to Germany.

May 1909   Mission of Baron Stumm to London.   He was instructed
to offer an agreement on naval affairs in return for a defensive alliance, a neutrality agreement or at least a general settlement of the
colonial questions.   Stumm was cooly received in England where
there was no desire to do anything that could weaken the Entente.
The British held the opinion that first a naval agreement must be
reached before there could be any consideration of other interests.

July 14, 1909   Resignation of Chancellor Bülow.   Bülow did not approve of the uncompromising naval policy of William II and Admiral
Tirpitz.   The Daily Telegraph affair also weakened his position.

1909-1917   Chancellorship of Dr. Theobald von Bethmann-Hollweg
(1856-1921).   He was the son of a wealthy Rhenish landowner.   He
studied law and entered the Prussian civil service in 1882.   He became the governor of the province of Brandenburg in 1899.   He was
appointed Prussian minister of the interior in 1905, gaining a high
reputation for the work he did in this position.   In 1907 he became
state secretary of the interior under Bülow.   Bethmann was a typical bureaucrat of the best type: sound, industrious, honest, well-
intentioned, but lacking in imagination and brilliance.   He was eager
for an agreement with England.

Nov.-Dec. 1909   Anglo-German negotiations between Gwinner and
Cassel.   The intention of the negotiations was to attempt to make a
general settlement of Anglo-German differences, but the discussions
dealt chiefly with the Baghdad Railway.   Germany was prepared to
denounce her sole claim, in favor of international control, of the
section of the railway extending from Baghdad to the Persian Gulf.
The British, however, demanded full control of this section for
themselves and were finally willing to make any agreement with Germany without consulting Russia and France.

Aug. 11, 1910   A German-Belgian agreement fixed the frontier between the Belgian Congo and German East Africa.

Nov. 4-5, 1910 Visit of Tsar Nicholas II and the new foreign minister, Sergei Sazonov, to Emperor William II at Potsdam. Tentative
agreements were reached regarding the Middle East. The Germans
gave the Russians a free hand in northern Persia. The Russians, in
return, promised that they would no longer oppose the Baghdad Railway. Russia also agreed to arrange for the connection of the Baghdad Railway with the Persian railways.

May 26, 1911 A law was passed organizing Alsace-Lorraine as a
state with a two chamber legislature and a large measure of autonomy.

April-May 1911 French advance in Morocco. The French entered
Fez on May 21, despite warnings from Germany that they were in
violation of the Algeciras Act.

June-Nov. 1911 Second Moroccan Crisis resulting from the advance
of the French on Fez and the German dissatisfaction with the working of the Algeciras Act of 1909. The French government was willing to offer Germany compensation. M. Jules Cambon, the French
ambassador at Berlin, engaged in secret conversations with the German foreign secretary, Kiderlen-Wächter, at Kissingen on June 20-
21. The Germans took the position that if the French had anything
to offer they should make the offer known, but the French on the
other hand wanted the Germans to make their demands known. Kiderlen-Wächter wanted to clear up the Moroccan question and improve
German relations with France and England.

July 1, 1911 The German gunboat Panther arrived at Agadir on the
coast of Morocco. The Germans said that they were there to protect German interests in Morocco, but were probably there to fright-
en the French into action.

July 15, 1911 Germany related to France that they would require
the whole of the French Congo as compensation for the abandonment
of German rights and interests in Morocco. To the French this

proposal was out of the question.

July 21, 1911   Mansion speech of David Lloyd George in which he
decried the fact that England had not been consulted about Morocco.
He phrased his remarks in such a way that the speech caused a
great stir and led to recriminations between the German ambassador
and Sir Edward Grey, British foreign secretary.   As Britain made
preparation for war, should it come, France and Germany continued
to negotiate and reached substantial agreement by October.   By the
convention of Nov. 4, Germany agreed to leave France a free hand
in Morocco and not to object to the erection of a French protectorate.   In return France ceded 100,000 square miles of the two strips
of territory connecting the German Cameroons with the Congo and
Ubangi Rivers.

Feb. 8, 1912   Haldane mission to Berlin.   The radicals in England
were dissatisfied with Grey's policy in the Agadir crisis and discontent with the Russian policy in Persia.   They wanted to improve relations with Germany.   In Germany both William II and Tirpitz
wanted to increase the fleet beyond the previous naval program, but
Bethmann and Kiderlen were anxious for better relations with England.   Haldane suggested that England would be willing to support
German colonial aspirations in Africa in return for German assurance that they would not increase the size of their fleet.   The Germans would not make a naval agreement without a political agreement.   Chancellor Bethmann demanded a promise of neutrality under
certain conditions.   Grey was willing only to give an assurance not
to attack or to take part in a hostile combination against Germany.

Feb. 26, 1912   Opening of the railway from Dar es-Salaam to Tab-
ora, the main line in German East Africa.

March 8, 1912   Publication of the new German naval bill, providing
for an increase in the number of ships, an increase in personnel,
and the establishment of a third squardon commission.   The publication of this bill ended the Anglo-German discussions, although con-

versations regarding the Baghdad Railway and colonial affairs continued and an effort was made by both England and Germany to put relations between the two countries on better footing.

July 22, 1912   The British admiralty decided to shift their battleships, which had been in the Mediterranean, to the North Sea. This move was prompted by the growing German naval strength. The French, on the other hand, withdrew their battleships from Brest and stationed them in the Mediterranean because of the growing power of Austria and Italy.

Nov. 24, 1912   The Austrians made public their opposition to territorial access to the Adriatic Sea for Serbia. Austria, at this time, also came out in support of an independent Albania. Germany, after some hesitation, promised that they would support Austria if she were attacked defending her interests.

Dec. 5, 1912   Last renewal of the Triple Alliance, for six years from July 1914. This reflected closer relations between Italy and Austria.

June 30, 1913   The German army and finance bills. The army bill provided for the addition of 4,000 officers, 15,000 non-commissioned officers, and 117,000 enlisted men. The objective of the bill was to increase the peacetime strength of the army from 544,000 to 870,000 men. The Socialists, Poles, and Alsatians voted against the bill; however, all other parties supported the government and the bill was passed. The cost of the measure was estimated at one billion marks, of which 435,000,000 was to fall due in 1913. In the finance law there was a provision for a special national defense tax (Wehrsteuer), to be levied only once on real and personal property and on income. This measure was a concession to the Socialists, and other radicals because it would be upon the well-to-do classes that this burden would fall. The Socialists therefore voted for the finance law, even though they had voted against the army bill for which the funds were intended.

Nov.-Dec. 1913 Crisis caused by the military mission of Liman von Sanders. He had been appointed by the Turkish government to reorganize the Turkish army. He was to have command of the First Army Corps at Constantinople and other far reaching powers. Initially the Russians had no objections to the plan, but when they learned of the extensive authority of the German mission they raised a protest. They demanded that Liman von Sanders be given a command at some place other than Constantinople. France supported Russia, but English support was at best lukewarm, being only a note sent to the Turkish government warning them against making concessions to Germany. The affair was closed in Jan. 1914 when the German government agreed that Liman von Sanders should give up the command and become inspector-general of the army. The incident left the Russians suspicious of German designs on Constantinople.

Overview of Colonial Situation in 1913

Togo, with Little Pope and Porto Seguro, in Upper Guinea between the Gold Coast Colony on the west and French Dahomey, was acquired in 1884, and administered by an imperial governor. It contained 33,700 sq. mi. 1913 pop., native: 1,081,975; European: 368, of whom 320 were German. The coast line was about 32 miles long but the island territory between the rivers Volta and Monu widened it to three or four times its breadth. The governor was assisted by a secretary, an inspector of customs, and a local unofficial council of seven members. The capital was located at Anechno.

The Cameroons protectorate was also acquired in 1884. The territory lay between British Nigeria and the French Congo, extending from the coast north eastwards to the southern shore of Lake Chad. An agreement settling the frontier between Nigeria and Cameroon from Yola to the sea was signed in London on March 11, 1913. Area: 191,130 sq. mi. 1913 pop., native: 2,648,720; European: 1,871, of whom 1,643 were German. Government: Imperial Governor at Buěa, was assisted by a chancellor, two secretaries, and a local council of three representative merchants.

German South-West Africa, acquired between 1884-1890, included the region lying between Portuguese West Africa and Cape Colony and extended eastward to the British sphere exclud-

ing Walfish Bay which belonged to Cape Colony.   Area:
322,450 sq. mi.   1913 pop., native: 79,556; European: 14,880,
of whom 13,292 were German.   The coast lands were held by
the Deutsche Kolonial Gesellschaft für Südwest Afrika which
gave the special names of Deutsche-Namaland to the southern
part of its territory and Deutsche-Damaraland to the northern.
The imperial governor's seat was at Windhoek; the last governor, Dr. Seitz.

German East Africa, acquired between 1885 and 1890 contained 384,180 sq. mi.   Its coast line extended for 620 miles.
Germany acquired the rights to the territory in 1890 for the
sum of four million marks.   The German protectorate extended
from the mouth of the Umba to Cape Delgado, or more accurate-
ly to 10° 40' south latitude.   It was governed, in Dar-es-Salaam,
by an imperial governor (the last, Dr. Schnee) who was assisted
by an advisory and largely unofficial council which met twice
yearly.   1913 pop., native: 7,645,770; European: 5,336, of
whom 4,107 were German.

Kiaochow on the north-east coast of the Chinese province of
Shantung was seized by Germany in Nov. 1897.   The town, harbor, and surrounding district were transferred to Germany for
a period of 99 years by a lease from China in March 1898.   In
April 1898 Germany declared the area a protectorate, ruled by
an imperial governor.   Area: 200 sq. mi.   1913 pop., native:
158,900; European: 4,470, of whom 3,806 were German.

Kaiser Wilhelm's Land, the northern section of New Guinea,
was declared a German protectorate in 1884, and administered
by an imperial governor.   The protectorate included Long Island, Dampier Island, and some other smaller islands which
made up an area of an estimated 70,000 sq. mi.   1913 pop.,
native: 531,000; European: 283, of whom 264 were German.

Bismarck Archipelago.   In Nov. 1884, the New Britain
Archipelago and several adjacent islands--Neu Pommern (formerly New Britain), Neu Mecklenburg (New Ireland), Neu Lan-
enburg (Duke of York Islands), and Neu Hanover, Admiralty,
Anchorite, Commerson, Hermit, and other islands were all declared a German protectorate administered by an imperial governor.   1913 pop., native: 188,000; Chinese: 396; and European:
685, of whom 482 were German.

The Solomon Islands were acquired in 1886 and included the
islands of Bougainville, and Buka.   Choiseul, Isabel (or Mah-
aga), and various smaller islands to the east of Bougainville
were transferred to Great Britain on Nov. 14, 1899.   The remaining islands were governed through the Kaiser Wilhelm's
Land group.

The Caroline, Pelew (or Palau), and Marianne (or Ladrone)
Islands.   By treaty on Feb. 12, 1899 these islands, with the

exception of Guam, passed on Oct. 1, 1899 from Spanish to
German possession for a payment of 16,800,000 marks. For
administrative purposes the islands were divided into two
groups: the Eastern Carolines with Ponape as the seat of government, and the Western Carolines, the Pelew Islands and the
Marianne Islands with Yap as the administrative center. They
all formed part of the German New Guinea protectorate and
were ruled by imperial governors. 1913 pop., native: 55,000;
European: 264, of whom 154 were German.

   The Marshall Islands, consisting of two chains or rows of
lagoon islands (several uninhabited), known respectively as
Ratack (with thirteen islands) and Ralick (with eleven islands),
were acquired in 1885 and administered by an imperial commis-
sioner on the island of Jaluit. 1913 pop., native: 15,000
(est.); European: 179, of whom 91 were German.

   Samoan Islands. Among German dependencies were included
Savai and Upolu, the largest of the Samoan or Navigator Islands.
By the Anglo-German Agreement of Nov. 14, 1899 (ratified by
the United States in Jan. 1900) Great Britain renounced all
rights over the islands in favor of Germany as regards Savaii
and Upolu, (and in favor of the United States as regards Tutuila
and other islands). Under the imperial governor was a native
high chief with a native council. Savaii has an area of about
660 sq. mi., Upolu, of 340. 1913 pop., native: 35,000; European: 544, of whom 329 were German and 132 British; Chinese:
1,354; and 1,003 non-native inhabitants of mixed races.

Dec. 1913   The Zabern affair, worsening Franco-German relations.
The incident involved a German officer striking and wounding a lame
cobbler with his sword and insulting Alsatian recruits.

June 15, 1914   An Anglo-German agreement concerning the Baghdad
Railway. The Germans promised not to construct the line south of
Basra and to recognize England's preponderent interests in the shipping on the Euphrates River. This agreement reflected a desire by
both England and Germany to settle outstanding colonial difficulties.

June 24, 1914   Austrian memorandum for Germany discussing the
Balkan situation as it emerged after the Treaty of Bucharest. Austria favored an alliance with Bulgaria and Turkey to render impossible a reconstruction of the Balkan League under Russian and French
auspices. Germany urged Austria to reconsider a reconciliation
with Serbia, Rumania, and Greece.

June 28, 1914 Assassination of the Archduke Francis Ferdinand of
Sarajevo.

July 5, 1914 Mission of Austrian Count Hoyos to Berlin with a revised memorandum on the Balkan situation calling for a need to settle at once Serbian activities in the Balkans. William II and Bethmann were of the opinion that the Austrian position, in regard to
Serbian activity in the Balkans, was justified. They promised German support, urging Austria to move at once to remedy the situation, while world opinion was still favorable to her. This German
promise is usually referred to as the "Blank Check." Germany
thought that a localized settlement could be made. Germany believed that Russia was not prepared to defend Serbia if fighting
should erupt.

July 23, 1914 Austrian ultimatum to Belgrade.

July 28, 1914 Austria declared war on Serbia. Germany urged the
Austrian occupation of Belgrade, to be used in negotiations with Russia regarding the Serbian reply on July 25 to the Austrian ultimatum
of July 23. Grey also favored this idea, but it was ignored by
Berchtold. France renewed assurances of support to Russia.

July 29, 1914 Chancellor Bethman-Hollweg, resisting pressure
from General von Moltke, chief of staff, urged for a resumption of
Austro-Russian negotiations. To achieve this end he started to
bring pressure to bear on the Austrian government. At the same
time the German Chancellor made a bid for English neutrality. Germany would give their assurance not to take any French or Belgian
territory in Europe if Britain would remain neutral. This proposal
was rejected by England.

July 29, 1914 Tsar Nicholas II yielded to pressure from Sazonov
and military men and agreed to a general mobilization. Then, re-
ceiving a telegram from Berlin telling of the German emperor's efforts to bring Austria in line, the Tsar changed the order for a

general mobilization to a mobilization against Austria.

July 30, 1914   Austro-Russian conversations resumed. Despite numerous German warnings, Russia reverted back to the order for a general mobilization.

July 31, 1914   Germany proclaimed a state of danger or threat of war and sent a twelve-hour ultimatum to Russia demanding that their mobilization on the German border be stopped;

   inquired in Paris in regard to what attitude the French would take in a Russian-German conflict; and

   refused a British request that Belgian neutrality be respected.

   At 5:00 P.M. Austria decreed general mobilization.

Aug. 1, 1914   France replied to Germany, in regard to the latter's inquiry of the previous day, that France would be guided by her own interests; and

   at 3:55 P.M. ordered general mobilization.

   Germany offered England a promise not to attack France if England would guarantee French neutrality;

   at 4:00 P.M. ordered general mobilization; and

   at 7:00 P.M. declared war on Russia after the latter's failure to answer the German ultimatum of July 31.

Aug. 2, 1914   The British Cabinet voted to give France assurances of her aid in protecting the French coast against German attack.

   Germany invaded Luxembourg and sent Belgium a demand for permission to cross her territory, promising in return to uphold Belgian integrity.

   Belgium rejected the German proposal.

Aug. 3, 1914   Germany declared war on France on the pretext of frontier violations by the French; and

   invaded Belgium.

Aug. 4, 1914 Great Britain declared war on Germany.

Chapter VII

An Annotated Bibliography of German Foreign Policy, 1890-1914, and Colonial Policy to 1914

FOREWORD

In compiling this bibliography I have tried to be selective. I have not included items that are of only marginal interest or use. Items of this nature can be found listed in the bibliographies of the works I have included here. The bibliography I have compiled is complete enough that if someone wishes to pursue a certain topic in German foreign policy for the period 1890-1914 he can use it as a more than substantial point of departure.

I have attempted to classify the materials in the bibliography according to subject. In some cases this was not possible. This was especially true in the case of memoirs which cover the entire period 1890-1914 and do not lend themselves well to classification. A considerable number of those materials placed under one classification may also be useful for the investigation of other subjects.

I have annotated the bibliography to make it a more useful tool for the researcher. In cases where the title is misleading or the contents require clarification, I have used a great deal of annotation. The amount of annotation following an entry in this bibliography does not in itself indicate the value of the work.

The various titles listed under each special classification do not follow in alphabetical, but in a complementary order. Nor does the order of the list indicate ascending or descending value. Each scholar will soon discover for himself which items are the most valuable for the specific topic on which he is working.

New studies are coming off the press each year at an ever

increasing rate, and this bibliography became dated soon after it
was compiled. However, it is possible to supplement my list, to
gain access to the very most recent works, by consulting the appropriate periodicals which either review or list nearly all articles,
books, and research undertaken in their fields.

It is highly improbable that many libraries will contain all
the items listed in this bibliography. Small libraries will not have
enough materials to conduct research in this area, yet this problem
need not be insurmountable. Any book in this bibliography can easily be obtained through normal interlibrary loan channels. It is a
different matter in regard to journals, newspapers, and other serials. Many libraries do not risk loss of their serials because they
are difficult or impossible to replace. However, all large libraries
in North America and nearly all libraries, museums, and archives
in Europe and Great Britain are willing to send photo copies of serial type material.

It is an easy matter to determine which library has the serial in which you may be interested. Library serial holdings are
listed in either: New Serial Titles; A Union List of Serials Commencing Publication After December 31, 1949; monthly supplements
are issued to keep the publication up to date; or Union List of Serials in the Libraries of the United States and Canada (New York,
1965) 5 v.; for serials which began publishing prior to 1950. Cosby
Brinkley Directory of Library Photoduplication Services in the United
States, Canada and Mexico (Chicago, 1962) is a convenient guide
listing libraries having photoduplication services, the different types
of services offered, and approximate cost estimates for this service.

The above union catalogs can be used to locate any serial,
but if it is a certain book that is needed for a research project, it
is often more difficult to locate a copy. If the book in question is
of particular significance the researcher might want to purchase a
photocopy, which nearly all libraries in North America are willing
to supply. The British Museum will microfilm a book. This is
also true of nearly all the large libraries in Germany, including the
university libraries.

The following list should help to locate most items desired:

Catalogue Générale des Livres Imprimés de la Bibliothèque Nationale (Paris 1897 ff.)

British Museum Catalog of Printed Books (London 1965) 261 v.

Library of Congress Catalog of Printed Books (Ann Arbor 1943-1946) 146 Vols. A 42 volume supplement was issued in 1948.

Library of Congress Author Catalog (Ann Arbor 1948) 42 Vols.

Library of Congress Author Catalog 1948-1952 (Ann Arbor 1953) 24 Vols.

Library of Congress: National Union Catalog Author List 1953-1957 (Ann Arbor 1958) 28 Vols.

Library of Congress: National Union Catalog Author List 1958-1962 (New York 1963) 54 Vols.

Library of Congress National Union Catalog Author List 1963, etc. (Washington 1964-) 5 Vols. Supplements to Union Catalog Author list appear annually.

Library of Congress Book Subjects: A Cumulative List of Works Represented by the Library of Congress Printed Cards (Ann Arbor 1955) 20 Vols.

Library of Congress Book Subjects: A Cumulative List of Works Represented by the Library of Congress Printed Cards 1955-1959 (Patterson, New Jersey 1961) 22 Vols.

Library of Congress Book Subjects: A Cumulative List of Works Represented by the Library of Congress Printed Cards 1960, etc. (Washington 1961-) (3 Vols. each year) Supplements are issued annually.

Library of Congress: The National Union Catalog 1952-1955 Imprints (Ann Arbor 1961) 30 Vols.

Many libraries have published catalogs of their holdings in certain subject areas. Several have published, usually on microfilm, their shelf lists, which can be of great assistance in locating books of a similar nature as it is normally arranged according to subject classification numbers. It is usually best to consult with the reference librarian to determine the exact holdings of a library in the area of printed catalogs and union shelf lists. Often these

works are not to be found on the public shelves. As a general rule
the items found in the bibliography area of a library represent only
a fraction of the library's resources in bibliographical aids.

Library of Congress Book Locating Service
    The Union Catalog Division of the Library of Congress pro-
vides libraries and scholars with a service of searching the National
Union Catalog and related files for the purpose of locating books.
In order to permit the division to provide the best and most efficient
service possible libraries and scholars requesting searching should
follow the procedures outlined below:

1. Verify the name of author, title, and imprint in some
   standard catalog or bibliography. Furnish as complete a
   citation as possible. State source of verification or, if
   item cannot be verified, give the original citation in full
   form. If a particular edition is not requested, state "any
   edition." If not all volumes of a multi-volume set (mono-
   graphic or serial) are required, designate which are.

2. A. Use separate sheets for listing items in the following
   catagories:

   1) Western language monographs. Imprints before 1952.

   2) Western language monographs. Imprints after 1951.

   3) Serials.

   4) Orientalia (Hebrew, Chinese, Japanese, etc.).

   5) Slavic material printed in the Cyrillic alphabet.

   Separate listings are requested because the searching
   must be done in separate files, each located in different
   places and buildings; use of separate lists permit more
   expeditious routing and searching of items falling in different categories.

   B. List the items to be searched in alphabetical order by
   author (or title where the author is not known or the work
   is anonymous) and, in the case of more than one work by
   the same author, sub-arrange alphabetically by title.

3. Prepare items in duplicate, leaving ample space between
   items and in both margins for annotations. Keep one copy

for your own record and send one copy to the Union Catalog Division, Library of Congress, Washington, D.C. 20540.

Local and nearby resources should be exhausted before a search of the National Union Catalog is requested. Because of the pressure of regular duties, the Union Catalog Division staff cannot undertake to search long lists, but competent persons can be suggested who will do the work for a fee. Microfilm or photostat copies of National Union Catalog cards may be obtained at prevailing photoduplication costs.

Research of Unfilled Library of Congress Card Orders

Through the Photoduplication Service, in cooperation with the Union Catalog Division, unfilled Library of Congress card orders may be re-searched in the National Union Catalog and photocopies of catalog cards from other libraries provided. There is a charge of 75 cents per title, including the cost of the pertinent National Union Catalog card.

This service is of real assistance for rare books and imprints, but for entries of 1952 and later it is advisable first to consult the National Union Catalog, 1952-1955 Imprints and the National Union Catalog, A Cumulative Author List before requesting this service.

BIBLIOGRAPHY

A. BIBLIOGRAPHIES AND HISTORIOGRAPHICAL ESSAYS

Those works which pertain to only one topic, such as colonial policy, will be found under that topic.

Bibliographies of Bibliographies

A 1. Besterman, Theodore. A World of Bibliography of Bibliographies. 3rd ed., 4 v. Geneva, 1955-56.

A 2. Bibliographic Index; A Cumulative Bibliography of Bibliographies. 6 v. New York, 1937 ff.
Issued quarterly and cumulates into annual and multi-
annual volumes. It is a subject index only and includes
bibliographies published separately as books and pamphlets and those published as parts of books, pamphlets, and periodical articles.

A 3. Coulter, E. M. and M. Gerstenfeld. Historical Bibliographies:
A Systematic and Annotated Guide. Berkeley, 1935.

A 4. International Bibliography of Historical Sciences. 32 v.
1930-1966.
Covers literature published in the years 1926-63.

A 5. Malclès, Louise-Noël. Les Sources du travail bibliographique.
Geneva, 1950 ff.
Lists outstanding bibliographies and standard reference
books of most countries, describing them in detail and
evaluating them with great care.

A 6. Winchell, Constance M. Guide to Reference Books. Chicago,
1950.
Three supplements bring it up to 1958.

A 7. Walford, A. J. Guide to Reference Material. Chicago, 1959.
The successor of the previous item; a supplement
brings it up to date.

General Bibliographies of European History

A 8. Jahresberichte der Geschichtswissenschaft. 56 v. Berlin,
       1878-1913.

       A comprehensive and accurate list of historical publi-
       cations in leading European languages appearing in the
       year concerned.

A 9. Jahresbericht der deutschen Geschichte. 1918 ff.

       This is an attempt to continue the above title, however,
       only the books and articles which appeared in German
       are covered. It has been published off and on under
       the same title down to the present day.

A 10. Bibliography of Historical Writings Published in Great Britain
       and the Empire 1940-1945. Oxford, 1947.

A 11. Lancaster, J.C. Bibliography of Historical Works Issued in
       the United Kingdom 1946-1956. London, 1957.

A 12. Kellaway, W. Bibliography of Historical Works Issued in the
       United Kingdom 1957-1960. London, 1962.

A 13. Historical Abstracts. 1955 ff.

       An annotated bibliography of the leading periodical lit-
       erature of the world. Very useful. Abstracts of arti-
       cles on diplomatic, political, economic, social, cul-
       tural, and intellectual history.

A 14. Langer, W.L. and H.F. Armstrong. Foreign Affairs Bibli-
       ography, 1919-1932. New York, 1933.

A 15. Wolbert, R.B. Foreign Affairs Bibliography, 1932-1942.
       New York, 1945.

A 16. Roberts, Henry L. Foreign Affairs Bibliography, 1942-1952.
       New York, 1955.

A 17. -- Foreign Affairs Bibliography, 1952-1962. New York,
       1964.

A 18. Bullock, Alan L. and A.J.P. Taylor. A Select List of Books
       on European History, 1815-1914. Oxford, 1957.

A 19. Franz, Guenther. Bücherkunde zur Weltgeschichte vom Unter-
       gang des Römischen Weltreiches bis zur Gegenwart. Munich,
       1956.

A 20. Herzfeld, Hanz. Die Moderne Welt 1789-1945. 2 v. Volume
       II Weltmächte und Weltkriege. Die Geschichte unseres
       Epoche 1890-1945. 1957.

A 21. Ragatz, Lowell J. A Bibliography for the Study of European
History 1815-1939. Ann Arbor, Mich., 1942. With 3 supplements I (1943), II (1945), III (1955).

A 22. Temperly, Harold and Lillian M. Penson. Short Bibliography
of Modern European History, 1789-1935. London, 1935.

A 23. Pinson, Koppel S. A Bibliographical Introduction to Nationalism. New York, 1935.

A 24. Deutsch, Karl W. Interdisciplinary Bibliography on Nationalism. Cambridge, Mass., 1956.

Bibliographies of German History and German Foreign Policy

A 25. Dahlmann, Friedrich C. and Georg Waitz. Quellenkunde der
deutschen Geschichte. 9th rev. ed., 2 v. Leipzig, 1931.

A 26. -- Quellenkunde der deutschen Geschichte. 10th rev. ed.
Stuttgart, 1965.

> The most recent edition of this famous bibliography;
> Abschnitt 393 of bk 8, and Abs. 358 of bk 7 are sec-
> tions relevant to the 1890-1914 period.

A 27. Franz, Guenther. Bücherkunde zur deutschen Geschichte.
Munich, 1951.

A 28. Leewe, Victor. Bücherkunde der deutschen Geschichte:
kritischer Wegweiser durch die neuere deutsche historische
Literatur. 1st-5th ed. Berlin, 1900-19.

> Annotated to indicate the value of each work; quite se-
> lective.

A 29. Ulrich, Hermann. Die besten deutschen Geschichtswerke.
Leipzig, 1923.

> Annotated; very selective.

A 30. Gilbert, Felix. "German Historiography During the Second
World War: A Bibliographical Survey," The American Historical Review. LIII (October, 1947):50-58.

A 31. Ritter G. and Holtzmann. Die Deutsche Geschichtswissenschaft im zweiten Weltkrieg; Bibliographie des historischen
Schriftums deutscher Autoren 1939 bis 1945. Marburg, 1951.

> Covers the historical writings published in Germany
> during the years 1939-1945.

A 32. Gunzenhäuser, Max. Bibliographie zur Aussenpolitik und Kolonialpolitik des deutschen Reichs, 1871-1914.   Stuttgart, 1943.

A 33. Thielen, Peter G.   "Die Aussenpolitik des deutschen Reichs

1890-1914, Literatur und Forschungsbericht für die Jahre

1945-1960, " Welt als Geschichte.   1962.   22(1/2):27-48.

Discusses the chief issues of German, English, and
American scholarship concerning the following aspects
of German foreign policy 1890-1914: 1) hegemony or
balance of power? 2) era of William II, 3) the "personal rule" of William II, 4) the new course, 5) Schlieffen
and the problem of German militarism, 6) Tirpitz and
German-English relations, and 7) Triple Alliance and
Eastern Europe.

A 34. Gebhardt, Bruno.   Handbuch der deutschen Geschichte.   8th

rev. ed., 4 v.   Stuttgart, 1954-1957.

A 35. Just, Leo. ed.   Handbuch der deutschen Geschichte.   5 v.

Konstanz, 1956 ff.

See especially in this work Bd III, Abs 3, by Walter
Bussmann: Das Zeitalter Bismarcks; and Bd IV, Abs
1, by Werner Frauendienst: Das Deutsche Reich 1890
bis 1914; and Bd IV, Abs 2, by Walter Hubatsch: Der
Weltkrieg 1914-1918. In addition to containing excellent
bibliographies each of the above mentioned works is a
substantial history of the period indicated by the title.

Bibliographies on the "War Guilt Question"

A 36. Barengo, U.   Contributo a una bibliografia della guerra mond-

iale.   Documenti e testimonianze politice-diplomatiche. Cause,

origini, responabilita, significato della guerra.   Rome, 1937.

A 37. Bibliothek für Zeitgeschichte, ehem Weltkriegsbücherei.   Ber-

lin, 1915 ff.

A systematic attempt to list all material published relating to the war.

A 38. Bücherschau der Weltkriegsbücherei.   Stuttgart, 1954.

A 39. Franz, Georg.   "Akten, Fakten ... Literatur zur Kriegs-

schuldfrage, " Osterreichische Furche.   1954.   10(33):6.

A 40. Historische Zeitschrift.   Band 179 (1954).

Contains an excellent bibliographical article on materials concerning the First World War published during
the years 1945-1954.

A 41. Die Kriegsschuldfrage, ein Verzeichnis der Literatur des In-

und Auslands.   Leipzig, 1925.

Contains about 1500 titles. It is not annotated but is cross-referenced.

A 42. Literatur zur Kriegsschuldfrage. Berlin, 1926.

A 43. Select Bibliography of Revisionist Books Dealing with the Two World Wars and their Aftermaths. Oxnard, Calif., 1959?

Annotated bibliography of books in English on the subjects indicated.

A 44. Renouvin, Pierre, and Edmond Préclin and George Hardy. La Paix Armée et la Grande-Guerre 1871-1919. 1947.

A 45. Vinogradov, K.B. Burzhuaznaia istoriografiia pervoi miro voi voiny: proiskhozhdenie voiny i mezhdunarodyne otnosheniia 1914-1917 GG. Moscow, 1962.

This book traces the "bourgeoisie historiography" of World War I and western writing on the origins of WW I and international relations in the months before the war. It is a competent survey of the principle sources and secondary works on WW I. There is a discussion of document collections, memoirs, and diaries, followed by a historiographic survey for the period 1914-1945. This survey is by countries and includes France, England, Germany, Italy, and the United States. A final section takes the historiography from 1945-1961 according to major issues and countries. Italy is omitted in this section. The author is critical of Wegerer, commends Renouvin, Pingaud, and Gooch. He has good words for Fay, although he disapproves strongly of Fay's disregard of economic factors. He praises Albertini's industry, while being critical of his method and his over-emphasis on diplomacy. Has high regard for Schmitt. Praises Gottlieb, Fischer, Gatzke, May, and Link. He is critical of Meyer's Mittel Europe, and J. Remak's Serajewo, both of which are deemed poor and misleading. He criticizes "bourgeois historians" for their narrowness of approach in limiting their investigations largely to diplomacy. They are "unwilling to take into account the sharpening of the economic and political struggle in the international arena and the class struggle within the capitalist countries in the era of imperialism." He states that these errors are not made by Soviet historians.

A 46. Wegerer, A. von. Bibliographie zur Vorgeschichte des Weltkriegs. Berlin, 1934.

A 47. Rich, Norman. Germany, 1815-1914. Washington, 1968.

A short listing, with comment, on books in the English language on German history. It is more useful for students and teachers who are not specialists in German history or for persons who are unable to read German.

A 48. Meyer, Henry Cord. Five Images of Germany: Half a Century of American Views of German History. Washington, 1966.

> Comments on American historical writing on Germany, pointing out how it has changed during the period since World War I.

B. ANNUALS AND YEARBOOKS

Often annuals and yearbooks and overlooked when working on a research project. They are a valuable source for establishing the chronology of a particular event. They contain a great amount of material not usually included in even the most detailed histories of an event, therefore they should be consulted.

American Annuals

B 1. International Year Book. Ed. by F.M. Colby. 1890-1902. Pub. con. under same ed. after 1907 with title The New International Year Book. 1907 ff.

B 2. The American Year Book; A Record of Events and Progress. Ed. by S.N.D. North. 1910 ff.

British Annual

B 3. Annual Register. London, 1758 ff.

> A good resume of political events. Half of the space in each volume is devoted to Great Britain and the other half to other countries.

French Annual

B 4. Annuaire historique universel. Paris, 1818-1861.

> Cont. by L'Année politique, ed. by André Lebon, Paris, 1874-1905, and La Vie politique dans les deux mondes, ed. by Archille Viallate, Paris, 1906 ff.

German Annuals

B 5. Schulthess' Europäischer Geschichtskalender. 79 v. Munich,

1860-1938.

    A very good source for the political events in Germany prior to the war.

B 6. Das Staatsarchiv: Sammlung der offiziellen Rechts der Gegenwart. Ed. by Georg Jellinek, Paul Laband, and Robert Piloty. 1907 ff.

B 7. Deutscher Geschichtskalender. Ed. by Karl Wippermann. Leipzig, 1885-1934.

Austrian Annual

B 8. Politische und volkswirtschaftliche Chronik. Ed. by Karl Neisser. 1912 ff.

    A semi-official monthly publication.

Special Reference Annuals

B 9. The Statesman's Year Book. 1864 ff.

    A statistical and descriptive annual of the countries of the world. Detailed information and a good bibliography of government publications is given for each of the German states.

B 10. Hazell's Annual. 1886 ff.

    Contains lists of principle officials in all countries, together with a brief review of main political events and a great deal of miscellaneous information.

B 11. Almanach de Gotha: annuaire généologique, diplomatique, et statistique. 1818 ff.

    Valuable for the relationships of royalty and the great noble families.

B 12. The Year Book of Social Progress. London, 1912 ff.

    Contains a summary of recent legislation, official reports, and voluntary efforts with regard to the welfare of the people of various countries.

B 13. Annuaire de la législation du travail. Brussels, 1897 ff.

    An annual digest of social legislation in all countries, published by the Belgian Office of Labor.

Statistical Handbooks and Yearbooks

B 14. Baedeker's Northern Germany. 16th ed. 1913.

B 15. The German Yearbook. London, 1914.

B 16. Handbuch über den Königl. Preussischen Hof und Staat.

Issued annually in Berlin.

B 17. Statistik des Deutschen Reichs. Berlin, 1873 ff.

B 18. Statistisches Handbuch für den Preussischen Staat.

Issued at various times in Berlin.

B 19. Statistisches Handbuch für das Deutsche Reich. Berlin, 1907.

B 20. Statistisches Jahrbuch für den Preussischen Staat.

Issued annually in Berlin.

B 21. Statistisches Jahrbuch für das Deutsche Reich. Berlin, 1880 ff.

B 22. Vierteljahrshefte zur Statistik des Deutschen Reichs. Berlin, 1882 ff.

C. ENCYCLOPEDIAS OF HISTORY, HANDBOOKS, ETC.

C 1. Bithell, Jethro. Germany: A Companion to German Studies. London, 1955.

C 2. East, William G. An Historical Geography of Europe. London, 1948.

C 3. Langer, William L. Encyclopedia of World History. New York, 1958.

This work is especially good on international relations for the pre-World War I period.

C 4. Roeder, William S. Dictionary of European History. New York, 1954.

D. BIOGRAPHIES

D 1. Allgemeine deutsche Biographie. 56 v. Leipzig, 1875-1912.

An invaluable dictionary of German biography with articles written mainly by scholars of the first rank.

D 2. Arnim, Max. International Personalbibliographie 1800-1943. 2 v. Leipzig, 1944-1952.

Index to personal bibliographies often leading to bibliographical information contained in books, periodicals, biographical dictionaries, Festschriften, etc; international, with emphasis on Germany.

D 3. Biographisches Jahrbuch und deutscher Nekrolog. 18 v. Berlin, 1897-1917.

Biographical articles on prominent persons deceased within the given years; highly selective.

D 4. Deutscher biographisches Jahrbuch. 11 v. Berlin, 1925-32.

D 5. Rössler, Hellmuth, and Günther Franz. Sachwörterbuch zur deutschen Geschichte. Munich, 1958.

D 6. Die grossen Deutschen. deutsche Biographie. 5 v. Berlin, 1956-57.

D 7. Wer ist wer. Berlin, 1905 ff.

The German who's who; publication interrupted at various times.

E. DISSERTATIONS

E 1. List of Doctoral Dissertations in History Now in Progress at Universities in the United States. Washington, 1902 ff. (Title varies.)

E 2. Doctoral Dissertations Accepted by American Universities, 1933-1955. New York, 1934-56.

E 3. Dissertation Abstracts: A Guide to Dissertations and Monographs Available in Microfilm. Ann Arbor, Mich., 1952 ff.

This is a continuation of Microfilm Abstracts: A Collection of Abstracts of Doctoral Dissertations and Monographs Available in Complete Form on Microfilm. 1938-51. (Subtitle varies.)

F. NEWSPAPERS AND PERIODICALS

Newspaper Indexes

F 1. Palmer's Index to "The Times" Newspaper, 1790-1943. 601 v. London, 1868-1943.

F 2. The Official Index to The Times. London, 1907 ff.

F 3. The New York Times Index. New York, 1851 ff.

> The index for September, 1851, through September,
> 1858; 1860; and 1863 through June, 1905, is available
> on microfilm. The index for the period since 1913 has
> long been available in printed form. The Times is
> presently in the process of bringing out in book form
> the index for the years 1851-1912.

F 4. New York Daily Tribune Index. 30 v. New York, 1876-1907.

Periodical Indexes

F 5. Poole's Index to Periodical Literature, 1802-1906. 7 v.

> Boston, 1888-1908.

F 6. Nineteenth Century Readers' Guide to Periodical Literature.

> New York, 1944 ff.

F 7. Reader's Guide to Periodical Literature. New York, 1900 ff.

F 8. International Index to Periodicals. 1907 ff. Prior to 1920,

> issued under title of Readers' Guide Supplement.

F 9. Bibliographie der deutschen Zeitschriften-Literatur. 1861 ff.

> Indexes over 4,000 German periodicals and newspapers.

F 10. Bibliographie der fremdsprachigen Zeitschriftenliteratur.

> 1911-1920, 1925 ff.

> About 3,000 periodicals in the principal non-German
> languages are indexed. Especially strong in English,
> French and Italian periodicals.

F 11. Catalogo metodico degli scitti contenati nelle publicazioni ital-

> iane e straniere. 10 v. Rome, 1885-1935.

> Index to foreign and Italian periodicals 1883-1930.
> Material covered is limited to biographical and critical
> information about persons.

F 12. Annuaire de la presse française et étrangère, et du monde

> politique. Paris, 1878 ff.

F 13. Scott, Franklin D., and Elaine Teigler. Guide to the Ameri-

> can Historical Review, 1895-1945: A Subject-Classified Ex-
> planatory of the Articles, Notes and Suggestions, and Docu-
> ments. Washington, 1945.

> There is also a supplement to this which covers the
> years 1945-1955.

F 14. Haskell, Daniel C. The Nation, Volumes 1-105, New York

> 1865-1917, Index of Titles and Contributors. 2 v. New York,

1951-1953.

F 15. Annual Magazine Subject-Index. 42 v. Boston, 1908-1949.

F 16. Bibliographie der Rezensionen. 77 v. Leipzig, 1901-1943.

A comprehensive index to book reviews in German periodicals and, for the years 1911-1915 and 1925-1943,
in other languages. Includes scholarly and specialized
books and covers many English and U.S. periodicals.

F 17. Book Review Digest. New York, 1905 ff.

F 18. An Index to Book Reviews in the Humanities. Detroit, 1960 ff.

Other Reference Books valuable for locating the exact title or dates
of a periodical or newspaper, or a library which contains the
periodical or newspaper.

F 19. Ulrich's International Periodicals Directory. 12th ed. New
York, 1967.

The first edition appeared in 1932.

F 20. Caron, Pierre, and Marc Jarye. World List of Historical
Periodicals. Oxford, 1939.

F 21. Boehm, Erich, and Adolphus Lalit. Historical Periodicals.
Santa Barbara, Calif., 1961.

An annotated list of 5,000 serials with a title index.

F 22. British Union Catalog of Periodicals: A Record of the Periodicals of the World, from the Seventeenth Century to the
Present Day in British Libraries. 4 v. London, 1955-58.

Supplement published in 1962. Lists 150,000 serials
in some 400 British libraries.

F 23. Union List of Serials in the Libraries of the United States and
Canada. 5 v. New York, 1965.

Lists the serials held by practically all libraries of any
size in North America. Contains information for each
library concerning loaning, microfilming, and photocopy-
ing of serials.

F 24. New Serial Titles: A Union List of Serials Commencing Publication After December 31, 1949. Washington, 1953 ff.

Monthly supplements are issued to keep it up to date.

F 25. Gregory, Winifred. A List of Serial Publications of Foreign
Governments, 1815-1931. New York, 1932.

F 26. Sperling's Zeitschriften- und Zeitungs- Addressbuch: Handbuch der deutschen Presse.   Leipzig, 1858 ff.

F 27. Willing's Press Guide.   London, 1874 ff.

Comprehensive for Great Britain, selective for other countries.

F 28. Newspaper Press Directory and Advertisers' Guide.   1846 ff.

Often refered to as "Mitchell's." Lists many news-papers and periodicals of the entire world.

F 29. Schwegmann, George A.   Newspapers on Microfilm: A Union Check List.   Washington, 1957.

Some of the best accounts of important events in German foreign and colonial affairs are to be found in the news section of contemporary periodicals, yet often these periodicals are not indexed by any of the guides mentioned above.   Even if they are indexed, the weekly or monthly news sections often are not.   Valuable and interesting information about a particular event can be found by leafing through the pages of contemporary issues of some of the newspapers and periodicals given below.   This method is time consuming and arduous but the rewards often compensate for the time spent.   The following selection of newspapers and periodicals are valuable for this purpose.   It should be noted that many of these are indexed by the above guides.

U.S. Newspapers and Periodicals

F 30. The New York Times, New York Daily Tribune, New Republic, Independent, Survey, Current Events, America, Review of Reviews, North American Review, American Journal of International Law, New Review, Pan-American Review, Nation, Annals of the American Academy of Political and Social Science, Atlantic Monthly, Chautauquan, Christian Union, Current Literature, Dial, Frank Munsey's Monthly, Harper's Monthly, Harper's Weekly, Forum, Literary Digest, Littell's Living Age, Century, McClure's Magazine, Outlook, Overland Review, Unpopular Review, World's Work.

English Newspapers and Periodicals

F 31. London Times, Westminster Gazette, Spectator, Nation, Tab-
let, Fortnightly, Contemporary, Nineteenth Century, West-
minster Review, Quarterly Review, National Review, Edin-
burgh Review, Near East, Russian Review, Dublin Review,
Far East, Hibbert Journal, Nineteenth Century and After,
The Round Table, New Statesman, Blackwood, The Cornhill
Magazine, Gentleman's Magazine, Douglas Jerrold's Shilling
Magazine, The Graphic, Macmillan's Magazine, North British
Review.

French Periodicals

F 32. Journal des débates, Revue politique et parlementaire, Le
Correspondant, Revue de Paris, Revué des deux mondes,
Revue bleu, L'Opinion, La Grande revue.

German Newspapers and Periodicals

F 33. Berliner Lokal Anzeiger was a popular and sensational daily
with a wide circulation among all classes. It was reputed to
be closely related to the Wilhelmstrasse and Potsdam, and
it served up the activities of royalty in popular form. In domestic politics it was conservative; in foreign affairs, intense-
ly nationalistic.

Berliner Tageblatt, a Jewish enterprise, was one of the most
important German dailies. It was radically liberal, and independent of any royal or official influence. The weekly review of foreign affairs by the editor, Arthur Levysohn, was
a conspicuous feature. It maintained its own foreign news
service; and its unbiased reports and opinions on foreign affairs enjoyed a high reputation. It circulated widely in middle class commercial and financial circles.

Berliner Neueste Nachrichten advertised itself as "non-parti-
san." It gave unqualified support to the government's foreign
policy, the Navy League, and Tirpitz' program. It was decidedly hostile to England and advocated "zu Lande ein starkes
Heer, zur See eine starke Flotte."

Die Post (Berlin) was a conservative reactionary organ and a loyal supporter of government policies, both foreign and domestic.   Occasional anti-English outbursts were contradicted by frequent expression of a desire to bring about more cordial relations with Great Britain.

Frankfurter Zeitung represented the financial and industrial interests of the new Germany as opposed to the agrarian Junker class of East Prussia.   It was liberal in domestic politics, but it usually struck an independent note on foreign affairs.   It advocated a fleet commensurate with the development of the German merchant marine, but heartily disapproved the tactics of the Navy League.

Hamburger Nachrichten, the old Bismarckian organ, distinguished itself by its Anglophobia.   It opposed the government's Moroccan policy.   It was reputed to have close connections with Russia and never ceased to advocate renewal of former treaty relations with the Tsar's empire.

Kölnische Zeitung, according to Bismarck, was worth an army corps on the Rhine.   It was still a frequent channel for official communications.   Telegrams from the Berlin correspondent were closely observed, and on subjects of international significance it was generally assumed that they reflected the views of the Wilhelmstrasse.   It also maintained an extensive foreign news service, ranking in this respect with Berliner Tageblatt and Frankfurter Zeitung.

Münchener Allgemeine Zeitung represented the conservative agrarian interests of Bavaria.   Frequently inspired from Berlin, it gave the official lead to south German public opinion in foreign affairs.   Toward England it appeared indifferent, although it supported the German naval program.

Neue Preussische Zeitung, usually referred to as the Kreuz-zeitung, was a Berlin daily representing the most reactionary elements in Germany--the Junkers, the army, and the Lutheran church.   Its masthead bore the words: "Vorwärts mit Gott für König und Vaterland."   Its most conspicuous feature was the Wednesday review of foreign affairs by Professor

Schiemann.

Norddeutsche Allgemeine Zeitung was the official organ of the Wilhelmstrasse. It represented no party, its circulation was small, and it had no special foreign correspondents. But it was to be found on every editor's desk, and its communications were quoted extensively at home and abroad.

National-Zeitung (Berlin), founded in 1848, was a National Liberal Party organ, occasionally inspired by the foreign office. It ceased publication on Jan. 1, 1905.

Reichsbote (Berlin) was an exceedingly reactionary chauvinistic organ much quoted in England as representative of the German Protestant clergy. It never recovered from its anti-English hysteria of the Boer war period. Its importance was grossly exaggerated in England.

Vossiche Zeitung (Berlin) was a scholarly liberal paper with large circulation among professional and upper-middle classes. It was an independent and unsparing critic of the more reactionary domestic policies of the government, but in foreign affairs it usually supported the chancellor. It was friendly toward England and never chauvinistic in discussing foreign affairs.

Vorwärts (Berlin) was the central organ of the Social Democratic party. It bitterly attacked Bülow's foreign policy, the Navy League, and the Pan-Germans. Foreign affairs were commonly used as a point of attack on the government.

Some of the more useful German periodicals are: Deutsche Rundschau, ed. by Julius Rodenberg, Berlin, 1874 ff; Deutsche Revue eine Monatschrift, ed. by Richard Fleisher, 47 v. Berlin, 1877-1922; Die Nation, Wochenschrift für Politik, Volkswirthschaft und Literatur, Berlin, 1883-1907; Deutsche Monatschrift, foreign ed. Theodor Schiemann; Preussische Jahrbücher, ed. by Hans Delbrück, 1858-1935; Die Zukunft, ed. by Maximillian Harden; Neue Rundschau; Zeitschrift für Politik; and Zeitschrift für Volkerrecht und Bundesstaatrecht.

A few German historical journals useful for this period are: Historische Vierteljahrschrift, 31 v., Freiburg and Leipzig, 1899-1939;

Historische Zeitschrift, Munich, 1859 ff.; Das Historische-politische Buch: ein Wegweiser durch das Schrifttum, Göttingen, 1953 ff.; Die Welt als Geschichte, Stuttgart, 1935 ff.; Beiträge zur Geschichte der deutschen Arbeiterbewegung, Berlin-East, 1958 ff.; Zeitschrift für Geschichtswissenschaft, Berlin-East, 1953 ff.

G. HISTORIES OF GERMANY

Some of the works listed below are of little value. They are included only because they reveal the general trend in the development of German historiography of the period.

G 1. Below, Georg A.H. von. Die deutsche Geschichtsschreibung von der Befreiungskriegen bis zu unsern Tagen. 2nd rev. ed. Munich, 1924.

Survey of German historiography.

G 2. Srbik, Heinrich, Ritter von. Geist und Geschichte vom deutschen Humanismus bis zur Gegenwart. 2 v. Munich, 1950-51.

Survey of German historiography.

G 3. Histoire et historiens depuis cinquante ans de 1876-1926. 2 v. Paris, 1927-1928.

Arranged according to country.

G 4. Bornhak, Conrad. Deutsche Geschichte unter Kaiser Wilhelm II. Leipzig, 1922.

G 5. Buehler, Johannes. Deutsche Geschichte. Berlin, 1934.

G 6. Conze, Werner. Die Zeit Wilhelms II und die Weimarer Republik deutsche Geschichte 1890-1933. Tübingen, 1964.

G 7. Dawson, William H. The German Empire 1867-1914. 2 v. 1919.

Vol. 2 deals largely with foreign affairs; old, but still useful.

G 8. Dill, Marshall. Germany: A Modern History. Ann Arbor, 1961.

G 9. Dorpalen, Andreas. "Wilhelmian Germany; A House Divided Against Itself," Journal of Central European Affairs. (Oct. 1955):240-247.

G 10. Endres, F.C. Tragödie Deutschlands. Im Banne d. Macht-
gedankens b. z. Zus. bruche d. Reichs von e. Dt. Stuttgart,
1925.

G 11. Eyck, Erich. Das Persoenliche Regiments Wilhelm II.
Zürich, 1948.

G 12. Fay, Sidney B. "Germany under Bismarck and his Successors, " Current History. 1955, 28 (164):211-217.

> Surveys German foreign and domestic policy 1871-1914.
> Germany's unification was political rather than social
> and cultural. A strong feeling of particularism still
> existed in Germany on the eve of World War I. Anglo-
> German and Russo-German relations did not deteriorate
> until after Bismarck's resignation in 1890. The small
> but fanatical Pan-German League supported the Kaiser's
> naval program and advocated a racist creed later as-
> sociated with Hitler.

G 13. Fife, Robert H. The German Empire Between the Wars.
Chautauqua, 1916.

> Traces the development of Germany in the years 1871-
> 1914.

G 14. Flenley, Ralph. Modern German History. New York, 1953.

G 15. Fletcher, Charles. The Germans: Their Emperor and How
They have Made it. London, 1914.

G 16. Frobenius, H. Germany's Hour of Destiny. 1914.

G 17. Göhring, Martin. Bismarcks Erben 1890-1945; Deutschlands
Weg von Wilhelm II bis Adolf Hitler. Wiesbaden, 1959.

G 18. Goldschmidt, Hans. Das Reich und Preussen im Kampf um
die Führung, von Bismarck bis 1918. Berlin, 1931.

G 19. Guttmann, Bernard. Schattenriss einer Generation 1888-1919.
Stuttgart, 1950.

G 20. Hammann, Otto. Deutsche Weltpolitik, 1890-1912. Berlin,
1925. English trans. The World Policy of Germany, 1890-
1912. New York, 1927.

> The author was the chief of the press division of the
> German foreign office. The book is based on his per-
> sonal recollections, and diaries and also contains valu-
> able memoranda and letters. It is highly readable and
> presents a breadth of view.

G 21. -- Der Neue Kurs. Berlin, 1918.

G 22. -- Um die Kaiser. Berlin, 1919.

G 23. Hammann, Otto. Zur Vorgeschichte des Weltkrieges. Berlin, 1918.

G 24. Hartung, Fritz. Deutsche Geschichte 1871-1919. Stuttgart, 1952.

G 25. Henderson, William O. A Short History of Germany 1815-1945. Cambridge, 1959.

G 26. Holborn, Hajo. A History of Modern Germany. 3 v. New York, 1959-1969.

G 27. Kaehler, Siegfried. Studien zur deutschen Geschichte des 19 und 20 Jahrhunderts: Aufsätze und Vorträge. Göttingen, 1961.

G 28. Mach, Edmund von. Germany's Point of View. 1915.

G 29. -- What Germany Wants. 1914.

G 30. Mann, Golo. Deutsche Geschichte des neunzehnten und zwanzigsten Jahrhunderts. Frankfurt A/M, 1959. Avail. in Eng. trans.

G 31. Pinson, Koppel S. Modern Germany: Its History and Civilization. 2nd ed. New York, 1966.

G 32. Rachfahl, Felix. Kaiser und Reich 1888-1913; 25 Jahre preuss. -dt. Geschichte Festschr. z. 25 jähr. Regierungsjubiläum Wilhelms II. 1913.

G 33. Renouvin, Pierre. L'Empire allemand de 1890-1918. Paris, 1951.

G 34. Rodes, John E. Germany: A History. New York, 1964.

G 35. Rohrbach, Paul. Der Krieg und die deutsche Politik. 1914. Eng. trans., Germany's Isolation.

G 36. Rosenburg, Arthur. The Birth of the German Republic 1871-1918. London, 1931.

G 37. Schnabel, Franz. Deutsche Geschichte in neunzehnten Jahrhundert. Freiberg, 1929.

G 38. Sexau, Richard. "Die Wilhelminische Epoche, " Neues Abendland. 1956, 11(3): 265-278.

G 39. Sybel, Heinrich von. Founding of the German Empire. 7 v. New York, 1890-1898.

     Sybel was the editor of the Historische Zeitschrift. He had Bismarck's permission to use the Prussian archives when writing the early volumes but after the fall of Bismarck he was denied this privilege.

G 40. Taylor, A.J.P. The Course of German History. A Survey
of the Development of Germany Since 1815. London, 1946.

G 41. Treitschke, Heinrich von. History of Germany in the Nineteenth Century. 7 v. New York, 1915-1919.
Treitschke was the editor of the Preussische Jahrbücher.

G 42. Wahl, Adalbert. Deutsche Geschichte von der Reichgrundung
bis zum Ausbruch des Weltkriegs 1871 bis 1914. 4 v. Stuttgart, 1926-36.
An attempt to explain the downfall of the German Empire.

G 43. Yamawaki, Shigeo. "Doitsu Sekai Seisaku No Ichilenici,"
Seiyo-shi-gaku. 1954, 23: 897-915.
Discussion of the period of Germany's shift to Weltpol-
itik. Concludes that the turning point came in 1900.

G 44. Ziekursch, Johannes. Politische Geschichte des neuen deutschen Kaiserreichs. 3 v. Frankfurt, 1927-1932.

G 45. Ramm, Agatha. Germany 1789-1919: A Political History.
New York, 1967.
A straightforward political and diplomatic history, which
avoids economic, social and cultural developments.

G 46. Simon, Walter. Germany: A Brief History. New York,
1966.
Covers economic, social, cultural, and political developments.

G 47. Passant, E.J. A Short History of Germany, 1815-1945.
Cambridge, 1962.
Covers political and economic developments.

G 48. Rodes, John E. Germany: A History. New York, 1964.
Primarily a political history of the period after 1850.

G 49. Ritter, Gerhard. The German Problem: Basic Questions of
German Political Life, Past and Present. Columbus, Ohio,
1965.

G 50. Meinecke, Friedrich. The German Catastrophe: Reflections
and Recollections. Boston, 1950.

G 51. Kohn, Hans. German History: Some New German Views.
New York, 1954.

A collection of interpretations of modern German history by eminent German historians.

G 52. Clapham, J.H. The Economic Development of France and Germany, 1815-1914. Cambridge, 1936.

Old but still very good. It has been reprinted in paperback.

G 53. Henderson, W.O. The Industrial Revolution on the Continent: Germany, France, Russia, 1800-1914. London, 1961.

Full of useful information.

G 54. Stolper, Gustav. German Economy, 1870-1940. New York, 1940.

Readable, but lacking in detail.

G 55. Bruck, W.F. The Social and Economic History of Germany, 1888-1938. New York, 1962.

H. DIPLOMATIC HISTORIES

Many of the works listed are now dated but are included because they point out the development of the historiography of German diplomatic history.

H 1. Albin, Pierre. La Guerre allemande: d'Agadir à Sarajevo 1911-1914. 1915.

H 2. Andrillon, Betrand P.H. L'Expansion de l'Allemagne, ses causes, ses formes, ses conséquences. Paris, 1914.

H 3. Anrich, E. Europas Diplomatie am Vorabend des Weltkrieges. Ein Bilanz der Wissenschaftlichen Forschung über die Vorgeschichte des Weltkrieges und der Julikrise 1914. Berlin, 1937.

H 4. Bartstra, J.S. Twaalf Jaren "Vrije-Hands-Politiek" 1890-1902. Leiden, no date.

A sound scholarly study of German foreign policy.

H 5. Baumont, Maurice, and Henry Germain-Martin, and Raymond Isay. L'Europe de 1900 à 1914. Paris, 1968.

H 6. Bernhardi, Friedrich von. Germany and the Next War. 1912.

H 7. Böhm, Wilhelm. "Diplomatisches Vorspiel zum ersten Weltkrieg, " Österreichsche Monatschefte. 1964, 20(7/8): 8-11.

H 8. Bullard, Arthur. The Diplomacy of the Great War. 1916.

H 9. Brandenburg, Erich. From Bismarck to the World War: A
History of German Foreign Policy, 1870-1914. New York,
1927.

> One of the first substantial accounts of German pre-
> war diplomacy. The author made good use of the Ger-
> man documents available to him.

H 10. Carroll, Malcolm E. Germany and the Great Powers 1866-
1914; A Study in Public Opinion and Foreign Policy. New
York, 1938.

> An exhaustive and valuable analysis of the German
> press and of the relation of public opinion to foreign
> policy.

H 11. Craig, Gordon A. From Bismarck to Adenauer: Aspects of
German Statecraft. Baltimore, 1958.

H 12. Dickenson, G.L. The International Anarchy 1904-1914. London, 1926.

> A severe condemnation of the pre-war international
> system.

H 13. DeLaisi, Francis. The Inevitable War. London, 1915.

H 14. Diercks, Gustav. Die Marokkofrage und die Konferenz von
Algeciras. 1906.

H 15. Dillon, Emile J. A Scrap of Paper: The Inner History of
German Diplomacy and her Scheme of World Conquest. London, 1914.

H 16. Drewer, Anton. Die "Daily Telegraph" Affaire vom Herbst
1908 und ihre Wirkungen. 1933.

H 17. European Politics in the Decade before the War as Described
by Belgian Diplomatists. 1915.

> Selections from the reports of Belgian representatives
> in London, Berlin, and Paris to the minister of foreign
> affairs in Brussels, 1905-1914. They were issued in
> the original French and also in an English translation
> by the German foreign office.

H 18. Feis, Herbert. Europe the World's Banker 1870-1914. New
Haven, 1930.

> Treats the subject of international loans for the period
> 1870-1914. The author sees political motives and con-

siderations behind financial transactions and relates
them to international diplomacy.

H 19. Gibbon, H.A.   The New Map of Europe 1911-1914:   The
Story of the Recent European Diplomatic Crisis and Wars and
of Europe's Present Catastrophe.   1914.

H 20. Gooch, G.P.   Before the War.   London, 1936.

H 21. -- Recent Revelations of European Diplomacy.   New York,
1940.

A critical review of the source materials dealing with
the years 1888-1914.

H 22. Gottlieb, W.W.   Studies in Secret Diplomacy During the First
World War.   London, 1957.

H 23. Hallgarten, George W.F.   Imperialismus vor 1914; die sozio-
logischen Grundlagen der Aussenpolitik europäischer Grossmächte vor dem ersten Weltkrieg.   2 v.   Munich, 1951.

H 24. Hanotaux, Gabriel.   La Politique de l'équilibre, 1907-1912.
1912.

H 25. Haselmayr, Friedrich.   Diplomatische Geschichte des zweiten
Reichs von 1871 bis 1918.   6 v.   Munich, 1950-1964.

This work consists of six very thick volumes and contains material on every aspect of German foreign policy for the years 1871-1918.   It is safe to say though
that some material on any aspect of German policy will
be found in Haselmayr and this work should be checked
as a first step in any study of German foreign policy
for the years 1871-1918.

H 26. Helmolt, H.F.   Die Geheime Vorgeschichte des Weltkrieges.
1914.

H 27. Heltner, Alfred.   Die Ziele unserer Weltpolitik.   Stuttgart,
1915.

H 28. Hintze, Otto, Friedrich Meinecke, Hermann Oncken and Hermann Schumacher.   Deutschland und die Weltkrieg.   1915.

All of this work except for one chapter was translated
into English with the title Modern Germany in Relation
to the Great War, 1916; (either book) is a good general
statement of Germany's position in regard to the war.

H 29. Hötzsch, Otto.   La Politique extérieure de l'Allemagne 1871
à 1914.   Geneva, 1933.

H 30. Hopfen, Otto H.   Kriegslehren zur äusseren Politik.   Berlin,

1915.

H 31. Ibbeken, Rudolf. Das Assenpolitische Problem Staat und Wirtschaft in der deutschen Reichspolitik, 1880-1914. Schleswig, 1928.

H 32. J'Accuse: von einem Deutschen. Zürich, 1914.

There are also French and English editions of this book which was supposed to have been written by a German citizen living in Switzerland. It is a striking indictment of German policy in the years before the war.

H 33. Jagow, K. "Der Potsdamer Kronrat. Geschichte und Legende," Süddeutsch Monatshefte. 24 (1928).

H 34. Knox, Samuel L.G. The Mailed Fist 1864-1939; The Background of Hitlerism. New York, 1943.

H 35. Langer, William L. The Diplomacy of Imperialism. New York, 1951.

A detailed study of the entire European diplomatic scene for the period 1890-1902. Each chapter contains exhaustive bibliographical references.

H 36. Lenz, Max. Deutschland im Kreis des Grossmachte 1871-1914. Berlin, 1925.

H 37. Lippmann, Walter. The Stakes of Diplomacy. New York, 1915.

An illuminating little volume setting forth the basic correlation of modern patriotism, business, and diplomacy.

H 38. Liv, Kwang-Ching. "German Fear of a Quadruple Alliance, 1904-1905," Journal of Modern History. 18(September, 1946): 222-240.

H 39. Macotta, Giuseppe W. Guglielmo II, la Germania e l'Europa, 1888-1914. Rome, 1934.

H 40. Prothero, George W. German Policy Before the War. New York, 1916.

H 41. Plehn, H. Bismarcks auswärtige Politik nach der Reichsgründung. 1920.

H 42. Rachfahl, Felix. Deutschland und die Weltpolitik 1871-1914. Stuttgart, 1923.

H 43. -- Die Deutsche Aussenpolitik in der wilhelminischen Ära. Berlin, 1924.

The author argues that Bismarck's successors continued
many of his policies.

H 44. Renouvin, Pierre. Histoire des relations internationales.

7 v. Paris, 1953 ff.

H 45. Reventlow, Ernst Graf zu. Deutschlands auswärtige Politik
1888-1914. Berlin, 1918.

Marked by strong nationalistic bias, but based on extensive reading.

H 46. Rohrbach, Paul. Der Deutsche Gedank in der Welt. Leipzig,
1912. Eng. trans., German World Policies. New York,
1915.

A patriotic defense of Germany's policies from an economic point of view.

H 47. Ruedorffer, J.J. Grundzüge der Weltpolitik in der Gegenwart.
Stuttgart, 1914.

H 48. Schiemann, Theodor. Deutschland und die Grosse Politik,
1901-1915. 14 v. Berlin, 1902-1915.

Reprint of weekly reviews of international affairs published in the Kreuzzeitung.

H 49. Schreiner, A. Zur Geschichte der deutschen Aussenpolitik,
1871-1945. Berlin, 1952.

H 50. Schwertfeger, Bernhard. Im Kampf um den Lebensraum.
Potsdam, 1940.

A competent and well written survey of German foreign
policy.

H 51. Seymour, Charles. The Diplomatic Background of the War
1870-1914. New Haven, 1916.

H 52. Sontag, Raymond. European Diplomatic History 1871-1932.
New York, 1933.

A good brief survey.

H 53. -- "German Foreign Policy 1904-1906," American Historical
Review. XXXIII (Jan. 1928): 278-301.

A good analysis of German Foreign Policy for this period, showing its manifold defects and inconsistancies.

H 54. Stieve, Friedrich. Deutschland und Europa 1890-1914. Berlin, 1926.

An analysis of the German diplomatic documents relating to the outbreak of the war.

H 55. Stowell, E.C. The Diplomacy of the War of 1914. 1915.

H 56. Sutten, Berthold. "Die Grossmächte und die Erhaltung des
Europäischen Friedens zu Beginn der Kreta-Krise von 1897, "
Südostorschungen. 1962, 21: 214-369.

   An analysis of the international political situation in
   1897. Traces the rebellion and massacres in Crete
   and the diplomatic activity of Russia, Great Britain,
   France, Austria-Hungary, Germany, and Italy. All
   were anxious to avoid a general clash but distrusted
   each other, and although all agreed that Greece was
   responsible for the war with Turkey each of them was
   afraid to take the first step against Greece, as it
   might provoke opposition in foreign as well as international politics--public opinion was strongly in favor
   of the Greeks. Only the unanimity of European powers
   prevented a general war, saved defeated Greece, and
   achieved autonomy for Crete.

H 57. Tardieu, André. La Conférence d'Algésiras: histoire diplo-
maitque de la crise marocaine. 1909.

H 58. -- Le Mystère d'Agadir. 1912.

H 59. Taylor, A.J.P. The Struggle for the Mastery in Europe,
1848-1919. Oxford, 1954.

   A good overview of the entire period with an excellent
   bibliography.

H 60. Valentin, Veit. Deutschlands Aussenpolitik von Bismarcks
Abgang bis zum Ende des Weltkrieges. Berlin, 1921.

   Treats the period 1890-1902 in a very cursory fashion
   but is good for the later period.

H 61. Welshert, Hans H. Als Bismarck gegangen war: intimitäten
der Weltpolitik 1890-1914. Hamburg, 1942.

H 62. Wolf, Theodor. The Eve of 1914. New York, 1936.

I. THE "WAR GUILT" QUESTION

   A large number of the books listed are "period pieces" and
consequently of little use; however, they are listed here to show
the trend in the historiography concerning the "war guilt" question. For bibliographies see: A 41-A 46.

I 1.   Adler, Georg. "Historikerkonferenz über den Ersten Welt-
       krieg, " Beiträge zur Geschichte der deutschen Arbeiterbe-
       wegung. East Berlin, 1964, 6(6): 1104-1108.

> The Historical Institute at the German Academy of Sci-
> ence, East Berlin, sponsored the conference Sept. 8-
> 10, 1964. Among the topics discussed were the aims
> of German imperialism and Karl Liebknecht's opposi-
> tion to the war.

I 2.   Albertini, Luigi.   The Origins of the War of 1914.   3 v.
       London, 1952 ff.

> The original appeared in Italian. The most comprehen-
> sive treatment available on the origins of the war,
> starting with the Congress of Berlin; unfortunately Al-
> bertini did not have access to the Italian documents
> which have only recently been published. Much other
> material has also been published since the Italian edi-
> tion of this work was published.

I 3.   Angelus, Oskar.   "Wer war am ersten Weltkrieg Schuld, "
       Politische Studien.   1964, 15(156): 429-439.

> Blames Russia because of her Balkan policy of support-
> ing Serbia and striving for possession of the Straits
> meant certain war. Author relates that Russia was al-
> so bent upon conquest in the Baltic region.

I 4.   Anrich, E.   Europas Diplomatie am Vorabend des Weltkrieges.
       Eine Bilanz der wissenschaftlichen Forschung über die Vor-
       geschichte des Weltkrieges und die Julikrise 1914.   1937.

I 5.   Armgaard, K.   Secrets of the German War Office.   New
       York, 1914.

I 6.   Barbagallo, C.   Come si scatenò la guerra mondiale.   Milan,
       1923.

I 7.   Barnes, Harry E.   The Genesis of the World War.   3rd ed.
       New York, 1929.

> A survey for the general reader of the revisionist point
> of view; with a useful annotated bibliography. Barnes
> also contributed a number of articles to Current His-
> tory in the 1920's and 1930's.

I 8.   --   In Quest of Truth and Justice.   New York, 1928.

> A summary of the revisionist controversy over the
> causes of World War I.

I 9.   --   World Politics in Modern Civilization.   New York, 1930.

> Surveys the war guilt literature in the last half of this
> book.

I 10. Bloch, Camile. Les Causes de la guerre mondiale. Paris,
1933. Eng. trans., The Causes of the World War: An Historical Summary. London, 1935.

I 11. Bornhak, Conrad. D. Kriegsschuld, Deutschlands Weltpolitik
1896-1914. Berlin, 1929.

A survey of German foreign policy 1890-1914, relying
almost entirely upon the German documents. The author makes a conscious effort to prove the innocence
of the Kaiser.

I 12. Cochran, M. H. Germany not Guilty in 1914. Boston, 1931.

A criticism of Bernadotte E. Schmitt's book The Coming of the War. See below I 55.

I 13. Delbrück, Hans. Deutsch-englische Schuld-Diskussion zwischen Hans Delbrück und J. W. Headlam-Morley. Berlin, 1921.

A debate on the question of war guilt.

I 14. Ewart, J. S. The Roots and Causes of the War. 2 v. 1925.

Especially severe on British policy.

I 15. Fabre-Luce, Alfred. The Limitations of Victory. New York,
1926.

French revisionist work which rejects the thesis of
primary German responsibility for World War I.

I 16. Fischer, Eugen. Kriegsschuldfrage und Aussenpolitik. Berlin, 1924.

I 17. -- Die Kritischen 39 Tage von Sarajewo bis zum Weltbrand.
1928.

I 18. Fischer, Fritz. Griff nach der Weltmacht. Düsseldorf,
1961. Eng. trans., Germany's Aims in the First World War.
New York, 1967.

See Fischer's answer to his critics in which he ex-
pounds further on his thesis: "Weltpolitik, Weltmachtstreben und deutsche Kriegsziele," Historische Zeitschrift. 199 (Oct. 1964): 265-346. Fischer has used
the files of the German foreign office and many of the
German ministries and offices and researched the archives at Vienna, Munich, and Stuttgart. His principal
thesis is that there was a continuity of German war
aims from the beginning of the war to its very end,
which was represented not only by the military leaders,
but equally by civilians, such as Chancellor Bethmann-
Hollweg, the high officials of the German foreign office,
of the imperial and Prussian ministries, and backed by
the political parties and their deputies, by the associa-

tions of German industry and trade, and by public opinion in general; between the military and the civilians
there were merely differences about the form in which
German rule should be exercised, but not, as hitherto
believed, contrasts of principle between annexationists,
whose war aims were virtually limitless, and moderates
who were opposed to annexation on a large scale.
Several interesting articles have been written on
the book. See: Klaus Epstein "German War Aims in
the First World War," World Politics, 15 (Oct. 1962):
163-185. James Joll "The 1914 Debates Continues;
Fritz Fischer and his Critics," Past and Present, No.
34, July, 1966. An article highly critical of Fischer's
thesis has been written by Gerhard Ritter "Eine neue
Kriegsschuldthese," Historische Zeitschrift, 194(1962):
646-668. See also Hans Herzfeld's article "Zur deutschen Politik im ersten Weltkriege; Kontinuität order
permanente Krise?" in Deutsche Kriegsziele 1914-1918,
Frankfurt A/M, 1964, p. 84-101. Eberhard von
Vietsch "Die Kriegsausbruch 1914 im Lichte der neusten
Forschung," Geschichte in Wissenschaft und Unterricht,
1964, 15(8): 472-486, relates that Fischer's interpreta-
tion is based on a faulty interpretation of the sources.
Dietrich Mende "Die Nicht Bewältigte Vergangenheit des
Ersten Weltkrieges," Europa Archiv, 1963, 18(19): 333-
354, is an unfavorable review. Fritz Epstein "Neue
Literatur zur Geschichte der Ostpolitik im Ersten Welt-
krieg," Jahrbücher für Geschichte Osteuropas, 1966,
14(1): 63-94, is generally favorable to Fischer's book.
Additional comment on Fischer's book may be found in:
The American Historical Review, 68 (1963): 443-445;
The English Historical Review, 78(Oct. 1963): 751-753;
The Journal of Central European Affairs, 23(April,
1963): 97-99; International Affairs, 39(Jan. 1963): 77-79;
Vierteljahreshefte für Zeitgeschichte, (1963): 224 ff;
Neue Politische Literatur No. 6(1962): 471; Cahiers
Pologne Allemagne, No. 4(1962): 108-113; Zeitschrift
für Geschichtswissenschaft, (1962): 1808; and Novaja i
novejsaja istorija, No. 2 (1963): 158-161. See: J 22,
Y 9-26.

I 19. Frauendienst, Werner. "Das Kriegsschuldreferat des Aus-
       wärtigen Amtes," Berliner Monatschefte. 15(1937).

I 20. Gutsche, Willibald. "Erst Europa--und dann die Welt; Prob-
       leme der Kriegszielpolitik der deutschen Imperialismus im
       Ersten Weltkrieg," Zeitschrift für Geschichtswissenschaft.
       East Germany, 1964. 12(5): 745-767.

       Germany planned to conquer all of Central Europe first
       and then use this continental hegemony as a basis for
       its conquest of the world.

I 21. Hale, Oron J. Germany and the Diplomatic Revolution.
Philadelphia, 1931.

> Points out that Germany was not responsible for the
> trend of European diplomacy which ended in World
> War I.

I 22. Headlam, J.W. History of Twelve Days, July 24-August 4,
1914. 1915.

I 23. Helmreich, E.C. The Diplomacy of the Balkan Wars. Cambridge, Mass., 1938.

> Detailed study of the Balkan situation and of the diplo-
> matic activities and intrigues which lay back of Austro-
> Russian friction and the outbreak of the war.

I 24. Hölzle, E. "Die Weltmächte und der Ausbruch des ersten
Weltkrieges," Aussenpolitik. 6, 2(1955).

I 25. Issac, J. "L'Histoire des origins de la guerre dans les man-
uels allemands," Revue d'histoire de la guerre mondiale.
10(1932).

I 26. -- "La Problème des origines de la guerre; Trois solutions
americaines," Rev. Hist. Mod. 7(1932).

I 27. -- Un Débat historique: 1914; La problème des origines de
la guerre. Paris, 1933.

> Discussion of the books by Fay and Schmitt.

I 28. Die Kriegsschuldfrage. Zeitschrift zur Vorgeschichte und
Geschichte des Weltkrieges. Berlin, 1923-28. Appeared under the title Berliner Monatschefte. Berlin, 1929-1944.

> Edited by Alfred von Wegerer 1923 to 1936 and by
> August Bach 1937 to 1944. A journal dedicated to
> proving Germany's innocence.

I 29. Lafore, Laurence. The Long Fuse: An Interpretation of the
Origins of World War I. Philadelphia, 1965.

> The book presupposes, on the part of the reader, a
> knowledge of the events leading up to 1914. The main
> emphasis is on the immediate crisis in July, 1914.
> The author concludes that the major responsibility for
> a general war rests on Germany and Austria and spe-
> cifically on Theobald von Bethmann-Hollweg, Gottlieb
> von Jagow, and Count Leopold Berchtold.

I 30. Lafajole, Faramond G.M.A. "Les Responsabilités de L'Allemagne," Revue Hist. Dipl. 45(1931).

I 31. Lutz, Hermann. Lord Grey and the World War. New York,

1928.

Traces the English responsibility for the war.

I 32. Lutz, Hermann. Die Europäische Politik in der Julikrise
1914. Berlin, 1930.

An early German interpretation of the events of July,
1914.

I 33. Mansergh, Nicholas. The Coming of the First World War.
1949.

I 34. Menczer, Bela. "New Light on July 1914," Quarterly Review.
1964, 302(640): 174-186.

An evaluation of Berchtold's part in the July crisis
which shows that Austria was moving toward a rapprochement with Russia.

I 35. Michon, Georges. The Franco-Russian Alliance, 1891-1917.
New York, 1929.

French revisionist study of the alliance, concluding that
it was the primary factor in producing World War I.

I 36. Montgelas, Maximilian. British Foreign Policy under Sir
Edward Grey. New York, 1928.

A sharp indictment of Grey.

I 37. -- Leitfaden zur Kriegsschuldfrage. Berlin, 1923. Eng.
trans., The Case for the Central Powers. New York, 1925.

An impeachment of the Versailles Treaty. The author
makes the point that had Germany wanted war, there
were many opportunities before 1914. He also states
that Germany was in a much better position to win a
war in 1905 than in 1914. He does not excuse Germany entirely, but blames the stupid bungling manner
in which German foreign policy was conducted during
the crisis in 1914. The English translation was poorly
done.

I 38. North, Robert C. "Perception and Action in the 1914 Crisis,"
Journal of International Affairs. 1967, 21(1): 103-122.

Summarizes events during the July crisis of 1914. Concludes that the reaction within the Triple Entente was
"appropriate to...environmental stimulus" whereas reaction within the Dual Alliance (Germany and Austria-
Hungary) were excessive because of a "relatively high
level of negative emotion or effect...."

I 39. Oncken, Hermann. Das Deutsche Reich und die Vorgeschichte
des Weltkrieges. Leipzig, 1933.

A synthesis of the materials published to that time on
the origins of the war; author concludes that the evidence supports the German thesis of revision.

I 40. Poletika, N.P. <u>Vozniznovenie pervoi mirovki voiny (iiul' skii</u>

<u>krizis 1914)</u>. Moscow, 1964.

This book on the origins of World War I with emphasis
on the July crisis is a new edition of an older work
first published in 1935. The author makes use of the
marxist formula to explain the causes of the war. The
war in his opinion resulted from a conspiracy of a
small band of capitalist stooges in the governments of
all the powers involved in the July crisis. They wished
for a war. Germany gets most of the blame for giving
the "blank check" to Austria and for her build-up in
armaments. England ranks second for giving a "blank
check" to both France and Russia and the denial to Germany of any possibility to retreat on the others. Behind British policy is her attempt to maintain mastery
of the seas. France ranks third for goading the Russians into the war which was conceived by France as
a means for getting even with Germany for the Franco-
Prussian war. Austria and Russia are blamed as willing partners to German and Anglo-French imperialism.
Both Austria and Russia had imperialist designs in the
Balkans.

I 41. Rassow, Paul. "Die Kriegsschuldfrage in ihren Abwandlungen

während des Krieges," <u>Berliner Monatschefte</u>. 13(1935).

I 42. Recouly, R. <u>Les Heures tragiques d'avant-guerre</u>. Paris,

1922.

I 43. -- "Les Origines de la guerre," <u>La Revue de France</u>.

5(1929).

I 44. Remak, Joachim. <u>The Origins of World War I.</u> New York,

1967.

Treats both the long and short range causes of the war
1871-1914.

I 45. Reiners, Ludwig. <u>The Lights Went out in Europe</u>. New York,

1956.

Revisionist book on the background of World War I.
Especially good for its treatment of the personalities
involved.

I 46. Renouvin, Pierre. <u>Les Origins immédiates de la guerre</u>.

Paris, 1927. Eng. trans., <u>The Immediate Origins of the War:</u>

<u>28 June-4 August, 1914.</u> London, 1928.

Tends to be revisionist in his attitude toward Germany.

I 47. Renouvin, Pierre. "L'Allemagne et les causes de la guerre,"
       La revue de Paris. 38 (1931).

I 48. -- "Les Historiens americaines et les responsabilités de la
       guerre," Revue des deux mondes. 8, 2(1931).

I 49. Rose, J.H. The Origins of the War. 1914.

I 50. Rosen, Fredrich. "Die europäischen Mächte im Sommer
       1914," Berliner Monatschefte. 12(1934).

I 51. Rumbold, Sir Horace. The War Crisis in Berlin July-August
       1914. London, 1940.

I 52. Salis, I.R. von. Die Ursachen des Ersten Weltkrieges. Stutt-
       gart, 1964.

I 53. Schilling, Baron. How the War Began. London, 1925.
       Places the blame on Russia.

I 54. Schücking, Walther. Die völkerrechtliche Lehre des Welt-
       krieges. Leipzig, 1918.

I 55. Schmitt, Bernadotte E. Coming of the War, 1914. New
       York, 1930.

       Is focused almost exclusively upon the immediate crisis.
       He considers the Central Powers more to blame, and
       found Germany in a particularly sensitive position of
       responsibility for European stability. Germany had led
       the way into the fatal alliance system, and had begun
       universal military conscription. He gives strong em-
       phasis to the Moltke-Conrad staff discussion of 1909
       and the Liman von Sanders mission of 1913-1914. Ger-
       man diplomatic conduct in 1914 aroused distrust and
       suspicion throughout Europe and the inexorable opera-
       tion of militarism and the alliance system did the rest
       automatically into war. Schmitt has reviewed all the
       document collections published by the European powers
       since the end of World War I. His review of the Rus-
       sian and French documents can be found in Foreign Af-
       fairs, XIII(1934): 133-153, XV(1937): 516-536. A re-
       view of the Italian documents is found in The Journal
       of Modern History, (Dec. 1965): 469-472. For an in-
       teresting article by Schmitt see The Journal of Modern
       History, XVI(Sept. 1944): 169-204 in which Schmitt re-
       views the origins of the war.

I 56. Schwertfeger, Bernard. Der Weltkrieg der Dokument; Zehn
       Jahre Kriegsschuldforschung und ihr Ergebnis. 1929.

I 57. Fay, Sidney B. Origins of the War. New York, 1930.

       Responsibilities for the war can be grouped as follows:
       (1) Austria, Russia, Serbia (2) Germany, France

(3) England. The most culpable diplomat was to be
found in Austria's Count Leopold Berchtold: He em-
phasizes the great underlying currents in Europe that
made the war possible: secret alliances, militarism,
aroused nationalism, economic imperialism, and irresponsibility of the press. (See also the numerous articles by Fay in Current History in the 1920's and 1930's.)

I 58. Siegler, J. "Entre la paix et la guerre (Juillet 1914), " Revue politique et parlementaire. 177(1938).

I 59. Source Records of the Great War. Vol. I Causes. 1923.

Contains government statements, individual narratives,
and documents covering the events which led up to the
war. Volume VII of this series contains a bibliography
on p. 213-216 of older studies on the origins of the
war.

I 60. Stieve, Friedrich. Isvolsky and the World War. New York,
1926.

Points out that Isvolsky and the French war group led
by Poincaré brought on the war.

I 61. Swain, J.W. Beginning of the Twentieth Century. New York,
1933.

A revisionist summary of the underlying diplomatic
causes of World War I.

I 62. Thomson, George M. The Twelve Days. New York, 1964.

A recent study of the period July 24 to Aug. 4, 1914.
Presents nothing new and overlooks much evidence presented by many other authors.

I 63. Toscano, Mario. L'Italia e la crisi europea del lugio 1914.
Milan, 1940.

A short treatment of the July crisis.

I 64. Trevor-Roper, H.R. "World War I--Start of an Age of Vio-
lence, " New York Times Magazine. Aug. 1, 1954.

Denies that the war was the inevitable result of any
economic or other development. Imperialist rivalries
led to "incidents" throughout the world but none of
these incidents led to war. It has been "proved" that
the war was caused "by deliberate German aggression"
following a policy determined by the German General
Staff.

I 65. Wegerer, Alfred von. Das Ausbruch des Weltkrieges 1914.
2 v. Hamburg, 1939.

The author was the editor of Die Kriegsschuldfrage,
later named the Berliner Monatshefte. In this position

he was the leader of the movement to disprove the charge that Germany was responsible for starting World War I. His two volumes are a synthesis of many years of work and discussion on the subject but contain little that was not already known. They contain a minute examination of the events between the assassination of Franz Ferdinand on June 28, 1914, and the English declaration of war on August 4. He does not pretend that Germany was without blame, but insists on Germany's right to arrange affairs in Central Europe without British interference. An extensive review by Bernadotte E. Schmitt is found in The Journal of Modern History, (June, 1941): 225-236.

I 66. Wegerer, Alfred von. Refutation of the Versailles War Guilt Thesis. New York, 1930.

I 67. Zeno, I. "La Germania e la Kriegsschuldfrage; Bilancio di 15 anni di ricerche e di polemiche," Riv. di polit. internazionale. 4(1937).

I 68. Fleming, D. F. The Origins and Legacies of World War I. New York, 1968.

J. ARCHIVAL SOURCES AND PUBLISHED DOCUMENTS

Archival Sources

J 1. Born, Lester K. "The Archives and Libraries of Post War Germany," The American Historical Review. (Oct. 1950): 34-57.

J 2. Case, Lynn M. and Daniel H. Thomas. Guide to the Diplomatic Archives of Western Europe. Philadelphia, 1959.

Contains an essay by Raymond J. Sontag on "Germany" p. 84-97 and one by Oron J. Hale on "Bavaria" p. 34-77.

J 3. Philippi, Hans. "Das Politische Archiv des Auswärtigen Amtes; Rückführung und Übersicht über die Bestände," Archivar. 13(1960): 201-218.

J 4. Schmid, Irmtraut. "Der Bestand des Auswärtigen Amts im deutschen Zentralarchiv Potsdam," Archivmitteilungen. 12(1962): 71-79, 123-132.

J 5. Skidmore, Thomas E. "Surveys of Unpublished Sources on

the Central Government and Politics of the German Empire
1871-1918, " The American Historical Review. (July, 1960):
848-859.

J 6. Stieg, Louis F. A Union List of Printed Collections of
Source Materials on European History in New York State Libraries. New York, 1944.

Published Collections of Documents including aids to help in using
the document collections, and catalogs of documents which
have been microfilmed.

J 7. Die Grosse Politik der europäischen Kabinette 1871-1914;
Sammlung der diplomatischen Akten des Auswärtigen Amtes.
Ed. by Johannes Lepsius, Albrecht Mendelssohn-Bartholdy,
and Friedrich Thimme. 40 v. Berlin, 1922-1927.

There is a French edition, La Politique extérieure de
l'Allemagne, Paris, 1928 ff., but it is incomplete and
for the moment ends with the 32nd volume and the year
1908. In the French edition the documents are organized chronologically, whereas the German edition is arranged topically. For a discussion of the manner in
which Die Grosse Politik was published, see: Mario
Toscano, The History of Treaties and International Politics; an Introduction to the History of Treaties and International Politics: The Documentary and Memoir
Sources, Baltimore, 1966, p. 134-138; and Fritz T.
Epstein, "Die erschliessung von Quellen zur Geschichte
der deutschen Aussenpolitik; die Publikation von Akten
d. Auswärtigen Amts nach d. beiden Weltkriegen, "
Welt als Geschichte, 22(1962): 204-219; and Raymond
J. Sontag, "The German Diplomatic Papers: Publication After Two Wars, " The American Historical Review,
(Oct. 1962): 57-68, which point out how important documents on military policy were omitted. Little was published on intelligence operations, including payments to
foreign newspapers. The files on economic and colonial activities were sparcely used. The files of the German embassy in London were not examined, nor was
Bismarck's study of public opinion in Austria published.
The edition refrained from publishing anything injurious
to neutral states and living statesmen. They showed
consideration, both in the text and in the footnotes, for
statesmen and enemy countries who had not been openly
anti-German, particularly if there was a possibility that
these statesmen might again exercise political influence,
for instance, in selecting material on the Moroccan
crisis of 1911 every effort was made to protect Joseph
Caillaux. Anyone working with Die Grosse Politik
should consult A Catalogue of Files and Microfilms of

the German Foreign Ministry Archives 1867-1920, Washington, 1959, to determine what was omitted because Die Grosse Politik, unlike other document collections, does not give details of file references or archival classification of the documents published. In this catalog, appendix II, p. 1248 ff., a cross-reference system has been prepared to point out the omission in Die Grosse Politik. For more detailed catalogs on the sections filmed by the University of Michigan and the University of California see: A Catalogue of German Foreign Ministry Archives 1867-1920, Ann Arbor, 1957, and Preliminary Index of German Foreign Ministry Archives 1867-1920, Berkeley, 1954. There is also a small catalog available for the sections filmed by the University of Florida. Many of the files listed in the general catalog mentioned above were not microfilmed. It is possible to have these files microfilmed at your own expense. For additional information write: Leiter des Politischen Archivs und Historischen Referats, Auswärtiges Amt, Koblenzer Strasse 99/103, 53 Bonn, Germany.

J 8. Die Auswärtige Politik des deutschen Reiches 1871-1914. Ed. by Albrecht Mendelssohn-Bartholdy and Friedrich Thimme.

4 v. Berlin, 1928.

An authorized abbreviated edition of Die Grosse Politik.

J 9. German Diplomatic Documents 1871-1914. Ed. by E.T.S. Dugdale. 4 v. New York, 1928-31.

A selection of the German foreign office documents taken from Die Grosse Politik.

J 10. Die Sammlung der deutschen diplomatischen Akten über die vorgehen der europäischen Mächte in ostasien; gewählt aus "Die Grosse Politik der europäischen Kabinette 1871-1914." Peking, 1940.

The documents in Die Grosse Politik relating to German Far Eastern relations.

J 11. Les Origines de la guerre et de la politique extérieure de l'Allemagne au debut du XXe siècle d'après les documents diplomatique publiés par le ministère allemand des affairs étrangères. Ed. by Edmond Vermeil. Paris, 1926.

A selection of the documents published in Die Grosse Politik translated into French.

J 12. Die Diplomatischen Akten des Auswärtigen Amts 1871-1914, Ein Wegweiser durch das grosse Aktenwerk der Deutschen

Regierung. Ed. by Bernhard Schwertfeger. 8 v. in 5.

Berlin, 1924-1927.

Prints the documents presented in Die Grosse Politik
which the editor thinks to be the most important.

J 13. Guides to German Records Microfilmed at Alexandria, Va;

No. 15: Records of Former German and Japanese Embassies
and Consulates. 1890-1945. Washington, 1960.

Some material on the German consulates in Tsingtao
and Hankow in China and in Yokohama, Japan for the
period prior to 1914.

J 14. N S D A P Hauptarchiv: Guide to the Hoover Institutional
Microfilm Collection. Comp. by Grete Heinz and Agnes Peterson. Stanford, Calif., 1964, p. 43-44.

See Reels 32 and 6 A, folders 610-611, & 616 which
contain photo copies of German documents relating to
the outbreak of the war, and the war guilt question.

J 15. Deutsche Gesandtschaftberichte zum Kriegsausbruch 1914:

Berichte und Telegramme der badischen, sächsischen, und

württembergischen Gesandlschaften in Berlin aus dem Juli

und August 1914. Im Auftrag des Auswärtigen Amtes. Ed.

by August Bach. Berlin, 1937.

Published in French in Revue d'histoire de la guerre
mondiale. (April, July, and Oct. 1935).
This collection, and also J 16, reveal many confidential statements of the chancellor, other government officials, and political leaders made to the diplomatic
representatives of these German states.

J 16. Bayerische Dokumente zum Kriegsausbruch und zum Versailles

Schuldspruch, im Auftrage des Bayerischen Landtages. Ed.

by Pius Dirr. Munich, 1922. 2nd ed., enl., 1923; 3rd. ed.,

enl., 1925.

J 17. Die Deutschen Dokumente zum Kriegsausbruch. Ed. by Karl

Kautsky. 4 v. Charlottenberg, 1919-1920. 2nd ed., enl.,

1927. Eng. trans., The Outbreak of the World War. Wash-

ington, 1924.

J 18. German Secret War Documents Covering the Period June 15-

August 1914, and Published by the German Government in

1919. New York, 1920.

A selection of some of the most important documents

from the four volume work edited by Karl Kautsky.

J 19. Völkerrecht im Weltkrieg.   Ed. by Eugene Fischer.   4 v.
Berlin, 1927.
A collection of source materials on the history of the
war.

J 20. Beilagen zu den stenographischen Berichten über die öffent-
lichen Verhandlungen des Untersuchungausschusses.   Berlin,
1921.   Eng. trans., Official German Documents Relating to
the World War.   2 v.   New York, 1923.
The reports of the Reichstag Commission of Inquiry
created in 1919 to investigate the war and its origins.

J 21. Das Werk des Untersuchungausschusses der Verfassunggebenden
deutschen nationalversammlung und des deutschen Reichstags.

Series I.   Unterausschuss zur Vorgeschichte des Weltkrieges.

Heft I.   Schriftliche Auskünfte deutscher Staatsmänner.   Ed.

by Walter Schücking.   Berlin, 1920.   Eng. trans., First Sub-

Committee Report found in Official Documents Relating to the

Outbreak of the War.   New York, 1923.   I, p. 1-120;

Heft II.   Militarische Rustungen und Mobilmachungen.   Berlin,

1921.

This is the report of the subcommittee which was to
look into the origins of the war.   It was a subcommittee set up in 1919 by the Reichstag Commission of Inquiry.   It made use of a questionnaire which was sent
to government officials who were in responsible positions during the pre-war period.   The statements
gathered as a result of this questionnaire were revealing regarding hitherto obscure phases of the July crisis,
such as: the real meaning of the Austro-German conversations at Potsdam, and the activities of the German
ambassador at Vienna, Tschirschky, whose personal
initiative was reported to have gone beyond his instructions.

J 22. Julikrise und Kriegsausbruch 1914: eine Dokumentensammlung.

Ed. by Imanuel Geiss.   2 v.   Hannover, 1963-1964.

The introduction to these volumes is by Fritz Fischer.
The collection is well edited.   An introduction is written to each day's dispatches.   There is also a handy
calendar of documents which are synchronized in parallel columns under the headings of the five major cap-
itals.   A list of principal ministers and diplomats of
each country is given.   A selected bibliography is also
included.   There is a summary by original collections

and with the original document numbers of all documents reproduced. The total number of documents presented in the two volumes is 1168. There are also valuable footnotes and well written appendices.

Geiss has his own conclusions on the causes of the war. He concludes that no power wanted World War I, but that it grew out of the continental war (Germany and Austria-Hungary vs. Russia and France) which in turn arose from a local war (Austria-Hungary vs. Serbia) a war that Austria-Hungary and Germany did not want. Since Berlin could have stopped this local war by its veto of the Austro-Hungarian action, Berlin played the decisive part in the chain reaction which led from Serajevo to the British declaration of war on August 4th.

Geiss rejects the idea that Germany wanted a preventive war as well as the idea that the entente would have attacked Germany in a few years. He is of the opinion that Britain's earlier failure to declare its solidarity with Russia and France places some responsibility on England for the war.

He states that Germany's change of heart on July 29 came too late; however, the Russian mobilization was started too early. Geiss believes that Germany played a more important role in the Balkans than merely giving a blank check to Austria. He is of the opinion that Germany was well aware of the risks they were taking and that to many people in high places the prospects of war were not unwelcome. The general tone of this document collection is anti-revisionist in nature.

The one volume abridged edition entitled Juli 1914, Munich, 1965, is available in English under the title July 1914; The Outbreak of the First World War: Selected Documents, New York, 1967. For Geiss' comments on the Fischer controversy (listed under I 18) see p. 9-16; there is a good bibliography included. Geiss also develops his ideas on the origins of the war in two articles: "Le Déclenchement de la première guerre mondiale, " Revue Historique, (1964): 415-426, and "The Outbreak of the First World War and German War Aims, " Journal of Contemporary History, I (July, 1966): 75-91. In these articles Geiss discusses his document collection concluding that: (1) Germany deserves most of the blame for both the outbreak of the local Austro-Serbian conflict and its escalation into a world war, (2) Bethmann-Hollweg deliberately failed to carry through William II's sincere desire to try to avert war following the Serbian reply to the Austrian ultimatum, (3) Germany planned from the outset to make

sure that the blame for a war would fall upon Russia,
(4) Germany would have mobilized on July 31 even if
Russia had not done so on July 30, (5) the entente
powers are exonerated, though it is conceded that they
may have contributed in a minor way.

J 23. Die Diplomatischen Akten des auswärtigen Amtes 1871, 1914.
Berlin, 1924.

A guide to the published documents of the German foreign office.

J 24. Meyor, Hermann. Das Politische Schriftwesen im deutschen
auswärtigen Dienst: ein Leitfaden zum Verständnis diplo-
matischer Dokumente. Tübingen, 1920.

A guide to the use of German foreign office documents.

J 25. Sass, Johann. Die Deutschen Weissbücher zur auswärtigen
Politik, 1870-1914; Geschichte und Bibliographie. Berlin,
1928.

A description of the German white books published by
the German Government before Die Grosse Politik was
published.

J 26. Aktenstücke über die schiedsgerechtliche erledigung der durch
den zwischenfall von Casablanca hervorgerufenen streitfrages
1908/09. Berlin, 1909. Text in German and French.

J 27. Aktenstücke zum Kriegsausbruch. Berlin, 1914.

An earlier and less complete edition of this collection
has the title Vorläufige Denkschrift und Aktenstücke zum
Kriegsausbruch. Berlin, 1914.

J 28. Strauss, Albert A. The Absolute Truth in Regard to the
Cause of the European War. New York, 1914.

Contains a translation of the German white paper entitled Die Reine Wahrheit über die Ursachen des europäischen Welt-Krieges, New York, 1914.

J 29. The German White Book; Authorized Translation: Documents
Relating to the Outbreak of the War, with Supplements. Berlin, 1914.

J 30. Why the War; the Official Documents and Other Diplomatic
Correspondence Relating to the European War. I White Paper
of England, II White Paper of Germany, III Orange Paper of
Russia, IV Grey Paper of Belgium, V Yellow Book of France.
New York, 1914.

There are numerous publications issued by The New
York Times of this nature. The titles all start the
same, "Why the War." Each time a new "Rainbow
Book" was published a new edition was published.
Originally this material was published in the Times
on Aug. 23, Sept. 24 & 27, Oct. 1, and other dates
during 1914.

J 31. Le Livre blanc allemand: memoire du chancelier von Bethmann-Hollweg; correspondance avec les représentants de l'empire Allemand à l'étranger; telegrammes du Tsar et de l'Empereur; ultimatum du Japon. Paris, 1914.

J 32. Das Deutsche Weisbuch: wie Russland Deutschland hinterging
und europäischen Krieg entfesselte; Denkschrift und Akten-
stücke mit den originaltelegrammen und Noten. Berlin, 1914.
Eng. trans., The German White Book: How Russia and her
Ruler Betrayed Germany's Confidence and thereby Caused the
European War. Berlin, 1914.

J 33. Collected Documents Relating to the Outbreak of the War.
London, 1915.
Contains a translation of the German White Book.

J 34. Auswärtiges Amt; Aktenstücke zum Kriegsausbruch. Berlin,
1915. Eng. trans. in J.B. Scott, Diplomatic Documents Relating to the Outbreak of the War, New York, 1916. Part II,
p. 769-780.

J 35. Deutschland Schuldig? Deutsches Weisbuch über die ver-
antwortlichkeit des urheber des Kriegen. Berlin, 1919.

J 36. Das Deutsche Weisbuch über die Schuld im Kriege mit Denkschrift der deutschen Viererkommission zum Schuldbericht
des alliierten und assoziierten Mächte. Charlottenburg, 1919.
2nd ed. enl. Berlin, 1927.

J 37. University of Michigan and Cambridge University Selection
(U.M./C.U.): Project 1 (G.F.M. 26). 1870-1930. 111 reels.
Selected files of the Marine Kabinett (1889-1922) of the
Admiralstab der Marine, Abteilung "A" (1885-1919) and
Abteilung "B" (1885-1917), and of the Reichs-Marine-
Amt (1870-1930), but mainly for the period 1889-1919.

J 38. University of Michigan Selection (U.M.): Project 1 (G.F.M.
27). 1900-1945. 22 reels.
Selected files of the Admiralstab der Marine, Abteilung

"A" (1900-1916), and Abteilung "B" (1912-1914), together with other files (1933-1945).

J 39. University of Michigan and Cambridge University Selection (U.M./C.U.): Project 2 (G.F.M. 31). 1872 to 1939. 19 reels.

Further selected files of the Admiralstab der Marine, Abteilung "A" (1874-1919) and Abteilung "B" (1880-1919), the Reichs-Marine-Amt (1872-1928) and the Marine-Kabinett (1877-1919).

J 40. University of Hawaii Selection (U.H.) (G.F.M. 28) 1867 to 1916. 25 reels.

Selected files of the Reichs-Marine-Amt (1867-1913), and of the Admiralstab der Marine, Abteilung "B" (1886-1916) relating to East Asia, Australia, and the south sea islands.

J 41. Australian Government Selection (Aus.) (G.F.M. 29). 1854 to 1944. 45 reels.

Selected files of the Reichs-Marine-Amt (1854-1913), and of the Admiralstab der Marine, Abteilung "B" (1800-1917), and of the Oberkommando der Marine Seekriegsleitung (1879-1944) relating to the Far East, Eastern Asia, south seas and Pacific Islands, and Australia.

J 42. Schlieffen Papers (Cab. 20). 1902-1912. 22 files and 11 maps.

Photostats of the papers of Graf von Schieffen, chief of the German general staff 1892-1906. The original papers were included in a collection of German army documents (Heeresarchiv). This material, which collectively forms what has become known as the Schlieffen Plan, has been almost completely copied. The originals are at Bonn.

J 43. Schriftwechsel mit der regierung der Vereinigten Staaten von Amerika betreffend den unterseehandelskrieg. Berlin, 1916.

Documents concerning German submarine warfare as it related to the United States.

J 44. Deutsche Reichsgeschichte in Dokumenten. Ed. by Johannes Hohlfeld. 4 v. Berlin, 1934.

Covers the period 1848-1933.

J 45. Publikationen aus den Königlichen Preussischen Staatsarchiven, veranlasst und unterstützt durch die Archiv-verwaltung. 9 v. Leipzig, 1878-1938.

J 46. Das Staatsarchiv, 1861-1914. 86 v. Leipzig, 1872-1919.

J 47. Verhandlungen des Reichstages; Stenographische Berichte.
Berlin, 1871-1938.

J 48. Stenographische Berichte über die Verhandlungen des Preussischen Landtages, Haus des Abgeorddeten. Berlin, 1848-
1917.

K. THE GERMAN GENERAL STAFF AND ITS INFLUENCE ON
FOREIGN RELATIONS

K 1. Ritter, Gerhard. Staatskunst und Kriegshandwerk: das Problem des "militarismus" in Deutschland. Vol. II. Die Haupt-
mächte Europas und das wilhelminische Reich 1890-1914.
Munich, 1960.

Ritter is interested in the influence of the German military on political decisions, and on the middle class in
Germany. He devotes closer scrutiny to the roles of
key personalities and groups including Tirpitz, whom
Ritter considers the strongest personality. He traces
the failure of the military to integrate military planning
with Germany's economic and political interests as well
as attributing the widening gap between the officer
corps and the civil society to the immunity of the army
from parliamentary criticism. Ritter is of the opinion
that the decisions of Schlieffen and Tirpitz placed German diplomacy in chains.

K 2. Förster, Gerhard. Der preussisch-deutsch Generalstab 1870-
1963. East Berlin, 1964.

This general survey points out the part the German
general staff played in the "imperialistic designs" of
Germany.

K 3. Craig, Gordon. The Politics of the Prussian Army. 1956.

Craig pictures the Prussian army as a state within a
state acquiescing in directions issued by the political
heads of the state for the most part only when it suited
its purpose to do so. This was a political danger
which increased when civilian control was weak.

K 4. Grieren, Gerhard. Vorkriegs und Kriegsstünden. Leipzig,
1926.

A popular, but suggestive account of the old military
system, the politico-military conflicts and the chief

operations of the war.

K 5. Die Generalstäbe in Deutschland, 1871-1945: Aufgaben in der
Armee und Stellung im Staate; Die Entwicklung der militärischen Luftfahrt in Deutschland 1920-1945: Planung und Mas-
snahmen zur Schaffung einer Fliegertruppe in der Reichwehr.
Stuttgart, 1962.

> A historical series produced by the Military History
> Research Institute of the West German Army. The
> first monograph in this volume surveys the organic
> development of the German general staff 1871-1945.

K 6. Demeter, Karl. The German Officer-Corps in Society and
State. New York, 1965.

> This is not a new book. It is Demeter's pioneering
> study, Das Deutsche Offizierkorps in seinen historisch-
> soziologischen Grundlagen (1930) brought up to date.
> The present book was translated from the revised Ger-
> man edition, which was published under the title, Das
> Deutsche Offizierkorps in Gesellschaft und Staat 1650-
> 1945. For the period prior to 1919 the book retains
> for the most part the original Demeter text. If possi-
> ble the German edition of this work should be used, in
> view of the fact that entire sections, often several
> pages in length, were omitted in the English transla-
> tion.

K 7. Förster, Gerhard. Der Preussisch-deutsche Generalstab
1640 bis 1965. East Berlin, 1966.

> Places much of the blame for both wars on the German
> general staff. Relates that the Bonn general staff is
> still up to its old imperialist ways.

K 8. Irvine, Dallas D. "The Origins of Capital Staffs," The Journal of Modern History. X(1938): 161-179.

K 9. Ritter, Gerhard. "The Political Attitude of the German Army
1900-1944: From Obedience to Revolt," in A.O. Sarkissian
(ed.) Studies in Diplomatic History in Honour of G.P. Gooch,
New York, 1962.

K 10. Fried, Hans E. The Guilt of the German Army. New York,
1942.

K 11. Krauss, Karl. "Vom Werden, Wesen und Wirken des preussischen Generalstabes," Geschichte in Wissenschaft und Unterricht. 1958. 9(5): 257-276.

> Discussion of the strategic planning of the general staff

1864-1918, emphasizing that the general staff was not solely the product of the reactionary power of old Prussianism, and concludes that the military was mainly responsible for the German defeat in World War I.

K 12. Schweppenburg, Leo Geyr von. "Der Kreigsausbruch 1914 und der deutsche Generalstab," Wehrwissenschaftliche Rundschau. 1963. 13(3): 150-163.

> Study of the outbreak of World War I based on the collected documents of the Russian section of the German general staff.

K 13. Helfritz, Hans. Geschichte der preussischen Heeresverwaltung. Berlin, 1938.

> A comprehensive history of the Prussian military administration up to World War I.

K 14. Görlitz, Walter. Die Deutsche Generalstab. Frankfurt, 1950. Eng. trans., The German General Staff. New York, 1953.

> A general history of the general staff covering the period 1657-1945.

K 15. Craig, Gordon A. "Military Diplomats in the Prussian and German Service: the Attachés, 1816-1914," Political Science Quarterly. 64(1949): 65-94.

K 16. Meisner, Heinrich O. Militärattaches und Militärbevollmächtigte in Preussen und im Deutschen Reich. Berlin, 1957.

K 17. Ritter, Gerhard. Die deutschen Militär-Attaches und das Auswärtige Amt. Heidelberg, 1959.

K 18. Schlieffen, Alfred, Graf von. Generalfeldmarshall Graf Alfred Schlieffen Briefe. Ed. by Eberhard Kessel. Göttingen, 1958.

> Letters to and from Schlieffen which give a view of the life, interests, attitudes, and problems of the father of the Schlieffen Plan. The editor has included an introduction in which he states a modification of the views held by Gerhard Ritter. He suggests criticisms of Ritter's attack on Schlieffen and the Schlieffen Plan. For Ritter's views see K 22. For the documents on the Schlieffen Plan see J 42.

K 19. -- Dienstschriften des Generalstabes der Armee Generalfeldmarshalls Graf von Schlieffen. 2 v. Berlin, 1937-38.

K 20. Müller-Brandenburg, Hermann. Von Schlieffen bis Ludendorff. Leipzig, 1925.

184   German Foreign Policy

A terse, but restrained criticism of German general staff leadership.

K 21. Bredt, Jah. Viktor. Die belgische Neutralität und der Schlieffensche Feldzugplan. Berlin, 1929. See: K 50.

K 22. Ritter, Gerhard. Der Schlieffenplan: Kritik eines Mythos. Munich, 1956. Eng. trans., The Schlieffen Plan. New York, 1958.

This book consists of a series of documents with an introductory essay. It is especially useful for Schlieffen's thought in connection with the role of England. Ritter attacks the Schlieffen legend. He maintains that the plan was not a recipe for victory, but a gamble, not even justified by the military risk, let alone the lamentable political implication, which put German foreign policy in a straight jacket and imposed on the generals and diplomats alike an "umheimliche Zeitdruck. " See K 1. Ritter asserts that neither Schlieffen nor Holstein advocated preventative war in 1905, during Russia's involvement with Japan. See K 26. Ritter blamed the political successors of Bismarck who regarded military planning as the private business of military specialists.

K 23. -- "Le 'Plan Schlieffen' de l'état-major Allemand de 1914: Considérations sur la critique militaire et politique, " Revue d'histoire moderne et contemporaine. 1960. 7(3): 215-232.

An analysis of the weakness of the plan and of the opposition to it by many of the German diplomats as well as General von Moltke.

K 24. -- "Le Plan Schlieffen, " Bulletin de la Société d'Histoire Moderne. 1960. 59(13): 7-9.

K 25. Flammer, Philip. "The Schlieffen Plan and Plan XVII: A Short Critique, " Military Affairs. 1966. 30(4): 207-212.

Argues that both the German and French war plans of 1914 were "outstanding examples of dogmatic hardening of military doctrine, completely dependent upon everything going exactly as planned--which rarely if ever happens. "

K 26. Rassow, Peter. "Schlieffen und Holstein, " Historische Zeitschrift. CLXXIII(1952).

Relates Holstein's intention during the first Moroccan crisis, although G. Ritter in K 22, p. 102-138, argues against the thesis that Holstein wanted war with France. But Wilhelm Groener's Lebenserinnerungen, ed. by F. Freiherr Heller von Gaertrengen, Göttingen, 1957, p. 83

ff, the author, a staff officer under Schlieffen, in 1905, relates that he believed that Schlieffen wanted war in 1905. Generaloberst von Einem's Erinnerungen eines Soldaten 1853-1933, Leipzig, 1933, shows that evidence for a preventative war psychology existed in the upper reaches of the army in 1905. But Eberhard Kessel in K 18, p. 13 f, 53 f, 205-208, denies that Schlieffen's war plan of 1905 had a preventative war character about it. He suggests that Schlieffen was willing and eager to come to grips with France in 1905.

K 27. Seyfert, Gerhard. Die Militärischen Beziehungen und Vereinbarungen zwischen dem deutschen und dem österreichischen
Generalstäbe vor und bei Beginn des Weltkrieges. Leipzig,
1934.

A useful collection of materials on the military agreements between the German and Austrian general staffs.
See: L 32.

K 28. Ritter, Gerhard. "Die Zusammenarbeit der Generalstäbe
Deutschlands und Österreich-Ungarns vor dem ersten Weltkrieg," in Festschrift für H. Herzfeld. 1958.

K 29. Kunner, Heinrich. Der Schlüssel zur Kriegsschuldfrage.
Munich, 1926.

An Austrian journalist's interpretation of the Moltke-
Conrad military conversation of Jan. 1908. See: J 21.

K 30. Waldersee, Alfred Graf von. Denkwürdigkeiten des General-
feldmarshalls Alfred Grafen von Waldersee. Ed. by Heinrich
O. Meisner. 3 v. Berlin, 1922-23. Eng. trans., Alfred
Graf von Waldersee, a Field Marshal's Memoirs from the
Diary, Correspondence, and Reminiscences. London, 1924.

An important source for the history of Bismarck's dismissal and the early years of William II's reign.

K 31. -- Aus dem Briefwechsel des Generalfeldmarshalls Alfred
Grafen von Waldersee. Ed. by Heinrich O. Meisner. 3 v.
Stuttgart, 1928.

K 32. Fornaschon, Wolfgang. Die Politischen Anschauungen des
Grafen Waldersee und seine Stellungnahme zur deutschen Politik. Berlin, 1935.

A good analysis of Waldersee's views on foreign affairs
as well as the part he played in formulating German
policy. Also very good in pointing out the process by
which he gradually drew away from the Bismarckian

        policy.

K 33. Kessel, Eberhard. Moltke. Stuttgart, 1957.

        This work supersedes all earlier studies of the elder
        Moltke.

K 34. Moltke, H. von. Erinnerungen, Briefe, Dokumente 1877-
        1916. Stuttgart, 1922.

K 35. Stone, N. "Moltke and Conrad, " The Historical Journal.
        (1966): 215-225.

K 36. Whitton, F.E. Moltke. London, 1921.

K 37. Falkenhayn, Erich General von. The General Staff and its
        Decisions 1914-1916. New York, 1920.

        There is some material on the pre-war period, but the
        greater share of the book deals with the early years of
        the war.

K 38. Zwehl, Hans General von. Erich von Falkenhayn: eine bio-
        graphische Studie. Berlin, 1926.

        Contains material from Falkenhayn's diaries; penetrat-
        ing study.

K 39. Kraft, Heinz. "Das Problem Falkenhayn; eine Würdigung der
        Kriegführung des Generalstabschefs, " Welt als Geschichte.
        1962. 22(1/2): 49-79.

        A discussion of the political and military considerations
        underlying the strategy employed by General Falkenhayn
        during his tenure as chief of staff 1914-1916. His pol-
        icies-maintenance of Italian neutrality, separate and
        early peace with Russia, recognition of England as the
        primary enemy in the West. Falkenhayn hoped to end
        the war by a series of limited but very fierce battles
        which were to make continuation of hostilities too costly
        to the enemy.

K 40. Hindenburg, Paul von. Aus meinem Leben. Leipzig, 1920.

        Eng. trans. avail.

K 41. Ludendorff, Erich. Urkunden der obersten Heeresleitung.
        Berlin, 1922.

K 42. -- The General Staff and its Problems. 2 v. London, 1920.

        Contains some material on the pre-war general staff
        and its relations with the German government. Based
        on official documents.

K 43. Haeussler, Helmut. General Wilhelm Groener and the Imper-
        ial German Army. Madison, Wisc., 1962.

K 44. Schweinitz, Hans Lother von. Briefwechsel des Botschafters Generals von Schweinitz. Berlin, 1928.

K 45. Wedel, Carl Graf von. Zwischen Kaiser und Kanzler; Aufzeihungen des General-Adjutanten Grafen Carl von Wedel aus den Jahren 1890-1894. Leipzig, 1943.

K 46. Sanders, Otto, Liman von. 5 Jahre Turkei. 1925.

K 47. Bernhardi, Friedrich von. Denkwürdigkeiten aus meinem Leben. Berlin, 1927.

> The author was a German general. He gives a picture of the old army and the old staff system.

K 48. Kloster, Walter. Der Deutsche Generalstab und der präventivkriegsgedanke. Stuttgart, 1932.

K 49. Turner, L.C.F. "The Role of the General Staffs in July 1914," The Australian Journal of Politics and History. (Dec. 1965): 312 ff.

K 50. Ritter, Gerhard. "Der Anteil der Militärs an der Kriegskatastrophe von 1914," Historische Zeitschrift. (1961): 72-91.

K 51. Steinberg, Jonathan. "A German Plan for the Invasion of Holland and Belgium, 1897," Historical Journal. VI (1963): 107-119.

K 52. Schmidt-Bückeburg, Rudolf. Das Militarkabinett der preussischen Könige und deutschen Kaiser 1787-1918. Berlin, 1933.

K 53. Kitchin, Martin. The German Officer Corps, 1890-1914. New York, 1968.

> The army by 1890 had lost the admiration of the nation. It was unwilling to make any concessions to liberalism or democracy, so under William II it adopted an extremely conservative position. Socially isolated and cut off politically by an ideology that no longer reflected the realities of the day, it alternated between active meddling in politics and critical isolation--contributing greatly to the lack of political equilibrium in Germany.

K 54. Rosinski, Herbert. The German Army. New York, 1966.

> Points out that the superiority of the German army was due to the development of the general staff and its consequent organizational superiority.

K 55. Jany, Curt. Geschichte der preussischen Armee vom 15 Jahrhundert bis 1914. Osnabrück, 1967.

K 56. Groener, Wilhelm. Lebenserinnerungen, Jugend, Generalstab, Weltkrieg. Göttingen, 1957.

K 57. Groener-Geyer, D. General Groener: Soldat und Staatsmann. Frankfurt A/M, 1954.

K 58. Görlitz, Walter. Hindenburg: ein Lebensbild. Bonn, 1953.

K 59. Hubatsch, Walter. Hindenburg und der Staat; aus den Papieren des Generalfeldmarschalls und Reichspräsidenten von 1878 bis 1934. Göttingen, 1966.

K 60. Ludendorff, Erich. Französische Fälschung meiner Denkschrift von 1912 über den drohenden Krieg. Berlin, 1919.

L. ADMIRAL TIRPITZ AND THE GERMAN NAVY: THEIR INFLUENCE ON FOREIGN, ESPECIALLY ANGLO-GERMAN, RELATIONS

See also: J 37-41, J 43.

Admiral Tirpitz

See: K 1, L 23-24, L 30, L 42, L 52, L 53.

L 1. Tirpitz, Alfred von. Erinnerungen. Berlin, 1920. Eng. trans., My Memoirs. New York, 1920.

L 2. -- Politische Dokumente. 2 v. Vol. I. Der Aufbau der deutschen Wehrmacht. Berlin, 1924. Vol II. Deutsche Ohnmachtspolitik im Weltkriege. Berlin, 1926.

> The political papers of the German navy collected and edited by Tirpitz to defend his pre-war policies.

L 3. Graham, Gerals S. "Admiral von Tirpitz and the Origin of Anglo-German Naval Rivalry," Canadian Defense Quarterly. (April, 1938): 305-312.

> A competent analysis of the trade and colonial rivalry as a background to Tirpitz's plans for coercing Britain.

L 4. Hassel, Ulrich von. "Tirpitz aussenpolitische Gedankenwelt," Berliner Monatshefte. XVII (April, 1939).

> A reconsideration of the Tirpitz doctrine by one of Tirpitz's closest associates.

L 5. -- Tirpitz, sein Leben und Werken mit Berücksichtigung seines Beziehungen zu Albrecht von Stosch. Stuttgart, 1920.

An important supplement to Tirpitz's memoirs, containing many letters.

L 6. Hallmann, Hans. Der Weg zum deutschen Schlachtflottenbau. Stuttgart, 1933.

Based on Tirpitz's papers; best single study of the origins of the first naval bill.

L 7. Hubatsch, Walther. Die Ära Tirpitz. Göttingen, 1955.

A rehabilitation of Tirpitz which relates that Tirpitz was naive in his foreign policy conceptions and that he tended toward a narrow "Ressortpartikularismus."

L 8. Michalik, Bernhard. Probleme des deutschen Flottenbaues. Breslau, 1931.

An analysis of the political and strategical views of Tirpitz.

L 9. Stadelmann, Rudolf. Die Epoche der deutsch-englischen Flottenrivalität. Laupheim, 1947.

A severe attack on the policies of Tirpitz.

L 10. Trotha, Vice Admiral Adolf von. Grossadmiral von Tirpitz. Breslau, 1933.

Primarily a character study and an attempt to put Tirpitz's policy in the larger national setting.

L 11. Becker, Willy. "Bülow contra Tirpitz. E. Beitr. z. d. Kontroversen über d. Flottenpolitik, " Zeitschrift für Politik. 16 (1926).

L 12. Kehr, Eckart. "Soz. und finanz. Grdl. d. Tirpitzschen Flottenpropaganda, " Gesellschaft. 5 (1928).

L 13. Hubatsch, Walther. "Die Gestalt von Tirpitz u. a. durch auswertung seiner Nachlasses in manchem deutlicher gezeichnet: Realität und Illusion in Tirpitz Flottenbau, " Schicksalswege deutsche Vergangenheit, Festschrift f. s. Kähler. 1954.

L 14. Woodward, Davis. "Admiral Tirpitz, Secretary of State for the Navy, 1897-1916, " History Today. 1963, 13(8): 548-555.

German Naval Program

L 15. Hurd, Archibald and Henry Castle. German Sea Power. London, 1913.

A general account, well-informed and generally fair, stresses the interrelationship of naval power with economics and politics.

L 16. Hopmann, Admiral A. Das Tagebuch eines deutschen Seeof-
fiziers. Berlin, 1924.

> A volume of recollections covering the period of Ger-
> man naval expansion.

L 17. Foerster, Raymond. Politische Geschichte der preussischen
und deutschen Flotte. Dresden, 1928.

> Deals strictly with the political aspects of naval expan-
> sion.

L 18. Kehr, Eckart. Schlachtflottenbau und Parteipolitik 1894-1901.
Berlin, 1930.

> A noteworthy contribution to the history of German na-
> val policy. The author is chiefly concerned with the
> social factors entering into the naval policy. It is a
> penetrating study of the relationship between German
> domestic politics and the naval building program.

L 19. Lehment, Jochim. Kriegsmarine und politische Führung.
Berlin, 1937.

> A general survey of the rise of the German navy.

L 20. Schuddekopf, Otto E. Die Stutzpunktpolitik des Reiches 1890-
1914. Berlin, 1941.

> A well documented book based on German and English
> sources. The author is critical of the failure of the
> Germans to appreciate the importance of naval bases.

L 21. Prowaseck, Hilde. Der Gedanke einer Kontinentalliga gegen
England unter Wilhelm II. Leipzig, 1928.

> A doctoral dissertation which summarizes the material
> in the published German documents.

L 22. Thalheimer, Siegfried. Das deutsche Flottengesitz von 1898.
Düsseldorf, 1926.

> A doctoral dissertation based on newspapers and other
> contemporary sources.

L 23. Hollyday, Frederic B.M. Bismarck's Rival: A Political
Biography of General and Admiral Albrecht von Stosch. Dur-
ham, N.C., 1960.

> Von Stosch was the founder of the Imperial German
> Navy. Excellent for the influence that the naval pro-
> gram in Germany had on the conduct of foreign policy.

L 24. Hubatsch, Walther. Der Admiralstab und die obersten Marine-
behörden in Deutschland 1848-1945. Frankfurt, 1958.

The author did a great deal of research in the files of the former marine archive.   The book contains an excellent appendix of documents and the author shows how Tirpitz sharply and successfully opposed the development of an admiral staff patterned on the army general staff, because he feared the growth of such a staff would endanger his own control of the navy.   This was especially true from the vantage point of the Reichsmarineamt (the civilian naval office which stood technically under the chancellor and was responsible for getting naval bills through the Reichstag).

L 25. Rosinski, Herbert.   "Strategy and Propaganda in German Naval Thought, " Brassey's Naval Annual.   (1945): 125-150.

Deals chiefly with Tirpitz and his methods of popularizing the German fleet.

L 26. Oldenhage, Gustav.   Die Deutsche Flottenvorlage von 1897 und die öffentliche Meinung.   Gutersloh, 1935.

A doctoral dissertation which supplies an excellent survey of German press opinion on naval expansion.

L 27. Marienfeld, Wolfgang.   "Wissenschaft und Schlachtflottenbau in Deutschland 1897-1906, " Marine Rundschau.   1957 (Spec. No. 2): 1-125.

An examination of the extremely favorable reaction of the German public to Germany's transition to Weltpolitik and battle fleet construction, with special reference to university teachers.   The author elucidates the economic, political, social, historical, geographical, and other arguments which many members of this group used in giving public propagandistic support to the Reich's leaders' goals, the necessity of which they stress.   Deals with the Reichsmarineamt, Deutscher Flottenverein, and Alldeutscher Verband whose fleet agitation was to a great extent sustained by university teachers.   Based on lectures, publications, etc., of the university teachers who participated in the agitation for a fleet.   See: L 31.

L 28. Steinberg, Jonathan.   "The Kaiser's Navy and German Society, " Past and Present.   1964, (28): 102-110.

L 29. Kehr, Eckart E.   "D. dt. Flotte in d. 90er Jahren und d. polit.-mil. Dualismus d. Kaiserreiches, " Archiv für Politik und Geschichte.   9 (1927).

L 30. -- Der Primat der Innenpolitik: Gesammelte Aufsätze zur preussisch-deutsch Sozialgeschichte im 19. und 20. Jahrhundert.   Veröffenlichung der Historischen Kommission zu Berlin, beim Friedrich-Meinecke-Institut der Freien Universität Berlin, No. 19. Berlin, 1965.

> With an introduction by Hans Ulrich Wehler and a forward by Hans Herzfeld. A series of essays by a scholar who died in 1933 at the age of 30. There is a very good essay on the naval armament and its relation to party politics in the 1890's.

L 31. Heidorn, Günther. "Bemerkungen zur Ersten Flottenrüstung und Flottenpropaganda des deutschen Imperialismus," Wissenschaftliche Zeitschrift der Universität Rostock Gesellschafts- und Sprachwissenschaftliche Reihe. East Germany, 1957/58, 7(1): 5-8.

> Tirpitz, a representative of the Alldeutscher Verband, initiated the construction of a strong navy. The naval bills of 1898 and 1900 were important stages prepared by ideological campaigns in which not only the press but such professors as Schmoller, Wagner, and Delbrück participated. The propaganda was mainly directed by the Flottenverein. In the Reichsmarineamt Tirpitz established a special department which constantly influenced the press according to the fleet policy of the ruling circles.

L 32. Jorberg, Friedrich, and Albert Röhr. "Der Einsatz der Kaiserlichen Marine während der beiden Balkankriege und die internationale Skutari-Unternehmung, 1912-1914," Marine Rundschau. (Dec. 1966).

L 33. Gabriele, Mariano. "Origin della convenzione navale italo-austro-germanica del 1913," Rassegna Storica del Risorgimento. 1955, 52(3): 325-344 and (4): 489-509.

> Traces the negotiations which led to the agreement between Italy, Germany, and Austria-Hungary for cooperative naval action against the Triple Entente powers.

L 34. Haselmayr, Friedrich. Diplomatische Geschichte des zweiten Reichs 1871 bis 1918. V: Die Ära des Flottenkaisers 1890-1918. Munich, 1962.

> Traces in detail the build up in the German navy and its effects on the foreign policy of Germany.

L 35. "Der Kulminationspunkt der dt. Flottenpolitik," Historische Zeitschrift. 1953.

L 36. Schramm, P.E. Deutschland und Übersee. 1950.

L 37. Schüssler, Wilhelm. Weltmachtstreben und Flottenbau. 1956.

An account of the part played by the German naval policies in the overall scheme for world power.

Effects of the German Naval Program on Anglo-German Relations

L 38. Galster, Vice Admiral Karl. England, deutsche Flotte und Weltkrieg. Kiel, 1925.

A general discussion of the earlier period.

L 39. Herzfeld, Hans. "Der Deutsche Flottenbau und die englische Politik, " Archiv für Politik und Geschichte. (Jan. 1926).

Detailed and scholarly. Covers the period 1898-1908.

L 40. Teleshev, L. "Anglo-germanskoe V 1898, " Krasnyi arkhiv. LVI (1933): 65-79.

A series of reports from the Russian ambassador at Berlin, revealing his uneasiness about the Anglo-German rapproachement. These documents have been translated into German in the Berliner Monatshefte, XI (1933): 492-510.

L 41. Woodward, Ernst L. Great Britain and the German Navy. New York, 1935.

A diplomatic study based on the published British and German documents.

L 42. Ziebert, Alexander. England und d. Bau d. dt. Schlachtflotte in d. Ära Bülow. Dissertation. Freiburg, 1929.

L 43. Steinberg, Jonathan. "The Copenhagen Complex, " Journal of Contemporary History. 1966, 1(3): 23-46.

Relates Tirpitz's reasons for concentrating a powerful German battle fleet in the home waters to force the British to make the line from the Elbe to the Thames the theater of war. The article covers the period 1896-1906. The policy was to prevent a premature British assault on the German navy.

L 44. Levy, H. England and Germany. London, 1949.

A very good account of the English-German naval rivalry.

L 45. Clark, John J. "Anglo-German Naval Negotiations 1898 to 1914 and 1935 to 1938, " Journal of the Royal United Service Institute. 1963, 108(632): 349-353.

L 46. Hallmann, H. Der Weg zum dt. Schlachtflottenbau. 1933.

Traces the development of German naval policy and how it came into conflict with England's naval ambitions.

194 German Foreign Policy

L 47. Stadelmann, Rudolf. "Die Epoche der deutsche-englische Flottenrivalität," Deutschland und Westeuropa. 1948.

L 48. "Warum kam e. Flottenverständigt mit England nicht zustande?" Süddeutsche Monatshefte. 23 (1923).

L 49. Kehr, Eckart E. "Englandhass und Weltpolitik E. Std. über d. innenpolitik und soz. Grdl. d. dt. Aussenpolitik um d. Jh. Wende," Zeitschrift für Politik. 17 (1928).

L 50. Widenmann, Wilhelm. Marine-Attache an der kaiserlich-deutsch Botschaft in London 1907-1912. Göttingen, 1952.

L 51. Müller, Georg A. von. Regierte der Kaiser? Kriegstagebücher, Aufzeichungen und Briefe des Chefs des Marinekabinetts 1914-1918. Ed. by W. Görlitz. Göttingen, 1959. Eng. trans. avail.

L 52. -- Der Kaiser: aus den Tagebüchern des Chefs des Marinekabinetts Admiral Georg Alexander von Müller. Ed. by Walter Görlitz. Göttingen-Berlin-Frankfurt A/M, 1965.

L 53. Steinberg, Jonathan. Yesterday's Deterrent; Tirpitz and the Birth of the German Battle Fleet. London, 1965.

The naval law of 1898 began a new era in which the emphasis in German military affairs shifted from land to sea. From April 1898, to Aug. 1914, the fleet which the Flottengesetz of 1898 called into being, dominated Germany's international relations. The ultimate aim of the program was to wrest from Great Britain her exclusive hegemony over the world's oceans.

L 54. Coler, Christfried. "Der Konflikt Bismarck-Stosch März/April, 1877," Wehrwiss. Rundschau (Oct. 1967).

L 55. -- "Palastrevolte in der Marine 1878/79," Wehrwiss. Rundschau (Nov. 1967).

L 56. -- "Der Sturz Albert von Stoschs März 1883," Wehrwiss. Rundschau (Dec. 1967).

M. TRIPLE ALLIANCE

M 1. Bourgeois, Emile. "Les Origines de la Triple Alliance et la question romaine," Revue de Paris. (Jan. 1, 1926).

M 2. Andrew, Christopher. "German World Policy and the Reshaping of the Dual Alliance," Journal of Contemporary History.

I (July, 1966): 137-151.

M 3. Cappelli, R. "La politica estera del Conte di Robilant, "
Nuova Antologia. (Nov. 1, 1897).

      The author was an authority on Robilant.

M 4. -- "Il Conte N. di Robilant, " Nuova Antologia. 1900.

M 5. Chabod, F. "Kulturkampf e Triplice Alleanza in una discus-
sione fra il Vaticano e il governo Austro-ungarico nel 1883, "
Rivista Storica Italiana. LXII (1950): 257-280.

M 6. Chiala, Luigi. Pagine di Storia Contemporanea. Vol. III:
La Triplice e la Duplice Alleanza, 1881-1897. Turin, 1898.

      A good account of the alliance, written from the Italian
point of view. The author made use of Robilant's papers.

M 7. Coolidge, Archibald C. The Origins of the Triple Alliance.
New York, 1926.

      Good account with critical notes on source materials
available at the time.

M 8. Corti, Egon. "Il Conte Corti al Congresso di Berlino, "
Nuova Antologia. (April 16, 1925).

M 9. -- "Bismarck und Italien am Berliner Kongress, " Historische
Vierteljahrschrift. (May 1, 1927).

M 10. Fellner, Fritz. Der Dreibund europäische Diplomatie vor
dem Ersten Weltkrieg. Munich, 1960.

      A good general account of the alliance and the part it
played in pre-World War I diplomacy; good bibliography.

M 11. Fopert, E.A. "Il Conte di Robilant, " Rassegna Nazionale.
1888.

M 12. Fuller, J.V. Bismarck's Diplomacy at its Zenith. 1922.

      Covers the period of the formulation of the Triple Alli-
ance.

M 13. Fraknoi, Wilhelm. Kritische Studien zur Geschichte des
Dreibundes. Budapest, 1917.

      A careful study but now quite dated.

M 14. Grabinski, J. La Triple Alliance d'après de nouveau documents. Lyon, 1904.

M 15. Granfelt, Helge. Das Dreibundsystem 1879-1916 eine histor-
ische-Völkerrechtliche Studie. Berlin, 1925.

M 16. Granfelt, Helge. Der Dreibund nach dem Sturze Bismarcks.

Vol. I: England im Einverstandnis mit dem Dreibund 1890-

1896. 1962. Vol. II: Der Kampf um die Weltherrschaft

1895-1902. 1964.

The author points out that the league of Germany, Austria, and Italy began to decline and Russia and France gradually gained the upper hand. The German decline can be shown by the change in English attitude toward Germany and also toward the entente powers. The author has made use of new material including recently published French and Italian documents as well as unpublished papers from the Austrian Staatsarchiv and the Public Record Office in London. More attention than usual is devoted to the smaller states; for example, to nationalist movement in Romania and the expansionist ambitions of Bulgaria. On the whole though the author's account is almost the same as earlier accounts. The real villain of these two volumes is Alfred von Tirpitz, whose obsession with the idea of naval supremacy drove England into the entente camp.

M 17. Gualtieri, Carlo Avarna di. L'Ultimo rinnovamento della

Triplice, 5 dicembre 1912. Milan, 1924.

M 18. Hartdegen, H.L. Die vatikanische Frage und die Dreibundes

Entstehung des Dreibundes. Bonn, 1938.

Dissertation. Reviews the problem of the Vatican and ...e Triple Alliance. The author made use of many materials from the archives in Vienna and Munich.

M 19. Italicus. Italiens Dreibundpolitik 1870-1896. Munich, 1926.

A scholarly account of the alliance.

M 20. Kalbskopf, Willy. Die Aussenpolitik der Mittelmächte in

Tripoliskriege und die letzte Dreibunderneuerung 1911-1912.

Erlangen, 1932.

M 21. Langer, William L. European Alliances and Alignments 1871-

1890. New York, 1950.

An excellent study of the Triple Alliance in relation to the greater sphere of European politics.

M 22. Manhart, George B. Alliance and Entente. New York, 1932.

A study of the Triple Alliance and the Entente.

M 23. Mendelssohn-Bartholdy, Albrecht. "Der Dreibund in der

europäischen Politik, " Archiv für Politik und Geschichte.

(June-July, 1924).

Examines the Triple Alliance and its relation to European politics.

M 24. Meyers, D. and J.C. D'Arcy. The Secret Treaties of Aus-
    tria-Hungary. Vol. I. Cambridge, 1925.

M 25. Iorga, Nicolae. Comment la Roumanie s'est détachée de la
    Triplice, d'après les documents Austro-Hongrois et des sou-
    venirs personnels. Bucharest, 1933.

M 26. Penson, Lillian M. "The New Course in British Foreign
    Policy 1892-1902, " Transactions of the Royal Historical So-
    ciety. Series IV, XXV (1943): 121-139.
        An analysis of the process by which Britain drifted
        away from the Triple Alliance.

M 27. Pribram, Alfred F. The Secret Treaties of Austria-Hungary.
    2 v. Cambridge, 1920-21.
        A good account of the renewal of the Triple Alliance
        based on papers from the Austrian foreign office.

M 28. Reemsten, Reemt. Spanisch-deutsche Beziehungen zur Zeit
    des ersten Dreibundvertrages 1882-1887. Berlin, 1938.

M 29. Salata, F. "L'Italia e la Triplice secondo: i nuovi documenti
    austro-germanice, " Le Nuove provincie. 1923.

M 30. Salvatorelli, Luigi. La Triplice alleanza 1877-1912. Milan,
    1939.
        A detailed study of Italy's part in the alliance.

M 31. -- "Cinquantenario della triplice alleanza, " La Cultura. XI
    (1932).

M 32. Salvemini, Gaetano. "La Triple alliance, " Revue des Nations
    Latines. (July, 1916).

M 33. Schmitt, Bernadotte. Triple Alliance and Triple Entente.
    1934.

M 34. Silva, Pietro. Come si formò la triplice. Milan, 1915.

M 35. Singer, Arthur. Geschichte des Dreibundes. Leipzig, 1914.
        Valuable for chronology and press comment. French
        edition has the title L'Histoire de la triple alliance,
        Paris, 1915.

M 36. Stieglitz, Baron de. L'Italie et la triple alliance. Paris,
    1906.

M 37. Sulliotti, A.I. La Triplice alleanza 1882-1915. Milan, 1915.
        War propaganda.

M 38. Volpe, Gioacchino. L'Italia nella triplice alleanza 1882-1915.
Milan, 1939.

    A convenient collection of key documents illustrating
the history and problems of the alliance.

M 39. Waldersee, Alfred Graf zu. "Von Deutschlands militärpoliti-
schen Beziehung zu Italien," Die Kriegsschuldfrage Zeitschrift zur Vorgeschichte und Geschichte des Weltkrieges.
(July, 1929): 642 ff.

M 40. Winckler, Martin. Bismarcks Bündnispolitik und das europäische Gleichgewicht. Stuttgart, 1964.

N. GERMANY AND THE HAGUE PEACE CONFERENCES

N 1. Documents Relating to the Program of the First Hague Peace
Conference. Oxford, 1921.

N 2. Holls, F.W. The Peace Conference at the Hague. New
York, 1900.

N 3. Junk, A. D. Mächte auf d. ersten Haager Friedenskonferenz.
Frankfurt, 1929.

    Dissertation.

N 4. Krafft, E. Die Ersten Internationalen Friedenskongresse und
ihre Entstehung. Frankfurt, 1922.

    Dissertation.

N 5. Meurer, Christian. Die Haager Friedenskonferenz. 2 v.
Munich, 1905.

    A substantial study dealing chiefly with the development
of arbitration.

N 6. Stengel, Karl von. "Die Haager Friedenskonferenz und das
Völkerrecht," Archiv für Öffentliches Recht. II (1900): 139-
201.

    A careful but not very favorable review of the work of
the conference by one of the German delegates.

N 7. Suttner, Berta von. Die Haager Friedenskonferenz Tagebuch-
blätter. Dresden, 1901.

    The recollection of the leading German pacifist; an in-
teresting account of the conference.

N 8. Tate, Merze. The Disarmament Illusion: The Movement for
a Limitation of Armaments to 1907. New York, 1942.
Deals with The Hague first peace conference

N 9. Zorn, Philipp. "Zur Geschichte der ersten Haager Friedenskonferenz, " Archiv für Politik und Geschichte. III (1924):
285-306.

N 10. -- "Z. Kriegsschuldfrage; betr. 1 Haager Friedenskonferenz,"
Archiv für Politik und Geschichte. 5 (1925).

N 11. Erdbrügger, Hermann W. England, Deutschland und die
zweite Haager Friedenskonferenz, 1907. Leipzig, 1935.

N 12. Bosak, Adam. "Uwagi Na Marginesie Pracy A.J. Kaminskie-
go 'Stanowisko Niemiec Na Pierwszej Konferencji Haskiej, '"
Slaski Kwartalinik Historyczny Sobótka. 1963, 18(3): 290-330.
Review article of a book by a Polish historian on The
Hague conference of 1899. Bosak is critical of the
conclusions arrived at by the author concerning the
part played by Germany at the conference.

N 13. Deutschland a. d. Haager Friedenskonferenz. Ed. by Walther
Shücking. 1929.

N 14. Foster, J.W. Arbitration and the Hague Court. 1904.

N 15. Fried, Alfred H. Handbuch der Friedenbewegungs. Leipzig,
1911.
One of the best German accounts of the conference.

N 16. Gottschalk, Egon. "Deutschlands Haltung auf den Haager
Friedenskonferenz, " Berliner Monatshefte. (May, 1930): 447-
456.
A review of German policy with special reference to
the evidence produced by the German parliamentary
commission.

N 17. The Hague Peace Conferences of 1899 and 1907. Ed. by
James B. Scott. 2 v. Baltimore, 1909.
The best documentary collection containing all the de-
bates.

N 18. Higgins, A.P. The Hague Conferences and Other International Conferences concerning the Laws and Usages of War.
1909.
A convenient resume of the achievements of various international conferences from that of Paris in 1856 to

that of London in 1909.

N 19. Hull, W.I.   The Two Hague Peace Conferences and their Contributions to International Law.   1908.

N 20. Meurer, Charles.   D. Haager Friedenskonferenz.   2 v. Munich, 1905-1907.

N 21. Nippold, Otfried.   Die Fortbildung des Verfahrens in Völkerrechtlichen Streitigkeiten.   Leipzig, 1907.

> A careful, scholarly treatment of the problem of arbitration.

N 22. Schücking, Walther.   Der Staatenverband der Haager Konferenzen.   Munich, 1912.

> The work of a leading German international jurist, who attempts to place the conference in the general development of international organization.

N 23. Die Vorgeschichte der Weltkrieges.   Vol. V: Deutschland auf den Haager Friedenskonferenzen.   Ed. by George Fradnauer.   Berlin, 1929.

> The testimony before the investigating commission of the German legislature, which confirms the German view that German intentions at The Hague conferences were good, but that the German tactics were mistaken and suspicious looking.

N 24. The Hague Arbitration Cases.   Ed. by G.G. Wilson.   1915.

N 25. Zorn, Philipp.   Deutschland und die beiden Haager Friedenskonferenz.   Berlin, 1920.

> A careful study of German policy at the conference by one of the German delegates.

O.   THE PAN-GERMAN MOVEMENT AND ITS INFLUENCE ON FOREIGN RELATIONS

O 1.   Alldeutsche Blätter.
>   Pan-German organ.

O 2.   Andler, Charles Philippe Théodore.   Les Origines du pan germanisme, 1800 à 1888.   Paris, 1915.

O 3.   -- Le Pangermanisme colonial sous Guillaume II.   Paris, 1916.

This is mainly a document collection, translated from German, pertaining to the effects of the Pan-German movement in the area of colonial affairs.

O 4. Andler, Charles Philippe Théodore. Le Pangermanisme continental sous Guillaume II, de 1888 à 1914. Paris, 1915.

This is a collection of documents, translated from German, pertaining to the Pan-German movement in continental Europe.

O 5. -- Le Pangermanisme philosophique, 1800 à 1914. Paris, 1917.

A collection of documents translated from German which traces the philosophical development of the Pan-German idea from 1800-1914.

O 6. Bonhard, O. Geschichte des Alldeutschen Verbandes. Berlin, 1920.

O 7. Chéradame, André. The United States and Pangermanism. New York, 1917.

The author was a French journalist whose books had a great influence in the United States. The conclusions in his books and articles were accepted as valid by men in the highest of positions in the United States Government. They had a formative influence on President Wilson's Flag Day address of June 14, 1917. His books and articles are decidedly anti-German in nature.

O 8. -- Pan-Germany, the Disease and the Cure. New York, 1918.

O 9. -- The Pan-German Plot Unmasked. New York, 1917.

O 10. Dorpalen, Andreas. Heinrich von Treitschke. New Haven, Conn., 1957.

A reassessment of the role played by von Treitschke and his relationship to Pan-Germanism in the period prior to the war; contains an excellent bibliography.

O 11. Foerster, E.T. Das Konzessionsunwesen in den deutschen Schutzgebieten; Vortrag Gehalten auf dem Alldeutschen Verbandstage am 12. September, 1903. Berlin, 1903.

O 12. Guralskii, A. "Iz Istorii Pan-germanizma," Istoricheski Zhurnal. No. 5 (1945): 22-33.

A general review of the subject but adds nothing new.

O 13. Handbuch des Alldeutschen Verbandes. Munich, 1914.

O 14. Harrison, Austin. Pan-German Doctrine. London, 1904.

Written from Pan-German sources. It has numerous
errors. Shows an accurate barometer of growing British concern about the Pan-German League.

O 15. Class, Heinrich. Wenn Ich der Kaiser wär' politische Wahr-
heiten und Notwendigkeiten. Leipzig, 1913.

O 16. Henderson, W.O. "The Pan-German Movement, " History.
(Dec. 1941).

An able compact evaluation of the literature on the subject up to 1941.

O 17. Jung, Dietrich. Der Alldeutsche Verband. Würzburg, 1936.

O 18. Koehl, Robert L. "Colonialism Inside Germany, 1886-1918, "
Journal of Modern History. XXV (Sept. 1953): 255-272.

O 19. Kruck, Alfred. Geschichte des Alldeutschen Verbandes 1890-
1939. Wiesbaden, 1954.

This account portrays the actual strength of the league.

O 20. N S D A P Hauptarchiv: Guide to the Hoover Institution
Microfilm Collection. Comp. by Grete Heinz and Agnes Peterson. Stanford, California, 1964.

See index for material on the Pan-German League.

O 21. Usher, Roland G. Pan Germanism. London, 1913.

This book is anti-German. Usher sees the ultranation-
alists as the major motivating force behind imperial
German foreign policy.

O 22. Werner, Lothar. Der Alldeutsche Verband 1890-1918; ein
Beiträge zur Geschichte der öffenlichen Meinung in Deutschland. Berlin, 1935.

One of the best works on the subject, stressing the
deeper roots of the movement in German development.

O 23. Wertheimer, Mildred S. The Pan-German League 1890-1914.
New York, 1924.

An investigation of the organization, membership, and
influence of the movement.

O 24. Wessely, Kurt. Pangermanismus: Geschichte und Widerle-
gung eines Schlagwortes. Lenz, 1938.

P. GERMAN PUBLIC OPINION ON FOREIGN POLICY AS RE-
    FLECTED IN THE PRESS

    See also: AE 24, 29. V 5.

P 1. Carroll, Malcolm E. Germany and the Great Powers; A
      Study in Public Opinion and Foreign Policy. New York, 1938.
      An exhaustive and valuable analysis of the German
      press and of the relation of public opinion to foreign
      policy.

P 2. Hale, Oron J. Germany and the Diplomatic Revolution: A
      Study in Diplomacy and the Press 1904-1906. Philadelphia,
      1931.
      The author presents the point of view that much of the
      ill feeling in England toward Germany, and the ill feel-
      ing in Germany toward England, came about as a re-
      sult of the German correspondents in England and Eng-
      lish correspondents in Germany. Both picked up the
      nationalistic sentiments of the press of the country in
      which they were working and sent it home in their re-
      ports which had a great influence, the author believes,
      on the newspaper reading public in both England and
      Germany.

P 3. Schmitt, Bernadotte. "The Relation of Public Opinion and
      Foreign Affairs Before and During the First World War,"
      Studies in Diplomatic History in Honour of G.P. Gooch. Ed.
      by A.O. Sarkissian. New York, 1962, p. 322-330.
      The British used public opinion as an excuse, while
      the French were less influenced by it. The German,
      Austrian, and Russian governments were influenced
      only by fear that public opinion might accuse them of
      insufficiently aggressive policies.

P 4. Heidorn, Günther. Monopole, Presse, Krieg: die Rolle der
      Presse bei der vorbereitung des ersten Weltkrieges; Studien
      zur deutschen Aussenpolitik in der Periode von 1902 bis 1912.
      East Berlin, 1960.
      This study contains an excellent bibliography.

P 5. Ris, Otto F. Das Verhältnis der deutschen Presse zur offi-
      ziellen deutschen Politik während der ersten Marokkokrise
      1904-1906. Cologne, 1949.

P 6. Leupolt, Erich. Die Stellung der bedeutendsten politischen
      Zeitschriften Deutschlands zum neuen Kurs der deutschen Aus-

senpolitik bis zum rücktritt Bülows, 14 Juli 1909. Mittweida,
1932.

> Relates the position of the German political periodicals
> in relation to the "new course" in German foreign pol-
> icy.

P 7. Theil, Hans J. Die Reichsdeutsche Presse und Publizistik
und das österreichungarische Verfassungs und Nationalitätenproblem in den Jahren 1903-1906. 1936.

P 8. Müller, W. Die Stellung der deutschen Presse von der Er-
mordung des österreichischen Thronfolgers Franz Ferdinand
am 28 Juni 1914 bis Ausbruch des Weltkrieges am 4 August
1914. Göttingen, 1924. Printed in part in Ab. der Philos.
Fak. der Georg-August-Univ. zu Göttingen. 1924.

P 9. Goebel, T. Deutsche Pressestimmen in der Julikrise 1914
in Beitrr. zur Geschichte der nachbismarckischen Zeit und
des Weltkrieges. 44 (1939).

P 10. Hale, Oron J. Publicity and Diplomacy, with Special Reference to England and Germany 1890-1914. New York, 1940.

> An excellent study of the German and British press,
> its organization, operation, etc; the author is especial-
> ly interested in the influence of the press on diplomacy.
> See: L 26.

P 11. Treue, Wilhelm. "Presse und Politik in Deutschland und
England während des Burenkrieges, " Berliner Monatshefte.
(August, 1933): 786-803.

> Deals with the unsuccessful efforts to influence the
> press; based on German and British documents.

P 12. Sell, Manfred. Das deutsch-englische Abkommen von 1890
über Helgoland und die Afrik Kolonien im Lichte der deutschen Presse. Berlin, 1926.

P 13. Meyer-Adams, Rudolf. Die Mission Haldanes im Februar
1912 in Spiegel der deutschen Presse. 1935.

P 14. Dreyer, Johannes. Deutschland und England in ihrer Politik
und Presse im Jahre 1901. Berlin, 1901.

P 15. Penner, C.D. "The Bülow-Chamberlain Recriminations of
1901-1902, " The Historian. (1943): 97-109.

> A study of newspaper polemics in Germany and England.

P 16. Bauermann, Werner. Die Times und die Abwendung Englands von Deutschlands im 1900. Cologne, 1939. Dissertation.

P 17. Voegtle, Erich. Die Englische Diplomatie und die deutsche Press, 1898-1914. Würzburg, 1936.

The author is interested in how the foreign policies of England and Germany were affected by the press in the two countries.

P 18. Anderson, Pauline R. The Background of Anti-English Feeling in Germany 1890-1902. Washington, 1939.

P 19. The History of the Times. III: The Twentieth Century Test, 1882-1912. New York, 1947.

This volume is especially valuable for the part played by correspondents of The Times of London, in Germany as informal diplomats. Often times these informal diplomats were able to work through channels closed to the official diplomats. See: Z 44.

P 20. Thimme, Annelise. Hans Delbrück als Kritiker der Wilhelminischen Epoche. Düsseldorf, 1955.

Delbrück was editor of the Preussische Jahrbücher. His commentaries on German domestic and foreign policies influenced a great many people in Germany in the period prior to World War I. See: AE 3.

P 21. Harnoch, Axel von. "Hans Delbrück," Neue Rundschau. No. 3 (1952).

P 22. Wolff, Theodor. Der Vorspiel. Munich, 1925.

Reminiscences by the editor of the Berliner Tageblatt; a moderate, sympathetic criticism of German pre-war policy with interesting sidelights on Bülow, Holstein, and Tirpitz.

P 23. Eigenbrodt, August. Berliner Tageblatt und Frankfurter Zeitung in ihrem Verhalten zu den nationalen Frage, 1887-1914. Berlin, 1917.

P 24. Young, Harry H. Maximillian Harden, Censor Germaniae: the Critic in Opposition from Bismarck to the Rise of Nazism The Hague, 1959.

Harden was editor of the political-literary journal Die Zukunft. The importance of Harden is to be found in his political and literary influence on thought in Germany. Harden was a close friend of Holstein and often times his attacks on William II bore close resemblence to ideas expressed by Holstein. For his close connection with Holstein see: AE 9, Z 2.

P 25. Leuss, Hans. Wilhelm Freiherr von Hammerstein, 1881-
      1895 Chefredakteur der Kreuzzeitung.   Berlin, 1905.
P 26. Ullstein, Ludwig.   Eugen Richter als Publizist und Herausge-
      ber. Leipzig, 1930.

Q. THE SOCIAL DEMOCRATIC PARTY AND GERMAN FOREIGN
    POLICY 1890-1914

         Any collection of materials examining German foreign pol-
    icy during the period 1890-1914 must include some materials
    on the Social Democratic Party (SPD), in view of the fact that
    the SPD has been seriously attacked for not doing more to
    avoid war and for their approval of the war credits.   The SPD
    was the largest single party in the Reichstag on the eve of the
    war, but its position in the unique parliamentary structure in
    Germany left it relatively powerless.   Anyone wishing to work
    on the topic of the SPD and the war would want to consult the
    archives of the SPD, located at the International Institute of
    Social History, Amsterdam.   The Institute contains the Bern-
    stein Archives which include a large number of his letters,
    speeches, and articles, newspaper clippings about him, as well
    as clippings concerning matters which interested him.   The In-
    stitute also has Kautsky's and Bebel's papers and much more
    material on the SPD.
         See also: AP 1, 32, 55, 70, 110, 126, 175, & AQ 10.

Bibliographies and Archival Guides
Q 1. Blumenberg, Werner.   Karl Kautskys Literarisches Werk;
      Eine bibliographische Übersicht.   The Hague, 1960.
Q 2. Schraepler, Ernst.   August-Bebel-Bibliographie.   Düsseldorf,
      1962.
Q 3. Matthias, Erich.   "Zur Geschichte der deutscher Arbeiter-
      bewegung, " Neue Politische Literatur.   III (1958).
Q 4. Fischer, Wolfram.   Blätter für deutsche Landesgeschichte.
      93 (1957), 94 (1958), 97 (1968), 99 (1963).
           Contains useful bibliographical articles.

Q 5. Maehl, William H. 'Recent Literature on the German Social-
      ist, 1891-1932, " Journal of Modern History. XXXIII (Sept.
      1961).

Q 6. Stammhammer, Joseph. Bibliographie des Sozialismus und
      Communismus. 3 v. Jena, 1893-1909.
            Useful for contemporary publications written by social
            democrats.

Q 7. Dolleans, Edouard and Michel Crozier. Mouvements ouvrier
      et socialiste; Chronologie et Bibliographie; Angleterre, France,
      Allemagne, États-Unis (1750-1918). Paris, 1950.

Q 8. Drahn, Ernst. Führer durch das Schriftum des deutscher
      Sozialismus. 2nd ed. Berlin, 1920.

Q 9. N S A D P Hauptarchiv: Guide to the Hoover Institutional
      Microfilm Collection. Comp. by Grete Heinz and Agnes Pe-
      terson. Stanford, Calif., 1964, p. 64, Reel 8A, Folders
      913, 914.
            Material on the Social Democratic Party and the out-
            break of the war. The admission of the Social Demo-
            cratic Party into the Kriegervereine. Also on the
            Deutsche Kriegerbund.

Q 10. A Catalogue of Files and Microfilms of the German Foreign
      Ministry Archives 1867-1920. Washington, 1959.
            The microfilms on the Social Democratic Party were
            filmed by the University of Michigan for the most part.
            For a detailed description of them see: A Catalogue
            of German Foreign Ministry Archives 1867-1920, Ann
            Arbor, 1957.

Q 11. Scheffler, Hildegard and Lutz Noach. Bibliographie zur
      Geschichte der deutschen Arbeiterbewegung; Eine Auswahl der
      seit 1955 im Gebiete der DDR erschienenen Veröffentlichungen.
      Leipzig, 1955.
            Bibliography of materials published in East Germany.

Q 12. Historische Forschungen in der DDR Analysen und Berichte;
      Sonderheft der Zeitschrift für Geschichtswissenschaft. East
      Berlin, 1960.
            Survey of materials published in East Germany.

Q 13. Spezialinventor des deutschen Zentralarchives. Abteilung
      Merseburg "Zur Geschichte der deutschen Arbeiterbewegung, "

ed. by Ministerium des Innern. 6 v. East Berlin, 1964.

Q 14. Schraepler, Ernst. "Neue Quellenpublikationen zur Geschichte der Arbeiterbewegung und des Sozialismus in Deutschland, " Internationale Wissenschaftliche Korrespondenz zur Geschichte der deutschen Arbeiterbewegung. Heft 4 (June, 1967): 1-14.

Q 15. Richter, Gregor and Wolfgang Schmierer. "Quellen zur Geschichte der Arbeiterbewegung im Hauptstaatsarchiv Stuttgart und im Staatsarchiv Ludwigsburg, " Internationale wissenschaftliche Korrespondenz zur Geschichte der deutschen Arbeiterbewegung. Heft 4 (June, 1967): 15-26.

Q 16. Obenaus, Herbert. "Materialien zur Geschichte der deutschen Arbeiterbewegung im Staatlichen Archivlager Göttingen, " Internationale wissenschaftliche Korrespondenz zur Geschichte der deutschen Arbeiterbewegung. Heft 4 (June, 1967): 26-28.

Q 17. Vogel, Hubert. "Quellen und zur Geschichte der Arbeiterbewegung im Stadtarchiv München, " Internationale wissenschaftliche Korrespondenz zur Geschichte der deutschen Arbeiterbewegung. Heft 4 (June, 1967): 28-30.

Q 18. Kolowski, Georg. "Zur Geschichte der Arbeiterbewegung in Mittel-und Ostdeutschland: ein Literaturbericht, " Jahrbuch für die Geschichte Mittel-und Ostdeutschlands. VIII (1959).

Journals Valuable for Bibliography

Q 19. International Review of Social History. Assen, 1956 ff. Pub. by International Institute for Social History, Amsterdam.

Q 20. Archiv für Sozialgeschichte. Hannover, 1961 ff. Pub. by Friedrich-Ebert-Stiftung.

Q 21. Beiträge zur Geschichte der deutschen Arbeiterbewegung. East Berlin, 1959 ff. Pub. by Central Committee of the Socialist Unity Party.

Each issue contains extensive bibliography.

Q 22. Annali. Milan, 1958 ff. Pub. by Giangiacomo Feltrinelli Institute.

Q 23. Internationale wissenschaftliche Korrespondenz zur Geschichte der deutschen Arbeiterbewegung. Pub. by Historischen Kommission zu Berlin beim Friedrich-Meinecke-Institut der Freien

Universität Berlin und in Verbindung mit dem Forschungsinstitut der Friedrich-Ebert-Stiftung.

General Works on the SPD in Pre-war Period

Q 24. Gilg, Peter. Die Erneuerung des demokratischen Denkens im Wilhelminischen Deutschland: eine Ideengeschichtliche Studie zur Wende vom 19. zum 20 Jahrhundert. Wiesbaden, 1965.

> Describes the attitude toward democracy among the Social Democrats and liberals; treats revisionism in the SPD.

Q 25. Gay, Peter. The Dilemma of Democratic Socialism: Eduard Bernsteins Challenge to Marx. New York, 1952.

Q 26. Schorske, Carl E. German Social Democracy, 1905-1917; the Development of the Great Schism. New York, 1955.

> A sound study with an excellent bibliography.

Q 27. Zechlin, Egmont. "Bethmann-Hollweg, Kriegsrisiko und SPD 1914," Der Monat. No. 208 (Jan. 1966): 17-32.

Q 28. Grünburg, Carl. Die Internationale und der Weltkrieg. Leipzig, 1916.

> The most useful collection of anti-war resolutions and actions taken by the Socialist International (1867-1914), and the national parties (1912-1914).

Q 29. Bernstein, Eduard. Die Heutige Sozialdemokratie in Theorie und Praxis. 3rd ed. Munich, 1912.

> Offers the best summary statement of the moderate revisionist position.

Q 30. Eisner, Kurt. Gesammelte Schriften. 2 v. Berlin, 1919.

> While primarily literary and philosophical, these writings do contain valuable material on the national question, though Eisner's views were not representative of revisionist thinking on the issue.

Q 31. Calwer, Richard. Das Sozialdemokratische Programm. Jena, 1914.

> Extremely nationalistic, representing the revisionist point of view.

Q 32. David, Eduard. Die Sozialdemokratie im Weltkriege. Berlin, 1915.

> A theoritical justification of the SPD war policy.

Q 33. Haenisch, Konrad. Die Deutsche Sozialdemokratie in und

nach dem Weltkriege. 2nd ed. Berlin, 1919.

> Interesting for the conversion experience of an apostate
> from radicalism.

Q 34. Heine, Wolfgang. Zu Deutschlands Erneuerung. Jena, 1916.

> A volume rich in promise of reward to labor for its
> cooperation in the war effort.

Q 35. Die Arbeiterschaft im neuen Deutschland. Ed. by Friedrich

Thimme and Carl Legien. Leipzig, 1916.

> The wartime attempt of right-wing Social Democrats
> and middle-class intellectuals to work together toward
> a Germany of class harmony and national power. In-
> cludes contributions by Meinecke, Natorp, Tönnies,
> Noske, and others.

Q 36. Schmoller, Gustav. "Der Weltkrieg und die Sozialdemokratie,"

Schmollers Jahrbuch. XXXIX (1915): 1103-1114.

> Schmoller hailed the labor bureaucracy as a synthesis
> of aristocratic and democratic principles. Contains
> some useful statistics on the party bureaucracy.

Q 37. Kautsky, Karl. Der Weg zur Macht. 2nd ed. Berlin, 1910.

Eng. trans., The Road to Power. Chicago. 1919.

> The classic centerist statement on Social Democratic
> theory and practice in the last pre-war decade and the
> first larger effort at analyzing the political implications
> of imperialism for the SPD.

Q 38. Hilfering, Rudolf. Das Finanzkapital. Vienna, 1923.

> The first major Marxist economic analysis of imperial-
> ism.

Q 39. Luxemburg, Rosa. Die Krise in der Sozialdemokratie.

Zürich, 1916.

> The classic Spartacist analysis of the economic and
> diplomatic origins of the war.

Q 40. -- Politische Schriften. Ed. by Ossip K. Flechtheim. 2 v.

Frankfurt, 1966.

Q 41. Nettl, J.P. Rosa Luxemburg. 2 v. London, 1966.

Q 42. Roth, Guenther. The Social Democrats in Imperial Germany;

A Study in Working Class Isolation and National Integration.

Totowa, N.J., 1963.

> Very good on SPD motives for backing the war effort.

Q 43. Maehl, William. "The Triumph of Nationalism in the German

Socialist Party on the Eve of the First World War, " Journal of Modern History. XXIV (March, 1952): 15-41.

Contains much bibliography.

Q 44. Schröder, Wilhelm. Handbuch der sozialdemokratischen Parteitage, 1863-1909. Munich, 1910.

Q 45. Walling, William E. The Socialist and the War. New York, 1915.

Q 46. Doerzbacher, E. Die Deutsche Sozialdemokratie und die Nationale Machtpolitik bis 1914. Gotha, 1920.

Q 47. Wallas, Graham. Human Nature in Politics. London, 1915.

> Wallas, a friend of Bernstein, pointed out to him in 1908 the possibility of a war between Germany and England. He relates that Bernstein was torn between his Anglophile sentiments and his love of Germany.

Q 48. Victor, Max. "Die Stellung der deutschen Sozialdemokratie zu den Fragen der Auswärtigen Politik, 1869-1914, " Archiv für Sozialwissenschaft und Sozialpolitik. LX (1928): 147-179.

> The author points out that as working conditions improved in Germany the SPD became more and more receptive to the policies of William II. He demonstrates that in foreign policy the SPD policy was negative; it opposed imperialism, condoned the Kaiser's inept utterances, decried militarism, and called for peace.

Q 49. Anderson, Pauline. The Background of Anti-English Feeling in Germany. 1939.

> Relates that the failure of the SPD to offer a thoroughgoing criticism of policy tended to give the bureaucrats in the German foreign office a free hand.

Q 50. Kerr, Eckart. "Englandhass und Weltpolitik, " Zeitschrift für Politik. XVII (1928): 500-526.

> Around the turn of the century, the SPD called for a German-English alliance, at a time when German industry and agriculture were joining forces in a "God-punish England" campaign.

Q 51. Erdmann, Karl. England und die Sozialdemokratie. 1917.

> Points out anti-British feeling in the SPD.

Q 52. Schippel, Max. England und Wir. 1917.

> Points out anti-British feeling in the SPD.

Q 53. Bernstein, Eduard. "Patriotismus, Militarismus und Sozialdemokratie, " Sozialdemokratische Monatshefte. XI (1907): 434-440.

Bernstein's position in regard to war.

Q 54. Bernstein, Eduard. "Sozialdemokratie und Imperialismus, "
Sozialistische Monatshefte. IV (1900): 238-251.

Bernstein's position in regard to imperialism.

Q 55. -- "Entwicklungsgang eines Sozialisten, " Die Volkswirtschafts-
lehre der Gegenwart in Selbstdarstellungen. I (Leipzig, 1924):
1-50.

Bernstein's position on the issue of new taxes for
greater armaments before the war. See also on this
same subject Protokoll über die Verhandlungen der
SPD 1913.

Q 56. -- Die Englische Gefahr und das deutsche Volk. Berlin,
1911. Eng. trans., The English Peril and the German People.

Bernstein's greatest contributions to the foreign policy
debate are to be found in this work in which he maintains that the "English Peril" has been artificially
created.

Q 57. -- Die Wahrheit über die Einkreisung Deutschlands. Berlin,
1919.

Shows in detail the efforts made by the British to come
to an understanding with Germany had been frustrated
by German blundering and ambition.

Q 58. Kautsky, Karl. Sozialisten und Krieg. Prague, 1937.

Q 59. Prager, Eugen. Geschichte der U.S.P.D. Berlin, 1922.

Q 60. La Chesnais, P.G. The Socialist Party in the Reichstag.
London, 1915.

Q 61. Bevan, Edwyn. German Social Democracy During the War.
London, 1918.

Q 62. Birnbaum, Immanuel. "Internationaler Syndikalismus, "
Grundsätzliches zum Tageskampfe. Breslau, 1925.

Bernstein's later reflections on the war credits issue
are revealed on p. 83-94.

Q 63. Lensch, Paul. Die Deutsche Sozialdemokratie und der Weltkrieg. Berlin, 1915.

Q 64. Bernstein, Eduard. "Die Internationale der Arbeiterklasse
und der europäische Krieg, " Archiv für Sozialwissenschaft
und Sozialpolitik. XL (1914-15): 267-322.

SPD and the War: East German Opinions

East German scholars have an abiding interest in the question of socialist war guilt in 1914. To substantiate their interpretations of the role of the SPD the East German historians have dug deeply into the documentary evidence. They have employed materials available in the Zentralarchiv located in Potsdam and Merseburg. They have also used the Länder archives, especially those in Brandenburg and Saxony. The Institut für Marxismus-Leninismus beim ZK der SED and the Internationales Institut für Sozialgeschichte, in Amsterdam, have also been probed by the East German scholars. In addition to this much of their research is based on the Klassiker des Marxismus-Leninismus. The results of their research have been published in a number of books and several journals. The most important journals are: Beiträge zur Geschichte der deutschen Arbeiterbewegung, Zeitschrift für Geschichtswissenschaft, Wissenschaftliche Zeitschrift der Friedrich Schiller Universität Jena, and Wissenschaftliche Zeitschrift der Martin Luther Universität Halle-Wittenberg. The historical institutes linked with the universities of Leipzig, Jena, Halle-Wittenberg, Greifswald, and Berlin have been used for the discussion and dissemination of material concerning the SPD.

Q 65. Kuczynski, Jürgen. Der Ausbruch des ersten Weltkrieges und die deutsche Sozialdemokratie. East Berlin, 1957.

The author asserts that the German working class was guilty in Aug. 1914, of agreeing with the German war aims. The SPD was in agreement with the war and thus betrayed the working class for their own benefit by making an agreement with the military leaders for personal gain. Kuczynski has been attacked for his view that the working class was in agreement with the war aims. Leading this attack are: Günther Benser, of Zeitschrift für Geschichtswissenschaft. See: Xaves Streb and Gerhard Winkler, "Partei und Massen bei Ausbruch des ersten Weltkrieges," Zeitschrift für Geschichtswissenschaft, VI (1958): 169-190; Josef Schleifstein, "Die Sozialdemokratie bei Ausbruch des ersten Weltkrieges," Zeitschrift für Geschichtswissenschaft, VI (1958): 190-214; and Heinz Fliegner, "Zu dem Buch Jürgen Kuczynskis, Der Ausbruch des ersten Weltkrieges," Zeitschrift für Geschichtswissenschaft, VI

(1958): 313-337. These writers accuse Kuczynski of playing down the importance of a disciplined Marxist party as a vehicle for the organization of the proletariat in the struggle against bourgeois war aims. Leo Stern, editor of Die Auswerkungen der Grossen Sozialistischen Oktoberrevolution auf Deutschland, I. Berlin-East, 1959 ff. 47-51, 72-84, declares that Kuczynski is mistaken in attributing to the workingmen in the SPD, a mass support for the war. Stern goes so far as to say that it is a documented fact that only the right-wing SPD leaders backed the war effort, doing this because of opportunism. The workingmen though, Stern relates, did not follow SPD leadership in this support of the war.

Q 66. Liebknecht, Karl. Gesammelte Reden und Schriften. East Berlin, 1960-1966.

The editorial work was done by the Institut für Marxismus-Leninismus beim ZK der SED.

Q 67. Evzerov, R. "Rosa Ljuksemburg-protiv germanskogo militarisma nakanune pervoj mirovoj vojny," Novaja i novejsaja istorija. (Moscow, 1966): 95-105.

Presents the efforts of Rosa Luxemburg in her struggle against militarism before World War I.

Q 68. Schumacher, Horst. "Der Kampf der deutschen Linken gegen Imperialismus, Militarismus und Opportunismus im ersten Weltkrieg," Geschichtsunterricht und Staatsbügerkunde. (Berlin, 1966): 301-307.

Q 69. Sumpf. Fredi. "Die Deutschen Linken im Kampf gegen den deutschen Imperialismus und Materialismus in der Arbeiterbewegung von der Jahrhundertwende bis 1914," Geschichtsunterricht und Staatsbügerkunde. (Berlin, 1966): 292-300.

Q 70. Geschichte der deutschen Arbeiterbewegung. East Berlin, 1966. 8 v. Ed. by Institut für Marxismus-Leninismus beim ZK der SED. V. I: Von den Anfängen der deutschen Arbeiterbewegung bis zum Ausgang des 19. Jahrhunderts and V. II: Vom Ausgang des 19. Jahrhunderts bis 1917 include material for 1890-1914.

Q 71. Haupt, Georges. "Une Rencontre Jaurès-Karl Liebknecht en Juillet 1914," Bulletin de la Société d'Études Jaurèsiennes. XIX (Paris, 1965): 3-7. This article also includes a letter by Karl Liebknecht of Aug. 1914.

Follows the East German line.

Q 72. Schneider, Kurt. "Der Kampf der Leipziger Arbeiterklasse
im Jahre 1914 gegen Imperialismus und Krieg und die ver-
räterische Haltung des SPD-Bezirksvorstandes Leipzig, "
Wissenschaftliche Zeitschrift der Karl-Marx-Universität
(Leipzig, 1965): 651-658.

Q 73. Gaponov, P. M. "Antimilitaristskie Uystapleniia Karla
Libknekhto Nakanune Pervoi Mirovoi, " Voprosy Istorii. 1957
(2): 32-45.

> An account of Liebknecht's activities against militarism.
> Liebknecht was the only member of the Social Demo-
> cratic Party to use the Reichstag as a tribunal to speak
> against militarism. Liebknecht did not receive any
> support from the "opportunist center faction of the
> party. "

Q 74. Müller, Günther. "Sozial demokratie und Kolonialpolitik vor
1914, " Das Parlament. No. 11(1968).

R. KRUGER TELEGRAM

R 1. Hallmann, Hans. Krügerdepesche und Flottenfrage. Stuttgart,
1927.

> With the use of material from the German marine ar-
> chives the author corrects Thimme's account of the in-
> fluence of the Transvaal crisis on the development of
> German naval policy. See also: R 5.

R 2. Hammann, Otto. "Die Entstehung der Krügerdepesche, " Archiv für Politik und Geschichte. IV (1924): 203-213.

> Written by the former director of the press bureau of
> the foreign office and based upon information received
> from Marshall and Holstein.

R 3. Lehmann, Konrad. "Die Vorgeschichte der Krügerdepesche, "
Archiv für Politik und Geschichte. V (1925): 159-177.

> A study dealing with the vexed question of the emperor's
> original draft.

R 4. Meyer, Arnold O. "Fürst Hohenlohe und die Krügerdepesche,"
Archiv für Politik und Geschichte. II (1924): 591-595.

> Includes a highly interesting account derived from
> Prince Radolin.

R 5. Thimme, Friedrich. "Die Krüger-Depesch Genesis und His-
      torische Bedeutung, " Europäische Gespräche. (May-June,
      1924): 201-244.

      The most valuable single study, based in part on the
      diaries of Marshall.

R 6. Haake, Paul. "Das Krügertelegramm, " Verhagen und Klo-
      sings Monatshefte. (July, 1925): 507-512.

      A minute study of the episode with special reference
      to the writings of Thimme and Meyer. See: R 4-5.

R 7. Sontag, Raymond. "The Cowes Interview and the Kruger
      Telegram, " Political Science Quarterly. XL (June, 1925):
      217-247.

S. HELGOLAND

S 1. Caprivi, Leo von. Die Ostafrikanische Frage und der Helgo-
      land-Sansibar-Vertrag. Bonn, 1934.

S 2. Hasenclever, Adolf. "Geschichte und Bedeutung des Helgo-
      landsvertrages, " Archiv für Politik und Geschichte. V (1925):
      507-524.

S 3. Hagen, M. von. "Geschichte und Bedeutung d. Helgoland-
      vertrages, " Weltkultur und Weltpolitik. VI (1916).

S 4. Sell, M. D. dt.-engl. Abkommen von 1890 über Helgoland
      und d. Afrik Kolonien im Lichte d. dt. Presse. 1926.

T. WILLIAM II

T 1. Goetz, Walter. "Kaiser Wilhelm II und die Deutsche Ge-
      schichtsschreibung, " Historische Zeitschrift. 1955. 179 (1):
      21-44.

      Distinguishes three major schools of thought in histori-
      cal accounts of the Wilhelmian era: 1) the court in-
      spired authors who treated William II as "a martyr and
      a hero, " 2) those who condemned the Kaiser as inade-
      quate for the role he was assigned by destiny and 3)
      scholarly writers who have, thus far vainly, sought to

provide a complete and objective portrayal of William II and his times. Goetz contends that the apologists have exercized a fateful influence in Germany, obscuring the real causes of the catastrophe of 1918.

T 2. William II. Ereignisse und Gestalten aus den Jahren 1878-1918. Leipzig, 1922. Eng. trans., The Kaiser's Memoirs. New York, 1922.

T 3. -- Erinnerungen an Korfu. Leipzig, 1924.

T 4. -- Verleichende Geschichtsabellen von 1878 bis zum Kriegs-ausbruch. Leipzig, 1921. Eng. & Fr. trans. avail.

T 5. -- Aus Meinem Leben. Berlin, 1927.

T 6. Briefe Wilhelm II und den Zaren 1894-1914. Ed. by Walter Goetz. Berlin, 1920. Fr. trans. avail.

T 7. Briefe und Telegramme Wilhelms II an Nikolaus II, 1894-1914. Ed. by Hellmuth von Gerlach. Vienna, 1920.

T 8. Letters from the Kaiser to the Tsar. Ed. by Isaac Don Levine. New York, 1920.

T 9. The Willy-Nicky Correspondence, being the secret and Intimate Telegrams Exchanged Between the Kaiser and the Tsar. Ed. by Herman Bernstein. New York, 1918.

T 10. Kaiserreden. Reden, Erlasse, Brr. Telegramme Kaiser Wilhelms II. Ed. by O. Klausmann. Leipzig, 1905.

T 11. Reden des Kaisers: Ansprachen, Predigten und Trinksprüche Wilhelms II. Ed. by Ernst Johann. Munich, 1966.

T 12. "Kaiser Wilhelm II 1896-1900," ed. by J. Penzler, Reclam. Leipzig, 1904. No. 4548-4550.

T 13. Gauss, Christian. The German Emperor as Shown in his Public Utterances. New York, 1915.

T 14. Kann, Robert A. "Emperor William II and Archduke Francis Ferdinand in their Correspondence," American Historical Review. (Jan. 1952): 323-351.

T 15. Boelcke, Willi. Krupp und die Hohenzollern: aus der Korrespondenz der Familie Krupp, 1850-1916. East Berlin, 1956. Gives some insight into the relationship between the Krupp family and the Hohenzollerns.

T 16. Chamberlain, Houston Stewart. Brr. 1882-1924 und Briefwechsel mit Kaiser Wilhelm II. 2 v. Munich, 1928.

T 17. Balfour, Michael. The Kaiser and his Times. London, 1964.

Pictures William II as an incompetent bungler prone to
rash statements. The war came about not because the
Kaiser willed it but because of his stupidity in international affairs or "Weltpolitik."

T 18. Benson, E.F. The Kaiser and English Relations. New York,
1936.

A systematic review of the Kaiser's relations with England; failed to make use of many materials available
in 1936.

T 19. Chamier, J.D. Fabulous Monster. New York, 1934.

A biography of William II which portrays him as the
scapegoat of ambitious intrigues by the men around him.

T 20. Cowles, Virginia. The Kaiser. New York, 1963.

The author sees William II as a sinister individual who
planned, plotted, and carried out World War I. The
book is reminiscent of the type of material written
about the Kaiser during World War I.

T 21. Davis, Arthur N. The Kaiser as I Know Him. New York,
1918.

An account of the Kaiser by a man who was his dentist
for fourteen years.

T 22. Eyck, Erick. Das Persönliche Regiment Wilhelm II; politische Geschichte des deutschen Kaiserreiches von 1890 bis
1914. Zürich, 1948.

A critical study of German history under William II.
The author also includes a good discussion of the era
of Count Caprivi and Prince von Hohenlohe and a fleet-
ing survey of pre-war European diplomacy ending with
a review of the war guilt question.

T 23. Fellner, Fritz. "Die Verstimmung zwischen Wilhelm II und
Eduard VII im Sommer 1905," Mitteilungen des Österreichischen Staatsarchivs. 11 (1958): 501-511.

The author holds that the importance of the personal
relations between the two rulers for the friction of the
pre-war period has not been adequately recognized and
examined; uses the Morocco Crisis as an example.

T 24. Fried, Alfred H. The German Emperor and the Peace of the
World. London, 1912.

T 25. Gerard, J.W. My Four Years in Germany. New York, 1917.

A very popular book in the United States during the war,
it went through numerous editions. Gerard was the

United States ambassador to Germany when the war broke out in 1914. A number of letters, newspaper accounts and documents are printed.

T 26. -- Face to Face with Kaiserism. New York, 1917.

T 27. Hammann, Otto. Um dem Kaiser. Berlin, 1919.

T 28. Harnoch, Axel V. "Der Aufruf Kaiser Wilhelms II beim Ausbruch der ersten Weltkrieges, " Neue Rundschau. No. 4 (1953).

T 29. Helfritz, Hans. Wilhelm II als Kaiser. Zürich, 1954.

An apologist for William II. The author uncritically accepts material from the Kaiser's memoirs, while ignoring more reliable and contradictory evidence. Neglects the youthful years of William II.

T 30. Henle, Adolf. Fürst Bülow und der Kaiser. Dresden, 1930.

T 31. Hill, David J. Impressions of the Kaiser. New York, 1918.

Hill was the U.S. ambassador to Germany 1908-1911. The first part of the book is a description of his relations with the Kaiser. The second part is concerned with the origins of the war and is not accurate.

T 32. Kautsky, Karl. Wie der Weltkrieg entstand: dargestallt nach dem Aktenmaterial des deutschen auswärtigen Amts. Berlin, 1919. Eng. trans., The Guilt of William Hohenzollern. London, 1920.

T 33. Kospoth, Graf C.A. Wie ich zu Kaiser stand. Persönl. Erinnerungen an Kaiser Wilhelm II. Breslau, 1921.

T 34. Krache, Friedrich. Prinz und Kaiser: Wilhelm II im Urteil seiner Zeit. Munich, 1960.

T 35. Küremberg, Joachim von. Das Leben Kaiser Wilhelms II. Bonn, 1951. Eng. trans., The Kaiser. New York, 1955.

A biography which is very favorable toward the Kaiser in respect to his responsibility for World War I.

T 36. Lamprecht, K. D. Kaiser, Versuch e. Charakteristik. 1913.

T 37. Lehmann, Konrad. "Zu Kaiser Wilhelms II England Politik, " Historische Zeitschrift. CXLVII (1933): 553-558.

Revises somewhat earlier opinion in the light of the Hohenlohe memoirs. See: W 2.

T 38. Lowe, Charles. The German Emperor William II. London, 1896.

T 39. Ludwig, Emil. Wilhelm Hohenzollern. New York, 1926.

T 40. Lüthy, Herbert. "Schicksalstragödie," Monat. 1964, 16(191):
21-33.

> Examination of the crisis of 1914. Author is critical
> of William II because he is of the opinion that Wil-
> liam's thinking was unrealistic and his attitude uncom-
> promising.

T 41. Mann, Golo. Wilhelm II. Munich, 1964.

> A collection of photographs of William II with an intro-
> duction. Useful for the insights that can be obtained
> from the pictures of tho Kaiser's life.

T 42. Melrose, Andrew. The Real Kaiser. New York, 1914.

T 43. Müller, Georg Alexander von. Regierte der Kaiser? Kriegs-
tagebücher Aufzeichnungen und Briefe des Chefs des Marin-
Kabinetts Admiral Georg Alexander von Müller 1914-1918.
Ed. by Walter Görlitz. Göttingen, 1959. Eng. trans., The
Kaiser and His Court: The Diaries, Note Books, and Letter
of Admiral Georg Alexander von Müller. London, 1961.

> Valuable for the Kaiser's relationship to the navy and
> for a picture of court life. See L 52.

T 44. Muret, Maurice. Guillaume II. Paris, 1934.

T 45. Niemann, A. Wandergn. m. Kaiser Wilhelm II. Leipzig,
1924.

T 46. Nowak, Karl F. Das Dritte deutsche Kaiserreich. 2 v.
Berlin, 1929-1931. Eng. trans., (V. I) Kaiser and Chancellor: The Opening Years of the Reign of Kaiser William II.
New York, 1930, (V. 2) Germany's Road to Ruin: The Middle Years of the Reign of Emperor William II. New York,
1932.

T 47. Paléologue, Maurice. Wilhelm II und Nicholas II. Bern,
1947.

T 48. Perris, G.H. Germany and the German Emperor. 1912.

T 49. Pfeil und Klein-Ellgurth, Graf H. von. M. Kaiser. D. Fall
Zeditz-tr. und Wilhelm's II; Neue wahres Geschichte. Leipzig, 1924.

T 50. Prince, Morton. The Psychology of the Kaiser. Boston,
1915.

T 51. Rachfahl, Felix. Kaiser und Reich. Berlin, 1913.

T 52. Rathenau, Walter. Der Kaiser. Berlin, 1919.

T 53. Reventlow, Ernst Graf zu. Der Kaiser und die Monarchisten.
Berlin, 1940.

T 54. -- D. Kaiser und d. Byzantiner. Berlin, 1906.

T 55. Rittholer, Anton. Ein Leben für den Liberalismus. Berlin,
1951.

T 56. Schmidt-Pauli, Edgar von. Das Wahre Gesicht Wilhelms II.
Berlin, 1928.

T 57. Shaw, Stanley. The Kaiser. London, 1914.
Good section on the 1901 Chinese nationalist attempt to
oust the Germans from China. There is also a good
account of William's dismissal of Bismarck in 1890.

T 58. Simon, E. L'Empereur Guillaume II et la première année
de son regne. Paris, 1889.

T 59. Stolberg-Wernigerode, Otto Graf zu. Wilhelm II. Lübeck,
1933.

T 60. Stutzenberger, Adolf. Die Abdankung Kaiser Wilhelms II.
Berlin, 1937.

T 61. Thielen, Peter G. "Die Marginalien Kaiser Wilhelms II, "
Welt als Geschichte. 1960, 20(4): 249-259.
The meaning to historians of the marginal notes written
by William II on official documents. The marginal advice was not intended to carry the full force of law.

T 62. Topham, Anne. Memoirs of the Kaiser's Court. New York,
1914. Fr. Trans., Souvenirs de la cour du Kaiser. Paris,
1916.

T 63. -- Chronicles of the Prussian Court. London, 1926.

T 64. -- Memoirs of the Fatherland. London, 1916.

T 65. Valbert, G. "L'Empereur Guillaume II et sa manière d'en-
tendre le government personnel, " Revue des deux mondes.
Vol. 101.

T 66. Valentini, Rudolf von. Kaiser und Kabinettschef. Oldenburg,
1931.

T 67. Viereck, George S. The Kaiser on Trial. New York, 1937.
A biography of the Kaiser which attempts to show him
as a much maligned man who would be justly acquitted
by fair trial under the available evidence.

T 68. Wendel, Erhard von. Wilhelm II in d. Karikatur. Dresden,
1928.

222   German Foreign Policy

T 69. Wile, Frederic. Men Around the Kaiser: Makers of Modern
      Germany. 1914.

T 70. Zechlin, Egmont. Staatsstreichpläne Bismarcks und Wilhelms
      II 1890-1894. Stuttgart, 1929.

T 71. Zedlitz-Truelzschler, Robert Graf. Zwölf Jahre an Deutschen
      Kaiserhof. Stuttgart, 1924. Eng. trans. avail.

T 72. Zwischen Kaiser und Kanzler: Aufzeichnungen des General
      Adjutanten Graften Carl von Wedel aus den Jahren 1890-1894.
      Ed. by Erhard von Wedel. Leipzig, 1943.
            Diary.

T 73. The Hohenzollerns Through German Eyes. London, 1917.
            Taken from Simplissimus during the years 1903-1914.

T 74. Ilsemann, Sigurd von. Der Kaiser in Holland; Aufzeichnungen
      des letzten Flügeladjutant Kaisers Wilhelms II. Munich, 1967.

T 75. William II. Wilhelm II; Was er sagt, was er denkt. Leip-
      zig, 1911.
            Taken from his speeches and writings.

T 76. -- Kaiserworte aus eiserner Zeit. Gelsenkirchen, 1915.

T 77. -- The War Lord; A Character Study of Kaiser William II
      by Means of his Speeches, Letters, and Telegrams. New
      York, 1914.

T 78. -- The German Emperor's Speeches; Being a Selection from
      the Speeches, Edicts, and Telegrams of Emperor William II.
      London, 1904.

T 79. -- Kaiser Wilhelm II; als denker; goldene Wörte Aussprüche
      ans seinen Reden, Erlässen, Gesprächen, Briefen und Tele-
      grammen. Lüneburg, 1913.

T 80. -- Kaiserreden; Reden und Erlasse, Briefe und Telegramme
      Kaisers Wilhelms des Zweiten, ein Charakterbild des deuts-
      chen Kaisers. Leipzig, 1902.

T 81. -- The Kaiser's Speeches, Forming a Character Portrait of
      Emperor William II. New York, 1903.

T 82. -- So sprach der Kaiser. Copenhagen, 1918. In Danish.

T 83. -- Die Reden Kaiser Wilhelms II. Ed. by Johs Penzler.
      4 v. Berlin, 1897-1913.

T 84. -- Meine Vorfahren. Berlin, 1929. Eng. trans., My Ancestors. London, 1929.

T 85. William II. My Early Life. New York, 1926.

T 86. -- My Ideas and Ideals. Boston, 1914.

U. BISMARCK'S FALL AND HIS INFLUENCE THEREAFTER

U 1. Bismarck, Otto von. The Kaiser vs. Bismarck. Trans. by Bernard Miall of v. III of Gedanken und Erinnerungen. New York, 1921.

U 2. Penzler, J. Fürst Bismarck nach s. Entlassg. 7 v. Leipzig, 1897-1898.

U 3. E. Reden Bismarck 1888-1898. 1899.

U 4. "Um Bismarcks 20 Brr. a. d. Weimarer Staatsarchiv, " Grenzboden. Ed. by F. Pischel. 81 (1922).

U 5. "Bismarcks Entlassung, " Berliner Monatshefte. Ed. by Erhard von Wedel. XX (April 1942): 167-185; (July 1942): 321-336; (Sept. 1942): 411-425; (Dec. 1942): 551-563.

This series of articles is part of the diary of General Adjutant Graften Carl von Wedel. They throw some interesting light on the crisis of March, 1890.

U 6. Daudet, E. "Les Dernières années de la dictature de Bismarck, " Revue des deux mondes. 30 (1915).

Based on the memoirs of Herbettes.

U 7. Delbrück, Hans. "Von d. Bismarck-Legende, " Historische Zeitschrift. 133 (1926).

U 8. -- "D. Hohenlohe-Memoiren und Bismarcks Entlassg, " Preussische Jahrbücher. 126 (1906).

U 9. "Dokumente zu Bismarcks Sturz, " Berliner Monatshefte. XVII (April 1939): 344-360.

A translation into German of the reports of the French Ambassador in Berlin as printed in volume III of the Documents diplomatique français.

U 10. "E. falsche Anklage gegen d. Fürsten Bismarck, " Deutsche Revue. XXXI (1906).

U 11. Egelhaaf, G. Bismarcks Sturz. Stuttgart, 1910.

U 12. Fürst Bismarcks Entlassung. Nach d. hinterlass., bish.

unveröff. Aufzeichngn. d. Staatssekretärs d. Innern von Boet-
ticher u. d. Chefs d. Reichskanzlei von Rottenburg. Ed. by
G. FrHr. von Epstein. 1922.

U 13. Frank, A. "A.d. Vorgeschichte von Bismarcks Sturz (Brr.
a. Stöckers Nachl.)," Süddeutsch Monatsheft. XXIV (1927).

U 14. Gagiardi, Ernst. Bismarcks Entlassung. Part II Der Ausgang. Tübingen, 1941.

         A detailed study making use of the materials published
         prior to 1930.

U 15. Gradenwitz, Otto. Bismarcks letzter Kampf, 1888-1898.
Berlin, 1924.

U 16. Kentaro, Hayoski. "Bisumaruku No Shikkyaku O Meguru
Shamondi," Shigaku-zasshi. 1958, 67(2): 96-157.

         Examines the causes of Bismarck's fall and its social
         significance. Concludes that the basic difference be-
         tween Bismarck and William II was their ideas on labor
         legislation (even though the immediate cause of the con-
         flict was the divergence of their tactics against the so-
         cialists). The differences of their ideas are closely
         connected with the development of Hochkapitalismus,
         some of whose characteristics may be noticed in the
         strikes which occurred in the Ruhr area in 1889, which
         the author also discusses.

U 17. Lange, K. Bismarcks Sturz u. d. öff. Meing. in Deutschland
und in Auslande. Stuttgart, 1927.

U 18. Mahn, P. Kaiser und Kanzler. 1924.

U 19. Mommsen, W. Bismarcks Sturz und d. Parteien. Stuttgart,
1924.

U 20. Richter, Hub. Sachsen und Bismarcks Entlassg. Dresden,
1928.

U 21. Röhl, John C.G. "The Disintegration of the Kartell and the
Politics of Bismarck's Fall from Power, 1887-1890," Historical Journal. IX (1966): 60-89.

U 22. Rothfels, Hans. "Bismarcks Sturz als Froschproblem,"
Preussische Jahrbücher. 191 (1923).

U 23. Schlitter, H. "Brr. Kaiser Franz Josefs I und Kaiser Wilhelms II über Bismarcks Rücktripp," Österreiche Rundschau.
LVIII (1919).

U 24. Schüssler, Wilhelm. Bismarcks Sturz. Leipzig, 1921.

U 25. Schüssler, Wilhelm. "Bismarcks Sturz im März 1890,"

Vergangenheit und Gegenwart. XXX (1940): 62-71.

U 26. Wertheimer, Ed. von. "D.k.u.k. Militärattache über d. politische Leben in Berlin 1880-1895," Preussische Jahrbücher.

20 (1925).

U 27. -- "Bismarcks Sturz. Nach neuen Quellen," Preussische
Jahrbücher. 184 (1921).

U 28. Eckardt, J. von. Aus d. Tagen v. Bismarcks Kampf gegen
Caprivi. Erinnerungen. Leipzig, 1920.

U 29. Gradenwitz, Otto. "Akten über Bismarcks grossdeutsche
Rundfahrt vom Jahre 1892," Sitzungsberichte der Heidelberger
Akademie der Wissenschaften. XII (1921).

U 30. -- Bismarcks letzter Kampf. 1888-1898. Skizzen nach d.
Akten. 1924.

U 31. Hofmann, H. Fürst Bismarck 1890-1898. 3 v. Stuttgart,
1922.

U 32. Liman, P. Fürst Bismarck nach s. Entlassg. 1904.

U 33. Poschinger, E. von. Bismarck und s. Hamb. Freunde.
Hamburg, 1903.

U 34. Röhl, John. The Crisis of Government in the Second Reich
1890-1900. Berkeley, Calif., 1967.

An analysis of the shortcomings of the Bismarckian
system of government. A detailed analysis of Bismarck's dismissal.

U 35. Schneidewin, Max. Ein Wenig mehr Licht über Bismarck,
Caprivi und die jüngst erlebte mobilmachung des Liberalismus.
Berlin, 1892.

U 36. Wertheimer, E. von. "Neues z. Geschichte d. Letzten Jahre
Bismarcks 1890-1898. Nach ungedr. Akten," Historische
Zeitschrift. 133 (1926).

U 37. Zechlin, Egmont. Staatsstreichpläne Bismarcks und Wilhelms
II 1890-1894. Stuttgart, 1929.

V. CAPRIVI

    See also: Z 22.

V 1. Die Reden des Grafen von Caprivi im deutschen Reichstag, Preussischen Landtage und bei besonderen Auslässen 1883-1893, mit der Biographie. Ed. by Rudolf Arndt. Berlin, 1894.

V 2. De Clery, Robinet. La Politique de L'Allemagne depuis l'avénèment de Caprivi jusqu'à nos Jours 1890-1925. Paris, 1925.
       A study of the Caprivi tariff policy and its effects.

V 3. Does, J.C. von der. "Het Kanseliership von Graaf Leo von Caprivi de Caprasa de Montecuculi," Historia. (Dec. 1950).

V 4. Ebmeyer, Major von. "Caprivis Entlassung," Deutsche Revue. XXXXVII (1922): 193-213.

V 5. Eckardt, Julius von. Aus den Tagen von Bismarcks Kampf gegen Caprivi. Leipzig, 1920.
       The reminiscences of a chief of the German press bureau on the period of the first years after Bismarck's fall and the opposition of Bismarck to Caprivi.

V 6. Geis, Robert. Der Sturz des Reichskanzlers Caprivi. 1930.

V 7. Gothein, Georg. Reichskanzler Graf Caprivi. E. kritische Würdigung. Munich, 1918.

V 8. Kröger, Karl H. Die Konservativen und die Politik Caprivis. Rostock, 1937.

V 9. Lotz, Walther. "Die Handelspolitik des deutschen Reich unter Graf Caprivi und Fürst Hohenlohe 1890-1900," Schriften des Vereins für Sozialpolitik. 92 (II). 1901.

V 10. Meisner, Heinrich Otto. "Der Reichskanzler Caprivi. Eine biographische Skizze," Zeitschrift für die gesamte Staatswissenschaft. III (1955): 669-752.
       A valuable biographical outline of Caprivi's career.

V 11. Nicholas, J. Alden. Germany After Bismarck: The Caprivi Era 1890-1894. Cambridge, Mass., 1958.
       The author made use of the Caprivi papers. He is sympathetic toward Bismarck and Holstein and calls Caprivi's chancellorship one of the brighter periods of

German history in the last hundred years.

V 12. Rachdau, Ludwig. Unter Bismarck und Caprivi. Erinnerungen eines Diplomaten aus den Jahren 1885-1894. Berlin, 1938.

Memoirs of a foreign office official.

V 13. Schneidewin, Max. Ein wenig mehr Licht über Bismarck, Caprivi, und die jüngst erlebte Mobilmachung des Liberalismus. Berlin, 1892.

V 14. -- D. politische System d. Reichskanzlers Caprivi. Danzig, 1904.

V 15. -- "Briefe des Toten Reichskanzlers Caprivi, " Deutsche Revue. XXXXVII (1922): 136-147, 247-258.

V 16. Schreck, Ernst. Reichskanzler Graf Leo von Caprivi. Düsseldorf, 1891.

V 17. Schutte, Dr. von. "Erinnerung an Graf Caprivi, " Deutsche Revue. XXIV (1899): 229-235.

V 18. Sempell, Charlotte. "The Constitutional and Political Problems of the Second Chancellor, Leo von Caprivi, " Journal of Modern History. XXVIII (Sept. 1953): 234-254.

The author reveals that Caprivi's attempts at reform were frustrated by the constitutional structure of Germany.

V 19. Werdermann, Johannes. Die Heeresreform unter Caprivi. Greifswald, 1928.

W. HOHENLOHE

W 1. Hohenlohe-Schillingsfürst, Fürst Chlodwig zu. Aus meinem Leben. Frankfurt, 1925.

W 2. -- Denkwürdigkeiten der Reichskanzlerzeit. Ed. by Karl Alexander von Müller. Stuttgart, 1931.

Chiefly devoted to German domestic policy, but has some very interesting notes and letters on foreign policy. For material that was omitted see: Z 6.

W 3. Lotz, Walther. "Die Handelspolitik des deutschen Reich unter Graf Caprivi und Fürst Hohenlohe 1890-1900, " Schriften des

Vereins für Sozialpolitik. 92 (II) (1901).

W 4. Meyer, A.O. "Fürst Hohenlohe und d. Krügerdepesche,"
Archiv für Politik und Geschichte. 2 (1924).

W 5. Zug, Josef. Versuche der Widerannäherung als Russland
unter Reichskanzler Fürst Chlodwig zu Hohenlohe-Schillingsfürst. Rottenburg, 1934.
A dissertation in which is found a good analysis of
Hohenlohe's policy toward Russia.

X. BÜLOW

X 1. Bülow, Bernhard H. Fürst von. Fürst Bülow und d. Kaiser
mit e. Wiedergabe a. ihrem geheim Briefwechsel. Dresden,
1930. Eng. trans., Prince Bülow and the Kaiser; with Ex-
cerpts from their Private Correspondence Preserved in the
Records of the German Foreign Office. London, 1931.

X 2. -- Deutschland und die Mächte vor dem Krieg. 2 v. Dresden, 1929. Eng. trans., Letters of Prince von Bülow; a Selection from Prince von Bülows Official Correspondence as
Imperial Chancellor During the Years 1907-1909 Including in
Particular Many Confidential Letters Exchanged Between Him
and the Emperor. London, 1930.

X 3. "Fürst Bülow und Germann von Rath. Noch unveröffentl.
Dokum," Preussische Jahrbücher. 223 (1931).

X 4. Fürst Bülows Reden. Ed. by Johannes Penzler and Otto
Hötzsch. 3 v. Berlin, 1907-09.

X 5. Bülow, Bernhard H. Fürst von. Deutsche Politik. Berlin,
1916. Eng. trans., Imperial Germany, New York, 1917.

X 6. -- Die Krisis Grundlinien der diplomatischen Verhandlungen
bei Kriegsausbruch. Berlin, 1922.

X 7. -- Denkwürdigkeiten. 4 v. Berlin, 1930-31. Eng. trans.,
Memoirs. Boston, 1931-32.
Bülow's memoirs are an indispensible source for the
study of his policies and of his personality. They are
especially valuable for the light they throw upon Bülow's
character and upon his methods of work. They show

Bülow 229

that personal relations played an inordinate part in the conduct of German foreign policy and that Bülow was more intent on the problem of dealing satisfactorily with the emperor than upon any other one thing. Though his memoirs were not intended to, they nevertheless show that Bülow's influence upon the emperor was detrimental. In his efforts to be agreeable with the emperor, he encouraged him to adopt courses of action, frequently with unfortunate results.

X 8. Gaertringen, Friedrich Freiherr Hiller von. Fürst Bülows Denkwürdigkeiten: Untersuchungen zu Entstehungsgeschichte und ihrer Kritik. Tübingen, 1956.

X 9. Thimme, Friedrich. Front Wider Bülow. Munich, 1931.

An imposing collection of rejoinders to Bülow's memoirs, by men who were in contact with him. This book throws considerable illumination on the style of writing used in Bülow's memoirs.

X 10. Hartung, F. "Bülows Denkwürdigkeiten," Zeitschrift für Politik. (1931): 44 ff.

X 11. Herre, P. "Fürst Bülow und s. Denkwürdigkeiten," Kriegsschuldfrage. 8/9 (1930-1931).

A review of Bülow's memoirs.

X 12. Schöler, Herm. D. Denkwürdigkeiten d. Fürst Bülow. Detmold, 1931.

X 13. Schmidt-Pauli, Edgar von. Fürst Bülows Denkwürdigkeiten, e. Protest. 1931.

X 14. Ancel, I. "L'Épreuve de force allemands en 1908-09; d'après les documents allemands; la crise austro-serbe et la politique de Bülow," Revue Historique. 127 (1928).

X 15. Becker, Willy. "Bülow contra Tirpitz. E. Beitr. z. d. Kontroversen über d. Flottenpolitik," Zeitschrift für Politik. XVI (1926).

X 16. Ziebert, A. England und d. Bau d. dt. Schlachtflotte in d. Ära Bülow. Freiburg, 1929.

X 17. Becker, Willy. Fürst Bülow und England. Greifswald, 1929.

A detailed study of Bülow's foreign policy in respect to England, based on the German documents.

X 18. Haller, Johannes. England und Deutschland um die Jahrhundertwende. Leipzig, 1929.

A severe criticism of Bülow.

X 19. Eckardstein, Hermann Frhr. von. D. Entlassung d. Fürst

Bülow. 1931.

X 20. Schüssler, Wilhelm. Die Daily-Telegraph-Affaire: Fürst

Bülow, Kaiser Wilhelm und die Krise des zweiten Reiches

1908. Göttingen, 1952.

The author points out the irresponsible part played by
Bülow in the Daily-Telegraph Affair. He shows that
Bülow never read the copy of the emperor's press re-
lease and then later in the Reichstag debates refused
to accept his share of the blame.

X 21. Eschenburg, Theodor. Das Kaiserreich am Scheideweg: Bas-

sermann, Bülow und der Block. Berlin, 1925.

Relates Bülow's irresponsibility in the Daily-Telegraph
episode.

X 22. -- Kaiser und Kanzler im Sturmjahre 1908. D. Wahrheit

nach d. Urkk. 1929.

X 23. -- Das Kaiserreich am Scheidewege; Bassermann, Bülow und

der Block; Nach unveröff Papieren aus d. Nachl. E. Basser-

manns. 1929.

Gustav Stressemann wrote an introduction to this work.

X 24. Haller, Johannes. Die Aera Bülow. Berlin, 1922.

A good critique of Bülow's foreign policy.

X 25. Hiltebrandt, Ph. Erinnerungen an d. Fürst Bülow. Bonn,

1930.

X 26. Henle, Adolf. Fürst Bülow und der Kaiser. Bresden, 1930.

X 27. Monts, Graf A. Erinnerungen und Gedanken. Berlin, 1932.

The memoirs of a former German ambassador containing an ex post facto criticism of German policy, especially that of Bülow; highly colored and prejudiced.

X 28. Münz, S. Fürst Bülow als Statesman und Mensch. 1930.

X 29. Spickernagel, Wilhelm. Fürst Bülow. Hamburg, 1921.

A sympathetic biography and defense of Bülow's policies.

X 30. Stein, L. "Erinnerungen an Fürst Bülow, " Nord und Süd.

52 (1929).

X 31. Tardieu, A. Le Prince Bülow. Paris, 1909.

X 32. Tenhaeff, N. B. Het rikskanseiierschap van von Bülow.

Utrecht, 1928.

X 33. Thimme, Friedrich. "Fürst Bülow und Graf Monts," Preussische Jahrbücher. Vol. 231, p. 193-219; Vol. 232, p. 17-
34.

Y.   BETHMANN-HOLLWEG

See also: I 18, J 22.

Y 1. Bethmann-Hollweg, Theobald von. Betrachtungen zum Weltkrieg. 2 v. Berlin, 1919. Eng. trans., Reflections on the
War. New York, 1920.

Y 2. -- Dispatch from His Majesty's Ambassador at Berlin,
Transmitting Translation of a Speech Delivered in the Reich-
stag on the Subject of the Events Preceeding the Franco-
German Morocco Agreement, on December 5, 1911. London,
Dec. 1911.

Y 3. -- Dispatches from His Majesty's Ambassador at Berlin,
Transmitting Translations of two Speeches Delivered in the
Reichstag, by the Imperial German Chancellor on the Subject
of the Franco-German Convention Respecting Morocco, on
November 9 & 10, 1911. London, Nov. 1911.

Y 4. "August 1914; Ein aufschlussreicher Briefwechsel; Reichskanzler von Bethmann-Hollweg über die deutschen Kriegserklärun-
gen," Berliner Monatshefte. XVII (1939).

Y 5. Haselmayr, Friedrich. Diplomatische Geschichte des zweiten
Reichs von 1871 bis 1918. Bd 6: Der Weg in die Katastro-
phe. Munich, 1964.

        Starts with Bethmann-Hollweg as chancellor in July
        1909, and traces events through the outbreak of the
        war. The second section of this volume is concerned
        with German diplomacy during the First World War.

Y 6. Hartung, F. Theobald von Bethmann-Hollweg. Stuttgart,
1927.

Y 7. Jarausch, Konrad H. A Political Biography of Theobald
von Bethmann-Hollweg 1856-1921.

        Doctoral dissertation, University of Wisconsin. Mr.
        Jarausch expects to publish a 2 volume biography on

Bethmann-Hollweg in 1970. The study draws on hither-
to unused material to shed new interpretational light on
the chancellor's controversial role during the First World
War. Based on material in Rest-Nachlass, Deutsches
Zentral Archiv Potsdam and Merseburg, Staatsarchiv
Potsdam, Hauptarchiv Berlin, Politisches Archiv of the
Foreign Ministry Bonn, Deutsche Staatsbibliothek East
Berlin and Marburg, Kiderlen--Wächter Nachlass at Yale,
and South German archives in Munich, Stuttgart and Karls-
ruhe. See: Central European History (March, 1969),48-76.

Y 8. Zmarzlik, Hans Günther. Bethmann-Hollweg als Reichskanzler
1909-1914: Studien zu Möglichkeiten und Grenzen seiner inner
Politischen Machtstellung. Düsseldorf, 1957.

The author makes careful use of unpublished material
concerning William II and Bethmann-Hollweg; however,
no new information or thesis about Bethmann-Hollweg
is presented. It is the clearest account we have of
his chancellorship, his attempts to implement his tax
policies, and his policies concerning Alsace-Lorraine.
The author clarifies Bethmann-Hollweg's relationship
with the Kaiser.

Y 9. Hillgruber, Andreas. "Riezlers Theorie des kalkulierten
Risikos und Bethmann-Hollwegs politische Konzeption in der
Julikrise 1914," Historische Zeitschrift. 202 (April 1966):
333-351.

Y 10. Augstein, Rudolf. "Bethmann-einen Kopf kürzer?" Die Zeit.
(Sept. 25, 1964).

Y 11. Dehio, Ludwig. "Deutschlands Griff nach der Weltmacht?
Zu Fritz Fischers Buch über den Ersten Weltkrieg," Der
Monat. No. 161 (Feb. 1962): 65-69.

Y 12. Erdmann, Karl Dietrich. "Zur Beurteilung Bethmann-Hollwegs," Geschichte in Wissenschaft und Unterrecht. 15 (Sept.
1964): 525-540.

Y 13. -- "Bethmann-Hollweg, Augstein und die Historiker-Zunft,"
Die Zeit. (Oct. 2, 1964).

Y 14. Freund, Michael. "Bethmann-Hollweg, der Hitler des Jahres
1914? Zu einer Spätfrucht des Jahres 1914 in des Geschichtsschreibung," Frankfurter Allgemeine Zeitung. 28/29 (March
1964).

Y 15. Gerstenmaier, Eugene. "Die Last des Vorwurfs. Zweimal
deutsche Kriegschuld?" Christ und Welt. (Sept. 2, 1964).

Also in Bulletin der Bundesregierung (Sept. 4, 1964).
See also the author's book, Neuer Nationalismus?
Stuttgart, 1965.

Y 16. Deutsche Kriegsziele 1914-1918.   Ed. by Graf Ernst W. Ly-
nar. Berlin, 1964.

Reprints a number of articles written about Fritz
Fischer's book Griff nach der Weltmacht and the part
Bethmann-Hollweg played; contains a bibliography on
the controversy.

Y 17. Mann, Golo. "Der Griff nach der Weltmacht, " Neue Züricher
Zeitung. April 28, 1962.

Y 18. Ritter, Gerhard. "Zur Fischer-Kontroverse, " Historische
Zeitschrift. 200 (June 1965): 783-787.

Y 19. -- "Die politische Rolle Bethmann-Hollwegs während des
Ersten Weltkrieges, " Congres international des sciences his-
toriques. IV (1965): 271-278.

Y 20. Wirsing, Giselher. "...auch am Ersten Weltkrieg Schuld?"
Christ und Welt. (May 8, 1964).

Y 21. -- "Der Bauchredner, " Christ und Welt. (July 10, 1964).

Y 22. Zechlin, Egmont. "Deutschland zwischen Kabinettskrieg und
Wirtschaftskrieg. Politik und Kriegführung in den ersten
Monaten des Weltkrieges 1914, " Historische Zeitschrift. 199
(Oct. 1964): 247-458.

Y 23. -- "Bethmann-Hollweg, Kriegrisiko und SPD 1914, " Monat.
1966, 18(208): 17-31.

An analysis of Bethmann-Hollweg's policy of July,
1914, a policy which, in the author's opinion, was designed to pin the guilt for a war on Russia. The decision of the SPD leaders in favor of voting for the
War Credits proved the chancellor right. Publishes a
telegram between Bethmann-Hollweg and the German
emperor.

Y 24. -- "Motive und Taktik der Reichsleitung 1914; ein Nachtrag, "
Der Monat. No. 209 (Feb. 1966): 91-95.

Y 25. Hagen, Maximilian von. "Deutsche Weltpolitik und kein
Krieg, " Historische Zeitschrift. 179 (April 1955): 297-307.

Y 26. Hubatsch, Walther. "So kam es zum Ersten Weltkrieg, "
Deutsche Korrespondenz. (July 4, 1964).

Y 27. Hillgruber, Andreas. Deutschlands Rolle in der Vorgeschichte der beiden Weltkriege. Göttingen, 1967.

>The author believes that the German lack of unity in
>policy making and their exaggeration of Russian might
>were the two most conspicuous features of Wilhelmian
>Germany. In 1914, believing that Germany's position
>could only be strengthened by "bluff"--a calculated
>risk of war--Bethmann-Hollweg spurred on Austria-
>Hungary. He hoped only to weaken Russia in the Bal-
>kans, but this aim, as he knew, ran directly counter
>to Moltke's strategic planning. It consciously extended
>war to France and Britain. By mid-July, Bethmann
>saw only two alternatives: capitulation to Russia, or
>war. Germany went to war unnecessarily, without ex-
>pansionist goals.

Y 28. Mommsen, Wolfgang J. "L'Opinion allemande et chute du

gouvernement Bethmann-Hollweg, " Revue d'histoire moderne

et contemp. (Jan.-March 1968).

Z. HOLSTEIN

See also: AB 4.

Z 1. The Holstein Papers. Ed. by Norman Rich and M.H. Fisher.

4 v. Cambridge, 1955-63.

>There is a German edition under the title Die Geheim
>Papiere, etc. The editors also prepared a typescript
>of the complete Holstein papers for microfilming.
>Friedrich von Holstein during the years 1890-1906 was
>the most influential director of German foreign policy.
>The Holstein papers contain his memoirs, political ob-
>servations, diaries, and correspondence. The material
>demonstrates the inadequacy of the usual view of Hol-
>stein. Holstein is shown in his papers as a conscien-
>tious public servant, deeply concerned about both the
>deterioration of public life and the aimlessness of Ger-
>man foreign policy under William II, rather than the
>sinister, conspiring "grey eminence" of historical tra-
>dition. They also show Holstein's opposition to the
>building of a German navy.

Z 2. Rogge, Helmuth. Holstein und Harden. Munich, 1959.

>A very revealing collection of letters exchanged be-
>tween Holstein and Harden, editor of Die Zukunft.

Z 3. -- Friedrich von Holstein, Lebensbekenntnis in Briefen an

eine Frau. Berlin, 1932.

>Letters from Holstein to his cousin Ida von Stülpnagel.

Z 4. Meisner, Heinrich O. "Gespräche und Briefe Holsteins, 1907-
       1909, " Preussische Jahrbücher. Volumes 228-229. 1932.

Z 5. "Zur Kenntnis der Vorkriegszeit. Briefe der Geheimrats von
       Holstein, " Süddeutsche Monatshefte. 1919, p. 420 ff.

Z 6. Rogge, Helmuth. Holstein und Hohenlohe: Neue Beiträge zu
       Friedrich von Holstein tatigkeit als Mitarbeiter Bismarcks
       und als Ratgeber Hohenlohes; nach Briefen und Aufzeichnungen
       aus dem Nachlass des Fürsten Chlodwig zu Hohenlohe-Schil-
       lingsfürst. Stuttgart, 1957.

       This book contains material omitted in the earlier Ho-
       henlohe publication of 1931. See: W 2. The new pa-
       pers presented in this volume show the heavy depend-
       ence of Hohenlohe on Holstein during the period of his
       chancellorship.

Z 7. Rich, Norman. Friedrich von Holstein: Politics and Diplo-
       macy in the Era of Bismarck and William II. 2 v. Cam-
       bridge, 1965.

       This book is more than a biography of Holstein. It is
       a diplomatic history of Germany, as well as a com-
       petent study of internal German history. The author
       has done a remarkable job of placing Holstein in the
       larger picture of German as well as European history.
       Holstein, often referred to as the "grey eminence" be-
       cause of his enigmatic personality, has been accused
       of many things by many people. Rich has to some ex-
       tent rehabilitated Holstein's character. The author
       made use of the Holstein Papers, which he co-edited,
       and also had access to many other items which are
       found in private collections. Holstein had an influence
       on German foreign policy not reflected in the position
       he held in the German foreign office. Rich concludes
       that Holstein was not a spy in the Arnim affair but
       that he did urge Bismarck to transfer him to Rome
       and later to Constantinople on the grounds that Arnim's
       policy was contrary to German interests and to Bis-
       marck's instructions. Rich is not convinced that Hol-
       stein engaged in speculation, using state secrets for
       personal gain. He feels that the evidence may have
       been forged. Holstein, as Rich points out, died a poor
       man. The author relates that it was Holstein who was
       largely responsible for the rejection of the Reinsurance
       Treaty by Caprivi and William II. Holstein was unable
       to understand Bismarck's policy toward Austria and
       Russia. He thought that the alliance with Austria and
       the Reinsurance Treaty with Russia represented an in-
       consistant policy. Holstein was in favor of the Austrian
       Alliance and was at one time even in favor of a preven-

tative war with Russia. Rich points out that Holstein
thought that eventually Britain would have to come to
terms with Germany on the question of the Triple Alli-
ance--terms that would be favorable to Germany. Holstein was strongly opposed to the emperor's naval ambitions, which he thought would prevent any lasting
agreement with England. Rich shows how Holstein
tried to control the actions of William II. He also
goes into some detail on Holstein's dislike of the emperor's colonial dream. In regard to Morocco, Rich
relates that Holstein did not deliberately try to provoke
a war with Franco in 1905 but that he was prepared
for it if it should come. It was William II who opposed Holstein on this issue.

Z 8. Enthoven, H.E. Fritz von Holstein en de Problemen van

zijn tijd. Utrecht, 1936.

A good account of the part Holstein played in the formulation of German foreign policy.

Z 9. Eyck, Erich. "Holstein as Bismarck's Critic, " in A.O. Sar-

kissian, ed., Studies in Diplomatic History in Honour of G.P.

Gooch. New York, 1962, p. 331-347.

Study of the period 1881-1888. Based on Holstein's
diaries. Indicates that Holstein was critical of Bismarck as a man and as a statesman. Holstein was
alert to Bismarck's character defects and to the cor-
roding effects of old age. Holstein was critical of
Bismarck's attempted annexation of the Carolines, the
Schnäbele incident, and the policy he followed toward
Russia.

Z 10. Eyke, Erich. "Holstein und Bismarck, " Deutsche Rundshau.

81(10): 1031-1039.

A review of volume I of the Holstein papers by Norman
Rich. See: Z 1.

Z 11. Feder, Ernst. Holsteins Börsenbriefe. Politik und Börsen-

spekulation unter dem Kaiserreich. Berlin, 1925.

Z 12. Fischer, Eugene. Holsteins grosses nein. Berlin, 1925.

A critical and hostile account of the policy of Bülow
and Holstein in relation to the English rapprochement.

Z 13. Frauendienst, Werner. "Friedrich von Holstein und Paul

Graf Wolff Metternich, " Geistiger Umgang mit der Vergangen-

heit. 1962, p. 168-250.

Z 14. Goltz, Hans von der. "Holstein, " Zeitschrift für Politik.

XXVII (April 1937): 217-225.

The author calls for a reassessment of Holstein's influence on foreign policy which he thinks has been exaggerated.

Z 15. Gooch, G.P. "Holstein Oracle of the Wilhelmstrasse," Studies in German History. London, 1948.

This study is free from invective and speculation about Holstein; and does not reflect the mass of memoirs containing evidence against him.

Z 16. Haenchen, Karl. "Friedrich von Holstein Herkunft und Jugend," Mecklenburg-Strelitzer Geschichtsblätter. III (1931): 109-130.

Z 17. Hammann, Otto. Bilder aus der letzten Kaiserzeit. Berlin, 1922.

Gives examples of the attempts made by Holstein to control the Kaiser's irresponsible conversations with diplomats and soldiers after the Krüger telegram.

Z 18. Hallgarten, George F.W. "Fritz von Holstein Geheimnis," Historische Zeitschrift. 177 (Feb. 1954): 75-83.

Z 19. Hutten-Czapsky, Bogdan Graf. Sechzig Jahre Politik und Gesellschaft. 2 v. Berlin, 1935-36.

Shows attempts made by Holstein to halt the constant, careless, tongue-wagging of the Kaiser in German foreign policy.

Z 20. Herz, Ludwig. "Rätsel um Friedrich von Holstein," Preussische Jahrbücher. Vol. 231, p. 155 ff.

Z 21. -- "Holstein, Harden, Eulenburg," Preussische Jahrbücher. Vol. 229, p. 248 ff.

Z 22. Klocke, Ernst. Der Einfluss Friedrich von Holsteins auf die deutsche Aussenpolitik während der Kanzlerzeit Caprivis. Cologne, 1937.

Dissertation.

Z 23. Krausnick, Helmuth. "Holsteins grosses Spiel im Frühjahr 1887," Geschichte und Gegenwartsbewusstsein. Göttingen, 1963.

Z 24. -- "Holstein und die deutsch-englische Verständigung von 1890-1901," International Jahrbücher für Geschichtsunterricht. (1951): 141 ff.

Z 25. Raschdau, Ludwig. "Zum Kapitel Holsteins," Deutsche Rund-

German Foreign Policy

schau. Vol. 201.

Z 26. Rassow, Peter. "Schlieffen und Holstein," Historische Zeitschrift. 173 (1952): 297-313.

Z 27. Rath, Hermann von. "Erinnerungen an Herrn von Holstein,"
Deutsche Revue. (1909): 11 ff.

Z 28. Rich, Norman. "Holstein and the Arnim Affair," Journal of
Modern History. 28 (1956): 35-54.

Z 29. -- "Eine Bemerkung über Friedrich von Holsteins Aufenthalt
in Amerika," Historische Zeitschrift. 186/1 (1958). 80-86.

Z 30. Rogge, Helmuth. Im Dienste Bismarcks: persönliche Erinnerungen. Berlin, 1936.

> The memoirs of Arthur von Bauer. They are valuable
> for the insights which they show into the character of
> Holstein.

Z 31. -- "Die Kladderadatschaffäre: ein Beitrag zu Innen Geschichte des Wilhelminischen Reichs," Historische Zeitschrift.
1962, 195(1): 90-130.

> An interpretation of the impact of the Kladderadatsch
> affair on German public life. In Dec. 1893, the satiri-
> cal weekly journal Kladderadatsch began a series of
> articles attacking three high ranking officials of the
> German foreign service--Holstein, Kiderlen-Wächter,
> and Philip zu Eulenburg. This series of articles
> stirred up a series of controversies involving censor-
> ship of the press, personal scandals, and even duels.

Z 32. -- "Friedrich von Holstein, Max Eyth und die Tau-Schlep-
pschiffahrt," Beilage für deutsche Landesgeschichte. (1952):
169-246.

Z 33. Schüssler, Wilhelm. Das Historische politische Buch.
V (1957).

> Contains a good article on the defects in Holstein's
> character.

Z 34. Schweinitz, Hans Lothar von. Denkwürdigkeiter des Botschafters General von Schweinitz. 2 v. Berlin, 1927.

> Von Schweinitz was one time ambassador in St. Peters-
> burg and knew Holstein as early as 1864 (he died in
> 1901). He points out fundamental defects in Holstein's
> personality which marred his good qualities.

Z 35. Stolberg-Wernigerode, Otto Graf zu. "Friedrich von Holstein
und die Krise der Reichsführung," Zeitwende. 1960, 31(5):

298-308.
> Examines the crisis in the leadership of imperial Germany which had begun already in the last year Bismarck was in power. The author sees the causes in the lack of unity of the supreme political and military authorities, a unity which could be guaranteed only by the Kaiser, who also determined the selection of personnel. Even if a constitutional change had been made it is very doubtful that the Reichstag would have been able to express a cohesive will.

Z 36. Trotha, Friedrich von. Fritz von Holstein als Mensch und Politiker. Berlin, 1931.
> An early favorable reappraisal of Holstein's political activities in the foreign office; the author does a lot to clear up the mystery surrounding the enigmatic personality of Holstein.

Z 37. Vogel, William C. "The Holstein Enigma: a Reappraisal of its Origins," Journal of Modern History. XIV (March 1942): 46-63.
> Deals chiefly with the Arnim Affair; the author exculpates Holstein.

Z 38. Erfurt, Erich. Bismarcks Sturtz und die Aenderund der deutschen Politik. Berlin, 1940.
> A good treatment of the influence of Holstein and Waldersee on the non-renewal of the Reinsurance Treaty. It does not make use of many Russian sources.

Z 39. Goldschmidt, Hans. "New Light on Bismarck's Fall," Contemporary Review. 152 (Nov. 1937): 584-591.
> Deals chiefly with Holstein's efforts to influence William II.

Z 40. Krausnick, Helmut. Holsteins Geheimpolitik in der Aera Bismarck, 1886-1890. Hamburg, 1942.
> The author makes use of documents in the Austrian archives to show that Holstein secretly exerted himself in behalf of the Austrians and the British to the detriment of Bismarck's policy toward Russia. Krausnick reveals Holstein's dislike of Russia and his attitude that Germany would support Austria even in a war of the latter's choosing.

Z 41. Kuei-yung, Chang. Friedrich von Holstein; Studien über den Charakter und die Methoden seiner Aussenpolitik. Leipzig, 1934.
> Deals with Holstein's responsibility for Bismarck's fall

from power in 1890. Also covers Holstein's methodology
in conducting foreign affairs.

Z 42. Lohmeyer, Hans. "Holstein und Bismarck, " Die Welt als
Geschichte. (1941): 243-258.

Covers the period 1885-1890.

Z 43. Baylen, Joseph O. "Valentine Chirol, Baron von Holstein,
and the Venezuelan Crisis of 1895-96: an Unpublished Memorandum, " The Historian. XXVI (Feb. 1965): 210-217.

The memorandum sheds some light on the German attitude toward the Venezuelan crisis and toward the
United States at a very critical time, but also adds
something to an understanding of the method of "informal diplomacy" as it was practiced by European diplomatic officials and the correspondents of The Times of
London.

Z 44. Chirol, Valentine. Fifty Years in a Changing World. New
York, 1928.

After a brief career in the British Foreign Office,
Chirol served as the London Standard's correspondent
in the Middle East from 1876 until his appointment in
1892 as the London Times correspondent in Berlin.
He came to Berlin at a time of mounting Anglo-German
rivalry in Africa and, with the encouragement of the
Times foreign editor, Sir Donald Mackenzie Wallace,
undertook between 1892 and 1894 to assuage the Germans by a series of articles explaining the German
point of view. Holstein responded by taking Chirol into his confidence on many matters pertaining to Anglo-
German relations, making him an informal diplomat
for the British Foreign Office.

Z 45. The Elmer Roberts Papers, at the University of North Caro-
lina Library, Chapel Hill, N.C.

These papers are a valuable source for a study of Holstein. Roberts, while Chief of the Associated Press
Bureau in Berlin, was one of the few foreign correspondents in whom Holstein confided and was for a long
time a personal friend. Among Roberts' papers is an
extensive manuscript biography of Holstein.

Z 46. Richter, Günther. Friedrich von Holstein. Ein Mitarbeiter
Bismarcks. Lübeck, 1966.

A collection of letters written by Holstein to the various
members of Bismarck's family. They are very revealing regarding the diplomatic methods employed by Holstein.

AA. LICHNOWSKY

AA 1.   Lichnowsky, K. M. Auf dem Weg zum Abgrund; Londoner
        Berichte, erinnerungen und sonstige Schriften. 2 v. Dres-
        den, 1927. Eng. trans., Heading for the Abyss. New
        York, 1928.
        Includes: My Mission to London, England Before the
        War Lichnowsky's London dispatches, and other docu-
        ments.

AA 2.   Thimme, Friedrich. "Fürst Lichnowskys 'Memoirenwerk, '"
        Archiv für Politik und Geschichte. X (1928).
        Review of Lichnowsky's memoirs.

AA 3.   Jagow, G. von and Wilhelm von Stumm. "Zuschrift, " Die
        Kriegsschuldfrage. VI (1928).
        Review of Lichnowsky's memoirs.

AA 4.   Lichnowsky, K. M. My Mission to London, New York,
        1918.

AA 5.   Smith, Monroe. The Disclosures from Germany. I: The
        Lichnowsky Memorandum. II: The Reply from Herr von
        Jagow. New York, 1918.
        The German text of the Lichnowsky memorandum is
        taken from Berliner Börsencourrier, No. 135, March
        21, 1918. The text of the reply from von Jagow is
        taken from the Norddeutsch Allgemeine Zeitung, March
        23, 1918.

AA 6.   Bach, August. "Das Angebliche (Missverständnis) des
        Fürsten Lichnowsky vom 1 August 1914, " Berliner Monats-
        hefte. VIII (1930).

AA 7.   Willis, Edward F. Prince Lichnowsky, Ambassador of
        Peace; A Study of the Pre-War Diplomacy, 1912-1914.
        Berkeley, 1942.

AB. EULENBURG
        See also: Z 1-3, Z 7, Z 21, Z 31.

AB 1.   Haller, Johannes. Aus den Leben des Fürsten Philipp zu
        Eulenburg-Hertefeld. Berlin, Leipzig, 1926. Eng. trans.,

Philip Eulenburg the Kaiser's Friend.   2 v.   New York, 1930.

> Written in an attempt to restore the reputation of Eulen-
> burg, a friend of William II, who became the victim of
> a scandalous accusation.   The work throws much light
> on Eulenburg's relationship with the emperor and is a
> valuable source for the study of the situation at the
> German court as well as in the foreign office.

AB 2.   Aus 50 Jahren: Erinnerungen, Tagebücher und Briefe aus dem Nachlass des Fürsten Philipp zu Eulenburg-Hertefeld. Ed. by Johannes Haller.   Berlin, 1923.

AB 3.   Baumont, Maurice.   L'Affaire Eulenburg et les origins de la grand guerre.   Paris, 1933.

AB 4.   Herz, Ludwig.   "Holstein, Harden, Eulenburg," Preussische Jahrbücher.   Vol. 229, p. 248 ff.

AB 5.   Muschler, Reinhold C.   Philipp zu Eulenburg; Sein Leben und seine Zeit.   Leipzig, 1930.

AC.   ECKARDSTEIN

AC 1.   Eckardstein, Hermann Freiherr von.   Lebenserinnerungen und politische Denkwürdigkeiten.   2 v.   Leipzig, 1919-20. Eng. trans., Ten Years at the Court of St. James 1895-1905.   New York, 1922.

> The recollections of the counsellor of the German em-
> bassy in London.   Full of sensational revelations, el-
> egantly written, but unreliable.   They are important be-
> cause they contain a number of private telegrams and
> letters that cannot be found in the German documentary
> collections.   For a critical review see: Heinz Trützz-
> schler von Falkenstein "Die Denkwürdigkeiten des Frh.
> v. Eckardstein im Lichte der grossen Aktenpublication
> des auswärtigen Amtes," Archiv für Politik und Ges-
> chichte, Hefte 5/6 (1924).

AC 2.   -- Die Isolierung Deutschlands.   Leipzig, 1921.

AC 3.   Roloff, Gustav.   "Die Bundnisverhandlung zwischen Deutschland und England 1898-1901," Berliner Monatshefte.   (Dec. 1929): 1167-1222.

> A detailed criticism of the works by Eckardstein as
> well as a very severe indictment of Eckardstein.

AC 4.   Stalinij, V.   "Popitka anglo-germanskogo sblisheniia v
        1898-1901, " Istorik Marksist.   (1928): 89-120.
        A marxian interpretation based almost exclusively on
        the Eckardstein memoirs and the German documents.

AD.   KIDERLEN-WÄCHTER
      See also: Z 31, AE 3.

AD 1.   Kiderlen-Wächter, Alfred von.   Der Staatsmann und Mensch;
        Briefwechsel und Nachlass.   Ed. by Ernst Jäckh.   2 v.
        Stuttgart, 1924.
        An important source for the study of German foreign
        policy, although the editor unduly magnifies Kiderlen's
        stature as a statesman.

AD 2.   Andreas, W.   "Kiderlen-Wächter: Randglossen zu seinem
        Nachlass, " Historische Zeitschrift.   CXXXII (1925).
        The author discusses papers left by Kiderlen-Wächter.
        He finds that the papers reflect Kiderlen-Wächter's
        lack of creativity, intellectual depth, or dedication to
        his work.

AD 3.   Kiderlen-Wächter, Alfred von.   Dispatch from His Majesty's
        Ambassador at Berlin forwarding Translation of the State-
        ment Made by the Secretary of State of the German Foreign
        Office Before the Budget Commission of the Reichstag on
        November 17 of the Franco-German Morocco Negotiations.
        London, Dec. 1911.

AE.   GENERAL MEMOIRS, COLLECTIONS OF LETTERS, ETC.

AE 1.   Bachem, Julius.   Erinnerungen eines alten Publizisten und
        Politikers.   Cologne, 1913.

AE 2.   Bernhardi, Fr. von.   Denkwürdigkeiten a. m. Leben nach
        gleichzeit. Aufzz u. im Lichte d. Erinnerungen.   1927.

AE 3.   Beyens, Napoleon Eugène Louis.   Deux années à Berlin.
        2 v.   Paris, 1931, and L'Allemagne avant la guerre; les
        causes et les responsabilités.   Paris, 1915.

The author was Belgian ambassador to Berlin. He
was a close friend of Kiderlen-Wächter.

AE 4.   Deimling, Berth. von. Aus d. alten in d. neue Zeit Le-
        benserinnerungen. 1930.

AE 5.   Delbrück, Hans. Vor und nach d. Weltkriege. Polit. und
        historische Aufsätze. 1902 bis 1924. 1926.

AE 6.   Elis. von Heyking, Tagebuch a. 4 Weltteilen, 1886-1904.
        Ed. by G. Litzmann. Leipzig, 1926.

AE 7.   Frhr. C. von d. Goltz, Denkwürdigkeiten. Ed. by Frhr.
        F. von d. Goltz and W. Foerster. 1928.

AE 8.   Freytag-Loringhoven, Frhr. H. von. Menchen und Dinge
        wie ich sie in m. Leben sah. 1923.

AE 9.   Harden, Maxim. Köpfe. 4 v. 1910-1924.
        Volume 3 contains the legal processes undertaken
        against Harden by the German government.

AE 10. Hohenlohe, A. von. "E. graue Eminenz. Erinnerungen as
        d. Auswärtige Amt," Deutsche Revue. XXXXIV (1919).

AE 11. Jagemann, E. von. 75 Jahre des Erlebens und Erfahrens.
        Heidelberg, 1925.

AE 12. Jagow, G. von. Ursachen und Ausbruch des Weltkrieges.
        Berlin, 1919.

AE 13. Jäckh, Ernst. Der goldene Pflug: Sebensernte eines Welt-
        bürgers. Stuttgart, 1954.

AE 14. Lancken-Wakenitz, Oskar Freiherr von der. Meine dreissig
        Dienstjahre 1888-1918. Berlin, 1931.

AE 15. Lerchenfeld-Koefering, Hugo Graf. Erinnerungen und Denk-
        würdigkeiten 1843-1925. Berlin, 1935.
        These reminiscences of the Bavarian minister in Berlin
        contain interesting sidelights on German policy in this
        period.

AE 16. Mach, R. von. A. Bewegter Balkanzt. 1879-1918. Erin-
        nerungen. 1928.

AE 17. Monts, Anton Graf von. Erinnerungen und Gedanken der
        Botschaft Anton Grafen Monts. Ed. by K.F. Nowak and
        Friedrich Thimme. Berlin, 1932.

AE 18. Namier, L.B. "Richard V. Kühlmann: the Study of a Ger-
        man Diplomatist," Quarterly Review. (July 1950).

AE 19. Pless, Fürsten D. von. Tanz auf d. Vulkan. Erinnerungen
        an Deutschlands und Englands Schichsalswende. Dresden,
        1929. Eng. ed. avail.

AE 20. Radowitz, Joseph Maria von. Aufzeichnungen und Erinne-
        rungen aus dem Leben des Botschafters Joseph Maria von
        Radowitz. Ed. by Hajo Holborn. 2 v. Stuttgart, 1925.

AE 21. Rheinbaden, Werner K. F. Viermal Deutschlands aus dem
        Erleben eines Seemanns Diplomaten Politikers 1895-1954.
        Berlin, 1954.

AE 22. Rosen, Friedrich. Aus einem diplomatischen Wanderleben.
        2 v. Berlin, 1931-1932.

AE 23. Reischach, Hugo Freiherr von. Unter drei Kaisern. Ber-
        lin, 1925.

AE 24. Schemann, L. Lebensfahrten e. Dt. Leipzig, 1925.

AE 25. Schmoller, Gustav. 20 Jahre deutsche Politik 1897-1917.
        Munich, 1920.

AE 26. Schönburg-Waldenburg, H. Prinz zu. Erinnerungen an
        kaiserl. Zeit. Leipzig, 1929.

AE 27. Schwabach, Paul H. Aus meinen Akten. Berlin, 1927.

        Memoranda and selections from his correspondence
        with the Rothschilds, Eyre Crowe, Luzzatti, Caillaux,
        and others. Also relative to this memoir is Frederich
        Thimme's "Auswärtige Polit. und Hochfinanz, " Eur.
        Gespr, VII (1929).

AE 28. Schweinitz, Lothar von. Briefwechsel. Berlin, 1928.

AE 28a. -- Denkwürdigkeiten. 2 v. Berlin, 1927.

        These two Schweinitz books are especially revealing in
        the areas of politics and German society in the era of
        William II. See also: Bogdan F. S. Graf von Hutten-
        Czopski's Sechzig Jahre Politik und Gesellschaft, 2 v,
        Berlin, 1936.

AE 29. Staatssekretät Graf Herbert von Bismarck: Aus seiner pol-
        itischen Privatkorrespondenz. Ed. by Walter Bussmann.
        Göttingen, 1964.

        This is the only major published collection of documents
        from the private papers of the oldest son of Chancellor
        Bismarck. The editor has contributed a long summary
        introduction and the editing itself has been competently
        done, with all documents arranged chronologically.
        There is a name index but no subject index. A con-

siderable part of the volume is made up of Herbert's
correspondence with his brother William, who served
as his father's private secretary; Count Rantzau, his
brother-in-law; Holstein, and Bülow, but almost nothing
from his father. The documents in this collection contain no revelations that could lead to a substantial re-
evaluation of any aspect of the Bismarck era. Yet
they are of interest because they frequently reveal the
motives and tendencies of German policy in a more
candid and direct, and occasionally also less discreet,
manner than official documents usually do. The letters
confer a conse of immediacy and personal contact with
personalities and problems of the period, and, in their
description of daily routine, they transmit a fascinating
picture of how the Bismarck family conducted politics.
The reader is given added insight into the personalities
of William II, Bülow, Holstein, and many others who
were involved in the politics of the period.

AE 30. Stein, August. Es war alles ganz anders. Aus den Werk-
stätte e. politische Journalisten. Frankfurt, 1922.

AE 31. Stein, L. Aus d. Leben e. Optimisten. 1930.

AE 32. Das Tagebuch der Baronin Spitzemberg. Ed. by R. Vier-
haus. Göttingen, 1960.

AE 33. Weber, Max. Ges. polit. Schrr. Munich, 1921.

AF.   GERMAN RELATIONS WITH THE FAR EAST
See also: J 10.

AF 1.   Bee, Minge C. "Origins of German Far Eastern Policy,"
Chinese Social and Political Science Review. XXI (April
1937): 65-97.

A scholarly review of German policy during the Sino-
Japanese war and the period of the Shimonoseki Treaty.

AF 2.   Brandt, Max von. Drei Jahre Ostasischer Politik, 1894-
1897. Stuttgart, 1897.

The author was for twenty years the German minister
to Japan and China; a detailed and well informed discussion especially of Korea.

AF 3.   Gollwitzer, Heinz. Die Gelbe Gefahr; Geschichte eines
Schlagwarts, Studien zum imperialistischen Denken. Götting-
en, 1962.

Traces the development of the idea of the "Yellow peril" and its influence on German Far Eastern policy for the period 1860-1914. The slogan, he concludes, rose in a mass society psychologically instable and prone to hysteria, social Darwinism, and cultural pessimism and in which there was a need by labor and business for high tariff lobbies to find broadly appealing rationalizations to promote their interests. The author found the symptoms of sensational journalism and its fixation on a "Yellow peril" common throughout Europe and America.

AF 4.   Ma Guerrero, Leon. "The Kaiser and the Philippines, " Philippine Studies. 1961, 9(4): 584-600.

Germany wanted to neutralize the islands in 1898 but their plans were frustrated by lack of British cooperation and growing American involvement. Based on documents from the political archives of the German foreign office.

AF 5.   Hoyningen, Heinrich Freiherr von (genannt Huene). Untersuchungen zur Geschichte des deutsch-englischen Bündnisproblems 1898-1901. Breslau, 1934.

An analysis of the Far East and other problems in relation to England.

AF 6.   Monger, G.W. "The End of Isolation: Britain, Germany and Japan 1900-1902, " Transactions of the Royal Historical Society. 13 (1963): 103-121.

AF 7.   Vagts, Alfred. "William II and the Siam Episode, " American Historical Review. XLV (July 1940): 834-841.

Prints a document for the year 1902 with the emperor's comments. These make clear that Roseberg was genuinely afraid of war but never actually requested German aid.

AF 8.   Joseph, Philip. Foreign Diplomacy in China 1894-1900. London, 1928.

A good general account based on contemporary materials and documents.

AF 9.   Kawai, Kazuo. "Anglo-German Rivalry in the Yangtze Region 1895-1902, " Pacific Historical Review. VIII (Sept. 1939): 413-434.

An excellent analysis of the published materials on the subject.

AF 10.   Morse, H.B.   The International Relations of the Chinese

Empire. 3 v. New York, 1918.

>This study is valuable because of the great amount of
periodical material the author uses.

AF 11. Stoecker, Helmuth. Deutschland und China im 19 Jahrhundert. East Berlin, 1958.

>Working with new material from previously unused Ger-
man public documents, business records, memoirs,
and contemporary newspapers and periodicals, the author wishes to set the historical record straight between Communist China and Communist East Germany
by showing that it was the German bourgeoisie which
led the German nation to participate with the other capitalist powers of the West in plundering, dividing, and
enslaving the Chinese people. In spite of his Marxist
bias he has much to contribute in the way of information and interpretation to our understanding of international affairs in the Far East during the period under
study. He shows that the German representatives in
the field were often at odds with the directing power
at home. Included are valuable statistics on German
business concerns and their ventures in the Far East.
Two such firms are Krupp and Carlowitz and statistics
are given for their trade with China.

AF 12. Wood, Carlton L. Die Beziehungen Deutschlands zu China.
Heidelberg, 1934.

>A dissertation covering the period 1894-1934 with slight
treatment of the earlier part.

AG. GERMAN RELATIONS WITH THE BALKANS AND THE MIDDLE
EAST, ESPECIALLY TURKEY AND PERSIA (BAGHDAD RAIL-
WAY)

Balkans

AG 1. Malzkorn, Richard. Die Deutsche Balkanpolitik in den neun-
ziger Jahren des vorigen Jahrhunderts. Cologne, 1934.
Dissertation.

AG 2. Michaelis, Herbert. Die Deutsche Politik während der Balkankriege 1912/13. Waldenburg, 1929.

AG 3. Meyer, Henry Cord. "German Economic Relations with
Southeastern Europe 1870-1914," American Historical Review. (Oct. 1951): 77-90.

See also: AG 87.

AG 4. Sasse, Heinz G. War das deutsche eingriefen in die bosnische Krise im März 1909 ein Ultimatium? Stuttgart, 1936.

General Works on Relations with the Middle East

AG 5. Yisraeli, David. German Palestine Relations 1889-1945. Doctoral dissertation, Bar-Ilan University.

AG 6. Kohn, Hans. Die Europäisierung des Orients. Berlin, 1934.

AG 7. Grothe, Hugo. Deutschland, die Turkei und der Islam; ein Beitrag zu den grundlinien der deutschen Weltpolitik im islamischem Orient. Leipzig, 1914.

AG 8. Lewin, Percy E. The German Road to the East; an Account of the "Drang nach osten" and of Teutonic Aims in the Near and Middle East. New York, 1917.

AG 9. Hurewitz, J.C. Diplomacy in the Near East. Princeton, 1956.

Valuable collection of documents.

AG 10. Raab, Alfons. Die Politik Deutschlands in Nahen Orient 1878-1908. Vienna, 1936.

A well documented, critical study.

AG 11. Christopher, Andrew. "German World Policy and the Reshaping of the Duel Alliance," Journal of Contemporary History. 1966, 1(3): 137-151.

Traces the French and Russian response to German policy at Kiaochow, the Pan-German policy, and German plans for the Baghdad Railway.

Turkey

AG 12. Benson, Edward F. Deutschland über Allah. London, 1917.

AG 13. Bondorevskii, Gregorii. Bagdadskaia doroga i proniknovenie germanskogo imprializma. 1955.

AG 14. Corrigan, H.S.W. "German-Turkish Relations and the Outbreak of the War in 1914: a Reassessment," Past and Present. 1967 (36): 144-152.

AG 15. Flaningam, M. L. "German Eastward Expansion, Fact and
        Fiction: a Study in German-Ottoman Trade Relations 1890-
        1914, " Journal of Central European Affairs. (Jan. 1955).

AG 16. Frauendienst, Werner. "Zur orientalischen Frage; eine
        diplomatischer Schriftwechsel, " Berliner Monatshefte. XX
        (Aug. 1942): 368-381.

        Prints a long letter of appraisal of the Middle East
        situation, from the German ambassador at Constanti-
        nople, dated Dec. 28, 1896.

AG 17. Helfferich, Karl. Die Deutsche Türkenpolitik. Berlin,
        1921.

AG 18. Grothe, H. Die Asiatische Türkei und die deutschen In-
        teressen. Halle, 1913.

AG 19. Holborn, Hajo. Deutschland und die Türkei 1878-1890.
        Berlin, 1926.

        Based in large measure on unpublished German ar-
        chival material.

AG 20. Langer, William L. "Russia, the Straits Question and the
        European Powers, 1904-1908, " English Historical Review.
        XLIV (Jan. 1929): 59-85.

AG 21. Mandelstam, Andrei N. Le Sort de l'Empire Ottoman.
        Lausanne, 1917.

AG 22. Morgenthau, Henry. Secrets of the Bosporus. London,
        1918.

AG 23. Pascha, Moukhtar. La Turquie, l'Allemagne et l'Europe
        depuis le traité de Berlin jusqu'à la Guerre Mondiale.
        Paris, 1924.

        The author was navy and war minister 1910-1912 and
        then ambassador to Germany until 1914; the book is
        based on his memoirs, and documentation drawn from
        the Turkish archives.

AG 24. Pascha, Ahmed Djemal. Erinnerungen eines Türkischen
        Staatsmannes. Munich, 1922.

        The author was the navy minister in 1914 and views
        the alliance with Germany of Aug. 2, 1914, as inevit-
        able; he adds that Germany was the only European
        power with no designs on Turkish territory.

AG 25. Mühlmann, Carl. "Deutschland und d. Türkei 1913/14, "
        Polit. Wissenschaft. Hefte 6 (1929).

AG 26. Mühlmann, Carl. Deutschland und die Turkei, 1913-1914;
        die Berufung der deutschen Militärmission nach der Turkei,
        1913; das deutsche-türkische Bundnis, 1914 und der eintritt
        Turkei in den Weltkrieg. Berlin, 1929.

AG 27. Nahmer, Ernst von der. "Deutsche Kolonisationspläne und
        Erfolge in der Türkei vor 1870, " Jahrbuch für Gesetzgebung
        des deutschen Reich. XL (1916): 915-976.

AG 28. Raschdau, Ludwig. Ein Sinkendes Reich, Erlebnisse einer
        deutschen Diplomaten in Orient 1877-1878. Berlin, 1933.

AG 29. Schmidt, Hermann. Das Eisenbahnwesen in der Asiatischen
        Türkei. Berlin, 1914.
        Deals with the later period.

AG 30. Schäfer, Carl. Deutsch-türkische Freundschaft. Berlin,
        1914.
        Deals chiefly with German interest in Turkey and con-
        tains some good statistical material.

AG 31. Baron Wlad. Giesl. Zwei Jahrzehnte im nahen Orient.
        Aufzeichungen. Ed. by Ritter von Steinnitz. 1927.

AG 32. Thimme, Friedrich. "Aus dem Nachlass des Fürsten Rado-
        lin. Fürst Radolin, Holstein und Friedrich Rosen, " Berliner
        Monatshefte. Vol. 15, p. 725-763, 844-902.

AG 33. Trietsche, Davis. Levante-Handbuch. 3rd ed. Berlin,
        1914.
        Contains a lot of useful statistical information.

AG 34. Trumpener, Ulrich. Germany and the Ottoman Empire
        1914-1918. 1968.
        A study of their political, economic and military rela-
        tions.

AG 35. Zechlin, Egmont. "Die türkischen Meerengen--ein Brenn-
        punkt der Weltgeschichte, " Geschichte in Wissenschaft und
        Unterricht. 17 (Jan. 1966): 1-31.

AG 36. Trumpener, Ulrich. "Liman von Sanders and the German-
        Ottoman Alliance, " Journal of Contemporary History. 1966.
        1(4): 179-192.
        Demonstrates how the documents in the Politisches Ar-
        chiv tend to substantiate what Liman von Sanders stated
        in his memoirs that his influence in Constantinople was

limited.

AG 37. Mühlmann, H. Deutschland und die Türkei 1913-1914.
Berlin, 1929.

The author was an adjutant of General Liman von
Sanders. This book, based on unpublished materials,
is a highly important contribution to the problem of
pre-war politics in Turkey.

AG 38. Sanders, Liman von. Fünf Jahre Türkei. Berlin, 1920.

AG 39. Kerner, R.L. "The Mission of Liman von Sanders,"
Slavonic Review. VI (June-Dec. 1927 & March, 1928):
12-27, 244-263, 543-569. VII (June 1928): 90-112.

AG 40. Lindow, Erich. Freiherr Marshall von Bieberstein als
Botschafter in Konstantinopel 1897-1912. Danzig, 1934.

A review of Marshall's ambassadorship at Constantinople.

AG 41. Wiewióa, B. "Frhr. Marshall von Bieberstein zum Problem d. völkerrechtlichen Anerkennung d. beiden deutschen
Regierungen," Pol. West. Affs. III (1962): 141-151.

AG 42. King, David Burnett. Marshall von Bieberstein and the
New Course 1890-1897. Doctoral dissertation, Cornell University, 1962.

This dissertation should be consulted by anyone working
on von Bieberstein, for it contains a large number of
valuable bibliographical references.

Persia and the Baghdad Railway

AG 43. "Neue Abstaz Märkten in Persien," Export. XXXI (1909):
642.

AG 44. "Deutschlands wirtschaftliche Interessen in Persien und die
russische Konkurrenz," Export. XXXI (1909): 642.

AG 45. Brandt, M. von. "Die wirtschaftlichen Verhältnisse in
Persien und Deutschlands Anteil und ihr Entwichlung,"
Bankarchiv. (1906-1907): 114-117.

AG 46. Brünner, E.R.J. De Bagdadspoorweg; bijdrage tot de ken-
nis omtrent het optreden der mogendheden in Turkije, 1888-
1908. Groningen, 1956.

Contains a comprehensive bibliography.

AG 47. Dehn, P. "Deutschland und Persien," Deutsche Kolonialzeitung. II (1885): 8-10.

The author presents the possibilities for German expansion in Persia.

AG 48. "Persien als Absatzgebiet für deutsche Waren, " Export. XXIX (1907): 483.

This article presents new commercial possibilities in Persia.

AG 49. Helfferich, Karl. Georg von Siemens. 3 v. Berlin, 1923.

The authorized biography of a German banker. Volume 3 contains what is probably the best single account of the Baghdad Railway project in the first phase.

AG 50. Huldermann, B. Albert Ballin. Berlin, 1922.

AG 51. Grothe, Hugo. Zur Natur und Wirtschaft von Vorderasien. VI, Persien series III, Heft 2. Frankfurt A/M, 1911.

This book is the outcome of a trip to Persia by the author in 1908-1909.

AG 52. Stolze, F. and F.C. Andreas. "Die Handerverhältnisse persiens, mit besondern Berücksichtigung der deutschen Interessen, " Petermanns Mitteilungen. LXXIII (1885).

An early German plea for increased German commercial expansion in Persia.

AG 53. "Unsere wirtschaftliche Interessen am Persischen Golf, " Kolonial Zeitschrift. III (1902): 5-7.

AG 54. "Englische Machenschaften gegen den deutschen Handel am Persischen Golf, " Deutsche Levante Zeitung. (1915): 311-312.

AG 55. Stanley, E. "Business and Politics in the Persian Gulf; the Story of the Wönckhaus Firm, " Political Science Quarterly. XXXXVIII (1933): 367-385.

Extremely useful for the details of this firm, which was concerned in the Abu Musa Incident of 1907-1908.

AG 56. Stauff, P. "Die Deutsche Bank in Tehran und der deutsch-persischen Handel, " Asien. VII (1908): 65-68.

AG 57. Gehrke, Ulrich. Deutschland in Persien während des ersten Weltkrieges. Hamburg, 1957.

This dissertation covers the period 1912-1918.

AG 58. -- Persien in der deutschen Orientpolitik während des ersten Weltkrieges. Tome 1, 2 in Darstellungen zur auswärtigen Politik. Stuttgart, 1960.

AG 59. Hildebrant, G. "Die Entwicklung Persiens und das Inte-
resse der deutschen Arbeiterklasse, " Sozialistische Monatshefte. III (1910): 1473-1478.

The author is interested in what will be the effect upon
the German working class of German policy in Persia.

AG 60. Jaeger, T. Persien und die persische Frage. Weimar,
1916.

An account of German achievements in Persia.

AG 61. Die Beziehungen Russlands zu Persien. Leipzig, 1903.

This account was written by a retired Prussian General
of Russophile inclinations. It contains much material
on Persia at the end of the 19th century not available
elsewhere.

AG 62. Martin, Bradford G. German-Persian Diplomatic Relations
1873-1912. Gravenhage, 1959.

AG 63. Moral, F. "Persien, Land und Leute, " No. 32, Bericht
der Wissenschaftliche Gesellschaft "Philomathie" in Neisse.
Neisse, 1905.

Gives details of the moral concession of 1895.

AG 64. Muzakerat-i-Majlis. Doureh-yi-dovvum-i-tagniniyeh. Tehran,
no date.

The Persian equivalent of the Congressional Record,
containing scattered material on German-Persian relations.

AG 65. Reventlow, E. "Das Deutsche Reich und der Islam, " Alldeutsche Blätter. XX (Aug. 1920): 290-292.

AG 66. Rohrbach, Paul. "Persien und die deutschen Interessen, "
Die Natur. LI (1902): 100-102, 111-114.

AG 67. -- "In Persien, " Preussische Jahrbücher. 106 (1901):
131-160.

AG 68. Vambery, H. "Die Europäische Rivalität in Persien und
die deutsche Bagdadbahn, " Deutsche Rundschau. 103 (1900):
206-220.

AG 69. Butterfield, Paul K. The Diplomacy of the Bagdad Railway
1890-1914. Göttingen, 1932.

Dissertation.

AG 70. Chapman, M. K. Great Britain and the Bagdad Railway

1888-1914. Smith Studies in History XXXI. Northampton, 1948.

> An exhaustive study of the British aims based on the British documents for the most part.

AG 71. Chéradame, André. Le Chemin de fer de Bagdad. Paris, 1926.

> Contains much contemporary material. Written by a well known propagandist.

AG 72. Hallgarten, G. W. F. Imperialismus vor 1914; eine soziologische Darstellung der deutschen Aussenpolitik bis zum ersten Weltkrieg. Munich, 1951.

> Deals with the German attempts to further their interests in Persia in connection with the Baghdad Railway.

AG 73. Grothe, Hugo. Die Bagdadbahn und das schwäbische Bauernelement in Transkaukasien und Palästina. Munich, 1902.

> An attempt to influence Germans to settle as colonists along the Baghdad Railway.

AG 74. Hüber, Reinhard. Die Bagdadbahn. Berlin, 1943.

> The entire story of the Baghdad Railway is covered including some of the technical aspects.

AG 75. Ibbeken, Rudolf. Das Aussenpolitische Problem Staat und Wirtschaft in der deutschen Reichspolitik 1880-1914. Schleswig, 1928.

> Contains a detailed discussion of the political aspects of the Baghdad Railway project. The author traces the influence of economic problems upon German foreign policy and discusses such matters as colonial activity, international finance, and commercial treaties.

AG 76. Jastrow, M. The War and the Bagdad Railway. Philadelphia, 1917.

> The feeling for Germany during the war is seen in this book. The fact that the author lets his personal feelings for Germany enter in, ruins his objectivity.

AG 77. Rathmann, Lothar. Berlin-Bagdad. East Berlin, 1964.

> This East German study of the Baghdad railway project is flavored by communistic ideology. It emphasizes that this policy was imperialistic.

AG 78. Rohrbach, Paul. "Die Bedeutung der Bagdadbahn," Verhandlungen des deutschen Kolonialkongresses, 1902. (Berlin,

1903): 800-808.

AG 79. Silki, Bekir. Das Bagdadbahn-Problem 1890-1905. Freiburg, 1935.

> A solid piece of work which makes use of many Turkish documents; especially strong on the period prior to 1901.

AG 80. Wolf, J.B. "The Bagdad Railway," University of Missouri Studies. XI (1936).

AG 81. Wagner, R. "Deutschland und England am Persischen Golf," Deutsche Kolonialzeitung. XVIII (1901): 431-432.

AG 82. -- "Deutschland und die neue Weltstrasse nach Indien," Alldeutsche Blätter. XIII (March 1901).

AG 83. Wirth, A. "Die Lage in Indien und Iran," Preussische Jahrbücher. 98 (1899): 417-441.

AG 84. -- "Eine Persisch-indische Reise," Neue Deutsche Rundschau. 12 (1901): 872-890.

AG 85. Witzeleben, E.U. "Die Bagdadbahn und die persische Meerbusen," Grenzboten. 61 (1902): 683-693.

AG 86. Seidenzahl, Fritz. "The Agreement Concerning the Turkish Petroleum Company: The Deutsche Bank and Anglo-German Understanding of 19th March 1914," Studies on Economic and Monetary Problems and on Banking History. (Aug. 1967).

AG 87. -- "Development Aid in 1914: Agreements Between the Disconto-Gesellschaft Syndicate and the Bulgarian Government," Studies on Economic and Monetary Problems and on Banking History. (March 1967).

AH. GERMAN RELATIONS WITH THE UNITED STATES, MEXICO, AND CENTRAL AND SOUTH AMERICA (INCLUDING GERMAN-U.S. RELATIONS REGARDING THE FAR EAST)

Bibliographies and Aids

AH 1. Bemis, Samuel Flagg and Grace Griffin. Guide to the Diplomatic History of the United States, 1775-1921. Washington, 1935.

Lists published as well as unpublished sources available for the study of the diplomatic history of the United States. It is valuable for German-United States relations. Even though it is only good for materials prior to 1935, it should not be overlooked.

AH 2.   Plischke, Elmer.   American Foreign Relations: A Bibliography of Official Sources. College Park, Md., 1955.

This bibliography lists only materials published in English. It includes references to various specific collections, compilations, series, and special reports. Although in large part it is a guide to official sources, in addition, selected unofficial bibliographies, periodicals, and collections of documents are included in the appendices.

AH 3.   Boyd, Anne and Elizabeth Rae Rips.   United States Government Publications. New York, 1949.

A standard work in researching government documents. For the investigator of foreign relations there is a section on the Department of State.

AH 4.   Schmeckebier, Laurence and Roy B. Eastin.   Government Publications and Their Use. Washington, 1961.

Under the sections on foreign affairs there is a discussion of diplomatic correspondence and congressional publications on foreign relations.

AH 5.   Hartwell, M. A.   Checklist of United States Public Documents 1789-1909. Washington, 1911.

This volume contains lists of congressional documents to the close of the 60th Congress, 1908, and of Department documents to the end of 1909. All the Department of State documents which were printed to 1909 have been listed, described, and their library classification numbers given. After 1909 the researcher should use the Document Catalogue, which is not as convenient; however, it is the only major aid available.

Documents

AH 6.   Papers Relating to the Foreign Relations of the United States. Washington, 1861 ff.

Contains many documents relating to German foreign policy. Volumes bound by years.

AH 7.   Dispatches from United States Ministers in Germany. Available on microfilm in many libraries.

AH 8.   Department of State Papers.

AH 9.   Consular Reports. Washington, 1879 ff.

> Reports on the commerce, manufacture, etc. of various
> consular districts. They include pertinent material on
> American trade with Germany, German trade with
> Japan, and many other topics.

AH 10. Special Consular Reports. Washington, 1890 ff.

> Reports prepared by the foreign officers of the State
> Department on a variety of topics. They provide an
> insight into the development of manufacturing, agricul-
> ture, and commerce in Germany.

AH 11. Reports of the Commercial Relations of the United States
With All Foreign Countries. Washington, 1856 ff.

> These are the annual reports of the consuls of the
> United States on the commerce, manufacturers, and
> industries of their districts.

AH 12. Department of Commerce Reports.

AH 13. The David Jayne Hill Papers, Rush Rhees Library, Univ.
of Rochester, Rochester, N.Y.

> These papers are a valuable source for the study of
> German-American relations for the period 1908-1911,
> during which time Hill was U.S. ambassador to Ger-
> many.

German-U.S. Relations

AH 14. Bailey, Thomas A. A Diplomatic History of the American
People. New York, 1958.

> See p. 418-595 for an overview of German-American
> relations as well as bibliography.

AH 15. -- "The United States and the Blacklist During the Great
War," The Journal of Modern History. VI (1934): 14-35.

AH 16. Bernstorff, Johann. My Three Years in America. New
York, 1920.

AH 17. -- Deutschland und Amerika; Erinnerungen aus dem fünf
jährigen Kriege. Berlin, 1920.

AH 18. -- Memoirs of Count Bernstorff. New York, 1936.

AH 19. Grew, Joseph C. Turbulent Era. Cambridge, Mass.,
1952. Vol. I.

AH 20. Grey, Edward G. Twenty-Five Years 1892-1916. New
York, 1925.

AH 21. Hendrick, B.J.   The Life and Letters of Walter H. Page.
2 v. New York, 1922.

AH 22. Seymour, Charles.   The Intimate Papers of Colonel House.
4 v. Boston, 1926.

AH 23. Keim, Jeanette.   Forty Years of German American Political Relations.   Philadelphia, 1919.

AH 24. Kunz-Lack, Ilse.   Die Deutsch-amerikanischen Beziehungen
1890-1914.   Stuttgart, 1935.

AH 25. Vagts, Alfred.   Deutschland und die Vereinigten Staaten in
der Weltpolitik. 2 v. New York, 1935.

> Based on German and American archival materials.
> An exhaustive sociological examination of German-
> American relations.

AH 26. Shippee, Lester B.   "German-American Relations 1890-
1914," Journal of Modern History. VIII (Dec. 1936): 479-
488.

> A critical review of the books by Alfred Vagts and
> Ilse Kunz-Lack.

AH 27. Gerard, James W.   My Four Years in Germany. New
York, 1917.

> Gerard was the United States ambassador to Germany
> in the years prior to the American entry into the war.

AH 28. --   Face to Face With Kaiserism. New York, 1917.

AH 29. Hanssen, Hans P.   Diary of a Dying Empire. Bloomington,
Indiana, 1955.

> Points out that the German minister of marine was of
> the opinion that the United States amounted to nothing
> from a military point of view.

AH 30. Leusser, Hermann.   Ein Jahrehnt deutsch-amerikanischer
Politik 1897-1906.   Munich, 1928.

AH 31. Kühnermann, Eugene.   Deutschland und Amerika; Briefe an
einem deutsch-amerikanischen Freund.   Munich, 1917.

AH 32. Livermore, Seward W.   "The American Navy as a Factor
in World Politics, 1903-1913," American Historical Review.
LXIII (July 1958): 863-879.

AH 33. Möckelmann, Jürgen.   Deutsch-amerikanische Beziehungen
in der Krise.   Studien zur amerikanischen Politik im ersten
Weltkrieg.   Frankfurt, 1967.

AH 34. N S D A P Hauptarchiv Guide to the Hoover Institutional
       Microfilm Collection.   Comp. by Grete Heinz and Agnes
       Peterson.   Stanford, Calif., 1964.   p. 86, 92, Reels 12A
       & 13A, Folder 1342.

           This material is on German immigration in America
           prior to World War I (1910-1912) and concerns the
           Phoenix Transport Gesellschaft Marktredwitz 1910-1912.
           Friedrich Maier, who was the German representative
           of the Phoenix Transport Gesellschaft in Rotterdam,
           presented this material to Martin Bormann in 1934.
           It was Maier's contention that heavy emigration from
           Germany and Austria to America from 1910 to 1913
           was partially an enemy conspiracy to drain Germany
           and Austria of manpower.   This loss of manpower, he
           states, contributed to military defeat in the war.

AH 35. Relations With the German Government; Address of the
       President of The United States, Delivered at a Joint Session
       of the Two Houses of Congress, April 19, 1916.   Washing-
       ton, 1916.

AH 36. Seymour, Charles.   American Diplomacy During the World
       War.   Baltimore, 1934.

AH 37. Zims, B.   D. Grossmächte und d. span.-amerikan. Krieg.
       Münster, 1929.   Dissertation.

AH 38. Shippee, L.B.   "Germany and the Spanish-American War,"
       American Historical Review.   XXX (1925).

           This article relates that Germany, France, and Austria-
           Hungary all favored effective mediation or intervention
           to prevent a war between Spain and the United States;
           however, it is pointed out that none of these countries
           were willing to assume the responsibility for leading
           such a movement.

AH 39. Scott, James B.   A Survey of International Relations Be-
       tween The United States and Germany August 1, 1914-April
       6, 1917, Based on Official Documents.   New York, 1917.

AH 40. Snyder, L.L.   "The American-German Pork Dispute 1879-
       1891," Journal of Modern History.   (1945).

           Traces the causes, developments, and outcome of the
           pork controversy between Germany and the United
           States.

AH 41. Spenser, Samuel R.   Decision for War, 1917: The Laconia
       Sinking and the Zimmermann Telegram as Key Factors in

the Public Reaction Against Germany. 1953.

The author shows how events of February and March 1917 increased anti-German sentiment in the United States. He rejects the revisionist arguments and his thesis is a defense of American entry into the war.

AH 42. Stolberg-Wernigerode, Otto Graf zu. Deutschland und die Vereinigten Staaten von Amerika im Zeitalter Bismarcks. Berlin, 1933.

AH 43. Thomas, Arnold W. German Ambitions as they Affect Britain and The United States of America. London, 1903.

AH 44. Tuchman, Barbara. The Zimmermann Telegram. New York, 1964.

AH 45. Dennett. Tyler. John Hay. New York, 1933.

Contains much material on German-American relations regarding the Far East and South America.

AH 46. Witte, Emil. Revelations of a German Attaché; Ten Years of German-American Diplomacy. New York, 1916.

AH 47. May, Ernst R. The World War and American Isolation, 1914-1917. Cambridge, Mass., 1959.

Presents an extensive narrative of the events in Berlin which shows that the Germans were driven along by circumstances and in the end faced little choice except to force a war with the United States.

AH 48. Millis, Walter. The Road to War, 1914-1917. Boston, 1935.

The author gives expression to the disillusioned view that was common in the Thirties, portraying the intervention in 1917 as the culmination of a series of tragic blunders.

AH 49. Tansil, Charles C. America Goes to War. Boston, 1938.

Argues that intervention was due to sinister machinations by Allied propagandists and arms makers and bankers with a financial stake in Allied victory.

AH 50. Borchard, Edwin M. and Lage, William P. Neutrality for The United States. 1937.

An advanced revisionist interpretation, highly critical of President Wilson. Holds Wilson and his advisors largely responsible for involving the nation in the war because they blundered in not adhering strictly to the recognized rules of neutrality in dealing with Germany and Great Britain.

AH 51. Leopold, Richard W. "The Problems of American Inter-
        vention 1917: an Historical Retrospect, " World Politics.
        II (April 1950): 404-425.
        A detailed survey of the literature on this subject.

AH 52. War Memoirs of Robert Lansing. Indianapolis, 1935.

AH 53. Smith, D. M. "Robert Lansing and the Formulation of
        American Neutrality Politics 1914-1915, " Mississippi Valley
        Historical Review. XLIII (1956): 59-81.

AH 54. Seymour, Charles. American Neutrality, 1914-1917. New
        Haven, Conn., 1935.
        Seymour concludes that from both the political and
        moral standpoints, Wilson had little choice but to op-
        pose unrestricted submarine warfare. The Germans,
        he argues, had the options of keeping America neutral
        or forcing American intervention, and they chose the
        latter course.

AH 55. Buchanan, Russell. "Theodore Roosevelt and the American
        Neutrality 1914-1917, " American Historical Review. XLIII
        (1938): 775-790.

AH 56. Hasenclever, Ad. "Th. Roosevelt und d. Morokkokrisis
        von 1904-06. E. Beitr. z. Geschichte d. dt.-Amerik.
        Beziehgn. vor d. Weltkriege, " Archiv für Politik und Ges-
        chichte. VI (1928).

AH 57. Peters, Evelene. Roosevelt und der Kaiser; ein Beitrag
        zur Geschichte der deutsch-amerikanischen Beziehungen
        1895-1906. Leipzig, 1936.
        Views the problem of German-American relations
        against the background of American-British and Amer-
        ican-Japanese relations.

AH 58. Kortmann, Bernhard. Präsident Theodore Roosevelt und
        Deutschland. Emsdetten, 1933.

AH 59. Baker, Ray Stannard. Woodrow Wilson: Life and Letters.
        8 v. New York, 1931-39.

AH 60. Buehrig, Edward H. Woodrow Wilson and the Balance of
        Power. Bloomington, Indiana, 1955.
        Presents evidence that shows that Wilson and his ad-
        visors were conscious of the long dangers of a German
        victory in the war. The United States entered the war
        because it shrank from the prospect of Germany sup-

planting British power which contributed to American security. Concern over American maritime rights was not the reason for the United States entering the war against Germany.

AH 61. Link, Arthur S. Wilson. Princeton, 1947 ff.

A multi-volume biography of Wilson. Presents the conventional treatment that submarine warfare brought on the war.

AH 62. The Fatherland. (June 9, 1915): 5-Col. 1.

The chief German-American propaganda paper in the United States, it was against sending munitions to England.

AH 63. Child, C.J. "German-American Attempts to Prevent the Exportation of Munitions of War 1914-1915," Mississippi Valley Historical Review. XXV (1938): 351-368.

AH 64. Bailey, Thomas A. "German Documents Relating to the Lusitania," The Journal of Modern History. VIII (1936): 320-337.

AH 65. -- "The Sinking of the Lusitania," American Historical Review. XLI (1935): 54-73.

AH 66. Bryan, William J. and M.B. Bryan. The Memoirs of William Jennings Bryan. Chicago, 1925.

Includes sections on the Lusitania and munitions sales to England.

AH 67. Manchester Guardian. (Jan. 27, 1920): 68.

The munitions sales to England in the early war years is discussed.

AH 68. New York Nation. (May 13, 1915): 527-528.

On the Lusitania.

AH 69. Bernbaum, Karl E. Peace Moves and U. Boat Warfare. A Study of Imperial Germany's Policy Towards the United States, April 18, 1916-January 9, 1917. Stockholm, 1958.

German Relations With Mexico and Central and South America

AH 70. Katz, Friedrich. Deutschland Diaz und die Mexikanische Revolution: die deutsche Politik in Mexiko 1870-1920. Berlin, 1964.

The author holds that in order to understand the German drive for world power before World War I one

264 German Foreign Policy

has to understand the German expansionist politics in
Latin America. In Katz's opinion, in Mexico devoloped
one of the more important stages in the struggle between the United States and the European powers for
domination in Latin America. The book is based in
large part on archival material and he used unpublished
material from the Deutsches Zentralarchiv in Potsdam,
and also materials from the German Auswärtiges Amt,
the Reichsamt des Innern, the Deutsche Reichsbank, the
Staatsarchiv in Hamburg and the Deutsches Wirtschafts-
institut in Berlin. The author has also made use of a
considerable amount of archival material from archives
located in the United States and Mexico. Katz contends
that German bankers in the late 1880's and 90's sought
to extend their influence into Mexico, but were handi-
capped by their American counterparts. He points out
that William II desired to set up a naval base in lower
California around 1903. The Zimmermann Telegram
is also discussed. This book is the most comprehensive treatment available on German policy in Mexico.

AH 71. "The Blockade of Venezuela 1902," History Today. 1965.
15(7): 475-485.

Describes the Anglo-German naval blockade of Venezuela from Dec. 8, 1902 to Feb. 14, 1903.

AH 72. Platt, D.C.M. "The Allied Coercion of Venezuela, 1902-
03--a Reassessment," Inter-American Economic Affairs.
1961/62. 15(4): 3-28.

Holds that the British-German-Italian blockade of Venezuela to obtain settlement of claims was a routine affair whose significance was exaggerated at the time and
in later writings, because of wholly extraneous factors.
The claims involved were of the same type that had led
to similar incidents in the past and the action of the
European powers was in accord with existing international law. Based largely on British foreign office
records.

AH 73. Perkins, Dexter. The Monroe Doctrine 1867-1907. Baltimore, 1937.

Shows how far the Kaiser went to curry favor with the
American people by conferring a medal on Roosevelt.
The Kaiser ordered a yacht built in the United States
and had Roosevelt's daughter Alice christen it. He
also sent Prince Henry to the United States to present
a statue of Frederick the Great. But German activities
in Venezuela tended to off-set these overtures.

AH 74. New York Times. (Jan. 23, 1903): 8 Col. 1.

On German activities in Venezuela.

AH 75. London Times. (Dec. 22, 1902): 9 Col. 5.

On Germany's activities in Venezuela.

AH 76. Baylen, Joseph O.   "Valentine Chirol, Baron von Holstein, and the Venezuelan Crisis of 1895-1896: an Unpublished Memorandum, " The Historian. XXVII (Feb. 1965): 210-217.

The memorandum sheds some light on the German attitude toward the United States in regard to the Venezuelan crisis at a very critical time.

AH 77. Wright, Almon R.   "German Interest in Panama's Piñas Bay 1910-1938, " Journal of Modern History. (March 1955).

German-U.S. Relations in the Far East

AH 78. Bailey, Thomas A.   "Dewey and the Germans at Manila Bay, " American Historical Review. XLV (1939): 59-81.

Points out German blunderings in the Philippines. Germany gathered five men-of-war at Manila and thus aroused suspicions in America that they were there to support the Kaiser's designs on the Philippines. The documents show that Germany did not want to provoke a war, but since she had entered the race for colonies late in the game she must employ all measures at her disposal to obtain colonies. Germany believed that if the United States would abandon the Philippines then the presence of a strong German fleet at Manila would buttress German claims to the islands.

AH 79. Literary Digest. XVII (July 1898): 92.

A contemporary account of the Manila incident.

AH 80. Schieber, C.E.   The Transformation of American Sentiment Toward Germany 1870-1914.   Boston, 1923.

Good for a variety of German-American issues including the Philippine incident. Goes into detail on the Danish West Indies question of 1902. Points out that there was considerable fear in the United States that Germany might try to acquire them to place naval bases near the projected canal across Panama. In 1902 Washington had concluded a treaty of annexation with Denmark only to have it rejected by the Danish Parliament. Some Americans felt that German pressure had thwarted ratification; however, the documents do not show it.

AH 81. Tansill, C.C.   The Purchase of the Danish West Indies. Baltimore, 1932.

Traces the German-American controversy over the

Danish West Indies.

AH 82.   Harpers Weekly. XLVII (March 21, 1903): 475.

On the Danish West Indies and German involvement.

AH 83.   Quinn, Pearle E.   "The Diplomatic Struggle for the Carolines 1898," Pacific Historical Review. XIV (Sept. 1945):
290-302.

This article was based primarily on German and British documents and shows how German assiduity, including pressure on American representatives in Washington and Paris, together with lukewarmness in the
United States, won the Carolines for Germany.

AH 84.   Ryden, George Herbert.   The Foreign Policy of The United
States in Relation to Samoa. New Haven, Conn., 1933.

Contains a great deal of material on German-American
relations in regard to Samoa.

AH 85.   Ellison, Joseph W.   "The Partition of Samoa: A Study in
Imperialism and Diplomacy," Pacific Historical Review.
VIII (Sept. 1939): 259-288.

AH 86.   Livermore, Seward W.   "American Strategy Diplomacy in
the South Pacific 1890-1914," Pacific Historical Review.
XII (March 1943): 33-52.

AH 87.   Vevier, Charles.   "The Open Door: An Idea in Action 1906-
1913," Pacific Historical Review. XIV (Feb. 1955): 49-62.

AH 88.   Hall, Luella J.   "The Abortive German-American-Chinese
Entente of 1907-1908," Journal of Modern History. I (June
1929): 219-235.

AI.   GERMAN-AUSTRIAN RELATIONS

See Also: Section M.

AI 1.   Bertil H. and A. Peterson.   "Das Österreich-ungarische
Memorandum an Deutschland vom 5 Juli 1914," The Scandia.
Sweden, 1964. 3(1): 138-190.

Traces the development of the Berchtold Memorandum
back to István Tisza's Memorandum of Aug. 25, 1913,
for a settlement in the Balkans. Points out how it was
changed by Berchtold.

AI 2.   Cramon, A. von. and P. Fleck. Deutschlands Schicksal-
         bund mit Österreich-Ungarn. Berlin, 1932.

         Cramon was the German representative at the Austrian
         headquarters. It is an important contribution to the
         recriminatory documents which have arisen between the
         former allies.

AI 3.   Förster, Leo. Das Bundesverhältnis Deutschlands zu
         Oesterreich-Ungarn in der Epoche Aenrenthal, 1906-1912.
         1934.

AI 4.   Goricar, Josef. The Inside Story of Austro-German In-
         trigue; or how the World War was Brought About. Garden
         City, N.Y., 1920.

AI 5.   Hatzfeld, Karl. Das Deutsch-österreichische Bündnis von
         1879- in der Beurteilung der politischen Parteien Deutsch-
         lands. Berlin, 1938.

AI 6.   Heller, Eduard. Das Deutsch-österreichesch-ungarische
         Bündnis in Bismarcks Aussenpolitik. Berlin, 1925.

AI 7.   Horsch, Wolfgang F. Unstimmigkeiten im deutsch-oester-
         reichischen Bündnis Ende 1888 und Anfang 1889. Urach,
         1931. Dissertation.

         This work is based on press material as well as on
         material from the Austrian archives.

AI 8.   Hoyos, Graf Alexander von. Der Deutsch-englische Gegen-
         satzund sein Einfluss auf die Balkanpolitik Österreich-
         Ungarns. Berlin, 1922.

AI 9.   Krausnick, Helmut. "Botschafter Graf Hatzfeldt und die
         Aussenpolitik Bismarcks," Historische Zeitschrift.
         CLXVII (1942): 566-583.

         An excellent study which concludes that Hatzfeld
         favored close relations with England and Austria
         rather than with Russia.

AI 10.   Kühlmann, Richard von. Thoughts on Germany. New York,
         1932.

         Contains very interesting reflections on German policy
         before the war, notably with respect to the German
         naval policy and the alliance with Austria.

AI 11.   Pribram, Alfred F. The Secret Treaties of Austro-
         Hungary 1879-1914. 2 v. Cambridge, 1920-21.

Contains a lot of material on the Austro-German Alliance of 1879, the League of the Three Emperors, and the Triple Alliance.

AI 12.   Stieve, Friedrich.   Die Tragödie der Bundesgenossen: Deutschland und Österreich-Ungarn 1908-1914.   Munich, 1930.

AI 13.   Schüle, Ernst.   "Zwei Briefe Kaiser Wilhelsm II an Kaiser Franz Josef I 1889-1893," Preussische Jahrbücher.   CCXI (June 1935): 251-250.

AI 14.   Schüssler, Wilhelm.   Österreich und das deutsche Schicksal. Leipzig, 1925.

A study of Austro-German relations before the war.

AI 15.   Theil, Hans J.   Die Reichsdeutsche Presse und Publizistik und das österreichungarische Verfassungs und Nationalitätenproblem in den Jahren 1903-1906.   1936.

AI 16.   Wedel, Oswald H.   Austro-German Diplomatic Relations 1908-1914.   Stanford, 1932.

AJ.   GERMAN-FRENCH RELATIONS

AJ 1.   Albin, Pierre.   La Paix armée: l'Allemagne et la France in Europe, 1885-1894.   Paris, 1913.

Favorable to France but not hostile to Germany.

AJ 2.   Bérard, Victor.   La France et Guillaume II.   Paris, 1907.

AJ 3.   Bracq, Jean C.   The Provocation of France; Fifty Years of German Aggression.   New York, 1916.

AJ 4.   Gontaut-Biron, E. de.   Mon Ambassade en Allemagne. Paris, 1906.

AJ 5.   Gooch, George P.   Franco-German Relations 1871-1914. London, 1923.

Brief and impartial.

AJ 6.   Mévil, André.   De la paix Francfort à la conference d'Algésiras.   Paris, 1909.

AJ 7.   Meynier, Victor.   France and Germany from the Peace of Frankfurt in 1871 to the Peace of Algeciras in 1906.   London, 1908.

AJ 8.   Naumann, Friedrich.   Deutschland und Frankreich.   Stutt-
        gart, 1914.

AJ 9.   N S D A P Hauptarchiv Guide to the Hoover Institutional
        Microfilm Collection.   Comp. by Grete Heinz and Agnes
        Peterson.   Stanford, Calif., 1964.   p. 91-92, Reel 12A,
        Folder 1341.
            Concerns the German and French iron industries 1914-
            1916.

AJ 10. Péguy, Charles P.   Par ce demi-clair Matin.   Paris, 1952.

AJ 11. Pinon, René.   France et Allemagne 1870-1913.   Paris,
        1913.

AJ 12. Playne, E.C.   The Neuroses of Nations: The Neurosis of
        Germany and France.   New York, 1925.
            A study in the national psychology of pre-war Europe.

AJ 13. Renouvin, Pierre.   "Les Relations franco-allemandes de
        1871 à 1914:   esquisse d'un programme de recherches, "
        Studies in Diplomatic History in Honour of G.P. Gooch.
        Ed. by A.O. Sarkissian.   New York, 1962.   P. 308-321.
            The essentials in the field of diplomatic history are
            known but much investigation remains to be done in
            demography, economics, and intellectual relations.
            The collective mentality in July, 1914, was more im-
            portant than economic interests.

AJ 14. Schoen, W. Freiherr von.   Erlebts: Beiträge zur Geschi-
        chte der neuesten Zeit.   Stuttgart, 1921.   Eng. trans.,
        The Memoirs of an Ambassador.   London, 1922.
            The author was the German ambassador to France
            1910-1914.

AJ 15. Turquan, Joseph.   Les Provacations allemandes de 1871 à
        1914.   Paris, 1917.

AJ 16. Wienefeld, Robert H.   Franco-German Relations, 1878-1885.
        Baltimore, 1929.

AJ 17. Ziebura, Gilbert.   Die Deutsche Frage in der öffenlichen
        Meinung Frankreichs von 1911-1914.   Berlin, 1955.

AJ 18. Bittner, Ludwig.   "Neue Beiträge zur Haltung Kaiser Wil-
        helms II in der Fashodafrage, " Historische Zeitschrift.
        CLXII (1940): 540-550.

Quotes unpublished Austrian documents to show that
the Emperor encouraged the British to expect German
benevolence in the event of an Anglo-French conflict.

AJ 19. Schimpke, Friedrich. Die Deutsche-französischen Beziehungen von Fashoda bis zum Abschluss der Entente Cordiale.
Emsdetten, 1935.

A sound doctoral dissertation based on the documents
as well as on extensive study of the contemporary
press.

AJ 20. Heinrich, David. "Noch Einmal: alte Diplomatic und der
Sturz Delcassés," Wissen und Leben. (April 20, 1925).

AJ 21. Kamplade, Walther. Delcassé und Deutschland, 1898-1911.
Emsdetten, 1940.

AJ 22. Nakayma, Jiichi. "Tanjiru Jiken No 'Shakaigakuteki Setsu-
mei,'" Jinbun Kenkyu. 1960, 11(9): 917-933.

A "sociological" interpretation of the Tangier affair.
The author maintains that a thesis by Hallgarten, that
William II was urged to land at Tangier by German
capitalists, especially by the Krupp firm, is not well
documented. The author concludes that the German
foreign office alone decided to precipitate the first
Moroccan crisis. See: W.F. Hallgarten Imperialismus
vor 1914. 2 v. Munich, 1951.

AJ 23. Ludwig, W. Frankreichs Haltung zur Deutschen Kolonialpolitik vom Marokko-Vertrag von 1911 bis zum Versailler
Diktat. Leipzig, 1940.

AJ 24. Edwards, E.W. "The Franco-German Agreement on Morocco, 1909," The English Historical Review. 78 (July
1963): 483-513.

Based on the documents published by England, France,
and Germany as well as the papers of the German foreign office microfilmed after World War II.

AJ 25. Balch, Thomas. France in North Africa. Philadelphia,
1906.

AJ 26. Bethmann-Hollweg, Theobald von. Dispatch from His Majesty's Ambassador at Berlin, Transmitting Translation of
a Speech Delivered in the Reichstag by the Imperial German Chancellor on the Subject of the Events Preceeding the
Franco-German Morocco Agreement, on December 5, 1911.
London, Dec. 1911.

AJ 27. Bethmann-Hollweg, Theobald von. Dispatches from His
        Majesty's Ambassador at Berlin, Transmitting Translation
        of two Speeches Delivered in the Reichstag by the Imperial
        German Chancellor on the Subject of the Franco-German
        Convention Respecting Morocco, on November 9 and 10,
        1911. London, Nov. 1911.

AJ 28. Kiderlein-Wächter, Alfred von. Dispatch from His Majes-
        ty's Ambassador at Berlin Forwarding Translation of the
        Statement made by the Secretary of State of the German
        Foreign Office Before the Budget Commission of the Reich-
        stag on November 17 of the Franco-German Morocco Nego-
        tiations. London, Dec. 1911.

AJ 29. Williamson, Francis T. Germany and Morocco Before
        1905. Baltimore, 1937.

        Investigates German commercial activities and foreign
        policy in relation to Morocco.

AJ 30. Anderson, E.N. The First Moroccan Crisis 1904-1906.
        Chicago, 1930.

AJ 31. Barlow, Irma. The Agadir Crisis. 1940.

AJ 32. Albin, Pierre. La Querelle franco-allemande: le "coup"
        d'Agadir, origines et dévelopement de la crise de 1911.
        Paris, 1912.

        Favorable to France but not anti-German.

AJ 33. -- La Guerre allemande: d'Agadir à Serajevo, 1911-1914.
        Paris, 1915.

AJ 34. Hazen, C.D. Alsace-Lorraine Under German Rule. 1917.

        Gives the French point of view.

AJ 35. Weill, B. Elsass-Lothringen und der Krieg. 1914.

        Written from the German point of view.

AJ 36. 'Der Fall Zabern. Rückblick auf eine Vervassungskrise
        der Wilhelminischen Kaiserreichs,'' Welt als Geschichte.
        1963, 23(1): 27-46.

        An examination of the Zabern case of autumn 1913 and
        the crisis it provoked, including the vote of non-con-
        fidence in Bethmann-Hollweg and William II's overruling
        of the Reichstag vote in favor of the military.

AJ 37. Mortimer, Jonne Stafford. "Commercial Interest and German Diplomacy in the Agadir Crisis, " Hist. Journal. No. 3. 1967.

AK.   GERMAN-RUSSIAN RELATIONS

AK 1.   Simon, Édouard.   L'Allemagne et la Russie; Origins de leuro rapports.   Paris, 1896.

   Traces the background of German-Russian relations for the period prior to the nineteenth century.

AK 2.   Narochnitskaia, Lidiia.   Rossiia voina Prussii.   Moscow, 1960.

   Traces the relations between Russia and Prussia for the years 1855-1881.

AK 3.   Müller, Manfred.   Die Bedeutung der Berliner Kongress für die deutsch-russischen Beziehungen.   Leipzig, 1927.

AK 4.   Raschdau, Ludwig.   "D. dt.-russ. Rückversicherungsvertrag, " Grenzboden.   77 (1918).

AK 5.   "D. Ende d. dt.-russ. Rückversicherungsvertrag, " D. Rote Tag.   (Oct. 17, 1920) No. 229.

AK 6.   "D. dt.-russ. Rückversich.-Vertr. E. Entgegnt, " Grenzboden.   80 (1921).

AK 7.   Lewin, J.   "Neue russ. Dokumente über d. Ende d. Rückversicherungsvertrag, " Osteuropa.   1 (1926).

AK 8.   Raschdau, Ludwig.   "Wie die deutsch-russische 'Freundschaft' zu Ende ging, " Berliner Monatshefte.   XI (Sept. 1937): 763-771.

   The author, who was directly concerned with the non-renewal of the Reinsurance Treaty tries to minimize the importance of the Treaty and argues that Bismarck, himself, had a low opinion of it.

AK 9.   Lambsdorf, Gustav Graf von.   "Bemerkungen zum deutsch-russischen Rückversicherungsvertrag, " Berliner Monatshefte. XV (Oct. 1937): 902-906.

   Takes issue with the preceding article by Raschdau, using as evidence Lambsdorf's diaries.   Raschdau's reply appears on p. 906-908 of the same issue.

AK 10.   --   Die Militärbervollmächtigten Kaiser Wilhelm II am zarenhofe 1904-1914.   Berlin, 1937.

AK 11. Seraphim, Ernst. "Der Sturz Bismarcks und die russische Politik, " Vergangenheit und Gegenwart. XXXI (1941): 197-213.

> An analysis of the material in the Lambsdorf diaries on this subject.

AK 12. Raschdau, Ludwig. "Das Ende des deutsch-russischen Geheimsvertrages von 1887, " Berliner Monatshefte. XVII (April 1939): 361-366.

> Maintains his original position as stated in the article cited in AK 9. He also takes issue with people who believe that Bismarck had a system.

AK 13. Griainov, Serge. "The End of the Alliance of the Emperors, " American Historical Review. XXIII (Jan. 1918): 324-350.

> Based primarily on the Russian documents.

AK 14. Hartung, Fritz. "Der Deutsch-russische Rückversicherungsvertrag von 1887 und seine Kündigung, " Die Grenzboten. (1921): 12-17.

AK 15. Pürschel, Erich. "Das Ende der Rückversicherungsvertrages, " Vergangenheit und Gegenwart. XV (1925): 144-159.

AK 16. Vebersberger, Hans. "Abschluss und Ende des Rückversicherungsvertrages, " Die Kriegschuldfrage. V (Oct. 1927): 933-966.

> Based on the German documents.

AK 17. Bornhak, Conrad. "Das Rätsel der Nichterneuerung des Rückversicherungsvertrages, " Archiv für Politik und Geschichte. II (1924): 570-582.

AK 18. Frankenberg, Richard. Die Nichterneuerung der deutsch-russischen Rückversicherungsvertrages im Jahre 1890. Berlin, 1927.

AK 19. Haake, Paul. "Der neue Kurs, " Zeitschrift für Politik. XV (1925): 320-347.

> An analysis of the non-renewal of the Reinsurance Treaty.

AK 20. Krausnick, Helmut. "Botschafter Graf Hatzfeldt und die Aussenpolitik Bismarcks, " Historische Zeitschrift. CLXVII

(1942): 566-583.

A study which shows that Hatzfeldt favored close relations with Britain and Austria rather than with Russia.

AK 21. Seraphim, Ernst. "Kaiser Alexander III und Fürst Bismarck, " Vergangenheit und Gegenwart. XXX (1940): 321-
326.

A review of the German-Russian relations based chiefly
on the Lambsdorf diaries.

AK 22. Raschdau, Ludwig. Unter Bismarck und Caprivi: Erinnerungen eines deutschen Diplomaten aus den Jahren 1885-
1894. Berlin, 1938.

Memoirs of a German foreign office official who was
primarily concerned with Russian affairs.

AK 23. Saburov, Petr A. The Saburov Memoirs; or, Bismarck
and Russia; Being Fresh Light on the League of the Three
Emperors, 1881. Ed. by J.Y. Simpson. Cambridge, England, 1929.

This book is a translation of Ma Mission à Berlin
which was printed for private circulation in St. Petersburg a few months before the outbreak of the war.

AK 24. Peters, Martin. Die Meerengen und die europäischen
Grossmächte 1890-1895. Erlangen, 1932.

An analysis of the straits question and the relation of
the great powers in Europe to this problem; based on
the German documents.

AK 25. Simon, Édouard. L'Allemagne et la Russie au XIXe siècle.
Paris, 1893.

AK 26. Röhl, John C.G. "A Document of 1892 on Germany, Prussia and Poland, " Historical Journal. VII (1964): 143-149.

AK 27. Reinach, J. Le Traité de Bjoerkoe (1905), un essai d'alliance de L'Allemagne la Russie et la France. Paris, 1935.

AK 28. MacDonald, Janet L. Russo-German Relations 1909-1914.
Chicago, 1942.

AK 29. The Willy-Nicky Correspondence. Ed. by Hermann Bernstein. New York, 1919.

AK 30. Briefe und Telegramme Wilhelms II an Nikolaus II, 1894-
1914. Ed. by Helmuth von Gerlach. Wien, 1920.

AK 31. Letters from the Kaiser to the Tsar. Ed. by Isaac Don

Levine. New York, 1920.

AK 32. Kurohane, Shigeru. "Kaizeru Uiruherumu Nisei No Tai-Ro Seisaku Ni Tsuite, " Seiyô-shi-gaku. 1954, 23: 933-947.

William II's policy toward Russia 1890-1904. The author regards William II's Russian policy as the first step in the creation of his Weltpolitik.

AK 33. "K Istorii Potsdamskogo soglasheniya 1911, " Krasnyi Arkhiv. 58 (1933): 46-57.

Valuable material on the Potsdam Conference and on German-Russian relations in regard to Persia.

AK 34. "Das Deutsche-russische Übereinkommen, " Alldeutsche Blätter. 20 (1910): 410.

German-Russian relations in regard to Persia.

AK 35. Reventlow, H. "Der Besuch des Zaren in Potsdam, " Alldeutsche Blätter. 20 (1910): 410.

German-Russian relations in relation to Persia.

AK 36. "Deutschlands wirtschaftliche Interessen in Persien und die russische Konkurrenz, " Export. 31 (1909): 642.

German economic interest in Persia and the attempts of Russian competition.

AK 37. Die Beziehungen Russlands zu Persien. Leipzig, 1903.

Written by a retired Prussian general of Russophile inclinations; much material on the German-Russian rivalry in Persia.

AK 38. Chirol, Valentine. Germany and the Fear of Russia. London, 1914.

AK 39. Grimm, Claus. Graf Witte und die deutsche Politik. Freiburg, 1930.

A doctoral dissertation based on the Russian materials but adding little not already known from the German documents.

AK 40. Hausser, Oswald. Deutschland und der englische-russische Gegensatz 1900-1914. Göttingen, 1958.

AK 41. Schüssler, Wilhelm. Deutschland zwischen Russland und England; Studien zur Aussenpolitik des Bismarckischen Reiches 1879-1914. Leipzig, 1940.

AK 42. Klein, Alfred. Der Einfluss auf die deutsch-russischen Beziehungen. Münster, 1931.

AK 43. Mitrofanoff, P. von. "Offener Briefe über das Verhältnis

von Russland und Deutschland, " Preussische Jahrbücher.

CLVI (June 1914): 385-398.

AK 44. Namier, Lewis B. Germany and Eastern Europe. London,

1915.

AK 45. Pourtalès, Friedrich. Meine letzten Verhandlungen in St.

Petersburg, Ende Juli, 1914; Tagesaufzeichnungen und

Dokumente. Berlin, 1927.

> Pourtalès was the German ambassador to Russia at the
> outbreak of the First World War. In this book, which
> includes his diary and other documents, he gives his
> rendition of the events that took place in St. Peters-
> burg during the last years before the war. An earlier
> edition published in 1919 under the title Am Scheide-
> wege zwischen Krieg und Frieden does not contain the
> author's official correspondence.

AK 46. Roloff, Gustav. Deutschland und Russland im Widerstreit

seit 200 Jahren. Stuttgart, 1914.

> Traces the development of the struggle between Russia
> and Germany for the 200 years prior to the First
> World War.

AK 47. Trampe, Gustav. "Elemente der deutsch-russische Bezie-

hungen, " Politische Studien. 1962, 13(144): 430-434.

> A summary of German-Russian relations since Bis-
> marck's fall, which points out that Russian distrust of
> Germany began during his chancellorship.

AK 48. Willkowski, G. Die Deutsch-russisches Handelsbeziehungen

in den letzten 150 Jahre. Berlin, 1947.

AK 49. Zug, Josef. Versuche der Wierannäherung an Russland

unter Reichskanzler Fürst Chlodwig zu Hohenlohe-Schillings-

fürst. Rottenburg, 1934.

> A dissertation in which is found a useful analysis of
> German-Russian relations in the years 1895-1898.

AK 50. Laqueur, Walter Z. Russia and Germany; a Century of

Conflict. London, 1965.

AL.   GERMAN-ENGLISH RELATIONS

   See also: L 38-53.

AL 1.   Schenk, Willy. Die Deutsch-englische Rivalität vor dem
        ersten Weltkrieg in der Sicht deutscher Historiker: Mis-
        sverstehen oder Machtstreben? Aarau, 1967.

        Reviews the writings of a number of leading Wilhelmian
        historians in light of whether the German-English rival-
        ry was more a hegemonial struggle for power or a fate-
        ful misunderstanding.

AL 2.   Benson, E.F. The Kaiser and English Relations. New
        York, 1936.

        A general survey of the part the Kaiser played in Ger-
        man relations with England. It does not go into the
        subject in any great depth.

AL 3.   Cramb, John Adam. Germany and England. 1914.

AL 4.   Pribram, A.F. England and the International Policy of the
        European Great Powers 1871-1914. Oxford, 1931.

        A series of lectures giving an excellent factual and
        interpretative account.

AL 5.   Schmitt, Bernadotte. England and Germany 1740-1914.
        Princeton, 1916.

        Pro-English and in favor of American alliance. The
        war was the outcome of German efforts to upset the
        European balance of power.

AL 6.   Bismarck's Relations with England. Ed. by E.T.S. Dug-
        dale. 1929.

        Translations of diplomatic documents.

AL 7.   Ritter, Gerhard. Bismarcks Verhältnis zu England und die
        Politik des 'neuen Kurses." Berlin, 1924.

        One of the keenest analyses of the Anglo-German prob-
        lem.

AL 8.   Krausnick, Helmut. "Botschafter Graf Hatzfeldt und die
        Aussenpolitik Bismarcks," Historische Zeitschrift. CLXVI
        (1942): 566-583.

        A careful study which points out that Hatzfeldt favored
        close relations with England and Austria rather than
        with Russia.

AL 9.   Moeller, Richard. "Bismarcks Bündnisangebot an England vom Januar 1889, " Historische Vierteljahrschrift. XXXI (1938): 507-527.

> The author is of the opinion that the alliance offer of 1889 was not intended to be taken literally by the English.

AL 10. Schüssler, Wilhelm. Deutschland zwischen Russland und England. Leipzig, 1940.

> A series of essays on relations with Russia and England. One essay is concerned with the problem of the 1889 alliance offer. The author takes issue with the preceding book by Moeller. Contains a discerning study of the negotiations of 1898-1901.

AL 11. Moeller, Richard. "Noch einmal Bismarcks Bündnisangebot an England vom Januar 1889, " Historische Zeitschrift. CLXIII (1941): 100-113.

> The author's reply to Schüssler's comments on his earlier book listed above.

AL 12. Schüssler, Wilhelm. "Noch einmal Bismarck zwischen England und Russland 1889, " Historische Zeitschrift. CLXIII (1941): 547-553.

> The author maintains his original opinion given in AL 10. He does, however, give some credence to the force of Moeller's arguments.

AL 13. Beazley, Raymond. "Britain and Germany in the Salisbury Era 1890-1892, " Berliner Monatshefte. (Oct. 1934): 839-852.

AL 14. Sontag, Raymond. Germany and England; Background of the Conflict 1848-1894. New York, 1938.

AL 15. Bayer, Theodore A. England und der neue Kurs 1890-1895; auf Grund unveröffentlicher Akten. Tübingen, 1955.

AL 16. Israel, Ludwig. England und der orientalische Dreibund 1887-1896. Stuttgart, 1938.

> A study which analyzes all phases of the Mediterranean situation and Britain's relationship to the Mediterranean agreements.

AL 17. "Englische Machenschaften gegen den deutschen Handel am Persischen Golf, " Deutsche Levante Zeitung. (1915): 311-312.

> German-English competition in Persia.

AL 18. Wagner, R. "Deutschland und England am Persischen
Golf, " Deutsche Kolonialzeitung. XVIII (1901): 431-432.

AL 19. Aydelotte, William O. Bismarck and British Colonial Policy; The Problem of South West Africa 1883-1885. Philadelphia, 1937.

AL 20. Beazley, Raymond. "Das Deutsche Kolonialreich, Gross-
britannien und die Verträge von 1890, " Berliner Monatshefte.
(May 1931): 444-458.
A general discussion of the Anglo-German colonial problem in 1890.

AL 21. Sell, Manfred. Das Deutsch-englische Abkommen von 1890
über Helgoland und die Afrik Kolonien im Lichte der deutschen Presse. Berlin, 1926.
A useful doctoral dissertation, stressing the factor of
public opinion in connection with Helgoland Treaty.

AL 22. Jantzen, Günther. Ostafrika in der deutsch-englischen Politik, 1884-1890. Hamburg, 1934.
The author goes over the Anglo-German relationship in
great detail making use of some unpublished material,
especially the papers of the German East African Association.

AL 23. Schwarze, Fritz. Das Deutsch-englische Abkommen über
die Portugiesischen Kolonien vom 30 August 1898. Göttingen, 1931.

AL 24. Convention and Declaration Between The United Kingdom
and Germany for the Settlement of the Samoan and Other
Questions; Signed at London, November 14, 1899; Ratification Exchanged at London and Berlin, February 16, 1900.
London, 1900.

AL 25. Springborn, Arnold. Englands Stellung zur deutschen Welt
und Kolonialpolitik in den Jahren, 1911-1914. Leipzig,
1939.

AL 26. Wingeroth, Carl G. Deutscher und englischer "Imperialismus" vor dem Weltkrieg. Bottrop, 1934.
Compares and contrasts the British and German conceptions of imperialism and its effects on international
trade and international relations.

AL 27. Banze, Angelika. Die Deutsche-englische Wirtschaftsrival-

ität; ein Beitrag zur Geschichte der deutsch-englischen
Beziehungen 1897-1907.   Berlin, 1935.

>An analysis which tends to minimize the importance of
>trade rivalry.

AL 28. Hoffmann, Ross J. S.   Great Britain and the German Trade
Rivalry 1871-1914.   Philadelphia, 1933.

>An excellent piece of work. The author gives a wealth
>of statistical material, but also studies the movement
>of opinion.

AL 29. Franke, Bruno W.   "Handelsneid und grosse Politik in den
englisch-deutschen Beziegungen, 1871-1914, " Zeitschrift für
Politik.   XXIX (1938): 455-475.

>Chiefly a critique of the Hoffmann book which the author
>thinks exaggerates the importance of trade rivalry be-
>tween England and Germany.

AL 30. Grabowsky, Adolf.   "Der Primat der Aussenpolitik, " Zeitschrift für Politik.   XVII (1928).

>The author is of the opinion that Anglo-German friction
>did not result from economic rivalry.

AL 31. Marti, Oscar A.   The Anglo-German Commercial and Colonial Rivalry as a Cause of the War.   Thesis presented at
Univ. of Southern Calif., Los Angeles, 1917.

AL 32. Bittner, Ludwig.   "Österreich-Ungarn und die deutsch-
englischen Bündnisverhandlungen im Frühjahr 1898, " Festschrift für Heinrich Srbik.   Munich, 1938.

>Adduces Austrian diplomatic reports which tend to show
>that Salisbury favored the planned agreement with Ger-
>many and that the entire British Cabinet supported
>Chamberlain.

AL 33. Garvin, J. L.   The Life of Joseph Chamberlain.   3 v. London, 1933.

>Volume 3 is an important source on the Anglo-German
>negotiations of 1898.

AL 34. Pick, Fritz.   "Das Deutsch-englische Bündnis, " Preussische
Jahrbücher.   (Jan. 1935): 56-65.

>A discussion of the third volume of Garvin's biography
>of Chamberlain.

AL 35. Roloff, Gustav.   "Die Englische-deutschen Bündnisverhand-
lung im Jahre 1898, " Berliner Monatshefte.   XIII (Oct.

1935): 849-876.

This article reviews relations with England in the light of British documents and the biography of Chamberlain by Garvin; concludes that Salisbury was basically opposed to the Chamberlain policy.

AL 36. Beazley, Raymond. "Joseph Chamberlain and die englisch-deutsch Beziehungen im Jahre 1898, " Berliner Monatshefte. XIII (Dec. 1935): 1011-1032.

Primarily a review of Garvin's biography of Chamberlain.

AL 37. Tümmler, Hans. "Die Deutsch-englischen Bündnisverhandlungen um die Jahrhundertwende 1898-1901, " Vergangenheit und Gegenwart. XXVIII (1938): 617-634.

A Nazi re-interpretation of the subject, drawing on the Garvin biography to demonstrate the ruinous policy of Bülow and Holstein.

AL 38. Jaenecke, W. A. Britisches Bündnisspiel um die Jahrhundertwende. Berlin, 1941.

A Nazi commentary on the failure of the Anglo-German negotiations.

AL 39. Rosen, Friedrich. "Die Deutsch-englischen Bündnisverhandlungen des Jahres 1898, " Berliner Monatshefte. (March 1934): 192-207.

AL 40. Löding, Walter. Die Deutsch-englischen Bündnisverhandlungen 1898 bis 1901. Hamburg, 1929.

AL 41. Pückler, Karl Graf von. Aus Meinem Diplomatenleben. Schweidnitz, 1934.

Contains some interesting material on Anglo-German relations in 1900.

AL 42. Thimme, Friedrich. "Der Ausklang der deutsch-englischen Bündnisverhandlungen 1901, nach Briefen des Botschafters Graf Wolff Metternich, " Berliner Monatshefte. XVI (June 1938).

Comments on the published British documents.

AL 43. Ritter, Gerhard. Die Legende von der verschmächten englischen Freundschaft 1898-1901. Freiburg, 1929.

Ritter used British and German documents and argues that the British offers were never concrete enough to lead to anything.

AL 44. Meinecke, Friedrich. Geschichte des deutsch-englischen

Bündnisproblems 1890-1901. Munich, 1927.

A good monograph on the subject.

AL 45. Becker, Otto. Deutsche-Literaturzeitung. (L): 903-925.

A review of the two preceding books of Meinecke and
Ritter. A penetrating and illuminating discussion of
the two conflicting views with regard to the alliance
negotiations.

AL 46. Kehr, Eckart. "Das Deutsch-englische Bündnisproblem der

Jahrhundertwende, " Die Gesellschaft. (July 1929); 24 31.

Elaborates the idea tentatively put forward by Meinecke
in AL 44 that the fundamental reason for the failure of
the negotiations was the objection of certain social
classes in Germany to any connection with England.

AL 47. Lehmann, Konrad. "Die Ablehnung des englischen Bündnis-

antrags, 1898-1901, " Preussische Jahrbücher. (Aug. 1930):

162-183.

Follows Meinecke's viewpoint.

AL 48. Mowat, R.B. "Great Britain and Germany in the Early

Twentieth Century, " English Historical Review. XLVI

(July 1931): 423-441.

A general survey of the period 1898-1914.

AL 49. Ehringhaus, Fritz. "Die Ergebnisse der englischen Akten

über die deutsch-englischen Bündnisverhandlungen 1899-

1901, " Vergangenheit und Gegenwart. XIX (1929): 471-480.

Very revisionary.

AL 50. Walter, Heinrich. "Die Deutsch-englischen Bündnisverhand-

lungen von 1906 und ihre Ergebnisse, " Historische Vier-

teljahrschrift. XXV (1931): 602-635.

AL 51. Löding, Walter. Die Deutsch-englischen Bündnisverhand-

lungen 1898-1901. Ihr Verlauf auf Grund der deutschen und

englischen Akten. Hamburg, 1929.

AL 52. Mecenseffey, Grete. "Die deutsch-englisch Bündnisverhand-

lungen 1898-1901 im Lichte der englischen Akten-publika-

tion, " Vierteljahrschrift für Politik und Geschichte. (1929):

175-191.

AL 53. Wolf, Marie-Luise. Botschafter Graf Hatzfeldt; seine Tätig-

keit in London 1885-1901. Speyer, 1935.

AL 54. Frauendienst, Werner.   "Deutschland und England an der
Jahrhundertwende; mit unveröffentlichen Dokumenten aus
dem Nachlass des Botschafters Grafen Paul von Hatzfeld, "
Berliner Monatshefte.   XVI (Dec. 1939): 970-988.

> Extracts from Hatzfeldt's papers to show Germany's
> readiness for an alliance with England.

AL 55. Salomon, Felix.   "Die Englisch-deutschen Bündnisverhandlungen von 1898-1901 im Weltpolitischen Zusammhang, "
Der Grenzboten.   (Aug. 29, 1920): 200-214.

AL 56. Bartstra, J.S.   Twaalf Jaren "Vrije-Hands-Politiek 1890-
1902. " Leiden, n.d.

> A sound study of German policy.

AL 57. Dittmar, Gustav.   Die Deutsch-englischen Beziehung in den
Jahren 1898-1899; die Vorbesprechunger zu den Bündnisverhandlungen von 1900-1901.   Stuttgart, 1938.

AL 58. Dreyer, Johannes.   Deutschland und England in ihrer Politik und Presse im Jahre 1901.   Berlin, 1934.

AL 59. Huene-Hoeningen, Heinrich von.   Untersuchungen zur Geschichte der deutsch-englischen Beziehungen 1898-1901.
Breslau, 1934.

AL 60. Johnson, E.N. and J.D. Bickford.   "The Contemplated
Anglo-German Alliance of 1890-1901, " Political Science
Quarterly.   XLII (March 1927): 1-57.

> One of the best treatments in English covering the at-
> tempts for an Anglo-German alliance in the years
> 1890-1901.

AL 61. Krausnick, Helmut.   "Holstein und das deutsch-englische
Verhältnis von 1890-1901, " Internationales Jahrbuch für
Geschichtsunterricht.   (1951): 141 ff.

AL 62. Monger, G.W.   "The End of Isolation: Britain, Germany
and Japan 1900-1902, " Transactions of the Royal Historical
Society.   XIII (1963): 103-121.

AL 63. Penson, Lillian M.   "The New Course in British Foreign
Policy 1892-1902, " Transactions of the Royal Historical
Society.   Series IV, v. XXV (1945): 121-139.

> An analysis of the process by which Britain drifted
> away from the Triple Alliance.

AL 64. Sargent, Charles William. Efforts Toward Anglo-German
        Reconciliation 1898-1901. 1951. Master's thesis, Mich.
        State Univ., East Lansing, Mich.

        The author failed to use most of the important mater-
        ials on the subject.

AL 65. Thomas, Arnold W. German Ambitions as They Affect
        Britain and The United States of America. London, 1903.

AL 66. Frauendienst, Werner. "Deutsche Weltpolitik; zur Prob-
        lematik der Wilhelminischen Reich, " Welt als Geschichte.
        1959, 19(1): 1-39.

        Discussion of the world policy of Germany after Bis-
        marck. Treats Anglo-German relations which the
        author calls a kind of a "cold war" from which World
        War I emerged. The three major zones of German-
        English rivalry were commercial, colonial, and naval.

AL 67. Rachfahl, Felix. Die Deutsche Aussenpolitik in der Wil-
        helminischen Ära. Berlin, 1924.

        The author argues that Bismarck's successors continued
        his policy of rapprochement with England.

AL 68. Cook, Sir Edward T. How Britain Strove for Peace; a
        Record of Anglo-German Negotiations 1898-1914 told from
        Authoritative Sources. London, 1914.

AL 69. Voegtle, Erich. Die Englische Diplomatie und die deutsche
        Presse 1898-1914. Würzburg, 1936.

AL 70. Hock, Walter. "Der Ursprung des deutsch-englischen Ge-
        gensatzes und die Lehren des Weltkrieges, " Archiv für Pol-
        itik und Geschichte. (March & May, 1923).

AL 71. Becker, Willy. Fürst Bülow und England 1897-1909.
        Greifswald, 1929.

AL 72. Erdbrügger, Hermann W. England, Deutschland und die
        zweite Haager Friedenskonferenz 1907. Leipzig, 1935.

AL 73. Eschenburg, Th. "Die Daily Telegraph-Affäre; Nach unver-
        öff; Dokumenten, " Preussische Jahrbücher. 214 (1928).

AL 74. Kühlmann, Richard von. Erinnerungen. Heidelberg, 1948.

        The memoirs of an important official in the colonial
        section of the foreign office. He was also counsellor
        in London, 1909-1914.

AL 75. Meyer-Adams, Rudolf. Die Mission Haldanes im Februar

1912 in Spiegel der deutschen Presse. 1935.

AL 76. Sarolea, Charles. Anglo-German Problems. London, 1912.
A bitter attack on German military build-up by a Belgian professor at Edinburgh University. He forcasts the war.

AL 77. Hauser, Oswald. Deutschland und der englisch-russische Gegensatz 1900-1914. Göttingen, 1958.

AL 78. Hoyos, Graf Alexander von. Der Deutsch-englische Gegensatz und sein Einfluss auf die Balkanpolitik Österreich-Ungarns. Berlin, 1922.

AL 79. England on the Witness Stand: the Anglo-German Case Tried by a Jury of Englishmen. New York, 1915.

AL 80. Spies, Heinrich. Deutschlands Feind: England und die Vorgeschichte der Weltkrieges. Berlin, 1915.

AL 81. Kordt, Erich. Nicht aus den Akten. Stuttgart, 1950.

AL 82. Kavanagh-Boulger, Demetrius Charles de. England's Arch-Enemy; a Collection of Essays Forming an Indictment of German Policy During the Last Sixteen Years. London, 1914.

AL 83. Reventlow, Ernst Graf zu. England der Feind. Stuttgart, 1914.

AL 84. -- Der Vampire des Festlandes; eine Darstellung der englischen Politik nach ihren Triebkraften, Mitteln und Wirkungen. Berlin, 1915. Eng. trans., The Vampire of the Continent. New York, 1916.

AL 85. Jagow, G. von. "Die Deutsche politische Leitung und England bei Kriegsausbruch, " Prussische Jahrbücher. 213 (1928).

AM.   COLONIAL--BIBLIOGRAPHIES

Background to sources

It is difficult to separate certain aspects of German colonial policy from German foreign policy; one is the appendage of the other. Jon Bridgman and David E. Clarke, in their introduction to

German Africa (AM 3), point out that "an understanding of the structure of German colonial administration greatly facilitates the finding of desired information.

"When Bismarck acquired the colonial empire in 1883-1884, he envisaged a very simple form of colonial administration in which the chartered companies would perform most of the administrative work. This arrangement soon proved inadequate, and the government had to take over the administration of the territories. From 1884 to his resignation in 1890, Bismarck, with the assistance of a few members of the Foreign Office, improvised the regulation of colonial affairs. In 1890 a new section of the Foreign Office, the Kolonialabteilung, was set up and charged with the responsibility for colonial affairs. It was empowered to prepare memoranda, give advice to missionaries and settlers, draft regulations, do preliminary work on the budget, and publish an official journal, the Kolonialblatt. The Kolonialblatt contained reports of missionaries, troop commanders, heads of expeditions, and explorers together with a wealth of statistical information. Publication of this journal continued without a break even when, on May 17, 1907, the Kolonialabteilung was replaced by a separate agency, the Kolonialamt.

"Besides the Kolonialabteilung, a Kolonialrat was established in 1890; it consisted at first of twenty, and later of forty, government members, chosen by the chancellor for their knowledge of, or interest in, colonial affairs. The chancellor summoned this group twice a year to advise him on colonial policy, and information about the meetings was published in the Kolonialblatt. The Kolonialrat was abolished in 1908. In addition to the Kolonialblatt, the Kolonialabteilung and its successor the Kolonialamt published the following: the Mitteilungen aus den deutschen Schutzgebieten, which contained scholarly and technical reports on such matters as rainfall, soil, climate, native customs, and flora and fauna; the Ergänzungshefte (supplements to the Kolonialblatt), which appeared at irregular intervals and generally included lengthy reports on scientific expeditions; the Medizinal-Berichte über die deutschen Schutzgebiete; a series of monographs entitled Veröffentlichungen des Reichskolonialamts; and many books and pamphlets.

"The publications of the legislative branch of the government

also contain much information on the colonies.   The stenographic
reports of the Reichstag debates give a complete record of all the
debates on colonial questions, and the Anlagebände have such items
as committee reports, texts of treaties, consular reports, and texts
of proposed laws.   Until 1900, these volumes also included the colonial budget, but after 1900 the budget is to be found in a separate
volume, the Haushalts-Etats für die Schutzgebiete.   All laws, orders,
and treaties pertaining to the colonies and the colonial empire were
brought together in two volumes of a semiofficial publication, the
Deutsche Kolonial-Gesetzgebung.

"The most important nongovernmental colonial agency was the
deutsche Kolonialgesellschaft.   This was formed in 1884 by the fus-
ing of two earlier agencies.   It met annually, and the proceedings
of its meetings appeared in its own periodical, the Kolonialzeitung.
As a rule this was a weekly publication, but sometimes it appeared
less frequently.   In 1899 the Kolonialgesellschaft began to publish
the Beiträge zur Kolonialpolitik und Kolonialwirtschaft, in which appeared articles of a more scholarly sort.   The Kolonialwirtschaftliches Komitee, the economic committee of the Kolonialgesellschaft,
published occasional monographs, its own journal (the Tropenpflanzer), and the annual Kolonial-Handels-Adressbuch.   This last publication listed the names and addresses of officials, traders, and
other people of importance in each of the colonies.

"Among the several colonial institutes in Germany, perhaps the
most important was the Hamburg Kolonialinstitut, which published a
scholarly series of monographs.   The student of the German colonies may need to refer to publications by other departments of the
Imperial government, such as the Statistisches Jahrbuch für das
deutsche Reich, published by the Statistisches Reichsamt, and the
Berichte über Handel und Industrie or the Deutsches Handelsarchiv,
both published by the Reichsamt des Innern. "

Bibliography

AM 1.   Austin, O. P.   Colonial Administration, 1800-1900.   Wash-
        ington, 1901.

AM 2.   Bielschowsky, Ludwig.   List of Books in German on South

Africa and South West Africa Published up to 1914, in the South Africa Public Library, Cape Town. Cape Town, 1949.

AM 3.   Bridgman, Jon, and David E. Clarke. German Africa; A Select Annotated Bibliography. Stanford, 1965.

A bibliography of the materials in the Hoover Institute on the subject of the German colonies in Africa. It is especially good for the literature of the Weimar and Nazi period. About one-third of the 907 items listed pertain to the pre-1914 period. The other two-thirds are concerned with the movement to regain Germany's lost colonies after World War I.

AM 4.   Brose, Maximilian. Die Deutsche Kolonialliteratur von 1884-1895. Berlin, 1897.

Lists many articles.

AM 5.   -- Die Deutsche Kolonialliteratur im Jahre 1896-1913. 18 v. Berlin, 1897-1914.

AM 6.   Charnyi, I.S. "Zapadnogermanskaia Publisistika i Istoriograffia o Kolonal noi politke Kaiserovskoi Germanii, " Novaia i Noveishia Istoriia. 1965, 9(1): 115-121.

The author has written an historiographical discussion, dealing with works written after 1952, of West German historical treatment of German colonial policy prior to World War I.

AM 7.   Die Deutsche Kolonialliteratur im Jahre 1901-1908. Berlin, 1908.

AM 8.   Deutsche Kolonien; ein Bücherverzeichnis. Leipzig, 1939.

AM 9.   Dietzel, Karl Heinrich. Die Deutschen Kolonien; eine historischgeographische Darstellung ihres Werdens und Wesens. Leipzig, 1935.

AM 10. Gunzenhäuser, Max. Bibliographie zur Aussenpolitik und Kolonialpolitik des deutschen Reichs, 1871-1914. Stuttgart, 1943.

AM 11. Koloniales Schrifttum in Deutschland. 1941. Pub. by Kolonialpolitische Amt der NSDAP.

AM 12. Kolonien in deutschen Schrifttum. 1936. Pub. by Reichskolonialbund.

AN. COLONIAL--HANDBOOKS, ANNUALS, LEXICONS, ATLASES,
      ETC.

AN 1.   Budget of the German Protectorates.   Berlin.   Annual.

AN 2.   Fitzner, R.   Deutsches Kolonial-Handbuch.

AN 3.   Kolonial Handbuch.   Berlin.   Issued annually by T.   Mensch
        and T. Hellmann.

AN 4.   Kolonial Rundschau.   Berlin.   Annual.

AN 5.   Meinecke, G.   Koloniales Jahrbuch.

AN 6.   Schneider, Karl.   Jahrbuch über die deutschen Kolonien.

AN 7.   Henoch, H.   Süsserotts illustrierter Kolonial-Kalender.

AN 8.   Herfurth, A.   Deutscher Kolonial-Kalender und statistisches
        Handbuch.

AN 9.   Deutscher Kolonial-Kalender.   Berlin.   Annual.

AN 10. Kolonialpraxis; Handbuch für Kaufleute, Industrielle, Banken,
        Behörden und Kapitalisen.   Berlin, 1911.

AN 11. Langhams, P.   Deutschlands Kolonial Atlas.   Gotha, 1895.

AN 12. Deutsches Kolonialatlas.   Berlin, 1936.

AN 13. Wirtschaftsatlas der deutschen Kolonien.   Berlin, 1906.

AN 14. Handwörterbuch des Grenz und Ausslanddeutschtums.   3 v.
        Breslau, 1933.
        Of some bibliographical value.

AN 15. Deutsches Kolonial Lexikon.   Ed. by Heinrich Schnee.
        3 v.   Leipzig, 1920.
        Schnee was the former governor of East Africa. This
        work, completed in 1914 and published unchanged after
        the war, represents the combined efforts of eighty ex-
        perts and was designed to furnish information of every
        description about all of the German colonies. It con-
        tains valuable photographs, maps, and diagrams.

AN 16. Die Deutschen Schutzgebiete in Afrika und der Südsee.   Hrg.
        von Reichskolonialamt.   Issued annually.

AN 17. Deutsche Kolonial-Gesetzgebung.
        A collection of treaties, laws, and instructions for the
        German colonies published during the years 1884-1909.

AO.   COLONIAL--PERIODICALS, INCLUDING ANNUAL PERIODI-
      CALS AND THEIR SUPPLEMENTS

AO 1.   Abhandlungen. Pub. by Kolonialinstitut, Hamburg, 1910-
        1921, irregular. 43 v. in 15.

        Concerned with various aspects of life in the colonies,
        language, and many other topics. Superseded by Ab-
        handlungen aus dem Gebiet der Auslandskunde.

AO 2.   Afrika; Monatschrift für die sittliche und soziale Entwick-
        lung der deutschen Schutzgebiete. Bielefeld, 1894-1912.
        Monthly. Pub. by Evangelischer Afrika-Verein.

AO 3.   Afrika und Übersee; Sprachen, Kulturen. Berlin, 1910 ff.
        Irregular.

AO 4.   Beitrage zur Kolonialpolitik und Kolonialwirtschaft. (Berlin,
        July 1899-Dec. 1903). Pub. by Der Deutsche Kolonialgesell-
        schaft.

AO 5.   Bericht über das Studienjahr. Hamburg, 1908/9 ff. An-
        nual. Pub. by Kolonialinstitut.

AO 6.   Deutsch-Ostafrikanische Zeitung; mit den Gratisbeilagen
        amtlicher Anzeiger für Deutsch-Ostafrika. (Dar-es-Salam).
        Semiweekly.

AO 7.   Das Deutsche Kolonialblatt. 1880 ff. Pub. by the colonial
        administration in Germany.

        Contains many official documents.

AO 8.   Deutsches Kolonialblatt; Amtsblatt des Reichskolonialamtes.
        Berlin, 1890-1921. Semimonthly.

        Earlier titles: 1890-1904, Amtsblatt für die Schutz-
        gebiete des Deutschen Reichs; 1905-1918, Amtsblatt für
        die Schutzgebiete in Afrika und in der Südsee. An of-
        ficial publication of the colonial office containing reports
        from officials and the proceedings of the Kolonialrat.

AO 9.   Deutsche Kolonialzeitung. Berlin, 1884-1942. Organ der
        Deutschen Kolonialgesellschaft. 1884-1887. Semimonthly;
        1888-1914, weekly; 1915-1942, monthly.

AO 10. Deutsche Monatschrift für Kolonialpolitik und Kolonisation.
        Charlottenburg, 1903-1905. 3 v. First 2 v. issued under
        title Nordafrika.

AO 11. Die Deutschen Schutzgebiete in Afrika und der Südsee.

Colonial--Periodicals   291

Berlin, 1891 ff. Annual. Pub. by Reichskolonialamt.

Earlier titles: 1891-1892, Entwicklung unserer Kolonien; 1906/07, Jahresbericht über die Entwicklung der
deutschen Schutzgebiete; 1908/09, Denkschrift über die
Entwicklung der Schutzgebiete in Afrika und der Südsee.
Appeared throughout as supplement to Deutsches Kolonialblatt, 1909/10-1912/13.

AO 12. Export: Organ des Centralvereins für Handelsgeographie
und Förderung Deutscher Interessen im Ausland. 1879 ff.

AO 13. Globus: Illustrierte Zeitschrift für Länder-und Völkerkunde
mit Besonderer Berücksichtigung der Anthropologie und
Ethnologie. 1862 ff. Bi-weekly.

This work contains information dealing with all parts
of the world.

AO 14. Koloniale Abhandlungen. Berlin, 1906 ff.

AO 15. Kolonial-Handels-Adressbuch. Berlin, 1897 ff. Annual.

Pub. by Kolonial-Wirtschaftlichen Komitee.

For the years 1898-1909 these supplementary volumes
to the Deutsches Kolonialblatt give the official report
of the colonial office, which was submitted to the
Reichstag each year. These reports contain an account of each colony's development, together with numerous statistics. Before 1898 they were included in
the Anlagebände of the Verhandlungen des Reichstag.
After 1908 the official reports are included in Die
Deutschen Schutzgebiete in Afrika und der Südsee.

AO 16. Koloniales Jahrbuch. Berlin, 1888-1898.

AO 17. Koloniale Monatsblätter; Zeitschrift für Kolonialpolitik, Kolonialrecht und Kolonialwirtschaft. Berlin, 1899-1914.

Monthly. Pub. by Deutschen Kolonialgesellschaft.

Earlier titles: Koloniales Jahrbuch; Beiträge zur Kolonialpolitik und Kolonialwirtschaft, 1899-1911.

AO 18. Kolonial-politische Korrespondenz Gesellschaft für deutsche
Kolonisation; Deutsch-Ostafrikanische Gesellschaft. Berlin,
1885-1887.

AO 19. Koloniale Rundschau; Monatschrift für die Interessen unserer
Schutzgebiete und ihrer Bewohner. Berlin, 1909-1941.
Monthly.

AO 20. Kolonie und Heimat; die deutsche Koloniale Bilderzeitung.
Munich, 1914 ff. Monthly.

AO 21. Koloniale Zeitschrift. Leipzig-Vienna, 1899-1919.

AO 22. Medizinal-Berichte über die deutschen Schutzgebiete. Berlin, 1903 ff. Annual.

Official report of Reichskolonialamt.

AO 23. Mitteilungen aus den deutschen Schutzgebieten. Berlin, 1889-1929. Annual.

Official report of Reichskolonialamt.

AO 24. Ergänzungshefte. Berlin, 1909-1920. Pub. by Kolonialamt.

A supplement to Mitteilungen aus den deutschen Schutzgebieten. Contains many reports of exploratory expeditions.

AO 25. Mitteilungen der Afrikanischen Gesellschaft in Deutschland. Berlin, 1878-1889.

AO 26. Mitteilungen für das Ausland. Hamburg, 1914 ff. Irregular.

AO 27. Mitteilungen von Forschungsreisenden und Gelehrten aus den deutschen Schutzgebieten. 1888 ff.

Contains many detailed reports of German explorers, and excellent descriptions of conditions in German colonies.

AO 28. Neue Allgemeine Missionszeitschrift. Berlin, 1874-1939. Monthly.

AO 29. Der Tropenpflanzer. 1897 ff.

AO 30. Über Land und Meer. Stuttgart, 1858-1923.

AO 31. Veröffentlichungen. Jena, 1911-1917. 9 v. in 10. Pub. by Kolonialamt.

Various monographs concerned with colonial questions.

AO 32. Zeitschrift für Ethnologie. Berlin, 1869-1944. Braunschweig, 1950 ff. Pub. as organ of Berliner Gesellschaft für Anthropologie, Ethnologie und Urgeschichte.

Suspended with Bd. 74 in 1944 and revived in 1950 (Bd. 75) as the organ of the Deutsche Gesellschaft für Völkerkunde.

AO 33. Zeitschrift für Kolonialpolitik.

AO 34. Zeitschrift für Volkskunde. Stuttgart, 1891-1940. Annual. Pub. 1891-1929 with title Zeitschrift des Vereins für Völkerkunde.

AP.   COLONIAL--GENERAL

AP 1.   Ascher, Abraham.   "Imperialists Within German Social
        Democracy Prior to 1914," Journal of Central European
        Affairs.   20(4): 397-422.
                   A detailed description of two groups of apoligists of
                   imperialism which emerged within the SPD.   The lead-
                   ing figures were Richard Calwer (1868-1927), Max
                   Schippel (1859-1928), and Gerhard Hildebrand.   Based
                   on SPD documents and writings.

AP 2.   Alype, Pierre.   La Provocation allemande aux colonies.
        Paris, 1915.

AP 3.   Andler, Charles Philippe Theodore.   Le Pangermanisme
        colonial sous Guillaume II.   Paris, 1916.
                   A collection of documents translated from German
                   which traces the influence of the Pan-German move-
                   ment on German colonial ambitions.

AP 4.   Baltzer, F.   Die Kolonialbahnen mit besonderer Berück-
        sichtigung Afrikas.   Berlin, 1916.

AP 5.   Barth C.G.   Unsere Schutzgebiete nach ihren wirtschaft-
        lichen Verhältnissen.   Leipzig, 1910.

AP 6.   Bast, Wilhelm.   Die Einfuhr des deutschen Reiches auf den
        Tropen, 1897-1932; eine handelsgeographische Untersuchung.
        Leipzig, 1936.

AP 7.   Bostian, Adolf.   Zwei Wörte über Colonial-Weisheit von
        Jemandem, dem dieselbe versagt ist.   Berlin, 1883.

AP 8.   Die Baumwollfrage; Denkschrift über Production und Ver-
        brauch von Baumwolle; Massnahmen gegen die Baumwollnot.
        Jena, 1911.

AP 9.   Der Baumwollbau in den deutschen Schutzgebieten; seine Ent-
        wicklung seit dem Jahre 1910.   Jena, 1914.

AP 10. Becker, Otto.   "Zu Bismarcks Kolonialpolitik," Berliner
        Monatshefte.   XVII (1939): 239-255.
                   A critique of A.J.P. Taylor's Germany's First Bid for
                   Colonies, and less thoroughly of other literature of the
                   1930's.   See also: AP 159.

AP 11. Besson, Maurice.   Les Colonies allemandes et leur valeur.
        Paris, 1919.

A history of German colonization and administration.

AP 12. Blum, Otto, and Erick Giese. <u>Wie erschliessen wir un-</u>
<u>sere Kolonien</u>? Berlin, 1907.

An investigation of the transportation facilities in the
colonies, with recommendations for improvements,
particularly for railroad construction.

AP 13. Bonn, Moritz J. <u>Die Neugestaltung unserer Kolonialen</u>
<u>Aufgaben</u>. Tübingen, 1911.

A speech describing the colonial reforms instituted by
Dernburg.

AP 14. -- <u>Nationale Kolonialpolitik</u>. Munich, 1910.

AP 15. Brackmann, Karl. <u>Fünfzig Jahre deutscher Afrikaschiffahrt</u>.
1935.

AP 16. Brunschwig, Henry. <u>L'Expansion allemande outre-mer du</u>
<u>XVe siècle a nos jours</u>. Paris, 1957.

Based on unspecialized secondary sources; a general
treatment.

AP 17. Buchner, Max. <u>Aurora Colonialis: Bruchstücke eines Tage-</u>
<u>buchs aus dem ersten Beginn unserer Kolonialpolitik, 1884/</u>
<u>85</u>. Munich, 1914.

AP 18. <u>Das Buch der deutschen Kolonien</u>. Leipzig, 1937.

AP 19. Cannstatt, Oscar. <u>Fürst Bismarcks Kolonialpolitisches In-</u>
<u>itiative</u>. 1908.

AP 20. Chéradame, André. <u>La Colonisation et les colonies alle-</u>
<u>mandes</u>. Paris, 1905.

The author was sent to Germany in 1899 to study colonization. His study is based on material from the library of the Kolonial Gesellschaft. He was influenced
very little, if at all, by French bias.

AP 21. Clark, Grover. <u>The Balance Sheets of Imperialism</u>. New
York, 1936.

AP 22. Class, Paul. <u>Die Rechtsverhältnisse der freien farbingen</u>
<u>Arbeiter in den deutschen Schutzgebieten Afrikas und der</u>
<u>Südsee</u>. Ulm, 1913.

AP 23. <u>Die Colonie der Tagesdebatte und Koloniale Vereinigungen</u>
<u>einige Fragestellungen</u>. Berlin, 1884.

AP 24. Coppius, Adolf. <u>Hamburgs Bedeutung auf dem Gebiete der</u>
<u>deutschen Kolonialpolitik</u>. Berlin, 1905.

AP 25. Decharme, P. Compagnies et sociétés coloniales allemandes. 1903.

AP 26. Dehn, Paul. Von Deutscher Kolonial-und Weltpolitik. Berlin, 1907.

A study of political and economic aspects of colonial
policy; of little use for Africa.

AP 27. Dernburg, Bernhard. Koloniale Finanzprobleme; Vortrag
(Gehaltung auf Veranlassung der Handelskammer in Frankfurt A. M. am 3. Februar 1907). Berlin, 1907.

AP 28. -- Koloniale Lehrjahre. Stuttgart, 1907.

AP 29. -- Zielpunkte des deutschen Kolonialwessens; zwei Vorträge. Berlin, 1907.

AP 30. Dernburg, E. Die Deutschen Kapitalinteressen in den
deutschen Schutzgebieten. 1907.

A study of the economic aspects of German colonial
policy.

AP 31. Deutsche Kolonialpolitik in Dokumenten. Ed. by Ernst G.
Jacob. Leipzig, 1938.

Mainly documents from biographies and diaries etc.

AP 32. Die Deutsche Kolonialpolitik. Berlin, 1906.

A socialist pamphlet.

AP 33. Die Deutsche Kolonialpolitik vor dem Gerichtshof der Welt.
Basel, 1918.

AP 34. Die Deutsche Kolonialgesetzgebung; Sammlung der auf die
deutschen Schutzgebiete bezüglichen Gesetze, Verordnungen,
Erlasse und internationalen Vereinbarungen. 2 v. Berlin,
1893, 1898.

Laws, statutes, etc.

AP 35. Das Deutsche Kolonialreich; eine Länderkunde der deutschen
Schutzgebiete. 2 v. Ed. by Hans H. J. Meyer. Leipzig,
1909-10.

Well indexed history and geography of the German colonies; contains a good bibliography.

AP 36. Das Deutsche Kolonialreich. Ed. by Hans Zache. Leipzig,
1909.

One of the most informed single volume works on German colonialism.

AP 37. Die Deutschen Kapitalinteressen in der deutschen Schutz-
        gebieten (ohne Kiautschou); grösse, Stand und Rentabilität.
        Berlin, 1907.

AP 38. Deutschland als Kolonialmacht; dreissig Jahre deutscher
        Kolonialgeschichte. Berlin, 1914.

AP 39. Deutschlands Weg zur Kolonialmacht. Ed. by Erich B. T.
        Schultz-Ewerth. Berlin, 1934.
            Well illustrated.

AP 40. Ditton, Ernst. Etatsrecht und Etatswesen in den deutschen
        Schutzgebieten. Philippsburg A. Rh., 1940.
            A study of taxation policy in the colonies.

AP 41. Doerr, Friedrich. Deutsches Kolonialstrafprozessrecht.
        Leipzig, 1913.

AP 42. Dreissig Jahre deutsches Kolonialpolitik. Ed. by Paul
        Leutwein. 1914.

AP 43. Engler, Gustav. Koloniales; eine umfassende Darstellung
        der Kolonialverhältnisse des deutschen Reichs und der
        übrigen europäischen Staaten. Hamburg, 1889.

AP 44. Englische Urteile über die deutsche Kolonisationsarbeit.
        Ed. by Alfred Mansfeld. Berlin, 1919.

AP 45. Die Entwicklung unserer Kolonien; sechs Denkschriften.
        Berlin, 1892.
            Contents: Togo, Cameroons, South West Africa, East
            Africa, New Guinea company, Marshall Islands.

AP 46. Epstein, Klaus. "Erzberger and the German Colonial Scan-
        dals, 1905-1910," English Historical Review. 1959. 74
        (293): 637-663.

AP 47. Erzberger, Matthias. Die Kolonial-Bilanz: Bilder aus der
        deutschen Kolonialpolitik auf Grund der Verhandlungen des
        Reichstags im Sessionsabschnitt 1905/06. Berlin, 1906.

AP 48. Faserstoffe und die deutschen Kolonien. Gesamteinfuhr in
        Deutschland, 1913: 166 millionen Mark. Berlin, 1916.
            Pam. (4p.) pub. by Kolonialwirtschaftliches Komitee.

AP 49. Fabri, Friedrich. Bedarf Deutschland der Colonien? Eine
        politisch-ökonomische Betrachtung. Gotha, 1884.
            This famous work, credited with awakening German

interest in the advantage of colonization, was first published in 1879 and argues that all powerful countries
need colonies.

AP 50. Fabri, Friedrich. Fünf Jahre deutscher Kolonialpolitik:
Rück-und Ausblicke. Gotha, 1889.

Discusses events in German East Africa and German
Southwest Africa and concludes that there is a need to
set up a German colonial office because rule by chartered companies is ineffective.

AP 51. Fischer, Ferdinand. Die Industrie Deutschlands und seiner
Kolonien. Leipzig, 1908.

A collection of statistics.

AP 52. Friedrich, Johann Karl Julius. Kolonialpolitik als Wissenschaft; ein neues Forschungsgebiet der Rechtsphilosophie.
Berlin, 1909.

A study of legal problems in relation to the colonies.
Colonial law should recognize and incorporate the con-
cepts of justice traditionally held by the people of the
colonial area.

AP 53. Fünfzig Jahre deutsche Kolonialgesellschaft, 1882-1932.
Berlin, 1932. Pub. by Deutsche Kolonialgesellschaft.

The first section of this publication written by Willibald
von Steumer Die deutsche Kolonialgesellschaft von der
Gründung bis zum Raub der Kolonien (1882-1919) is a
good survey of German pre-war colonial policy.

AP 54. Gareis, D.K. Deutsches Kolonialrecht. Giessen, 1902.

AP 55. Gemkow, Heinrich. "Dokumente der Kampfes der deutschen
Sozialdemokratie gegen Bismarcks Kolonialpolitik und gegen
den Reichsopportunismus in den Jahren 1884/85," Beitrage
zur Geschichte der deutschen Arbeiterbewegung. East Germany, 1959, 1(1): 350-367.

Points out that the Social Democrats of the 1880's opposed Bismarck's colonial policy.

AP 56. German Possessions in Africa and the Pacific, and to the
Congo, Egypt, and East Asia. 20 v. Berlin, 1884-1900.

AP 57. Geschichte der deutschen Kolonialpolitik. Ed. by Gustav
Schmoller and Alfred Zimmermann. 1914.

AP 58. Gothard W. Germany's Colonial Work in Africa. Bielefeld,
1931.

AP 59. Häute und Gerbstoffe und die deutschen Kolonien. Gesamt-

einfuhr in Deutschland, 1913: Häute für 39 millionen Mark.
Berlin, 1915.   Pam. (4p.) pub. by Kolonialwirtschaftliches
Komitee.

AP 60. Hagen, Maximilian von.   Bismarcks Kolonialpolitik.   Stuttgart, 1923.

Contains a very good bibliography on German colonialism on pages xii-xxv.   A well-informed study by a vigorously pro-colonialist, anti-liberal admirer of Bismarck.

AP 61. Hallgarten, George W. F.   Imperialismus vor 1914.   2 v.
Munich, 1951.

An interesting and informed effort to establish a non-Marxist social theory of foreign policy.

AP 62. Der Handel der deutschen Kolonien.   Berlin, 1914.   Pam.
(8p.) pub. by Kolonialwirtschaftliches Komitee.

AP 63. Handels und Machtpolitik.   1900.

An important study on the relationship between business and colonial expansion.

AP 64. Hansen, Marcus L.   German Schemes of Colonization Before 1860.   Smith College Studies in History.   Northampton,
Mass., Oct. 1923-Jan. 1924.   Vol. IX, Nos. 1 & 2.

The footnotes of this volume contain many references to German colonial schemes for the period prior to 1860.

AP 65. Harms, Heinrich.   Deutschlands Kolonien.   Leipzig, 1909.

Facts and figures on each colony.

AP 66. Harris, J. H.   Germany's Last Colonial Empire.   London,
1917.

AP 67. Hassert, K.   Deutschlands Kolonien: Erwebungs und Entwicklungs Geschichte, Landes und wirtschaftliche Bedeutung
unserer Schutzgebiete.   Leipzig, 1910.

A thorough account of each of the German colonies including history, economic, geographic and ethnographic aspects.

AP 68. Heilborn, Adolf.   Die Deutschen Kolonien.   Leipzig, 1912.

AP 69. Helfferich, Karl T.   Zur Reform der kolonialen Verwaltungs-
organisation.   Berlin, 1905.

Suggests needed governmental reforms in the colonies.

AP 70. Helphand, Alexander.   Die Kolonialpolitik und der Zusammenbruch. Leipzig, 1907.

A socialist tract.

AP 71. Hermann, Rudolf. Die Handelsbeziehungen Deutschlands zu seinen Schutzgebieten. Berlin, 1899.

AP 72. Herrfurth, Kurt. Fürst Bismarck und die Kolonialpolitik. Berlin, 1909.

Traces Bismarck's conversion to colonialism.

AP 73. Henderson, William O. Studies in German Colonial History. Chicago, 1962.

These nine essays on various aspects of German colonial policy comprise the best general work in English on the German colonial empire. The development of the colonial empire, its loss during World War I, and colonial dreams after the war are all covered. The appendix contains many statistical tables and maps of all the German colonial possessions.

AP 74. Hertz, R. Das Hamburger Seehandelhaus J.C. Godeffroy & Sohn. 1922.

AP 75. Hessler, Carl. Die Deutschen Kolonien. Leipzig, 1905.

A description of each of the colonies; illustrated.

AP 76. Hieke, Ernst. Zur Geschichte des deutschen Handels mit Ostafrika. Das Hamburgische Handelhaus Wm. Oswald & Co. 1939.

AP 77. Hoffmann, Paul. Die Deutschen Kolonien in Transkaukasien. Berlin, 1905.

Based on primary sources.

AP 78. Ibbeken, Rudolf. Das Aussenpolitische Problem; Staat und Wirtschaft in der deutschen Reichspolitik, 1880-1914. Schleswig, 1928.

An excellent account of the relationship between German foreign policy and economics.

AP 79. Jacob, Ernst Gerhard. Deutsche Kolonialbunde; 1884-1934. Dresden, 1934.

AP 80. Jäckel, Herbert. Die Landgesellschaften in den deutschen Schutzgebieten; Denkschrift zur kolonialen Landfrage. Jena, 1909.

AP 81. 40 Jahre deutsche Kolonialarbeit; Gedenkschrift zum 24 April. Berlin, 1924. Pub. by Kolonialen Reichsarbeitsgemeinschaft.

AP 82. Jambo Watu! Das Kolonialbuch der deutschen. Ed. by
Willy Bolsinger and Hans Rauschnabel. Stuttgart, 1927.

AP 83. Jagd und Wildschutz in der deutschen Kolonien. Jena, 1913.

AP 84. Jerussalimski, A.S. Die Aussenpolitik und die Diplomatie
des deutschen Imperialismus am Ende des 19 Jahrhunderts.
Berlin, 1954.

AP 05. Jöhlingor, Otto. Die Wirtschaftliche Bedeutung unserer
Kolonien; sechs Vorlesungen für Kaufleute. Berlin, 1910.

AP 86. Karstedt, Oskar. Was war uns deutscher Kolonialbesitz?
Was muss es uns werden? Berlin, 1918.

AP 87. -- Deutschlands koloniale Not. Stuttgart, 1938.

AP 88. -- Warum brauchen wir deutschen Kolonialbesitz? 1918.

AP 89. Kautschuk und die deutschen Kolonien; Gesamteinfuhr in
Deutschland, 1913: 126 millionen Mark. Berlin, 1916.
Pamp. (3p.) pub. by Kolonialwirtschaftliches Komitee.

AP 90. Köbner, Otto. Einführung in die Kolonialpolitik. Jena,
1908.
A detailed description of the administrative system of
the German colonial possessions. Has a good bibliography.

AP 91. Köhler, Arthur. Der Deutsche Anteil an der Entdeckung
und erforschung der Erdteile. Karlsruhe, 1929.
Biographical notes on various German explorers.

AP 92. Koloniale Zeitfragen. Berlin, 1916.

AP 93. Koschitzky, Max von. Deutsche Kolonialgeschichte. Leipzig, 1888. 2 v.
Detailed and thorough.

AP 94. Kühlmann, Richard von. Erinnerungen. Heildelberg, 1948.
The memoirs of a man who held important positions in
the colonial section of the foreign office. He was
chargé d'affairs at Tangier in 1905.

AP 95. Kuczynski, Jürgen. Studien zur Geschichte des deutschen
Imperialismus. 2 v. East Berlin, 1952.

AP 96. Kuckleutz, K. Das Zollwessen der Deutschen Schutzgebiete.
Berlin, 1914.

AP 97. Langheld, Wilhelm. Zwanzig Jahre in deutschen Kolonien.

Berlin, 1909.

AP 98. Langer, William L.   The Diplomacy of Imperialism.
New York, 1950.

AP 99. Lensch, Paul.   Der Arbeiter und die deutschen Kolonien.
Berlin, 1917.

AP 100. Lessner, Paul.   Was müssen wir von unsern Kolonien
wissen? Berlin, 1911.

AP 101. Die Letzten Kolonialdebatten im aufgelösten Reichstag, November und Dezember 1906. Berlin, 1907.

AP 102. Leutz, Heinrich.   Die Kolonien Deutschlands; ihre Erwer-
bung, Bevölkerung, Bodenbeschaffenheit und Erzeugnisse.
Karlsruhe, 1900.
Illustrated with maps and steel engravings.

AP 103. Lewin, Evens.   The Germans and Africa. 1915.

AP 104. Loehnis, H.   Die Europäischen Kolonien; Beiträge zur
Kritik der deutschen Kolonialprojekte. Bonn, 1881.

AP 105. Lüders, Ewald.   Das Jagdrecht der deutschen Schutzgebiete.
Hamburg, 1913.

AP 106. Lüttich, Georg.   Bundesrat und Reichstag bei der Kolonial-
gesetzgebung. Münster, 1914.

AP 107. Ludwig, Walter.   Frankreichs Haltung zur deutschen Kolonialpolitik vom Marokko-Vertrag von 1911 bis zum Versailler Diktat. Würzburg, 1940.

AP 108. Ludwig Scholz, ein deutscher Kolonialpionier. Düsseldorf,
1934.

AP 109. Maclean, Frank.   Germany's Colonial Failure; Her Rule
in Africa Condemned on German Evidence. Boston, 1918.

AP 110. Mansfeld, Alfred.   Sozialdemokratie und Kolonien. Berlin, 1919.

AP 111. Marti, Oscar A.   The Anglo-German Commercial and Colonial Rivalry as a Cause of the War. Thesis presented
the Univ. of Southern Calif., Los Angeles, 1917.

AP 112. Mathies, Otto.   Hamburgs Reederei 1814-1914. 1924.

AP 113. -- Die Beschränkung der Gewerbe- und Handelsfreiheit in
den deutschen Schutzgebieten; eine Monographie. Hamburg,
1916.

AP 114. Mayer, Otto. Die Entwicklung der Handelsbeziehungen
         Deutschlands zu seinen Kolonien. Munich, 1913.
         A statistically supported argument that the colonial
         empire was necessary for the German economy.

AP 115. Medina, Angel. El Imperialismo Aleman; origines, Desa-
         rollo fin del imperio Aleman. Barcelona, 1915.

AP 116. Medizinal-Berichte über die deutschen Schutzgebiete. Ber-
         lin, 1903-1912.
         Reports of public health in the colonies.

AP 117. Mellem, Wilhelm. Der Deutsche Kolonialanspruch. Er-
         langen, 1938.

AP 118. Meyer, Annaliese. Das Werden des Bismarckischen Kolo-
         nialreiches. Hamburg, 1937.

AP 119. Meyer, Erwin. Das Finanzwesen der deutschen Schutzge-
         biete. Erlangen, 1912.

AP 120. Meyer, Hans. Die Entwicklung unserer Kolonien. Leip-
         zig, 1893.
         The author approves of the colonial policy of the Ger-
         man government.

AP 121. -- Gegenwart und Zukunft der deutschen Kolonien. Ber-
         lin, 1916.

AP 122. Mirbt, Carl. Mission und Kolonialpolitik in den deutschen
         Schutzgebieten. Tübingen, 1910.

AP 123. Moon, Parker T. Imperialism and World Politics. New
         York, 1926.

AP 124. Moszkowski, Walter. Bernhard Dernburg. Berlin, 1908.
         Pamphlet.

AP 125. Naendrup, Hubert. Die Entwicklung des Geldwessens in
         den deutschen Kolonien (unter Berücksichtigung der inter-
         nationalen Einflüsse); Vortrag, Gehalten in der internation-
         alen Vereinigung für vergleichende Rechtswissenschaft und
         Volkswirtschaftslehre zu Berlin am 16 Dezember 1911.
         Berlin, 1912.

AP 126. Noske, Gustav. Kolonialpolitik und Sozialdemokratie.
         Stuttgart, 1914.

AP 127. Nowak, Karl F. Germany's Road to Ruin. New York,

1932.

Contains an account of the Cowes episode based upon evidence furnished by the Kaiser. It is considered to be quite fantastic.

AP 128. Nussbaum, Manfred. Vom "Kolonialenthusiasmus" zur Kolonialpolitik der Monopole: zur Kolonialpolitik unter Bismarck, Caprivi, Hohenlohe. East Berlin, 1962.

The original acquisition of colonies by Germany in the 1880's preceded the establishment of monopoly capitalism which was the directing force of German policy. It was motivated by the desire for commodity markets, affecting only a part of the capitalistic community.

AP 129. Okabe, Takehiko. "Shin-Koro" No Tsusho Seisaku," Seiyoshi-gaku. 1954, 23: 916-932.

This article deals with the German trade policies during the Caprivi era and concludes that Caprivi's trade policies did not necessarily involve active advance into overseas regions but that they helped pave the way for the national and international development of German imperialism.

AP 130. Partsch, Josef F. Die Schutzgebiete des deutschen Reichs. Berlin, 1893.

AP 131. Phillips, Walter A. A Short History of Germany and her Colonies. London, 1914. Reprod. from the 11th ed. of Encyclopedia Britannica.

AP 132. Pierard, Richard V. "Colonial Propaganda in the German Schools Prior to World War I, " Teachers Coll. Journal. (May 1967).

AP 133. Prager, Erich. Die Deutsche Kolonialgesellschaft, 1882-1907. Berlin, 1908.

An authorized account.

AP 134. Radlauer, Ernst L. Die Lokale Selbstverwaltung der kolonialen Finanzen. Breslau, 1909.

AP 135. Rehbein, Elfriede. "Studien zur Geschichte der imperialistischen deutschen Eisenbahnpolitik in den Jahren von 1890-1914, " Wissenschaftliche Zeitschrift der Martin-Luther-Universität Halle-Wittenberg. Gesellschafts- und Sprachwissenschaftliche Reihe. East Germany, 1958/59. 13(3): 357-358.

Presents as factors which must be considered in a comprehensive treatment of this topic: 1) the general status of German railroads, 2) international considerations, 3) the relationships of imperialism and colonization to railroad expansion, 4) the subsidizing of the Junkers and monopolists by imperialist railroad policy, and 5) the active preparation in the railroad system for war between 1890-1914.

AP 136. Rohrbach, Paul. Das deutsches Kolonialwesen. Leipzig, 1911.

AP 137. Roscher, W. and J. Jannasch. Kolonien, Kolonialpolitik und Auswanderung. Leipzig, 1885.

AP 138. Sadebeck, R. Die Kulturgewächse der deutschen Kolonien. Jena, 1899.

AP 139. Schanz, Johannes. Neu-Deutschland; ein kolonial-Handbüchlein. Kreunznach und Leipzig, 1889.

AP 140. Schanz, Moritz. Cotton Growing in German Colonies. Manchester, 1910.

AP 141. -- Die Deutsche Kolonialschule in Witzenhausen. Berlin, 1910.

AP 142. Schaumberg, Paul E.B. Hermann von Wissmann, ein deutscher Kolonialpionier. Reutlingen, 1939.

AP 143. Scheel, Willy. Deutschlands Kolonien in achtzig farbenphotographischen Abbildungen. Berlin, 1914.

AP 144. Schlunk, Martin. Die Schulen für Eingeborne in den deutschen Schutzgebieten am 1. Juni 1911. Hamburg, 1914.

AP 145. Schmidt, Rochus. Hermann von Wissmann und Deutschlands Kolonialeswirken. Berlin, 19??.

The author was an immediate subordinate and close friend of Wissmann.

AP 146. Schmokel, Wolfe W. Dream of Empire: German Colonialism, 1919-1945. New Haven, 1964.

An account of the German colonial aspirations during the Weimar and Nazi periods; with bibliography.

AP 147. Schnee, Heinrich. German Colonization Past and Future: the Truth About the German Colonies. London, 1926.

A defense of German colonial administration before the war by a well known former colonial governor of German East Africa.

AP 148. Schramm, P.E. Deutschland und Übersee. 1950.

AP 149. Schütz, Jacob H. Kolonien; die geschichtliche Entwicklung
und Bedeutung derselben unter Berücksichtigung der deutschen Besitzungen. Leipzig, 1909.

AP 150. Schwabe, Kurd. Die Deutschen Kolonien. 2 v. Berlin,
1910.

A popular work with many color plates.

AP 151. Seidel, A. Der Gegenwärtige Handel der deutschen Schutzgebiete und die Mittel zu seiner Ausdehnung. Giessen,
1907.

AP 152. Seitz, Theodor. Vom Aufstieg und Niederbruch deutscher
Kolonialmacht. 3 v. Karlsruhe, 1927-29.

AP 153. Sommerlad, T. Der Deutsche Kolonialgedanke und sein
Werden im 19en Jahrhundert. 1918.

AP 154. Spellmeyer, Hans. Deutsche Kolonialpolitik in Reichstag.
Stuttgart, 1931.

This work is a study of the connection between colonialism and German domestic politics from 1884 to
1914 and it examines in detail the role of the colonial
in the Reichstag debates. Special attention is given
to the policies of the Social Democrats.

AP 155. Springborn, Arnold. Englands Stellung zur deutschen Welt
und Kolonialpolitik in den Jahren, 1911-1914. 1939.

AP 156. Stengel, Karl M.J.L. Deutsche Kolonialpolitik. Berlin,
1907.

AP 157. Stuhlmacher, Walther. Bismarcks Kolonialpolitik. Halle,
1927.

AP 158. Stürmer, Willibald von. Fünfzig Jahre deutsche Kolonialgesellschaft 1882-1932. Berlin, 1932.

Stürmer describes colonial policy to 1919 and a concluding essay written by Erich Düms covers the period
1919-1932.

AP 159. Taylor, A.J.P. Germany's First Bid for Colonies, 1884-
1885; A Move in Bismarck's European Policy. London,
1938.

Taylor overstates his thesis, which is based on very
narrow evidence.

AP 160. Tesch, Johannes. Die Laufbahn der deutschen Kolonialbeamten, ihre Pflichten und Rechte. Berlin, 1902.

AP 161. Townsend, Mary E. Origins of Modern German Colonialism 1871-1885. New York, 1921.

> A valuable approach through domestic party politics
> which, however, often errs in documentation and de-
> tail.

AP 162. -- The Rise and Fall of Germany's Colonial Empire 1884-
1918. New York, 1930.

> A standard treatment of Germany's colonial policy.

AP 163. -- European Colonial Expansion Since 1871. New York,
1941.

> In this general history of colonialism it is possible
> to see clearly the part played by Germany. There is
> a good chapter on Germany in Africa and also mater-
> ial on German colonial ambitions in the Middle East
> and Far East and on German colonial agreements with
> Russia, France, and England.

AP 164. Das Überseeische Deutschland; die deutschen Kolonien in
Wort und Bild. 2 v. Stuttgart, 1911.

> A textbook treatment of the period.

AP 165. Unserer Kolonialwirtschaft in ihrer Bedeutung für Industrie und Arbeiterschaft. Berlin, 1909. Pub. by Kolonialwirtschaftliches Komitee.

AP 166. Verhandlungen des deutschen Kolonialkongresses. 3 v.
Berlin, 1903, 1906, & 1911.

> Published proceedings and resolutions of the con-
> gresses of 1902, 1905, 1910 sponsored by the colonial
> society.

AP 167. Vietor, Johann K. Geschichtliche und kulturelle Entwicklung unserer Schutzgebiete. Berlin, 1913.

> The author traveled widely in the colonies.

AP 168. Vietsch, Eberhard. Wilhelm Solf, Botschafter; zwischen
den Zeiten. Tübingen, 1961.

AP 169. Wagner, Hermann. Über gründung deutscher Colonien.
Heidelberg, 1881.

AP 170. Walker, Mack. Germany and the Emigration 1816-1885.
Cambridge, Mass., 1964.

> This book though not directly concerned with German
> colonial history, nevertheless contains some good ma-

terial on the subject. The bibliography for the early period is extensive.

AP 171. Warneck, Gustav. Welche Pflichten legen uns unsere Kolonien auf? Ein Appell und das christliche deutsche Gewissen. Heilbronn, 1885.

The author argues that Germany must fulfill three obligations to the natives in the colonies: protect them, educate them, and Christianize them. He criticizes economic exploitation and examines the role of the German missions.

AP 172. Weber, Ernst von. Die Erweiterung des deutschen Wirtschaftsgebiets und die Grundlegung zu überseeischen deutschen Staaten; ein dringendes Gebot unserer wirtschaftlichen Notlage. Leipzig, 1879.

AP 173. Weber, Friedrich. Die Koloniale Finanzhoheit. Münster, 1909.

AP 174. Westermann, Diedrich. Beiträge zur deutschen Kolonialfrage. Essen, 1937.

Articles on subjects such as the German role in the exploration of Africa, native education in the German colonies, and German colonial policy.

AP 175. Weinberg, Gerda. "Die Deutsche Sozialdemokratie und die Kolonialpolitik, " Zeitschrift für Geschichtswissenschrift. No. 3. (1967).

AP 176. Weissborn, W. Sechs Jahre deutscher Colonialpolitik. 1890.

AP 177. Wiese, Josef. Neu-Deutschland; unsere Kolonien in Wort und Bild, der deutschen Jugend und dem deutschen Volke geschildert. Berlin, 1908.

AP 178. Wünsche, Alwin. Die Deutschen Kolonien; für die Schule dargestellt. Leipzig, 1912.

AP 179. Yerussalimski, A.S. "George W. F. Hallegarten und seine Darstellung der Aussenpolitik des deutschen Imperialismus," Zeitschrift für Geschichtswissenschaft. East Germany, 1962, 10(4): 844-882.

The article is a German translation of the author's introduction to the Russian edition of Hallgarten's book. He relates that even though Hallegarten is a bourgeois historian and sometimes fails to understand certain

historical factors due to the lack of comprehension of
Marxist principles, he has not only contributed "extensive and interesting facts" but has also advanced
explanations of "how the greedy interests of ruling
classes put into operation the mechanism of imperialist expansion, aggression, and war." See also: AP
61.

AP 180. Yerussalimsky, A.S. "Vneshniaia Politika i Diplomatiia
Germanskogo Imperializma v Nachale XX Veka," Novaia:
Noveishaja Istoriia. 1961, 5(6): 45-60.

An examination of German foreign policy and imperialism in the early part of the 20th century.

AP 181. Zdeněk, Jindra. "K Hospodářskym Kořenům Agresivity
Německého Vilémovské Éry," Ceskoslovenský Časopis His-
toricky. 1961, 9(2): 174-197.

A brief comparative study of the economic progress
made by Western countries in the period 1860-1915,
with emphasis on Germany, which made the most
marked progress. Politics, capital, and raw materials played an important part in the German colonial
expansion, which was primarily supported by the Prussian Junkerdom and militarism. Based on published
sources.

AP 182. Zehn Jahre Frauenbund der deutschen Kolonialgesellschaft.
Berlin, 1918.

AP 183. Zimmermann, Alfred. Geschichte der deutschen Kolonialpolitik. Berlin, 1914.

The author was prominent in German colonial service
before the war which gave him an unusual opportunity
to observe colonial affairs from the inside. He had
access to German colonial records in writing this
book, which contains a notable lack of bias or parti-
sanship. It is detailed and covers the period 1884-
1913.

AP 184. Zimmermann, Emil. Unsere Kolonien. Berlin, 1912.

AQ. COLONIAL--FAR EAST
     See also: AF 1-12, AH 78-88.

General
AQ 1. Chubb, O.E. 20th Century China. New York, 1964.

AQ 2.   Harris, N.D.   Europe and the East.   New York, 1926.

AQ 3.   Tan, C.C.   The Boxer Catastrophe.   New York, 1955.

AQ 4.   Owen, D.E.   Imperialism and Nationalism in the Far East.
New York, 1929.

AQ 5.   Churchill, William.   "Germany's Lost Pacific Empire, "
Geographical Review.   X (1920): 84-90.

AQ 6.   Grote, Gerhard.   Untersuchungen zur deutschen Kolonialpolitik um die Jahrhundertwende.   Berlin, 1940.

> A solid monograph which provides a systematic review
> of the German acquisition of Samoa, Kiao Chow, the
> Carolines, and other colonial possessions.

AQ 7.   Hesse-Wartegg, E. von.   Samoa, Bismarckarchipel und Neu
Guinea.   Leipzig, 1902.

AQ 8.   Masterman, Sylvia.   The Origins of International Rivalry in
the Pacific 1845-1884.   1934.

AQ 9.   Pfeil, J. Graf.   Studien und Beobachtungen aus der Südsee.
Brunswick, 1899.

AQ 10.   Elm, Ludwig.   "Die Sozialdemokratische Partei Deutschlands und der antiimperialistische Volksaufstand (Borenauf-
stand) in China im Jahre 1910, " Wissenschaftliche Zeitschrift der Friedrich-Schiller-Universität Jena Gesellschafts-
und Sprachwissenschaftliche Reihe.   1957/58.   7(2/3): 307-
316.

> The German Social Democrats opposed the government
> policy, with the exception of the revisionists led by
> Eduard Bernstein.

AQ 11.   Wegner, G.   Deutschland in der Südsee.   Bielefeld, 1903.

AQ 12.   Stepman, E. and F. Grabner.   Die Küste von Umuddu bis
Kap St. George.   Berlin, 1907.

AQ 13.   Stevenson, Robert L.   A Footnote to History-Villima Letters.
London, 1895.

AQ 14.   Staatsvertrag zwischen Deutschland und Spanien über den
kauf der Karolinen-, Palau- und Marianeninseln in der Südsee, 30, Juni 1899.   Madrid, 1899.

> German and Spanish in opposite columns.   Appendix
> contains the authorization by King Alfonso XII and
> Queen Maria Christina of Spain for Francisco Silvela
> to conclude and ratify the treaty.

AQ 15. Hörmann, Bernhard Lothar. The Germans in Hawaii.
        Master's thesis, Univ. of Hawaii, 1931.

AQ 16. Kaiserlicher Schutzbrief für Deutsch-Neuguinea vom 17.
        Mai 1885. Berlin, 1885.

> Letter of protection granted by William I in favor of
> the Neu-Guinea Kompagnie for its acquisitions in Ger-
> man New Guinea.

Kiao Chow

AQ 17. Becker, Willy. "Die Deutsch-russische Krise bei der Er-
        werbung von Kiautschou, " Zeitschrift für Politik. XV
        (1925): 58-71.

> A careful study, based primarily on the German docu-
> ments.

AQ 18. Bohme, F. and M. Krieger. Guide to Tsingtau and its
        Surroundings. Wessel, 1906.

AQ 19. Kiautschou. (Eine Reise durch die deutschen Kolonien).
        Vol. 6. Berlin, 1912.

AQ 20. Franzius, Georg. Kiautschou, Deutschlands Erwerbung in
        Ostasien. Berlin, 1898.

AQ 21. -- Kiautschou. Berlin, 1900.

> The author investigated the Bay of Kiao Chow for the
> German government in 1897 and gives a detailed survey
> of the territory.

AQ 22. Hesse-Wartegg, E. von. Schantung und Deutsch-China.
        Leipzig, 1896.

AQ 23. Irmer, Arthur J. Die Erwerbung von Kiautschou 1894-1898.
        Cologne, 1930.

AQ 24. Janson, A. von. Tsingtau: Erweb, Blüte und Verlust.
        Berlin, 1915.

AQ 25. Richthofen, Ferdinand, Freiherr von. "Kiautschou, seine
        Weltstellung und voraussichtliche Bedeutung, " Preussische
        Jahrbücher. (Jan. 1898): 167-191.

> Written by an eminent authority on the geography of
> China. This is a compact and in every way excellent
> study of the importance and prospects of the German
> acquisitions.

AQ 26. -- Schantung und seine Eingangspforte Kiautschou. Berlin,

1898.

AQ 27. Schrameier, W.L. Die Grundlagen der wirtschaftlichen
Entwicklung in Kiautschou. Berlin, 1903.

Kaiser Wilhelmsland and Bismarck Archipelago

AQ 28. Nachrichten über Kaiser Wilhelms Land und den Bismarck-
archipel. 3 v. 1875-1880. Issued by the New Guinea
Company.

AQ 29. Nachrichten über Kaiser Wilhelms Land und den Bismarck-
archipel. Berlin, 1885-1898. Issued by the New Guinea
Company.

AQ 30. Parkinson, R. Dreissig Jahre in der Südsee. Land und
Leute, Sitten und Gebräushe auf dem Bismarck-Archipel.
Stuttgart, 1909.

AQ 31. Schnee, H. Bilder aus der Südsee (Bismarck-Archipelogo).
Berlin, 1904.

Caroline and Marianas (See also: AQ 14)

AQ 32. Christen, F.W. The Caroline Islands. London, 1899.

AQ 33. Finsch, Otto. Karolinen und Marianen. Hamburg, 1900.

AQ 34. Garcia, L. de Ibaflez y. Historia de las Islas Marianas....
Granada, 1886.

Samoa

AQ 35. Beazley, Raymond. "Samoa: eine deutsche-englische Kolo-
nialverständigung, " Berliner Monatshefte. XV (Dec. 1937):
1940-1959.
A detailed examination of the events of 1898-1899.

AQ 36. Boyd, Mary S. Our Stolen Summer. London, 1900.

AQ 37. Churchill, L.P. Samoa Uma. London, 1902.

AQ 38. Churchward, W.B. My Consulate in Samoa. London, 1887.

AQ 39. Convention and Declaration Between the United Kingdom and
Germany for the Settlement of the Samoan and other Questions; Signed at London, November 14, 1899; Ratification
Exchanged at London and Berlin February 16, 1900. London, 1900.

AQ 40. Correspondence Respecting the Affairs of Samoa. London, 1887.

AQ 41. Ehlers, O.E. Samoa die Perle der Südsee à jour gefasst. Berlin, 1900.

AQ 42. Ellison, Joseph W. "The Partition of Samoa," Pacific Historical Review. VIII (Sept. 1939): 259-288.

AQ 43. Krämer, A. Die Samoa Inseln. Stuttgart, 1902.

AQ 44. Kurze, G. Samoa, das Land, die Leute und die Mission. Berlin, 1899.

AQ 45. Reinecke, F. Samoa. Berlin, 1901.

AQ 46. Stain, J.E. Old Samoa. London, 1897.

AQ 47. Weck, Alfred. Deutschlands Politik in der Samoafrage. Leipzig, 1933.

> This dissertation covers the subject from 1876-1899, making an analysis of the published sources.

AR. COLONIAL--AFRICA--GENERAL

AR 1. Banse, Ewald. Unsere grossen Afrikaner, das Leben deutscher Entdecker und Kolonialpioniere. Berlin, 1943.

AR 2. Batson, Adolf. African Intrigues. Garden City, N.Y., 1933.

AR 3. Boshart, August. Zehn Jahre afrikanischen Lebens. Leipzig, 1898.

> The author lived in the Congo German East Africa, and in South West Africa.

AR 4. Britain and Germany in Africa: Imperial Rivalry and Colonial Rule. Ed. by Prosser Gifford and Wm. Roger Louis. New Haven, 1967.

> A series of twenty-four essays spanning the period 1880-1939.

AR 5. Calver, Albert F. The German African Empire. London, 1916.

> An economic, ethnic, and geographic survey of the colonies, seen in an anti-German light.

AR 6. Crowe, Sybil E. The Berlin West African Conference,

1884-1885. New York, 1942.

AR 7. Darmstaedter, P. Geschichte der Aufteilung und Kolonisation Africas. Berlin, 1914.

AR 8. Europäische Colonien in Afrika und Deutschlands Interessen sonst und jetzt. Berlin, 1884.

> Argues that Germany should develop colonies in Africa and examine trade possibilities.

AR 9. Friererich, Adolf. (Duke of Mäcklenburg). From the Congo to the Niger and the Nile. London, 1913.

AR 10. Frobenius, Leo. The Voices of Africa. London, 1913. Eng. trans. of a German work.

AR 11. Hallgarten, Wolfgang. "L'Essor et l'échec de la Politique Boer de l'Allemagne 1890-1898, " Revue Historique. CLXXVII (1936): 505-536.

> A thorough analysis of German economic interest and activity, based in part on unpublished material.

AR 12. Johnston, Sir Harry Hamilton. A History of the Colonization of Africa by Alien Races. Cambridge, 1930.

> For the material on Germany see p. 403-422.

AR 13. Harris, N.D. Europe and Africa. New York, 1927.

AR 14. Hoskins, H.L. European Imperialism in Africa. New York, 1930.

AR 15. Junker, Wilhelm Johann. Travels in Africa During the Years 1875-1886. 3 v. London, 1890-1892.

> The travels of a famous German explorer.

AR 16. Johnston, H. The Colonization of Africa. Cambridge, 1899.

AR 17. Keltic, K.S. The Partition of Africa. London, 1895.

AR 18. Lent, Carl. Tagebuch-Berichte der Kilimanjaro-Station. Berlin, 1894.

> The Kilimanjaro Station was one of the two research stations set up and financed by the Kolonialgesellschaft. The other was at Windhoek in German South West Africa.

AR 19. Lettow-Vorbeck, Paul Emil von. Afrika, wie ich es Wiedersah. Munich, 1955.

> The author began his African service in German South West Africa in 1904. He was transfered to East Africa

in 1914.

AR 20. Lewin, Percy E. The Germans and Africa, Their Aims on
the Dark Continent and how they Acquired their African
Colonies. London, New York, 1915.

> Anti-German but contains much detail and documenta-
> tion about Germans in Africa.

AR 21. Lücke, Joachim H. Bevölkerung und Aufenthalsrecht in den
deutschen Schutzgebieten Afrikas. Hamburg, 1913.

AR 22. Meyer, Hans. Die Eisenbahnen im tropischen Afrika; eine
kolonialwirtschaftliche Studie. Leipzig, 1902.

AR 23. Müller-Rüdersdorff, Wilhelm. Deutsche Kolonialpioniere in
Afrika. Leipzig, 1938.

AR 24. Salzburg, Edith. Karl Peters und sein Wolk: Der Roman
des deutschen Kolonialgründers. Weimar, 1929.

AR 25. Peters, Karl. Afrikanische Köpfe. Berlin, 1915.

> Sketches of the lives of explorers of Africa.

AR 26. -- Carl Peters nationalpolitisches Vermächtnis. Hannover,
1938.

> A selection of Peter's writings.

AR 27. -- Gesammelte Schriften. 3 v. Munich, 1943-1944.

AR 28. -- New Light on Dark Africa. London and New York,
1891.

> An English translation of Die Deutsche Emin-Pascha-
> Expedition. The Dutch translation is Door Afrika's
> Wildernissen. Leiden, 1891. It is Volume II of
> Peters' Gesammelte Schriften. This work is an ac-
> count of the journey made in 1889-1890 by Dr. Karl
> Peters (1856-1918) from Bagamoyo, opposite Zanzibar
> on the German East African coast, inland to Lake Vic-
> toria, around the western and northern shores of this
> lake, and then east past Mt. Kenya, and down the Tana
> Valley to the coast. This journey, known as the
> Emin-Pasha-Expedition and under Peters' command,
> was to bring supplies to Dr. Eduard Schnitzer, known
> as Emin Pasha, who had been cut off from the outside
> world for several years.

AR 29. -- Zur Weltpolitik. Berlin, 1912.

> A collection of articles.

AR 30. Pick, F.W. Searchlight on German Africa: the Diaries
and Papers of Dr. W. Ch. Regendanz; a Study in Colonial

Ambitions. London, 1939.

A large part of this book is devoted to the Agadir crisis. Ragendanz prior to World War I was in the confidence of Wilhelmstrasse. German efforts to secure Nyasaland, a district of the Portuguese colony of Mozambique, is also outlined.

AR 31. Rohrbach, Paul. Wie machen wir unsere Kolonien rentabel. Halle, 1907.

The author, who had first hand knowledge of Togo, Cameroon, and German South West Africa, argues that if the colonies are to enrich the economy a great deal of effort and capital must first be invested and that careful planning must be carried out. The condition of each colony is discussed in detail and suggestions for economic development are made.

AR 32. Sanderson, G. N. "The Anglo-German Agreement of 1890 and the Upper Nile, " The English Historical Review. 78 (Jan. 1963): 49-72.

AR 33. Schloifer, Otto. Bana Uleia, ein Lebenswerk in Afrika; aus den Tagebüchern eines alten Kolonialpioniers. Berlin, 1939.

Describes the author's extensive travels in Africa between 1892-1913 as a mining engineer and promoter of mining enterprises.

AR 34. Schmidt, Rochus. Deutschlands koloniale Helden und Pioniere der Kultur im schwarzen Kontinent. 2 v. Braunschweig, 1896.

AR 35. Schramm, P. E. Deutschland und übersee; der deutsche Handel mit den anderen Kontinenten, insbesondere Afrika, von Karl V bis zu Wirtschaftsleben. Braunschweig, 1950.

AR 36. Schreiber, Hermann. Deutsche Tat in Afrika; Pionierarbeit in unseren Kolonien. Berlin, 1942.

AR 37. Schuetze, Woldemar. Schwarz gegen Weiss; die Eingebotenenfrage als Kernpunkt unserer Kolonialpolitik in Afrika. Berlin, 1908.

AR 38. Schurtz, Heinrich. Das Afrikanische Gewerbe. Leipzig, 1900.

AR 39. Schwarze, Fritz A. Das Deutsch-englische Abkommen über die portugiesischen Kolonien vom 30. August 1898. Göttingen, 1931.

AR 40. Schweinfurth, Georg A. Georg Schweinfurth; Lebenbild
eines Afrikaforschers: Briege von 1857-1925. Stuttgart,
1954.

AR 41. Sell, Manfred. Das deutsch englische Abkommen von 1890
über Helgoland und die Afrik Kolonien im Lichte die deutsche Presse. Berlin, 1926.

AR 42. Steer, George L. Judgement on German Africa. London,
1030.
         An indictment of the whole German colonial system.

AR 43. Steegmüller, Walter. Die Erwerbung und der rechtliche
Charakter der deutschen Schutzgebiete. Borna-Leipzig,
1912.
         An analysis of legality of Germany's position in Africa.

AR 44. Vignes, K. "Étude sur la rivalité d'influence entre les
puissances Européenes en Afrique Équatoriale et Occidentale
depuis l'acte General de Berlin jusqu'au seuil du XXe Siècle, " Revue Francaise Hist. d'outre-mer. 1961, 48(1):
5-95.

         This analysis of the Berlin Conference of 1884 and the
         Brussels Conference of 1899 traces the Anglo-France,
         and Franco-German rivalries during the years 1884-
         1900.

AR 45. Wissmann, Hermann von. Durchquerung Afrikas. Berlin,
1907. 2 v. in 1. I: Unter deutscher Flagge quer durch
Afrika von west nach ost. II: Meine zweite Durchquerung
Aequatorial-Afrikas vom Kongo zum Zambesi. Eng. trans.,
My Second Journey Through Equatorial Africa from the Con-
go to the Zambesi in the Years 1886-1887. London, 1891.

         The journey described in vol. I took place in 1880-
         1883; that in vol. II, in 1886-1887. Wissmann re-
         ceived military command in German East Africa in
         1889 and became governor of this colony in 1895.
         He left Africa for good in 1896 and accidentally shot
         himself in a hunting accident in 1905.

AR 46. Schaumberg, P.E.B.R. Hermann v. Wissmann, ein deutscher Kolonialpionier. Reutlingen, 1939.

AR 47. Schmidt, Rochus. Hermann v. Wissmann und Deutschlands
koloniales Wirken. Berlin, 19??.

AR 48.   Hermann von Wissmann Deutschlands grösser Afrikaner;
         sein Leben und Wirken, unter Benutzung des Nachlasses.
         Ed. by A. Becker and C. von Perbandt. Berlin, 1907.

AR 49.   Zimmermann, Emil.   The German Empire of Central Af-
         rica.   London, 1918.

AS.   COLONIAL--SOUTH WEST AFRICA
      See note to Chapter IV.

AS 1.   Angra Pequeña Copy of Dispatch from the Earl of Derby to
         H.M.'s High Commission in South Africa Relative to the
         Establishment of a Protectorate at Angra Pequeña and
         Along the Coast.   London, 1884.

AS 2.   Hodge, Amelia L.   Angra Pequeña.   Munich, 1936.

AS 3.   Alverdes, Hermann.   Mein Tagebuch aus Südwest; Erin-
         nerungen aus dem Feldzuge gegen die Hottentotten.   Olden-
         burg, 1906.

AS 4.   Anonymous (Fritz Heilbron).   "Deutsche Intrigen gegen Eng-
         land während des Burenkrieges, " Deutsche Revue.   (Sept.
         1908): 257-263.

              This article was written from German documents and
              published anonymously by the German foreign office.
              It says substantially what the Emperor said in his fa-
              mous Daily Telegraph interview of Oct. 28, 1908.

AS 5.   Anton, Günther K.   Die Siedelungsgessellschaft für deutsch-
         Südwestafrika; Vortrag, Gehalten am 21. November 1907.
         Jena, 1908.

              A 61 page pamphlet to encourage settlement.

AS 6.   Aydelotte, William O.   Bismarck and British Colonial Pol-
         icy; The Problem of South West Africa, 1883-1885.   Phila-
         delphia, 1937.

AS 7.   Baum, H.   Kolonial wirtschaftliches Komitee; Kunene Sam-
         besi Expedition.   Berlin, 1903.

AS 8.   Bayer, Maximilian G.S.   Mit dem Hauptquartier in Südwest-
         afrika.   Berlin, 1909.

              A lengthy account of the Herero war with illustrations

and bibliography.

AS 9.   Die Behandlung der Einheimischen Bevölkerung in den kolonialen Besitzungen Deutschlands und Englands; Eine Erwider-
ung auf das englische Blaubuch vom August 1918: Report
on the Natives of Southwest Africa and their Treatment by
Germany. Berlin, 1919. Eng. trans., The Treatment of
Native and Other Populations in the Colonial Possessions of
Germany and England; an Answer to the English Blue Book
of August 1918: "Report on the Natives of Southwest Africa
and Their Treatment by Germany." Berlin, 1919.

AS 10. Bixler, Raymond. Anglo-German Imperialism in South Africa. Baltimore, 1932.

A digest of the British and German material on the
Portuguese treaty of 1898.

AS 11. Botha, Philip. Die Staatkundige Ontwikkeling van die Suid
Afrikaanse Republiek onder Kruger en Leyds. Amsterdam,
1924.

This history of the transvaal from 1844-1899 is a study
of the Boer side, using German documents and other
official papers.

AS 12. Bruck, Felix F. Noch Einmal die Deportation und deutsch-
Südwestafrika. Breslau, 1906.

A pamphlet proposing to use Southwest Africa as a re-
ceiving area for deported criminals.

AS 13. Bülow, F.J. von. Deutsch Südwest Africa: Drei Jahre im
Lande Hendrik Witbois. Berlin, 1899.

AS 14. Büttner, Carl G. Kolonialpolitik und Christentum, Betrach-
tet mit Hinblick und die deutschen Unternehmungen in Südwestafrika. Heidelberg, 1885.

AS 15. Calvert, Albert F. South-West Africa During the German
Occupation, 1884-1914. London, 1916. Contains 230 plates.

Propaganda.

AS 16. Deimling, Berthold von. Südwestafrika; Land und Leute,
unsere kämpft, Wert der Kolonie; Vortrag, gehalten in
einer Anzahl deutscher Städte. Berlin, 1906.

The author was the commander of the 2nd Field Regiment during the Herero war.

AS 17. Dernburg, Bernhard. Südwestafrikanische Eindrücke. In-
        dustrielle Fortschritte in den Kolonien. Berlin, 1909.

        Text of a speech given by the author, who was colonial
        minister, in the Reichstag upon his return from South
        West Africa.

AS 18. Bongard, Oskar. Staatssekretär Dernburg in British und
        Deutsch-Süd-Afrika. Berlin, 1908.

        Dernburg's visit to German South West Africa is de-
        scribed in a series of letters by one of his companions.

AS 19. Deutsche Reiter in Südwest; Selbsterlebnisse aus den
        Kämpfen in Deutsch-Süd-Westafrika; Nach persönlichen
        Berichten bearb. Ed. by Freiherr Friedrich von Dincklage-
        Campe. Berlin, 1909.

AS 20. Dinter, K. Deutsch-Südwestafrika. Leipzig, 1909.

AS 21. Dove, Karl. Deutsch-Südwest-Afrika. Berlin, 1903.

        An exhaustive reference work of the time. Deals with
        history, geography, mineral deposits, climate, flora,
        fauna, native and white population.

AS 22. -- Südwest-Afrika; Kriegs- und Friedensbilder aus der
        ersten deutschen Kolonie. Berlin, 1896.

        The author was a professor of geography at the Univer-
        sity of Berlin and a specialist in African studies. He
        was in charge of the Windhoek research station opened
        by the Deutsche Kolonialgesellschaft in 1892 and lived
        there during 1892-1893. During this period he made a
        number of research excursions and became involved in
        the wars with Hendrik Witboi. This book is an ac-
        count of his stay in Africa.

AS 23. Drecksler, Horst. Südwestafrika unter deutscher Kolonial-
        herrschaft: Der Kampf der Herero und Nama gegen den
        deutschen Imperialismus, 1884-1915. East Berlin, 1966.

        The author made extensive use of the German colonial
        archives. The Germans, except for some missionaries,
        are portrayed as proceeding against the Africans, con-
        sciously disregarding treaties, laws, promises, and
        humanitarian principles. Some even advocated exter-
        mination of the natives, a policy opposed by those who
        insisted that the colony could not exist without cheap
        labor. This policy is fully documented. The author
        compares the published writings of official participants
        in the administration with their actual views and deeds
        as revealed in the documents of the colonial archives.

AS 24. Die Kämpfe der deutschen Truppen in Südwestafrika. Berlin, 1906.

Official history of the wars against Herero.

AS 25. Patte, Henri. Le Sud-Ouest Africain Allemand; Révolte des Hereros. Paris, 1907.

An analysis of the revolt by a member of the French general staff.

AS 26. Schmidt, Max. Aus unserem Kriegsleben in Südwestafrika; Erlebnisse und Erfahrungen. Berlin, 1913.

Diary of a preacher during the Herero war.

AS 27. Drechsler, Horst. "Deutsche versuch, das deutsch-englische Abkommen von 1898 über die portugiesischen Kolonien zu Realisieren," Zeitschrift für Geschichtswissenschaft. East Germany, 1961, 9(7): 1619-1631.

The background and motives behind the Anglo-German Agreement of 1898 aimed at dividing the Portuguese colonies between Germany and England. That Germany did not succeed in getting South Angola, which it had desired, was due to a lack of unity among the financial circles involved.

AS 28. Lopes, Arthur R. A Convençao Secreta entre a Allemanha e a Inglaterra sobre a Partilha das Colônias Portuguesos. Lisbon, 1933.

Deals with the secret treaty of 1898.

AS 29. Schwarze, Fritz. Das Deutsch-englisch Abkommen über portugiesischen Kolonien vom 30 August 1898. Göttingen, 1931.

A doctoral dissertation that uses both British and German documents. Written with a keen understanding of the broader issues involved.

AS 30. Beazley, Raymond. "Britain, Germany and the Portuguese Colonies 1898-1899," Berliner Monatshefte. XIV (Nov. 1936): 866-887.

A digest of the German and British documents.

AS 31. Dubois, Pierre. "Le Traité Anglo-Allemand du 30 aôut 1898 relatif aux Colonies Portugais," Revue d'histoire de la guerre mondiale. XVII (July 1939): 232-246.

A re-examination of the subject in the light of the German, British, and French documents.

AS 32. Falkenhausen, Helene von. Ansiedlershicksale; elf Jahre in deutsch-südwestafrika, 1893-1904. Berlin, 1906.

AS 33. François, H. von. Nama und Damara; Deutsch-Süd-West-Afrika. Magdeburg, 1895.

AS 34. Gorges, E.H. Report on the Natives of Southwest Africa and Their Treatment by Germany. 1918.

AS 35. Haussleiter, G. Zur Eingeborenen-Frage in Deutsch-Südwest-Afrika; Erwägungen und Vorschläge. Berlin, 1906.

The author was an inspector of the Rheinish mission.

AS 36. Hesse, Hermann. Die Landfrage und die Frage der Rechts-gültigkeit der Konzessionen in Südwestafrika. 2 v. Jena, 1906.

An account of land law with the relevant documents.

AS 37. Hintrager, Oskar. Südwestafrika in der deutschen Zeit. Munich, 1955.

AS 38. Hoppe, Theodor. Wirtschaftsstruktur und Wirtschaftsent-wicklung von Deutsch-Südwestafrika. Borna, 1936.

There are sections on history and German colonial native policy and a bibliography.

AS 39. Irle, I. Die Herrero. Gütersloh, 1906.

AS 40. Die Kämpfe der deutschen Truppen in Süd-West Afrika. 2 v. 1906-07.

An official account by the German general staff of the native uprising.

AS 41. Leiner, F. Bergtourer und Steppenfahrten in Hereroland. Berlin, 1904.

AS 42. Leutwein, Theodor. Deutsch-Südwest-Afrika; Vortrag, ge-halten in der Abt. Berlin-Charlbg. Der Deutschen Kolonial-gesellschaft. Berlin, 1898.

AS 43. -- Elf Jahre Gouverneur in Deutsch-Südwestafrika. Berlin, 1908.

AS 44. Leutwein, Paul. Afrikanerschiksal; Gouverneur Leutwein und seine Zeit. Stuttgart, 1929.

Theodor Leutein went to South West Africa as an officer in the colonial army in 1893 and became Landeshaupt-mann (the post later known as Governor) from 1895-1904. This book is written by his son and is concerned mainly with his father's handling of the native uprisings, particularly those of the Hereros and Hendrik Witboi.

AS 45. Leutwein, Paul. Die Leistungen der Regierung in der Süd-
        westafrikanischen Land- und Minenfrage. Göthen, 1911.

AS 46. Lovell, Reginald I. The Struggle for South Africa 1875-
        1899; a Study in Economic Imperialism. New York, 1934.
        Traces the Anglo-German estrangement over Africa.

AS 47. Die Erschliessung von Deutsch-Südwest-Afrika durch Adolf
        Lüderitz; Akten, Briefe und Denkschriften. Ed. by C.A.
        Lüderitz. Oldenburg, 1945.

AS 48. Schüssler, Wilhelm. Adolf Lüderitz; ein deutscher Kampf
        um Südafrika, 1883-1886; Geschichte des ersten Kolonial-
        pioniers im Zeitalter Bismarcks. Bremen, 1936.

AS 49. Lunkenbein, Anton. Die Mine im Urwald; abenteurliche
        Schicksale Lunkenbeins in Deutsch-Südwestafrika von ihm
        selbst erzählt. Reutlingen, 1939.

AS 50. Neumann, Johannes. Die Verwendung von deutschem Zucht-
        vieh in Deutsch-Südwestafrika in Reinzucht und zur Veredel-
        ung der dortigen Rindviehbestände. Hamburg, 1914.

AS 51. Oelhafen, H. von. Die Besiedlung Deutsch-Südwestafrikas
        bis zum Weltkriege. Berlin, 1926.
        This account of the German migration to South West
        Africa has sections on the railways, water, land, etc.
        and includes documents and a bibliography.

AS 52. Oestertag, Robert von. Das Veterinäwesen und Fragen der
        Tierzucht in Deutsch-Südwestafrika; Reisebericht. Jena,
        1907.

AS 53. Opitz, W. In Südwestafrika. Leipzig, 1909.

AS 54. Portora (pseud.). Im Dienste von Downing Street; aus der
        Aktenmappe eines politischen Geheimagentem. Paris, 1908.
        German-English relations in South West Africa; based
        on secret documents.

AS 55. Penner, C.D. "Germany and the Transvaal Before 1896,"
        Journal of Modern History. XII (March 1940): 31-59.
        A careful re-examination drawing heavily on contempo-
        rary materials.

AS 56. Quiring, Erich. Die Eisenbahn Deutsch-Südwestafrikas und
        ihre Bedeutung für die wirtschaftliche Entwicklung der Kolo-
        nie. Borna, 1911.

AS 57. Range, Paul T. Beiträge und Ergänzungen zur Landeskunde des deutschen Namalandes. Hamburg, 1914.

This work contains a detailed description of the exploration of Namaland, including the flora, fauna, and geology, and an outline of German activity in the area. Maps, photographs, and a bibliography are included.

AS 58. Rehbock, Theodor. Deutschlands Pflichten in Deutsch-Südwest-Afrika. Berlin, 1904.

The water problem is discussed.

AS 59. Rohrbach, Paul. Dernburg und die Südwestafrikaner; Dimantenfrage, Selbstverwaltung, Landeshilfe. Berlin, 1911.

AS 60. -- Deutsch-Südwest-Afrika ein Ansiedlungs- Gebiet. Berlin, 1904.

AS 61. -- Deutsche Kolonialwirtschaft. Berlin, 1907. Vol. I: Südwest Afrika.

AS 62. Rupp, Erwin. Soll und Haben in Deutsch-Südwest-Afrika. Berlin, 1904.

Advocates further development in South Africa by Germany.

AS 63. Sander, Ludwig. Geschichte der deutschen Kolonialgesellschaft für Südwest-Afrika von ihrer Gründung bis zum Jahre 1910. 2 v. Berlin, 1912. I: Geschichtliche Darstellung, II: Grundlegende Urkunde.

AS 64. Schulze, L. Südwestafrika. Berlin, 1910.

AS 65. Schwabe, Kurd. Im deutschen Diamantenland; Deutsch-Südwest-Afrika von der Errichtung der deutschen Herrschaft bis zur Gegenwart, 1884-1910. Berlin, 1909.

AS 66. -- Der Krieg in Deutsch-Südwest-Afrika, 1904-1906. Berlin, 1907. Illus.

The author was involved in the fighting.

AS 67. -- Mit Schwert und Pflug in Deutsch-Südwest-Afrika; vier Kriegs- und Wanderjahre. Berlin, 1899.

AS 68. Semler, Johannes. Meine Beobachtungen in Süd-West-Afrika; Tagebuchnotizen und Schlussfolgerungen. Hamburg, 1906.

AS 69. Thomsen, Hermann. Deutsches Land in Afrika. Munich, 1911.

AS 70. Tönjes, Hermann. Ovamoland; Land, Leute, Mission, mit besonderer Berücksichtigung seines grössten Stammes Oukuanjama. Berlin, 1911.

The author was a missionary and he gives a complete account of the lives and customs of the people who inhabited the northern portion of the colony.

AS 71. Walter, M. Duitschland en de Holland Republieken in Zuidafrika. Amsterdam, 1918.

AS 72. Vedder, H. Das Alte Südwestafrika. 1934.

AS 73. Wüd, Johannes. Die Rolle der Burenrepubliken in der auswärtigen und Kolonialen Politik des deutscher Reichs in den Jahren 1883-1900. Nuremberg, 1927.

A dissertation based primarily on German documents, making use of some unpublished material.

AT. COLONIAL--EAST AFRICA

AT 1. Baumann, Oskar. Afrikanische Skizzen. Berlin, 1900.
A travel book.

AT 2. -- In Deutsch-Ostafrika während des Aufstand. Wien, 1890.

AT 3. Bell, R.M. "The Maji-Maji Rebellion in the Liwale District," Tanganyika Notes and Records. No. 28, Jan. 1950.

AT 4. Blöcker, Hans. Deutsch-Ostafrika (Tanganyika Territory und Ruanda-Urundi in der Weltschaft). Berlin, 1928.

Compares the German administration between 1907 and 1913 with the first five years of British rule.

AT 5. Büttner, Kurt. Die Anfänge der deutschen Kolonialpolitik in Ostafrika; eine kritische Untersuchung an Hand unveröffentlicher Quellen. East Berlin, 1959.

AT 6. Caprivi, Leo von. Die Ostafrikanische Frage und der Helgoland-Zansibar-Vertrag. Bonn, 1934.

AT 7. Deutsche Zentral-Afrika-Expedition, 1907-1908. Wissenschaftliche Ergebnisse. 7 v. Leipzig, 1910.

AT 8. Dietzel, Karl H. Versuch einer geographischen Charakterisierung des ostafrikanischen Zwischenseengebietes. Weida, 1917.

AT 9.   Dove, Karl. Ostafrika. Leipzig, 1912.

AT 10. -- Vom Kap zum Nil; Reiseerinnerungen aus Süd-Ost und Nordafrika. Berlin, 1898.

        A description of a journey by the author, from Cape Town to Alexandria via Natal, German East Africa, Zanzibar, the Nile Valley, and Cairo.

AT 11. East African Explorers. Ed. by Charles G. Richards. London, 1960.

AT 12. Fabri, Friedrich. Der Deutsch-englische Vertrag; Rede, auf der am 1. Juli 1890 zu Köln veranstalteten Volks-Versammlung mit Wissmann-Feier. Cologne, 1890.

AT 13. Förster, Brix. Deutsch-Ostafrika; Geographie und Geschichte der Kolonie. Leipzig, 1890.

        Detailed description of flora, fauna, and native tribes.

AT 14. Fouck, H. Deutsch-Ostafrika. Berlin, 1909.

AT 15. Fronck, Heinrich. Deutsch-Ostafrika; eine Schilderung deutscher Tropen nach 10 Wanderjahren. 5 v. Berlin, 1910.

        Covers the colonial army, history, explorations, geography, natives, hunting and economics.

AT 16. Götzen, Gustav A. von. Deutsch-Ostafrika im Aufstand 1905/1906. Berlin, 1909.

        The author was a former governor of East Africa.

AT 17. Gurlitt, Friedrich. Die Ersten Baujahre in Deutsch-Ostafrika. Berlin, 1905.

AT 18. Handbook of German East Africa. London, 1920.

AT 19. Handbook of Tanganyika. Ed. by J.P. Moffett. Dar-es-Salaam, 1958.

        Contains an account of the period of German rule.

AT 20. Heuglin, Theodor von. Die Deutsche Expedition in Ost-Afrika 1861 und 1862. Gotha, 1864.

AT 21. Hofmeister, Rudolf. Kulturbilder aus Deutsch-Ost Afrika. Bamberg, 1895.

AT 22. Jaeger, Fritz. Das Hochland der Eiesenkrater und die umliegenden Hochlander Deutsch-Ostafrikas. Berlin, 1911.

AT 23. Jantzen, Günther. Ostafrika in der deutsch-englischen Politik 1884-1890. Hamburg, 1934.

AT 24. Jungblut, Carl. Vierzig Jahre Afrika, 1900-1940. Frie-
denau, 1941.

A settler's account of his experiences.

AT 25. Keller, Konrad. Reisebilder aus Ostafrika und Madagaskar.
Leipzig, 1887.

AT 26. Kollman, P. The Victoria Nyanza. London, 1900. Eng.
trans. of a German work.

AT 27. Kurtze, Bruno. Die Deutsche-ostafrikanische Gesellschaft
ein Beitrag zum Problem der Schutzbriefgesellschaften und
zur Geschichte Deutsch-Ostafrikas. Jena, 1913.

AT 28. -- Die Wirtschaftstätigkeit der Deutsch-Ostafrika-Nischen
Gesellschaft in den Jahren 1887-91 und ihre wichtigsten
Voraussetzungen. Jena, 1913.

AT 29. Leue, A. Dar-es-Salaam. Berlin, 1903.

AT 30. Monte, Santa Maria (G. Bourbon del). L'Africa orientale
tedesca. 3 v. Città di Castello, 1918.

AT 31. Meyer, Hans H.J. Ergebnisse einer Reise durch des Zwis-
chenseegebiet, 1911. Berlin, 1913.

AT 32. -- Ostafrikanische Gletscherfahrten; Forschungsreisen im
Kilimandscharo-Gebiet. Leipzig, 1890.

AT 33. -- Der Kilimandjaro. Berlin, 1900.

AT 34. Müller, Fritz. Deutschland-Zanzibar-Ostafrika: Geschichte
einer deutschen Kolonialeroberung, 1884-1890. East Berlin,
1959.

The opening sketch on the origins of colonialism offers
a less rigid schematization of social elements than even
the non-Marxist study by Hallgarten. See also: AP
64. It is kept precariously within the Marxist fold by
the perfunctory use of the concept of unwitting tools of
bourgeois ruling circles; this device permits considerable accuracy of detail and substantive analysis.
Based on documents from the former Kolonialarchiv
now located in Potsdam.

AT 35. Paasche, Hermann. Deutsch-Ostafrika: wirtschaftliche
Studien. 1906.

AT 36. Peters, Karl. Das Deutsch-ostafrikanische Schutzgebiet.
Munich, 1895.

AT 37. -- Die Gründung von Deutsch-Ostafrika. Berlin, 1906.

This work is autobiographical in style and critical of
German attitudes in colonial matters and foreign policy.
Peters spent much time in England, where he had come
to admire the British colonial system, and decided that
Germany needed colonies. After his return to Germany
in 1882, he successfully campaigned for a well-financed
colonizing expedition and himself became one of the
leading figures in the founding of German East Africa.
This book is concerned with the period from the founding up to 1890.

AT 38. Peters, Karl. Wie Deutsch-Ostafrika Entstand. Leipzig,

1912.

AT 39. Wichterich, Richard. Dr. Karl Peters; der Weg eines

Patrioten. Berlin, 1934.

AT 40. Böhme, Hermann. Carl Peters, der Begründer von Deutsch-

ostafrika. Leipzig, 1939.

AT 41. Coerver, Herbert. Carl Peters, ein Kämpfer um deutschen

Raum. Leipzig, 1937.

AT 42. Buchhorn, Josef. Weg in die Welt; ein Schauspiel um den

deutschen Mann Karl Peters. Berlin, 1940.

AT 43. Klampen, Erich zu. Carl Peters; ein deutsches Schicksal

im Kampf im Ostafrika. Berlin, 1939.

AT 44. Pfeil, Joachim von. Die Erwerbung von Deutsch-Ostafrika.

1907.

AT 45. Plumon, Eugéne. La Colonie Allemande de l'Afrique orien-

tale. Dissertation, Univ. of Rennes, 1905.

AT 46. Reche, Otto. Zur Ethnographie des Abflusslosen Gebietes

Deutsch-Ostafrika. Hamburg, 1914.

Based on the findings of the Ostafrika-Expedition der
geographischen Gesellschaft in Hamburg.

AT 47. Redeker, Detrich. Die Geschichte der Tagespresse Deutsch-

Ostafrikas 1899-1916. Berlin, 1937.

AT 48. Richard, Paul. Deutsch-Ostafrika. Leipzig, 1891.

Detailed account of the acquisition of German East
Africa.

AT 49. Richter, Julius. Tanganyika and its Future. London, 1934.

AT 50. Reusch, Richard. History of East Africa. Stuttgart, 1954.

Useful for period prior to 1870.

AT 51. Ried, H.A. Zur Anthropologie des Afbflusslosen Rumpfschollenlandes im NordÖstlichen Deutsch-Ostafrika. Hamburg, 1915.

> Based on the findings of the Ostafrika-Expedition der Geographischen Gesellschaft in Hamburg.

AT 52. Rodemann, William H. Tanganyika, 1890-1914; Selected Aspects of German Administration. Doctoral dissertation, Univ. of Chicago, 1961. Avail. on microfilm.

AT 53. Rornau, Friedrich. Die Goldvorkommen Deutsch-Ostafrikas, insbesondere Beschreibung der neu Entdeckten Goldgänge in der Umgegend von Ikoma. Heidelberg, 1905.

AT 54. Rousse, A. Zwanzig Jahre Ansieder in Deutsch Ost-Afrika. 1929.

AT 55. Samessa, Paul. Die Besiedlung Deutsch-Ostafrikas. Berlin, 1909.

AT 56. Schmidt, Rochus. Geschichte des Araberaufstandes in Ostafrika. Frankfurt, 1892.

AT 57. -- Aus Kolonialer Frühzeit. Berlin, 1922.

> An account of the author's activities in German East Africa between 1885-1891; he was intimately acquainted with Stanley and Emin Pasha (Dr. Eduard Schnitzer).

AT 58. -- Kolonialpioniere; persönliche Erinnerungen aus kolonialer Frühzeit. Berlin, 1938.

AT 59. Siebenlist, Th. Fortswirtsschaft in Deutsch-Ostafrika. Berlin, 1914.

AT 60. Spring, Kapitän. Selbsterlebtes in Ostafrika. Dresden, 1896.

AT 61. Stuhlmann, Franz. Die Wirtschaftliche Entwicklung Deutsch-Ostafrikas. Berlin, 1898.

> Written by a former colonial administrator. Gives names of planters, maps of plantations.

AT 62. -- Wissenschaftliche Forschungsresultate über Land und Leute unseres ostafrikanischen Schutzgebiets und der angrenzender Länder. Berlin, 1909.

AT 63. Thomsen, Hermann. Deutsches Land in Afrika. Munich, 1911.

AT 64. Wagner, J. Deutsch Ostafrika; Geschichte der Gesellschaft für deutsche Kolonisation und die deutsche Ostafrikanische

Gesellschaft. 1886.

AT 65. Weishaupt, Martin. Ostafrikanische Wandertage; durch des Gebiet der Leipziger Mission in Deutsch-Ostafrika. Leipzig, 1913.

AT 66. Werth, Emil. Das Deutsch-ostafrikanische Küstenland und die Vorgelagerten Inseln. 2 v. Berlin, 1915.

Description of flora, fauna, natives, many maps.

AT 67. Werther, C. Waldeman. Die Mittleren Hochländer des nördlichen Deutsch-Ost-Afrika. Berlin, 1898.

An account of an expedition which took place in 1896-1897.

AT 68. "Die wirtschaftliche Entwicklung Deutsch-Ostafrika, 1885-1935," Jahresbericht der Klosterschule Rossleben. (1906): 3-28.

AT 69. Austen, Ralph A. Northwest Tanzania Under German and British Rule; Colonial Policy and Tribal Politics 1889-1939. New Haven, 1968.

Offers fresh insights into German administration and provides an understanding of the impact of the colonial administration on the native peoples of East Africa.

AT 70. Schröter, Hermann. "Essen und die Kolonialfrage, Gründung und Geschichte der Sigipflanzung in Deutsch-Ostafrika," Tradition (Oct. 1967).

AT 71. Iliffe, John. Tanganyika under German Rule 1905-1912. Cambridge, 1969.

AU. COLONIAL--TOGOLAND

AU 1. Calvert, Albert F. Togoland. London, 1918.

AU 2. Full, August. Fünfzig Jahre Togo. Berlin, 1935.

The author was a colonial official.

AU 3. Gärtner, Karl. "Togo"; finanztechnische Studie über die Entwicklung Schutzgebietes unter deutscher Verwaltung. Darmstadt, 1924.

AU 4. Gehrts, M. A Camera Actress in the Wilds of Togoland. London, 1914.

AU 5.   Hutter, F.   Wanderungen und Forschungen im Nord-Hinter-
        land von Kamerun.   Braunschweig, 1902.

AU 6.   Metzger, O.F.   Die Forstwirtschaft im Schutzgebiet Togo.
        Jena, 1911.

AU 7.   Och, Helmut.   Die wirtschaftsgeographie Entwicklung der
        früheren deutschen Schutzgebiete Togo und Kamerun.
        Königsberg, 1931.

AU 8.   Passarge, Siegfried.   Togo.   Berlin, 1910.

AU 9.   Schlunk, Martin.   Die Norddeutsche Mission in Togo.   2 v.
        Bremen, 1910-1912.

AU 10. Togo; die Geschichte einen afrikanischen Staater von der
        Vergangenheit bis zur Gegenwart.   Bühl-Baden, 1961.

AU 11. Trierenburg, G.   Togo.   Berlin, 1914.

AU 12. Zöller, Hugo.   Das Togoland und die Sklavenküste.   Berlin,
        1885.

AV.   COLONIAL--CAMEROONS

AV 1.   Amtsblatt für das Schutzgebiet Kamerun.   1908 ff.
        The official decrees and legislation were published in
        this work, by the Cameroons administration.

AV 2.   Autenrieth, F.   Ins Inner-Hochland von Kamerun.   Stutt-
        gart, 1909.

AV 3.   Buchner, Max.   Kamerun.   Leipzig, 1887.

AV 4.   --   Aurora Colonialis; Bruchstücke eines Tagebuchs aus
        dem ersten Beginn unwerer Kolonialpolitik, 1884-1885.
        Munich, 1914.

AV 5.   Calvert, Albert F.   The Cameroons.   London, 1917.

AV 6.   Danckelmann, Alexander S.F.E. von.   Das Kamerungsbkom-
        men vom 4 November 1911 im Reichstag und in der Budget-
        kommission.   Berlin, 1912.
        The debate in the Reichstag on the Cameroons Treaty.

AV 7.   Detzner, Hermann.   Im Lande des Dju-Dju; Reiseerlebnisse
        im östlichen Stromgebiet des Niger.   Berlin, 1923.
        A participant's account of a 1912 expedition to northern

Cameroons.

AV 8. Dominik, Hans. Kamerun: Sechs Kriegs- und Friedens-
jahre in den deutschen Tropen. Berlin, 1901.

AV 9. Dove, Karl. Die Deutschen Kolonien: Togo und Kamerun.
Leipzig, 1909.

AV 10. Escherich, Georg. Quer durch den Urwald von Kamerun.
Berlin, 1923.

An account of the expedition which the author led to
explore the Cameroons in 1912.

AV 11. -- Kamerun. Berlin, 1938.

AV 12. Der Handel in Südkamerun in den Jahren 1908 bis 1911.
Berlin, 1912.

AV 13. Hutter, Franz K. Wanderungen und Forschungen im Nord-
hinterland von Kamerun. Braunschweig, 1902.

Account of the 1891-1893 expedition.

AV 14. Kamerun als Ein- und Ausfuhrmarkt 1910, 1911, 1912.
Berlin, 1910-12.

AV 15. Külz, Ludwig. Blätter und Briefe eines Artes aus dem
tropischen deutschafrika. Berlin, 1906.

AV 16. Lenz, Oskar. Skizzen aus Westafrika; Selbsterlebnisse.
Berlin, 1878.

AV 17. Lux, Anton E. Von Loanda nach Kimbudu; Ergebnisse der
Forschungsreise in Äquatorialen West-Afrika, 1875-1876.
Vienna, 1880.

AV 18. Mansfeld, Alfred. Urwald-Dokumente. Vier Jahre unter
den Crossflussnegern Kameruns. Berlin, 1908.

AV 19. Morgen, Curt. Durch Kamerun von Süd nach Nord. Leipzig, 1893.

AV 20. Och, Helmut W.A. Die Wirtschaftsgeographische Entwicklung der früheren deutschen Schutzgebiete Togo und Kamerun.
Königsberg, 1931.

AV 21. Passarge, Siegfried. Adamaua; Bericht über die Expedition
des deutschen Kamerun-Komitees in den Jahren 1893/94.
Berlin, 1895.

The author was the leader of the expedition.

AV 22. Puttkamer, Jeske von. Gouverneusjahre in Kamerun. Berlin, 1912.

Puttkamer was governor from 1895-1906.

AV 23. René, C. Kamerun und die deutsche Tsadsee Eisenbahn.
Berlin, 1912.

AV 24. Kamerun unter deutscher Kolonialherrschaft; Studien. Ed.
by Helmuth Stoecker. East Berlin, 1960.

> Describes the character of the colonial policies and ad-
> ministration of the colony. Makes use of unpublished
> material from private sources in addition to material
> from the colonial archives. Several documents are
> published. An appendix lists the colonial secretaries
> and the governors of Cameroons. Excellent map.

AV 25. Riebe, Otto. Drei Jahre unter deutscher Flagge im Hinterland von Kamerun. Berlin, 1897.

> The diary of Carl Hörhold, an explorer in the Came-
> roons 1888-1891.

AV 26. Ritter, Karl. Neu-Kamerun; das von Frankreich an Deutschland im Abkommen vom 4 November 1911 abgetretene Gebiet.
Jena, 1912.

> Account of flora, fauna, resources, natives, etc.

AV 27. Roskoschny, Hermann. West-Afrika vom Segegal zum
Kamerun. Leipzig, 1890.

> Mainly illustrations.

AV 28. Rudin, Harry R. Germans in the Cameroons 1884-1914; a
Case Study in Modern Imperialism. New Haven, 1938.

> The most comprehensive treatment in English on Ger-
> man policy in the Cameroons. The sub-title is indica-
> tive of the author's conclusions, however, they are
> moderated by the fact that the Germans were only fol-
> lowing accepted colonial practices of the period. It
> gives a good picture of German colonial practices and
> procedures, economic exploitation, native administra-
> tion, and public control. It has a good bibliography.

AV 29. Ruppel, Julius. Die Landesgesetzgebung für das Schutzgebiet Kamerun. 1912.

> A selection of the colonial legislation and ordinances
> for the Cameroons.

AV 30. Seidel, August. Deutsch-Kamerun; wie es ist und was es
verspricht; Historisch, Geographisch, Politisch, Wirtschaft-
lich Dargestellt. Berlin, 1906.

AV 31. Seitz, Theodor. Vom Aufstieg und Niederbruch deutscher Kolonialmacht. Karlsruhe, 1929.

Volume 2 deals with the author's years as governor of the Cameroons.

AV 32. Sembritzki, Emil. Kamerun. Berlin, 1908.

AV 33. Steiner, P. Kamerun als Kolonie und Missionsfeld. Basel, 1909.

AV 34. Togoland und Biafra-Bai. No. 41, Anlagen zu den Reichstagverhandlungen, 1884-85.

The official German account of the occupation of the Cameroons. A convenient reprint of this may be found in Das Staatsarchiv, XLIII, Leipzig, 1884, documents 8269-8282, p. 224-274. On the conversations at Berlin between Meade, Bismarck, and Busch, see: Das Staatsarchiv, XLIV, Leipzig, 1885, documents 8510-8552, p. 289-312.

AV 35. Westafrikanische Kautschuk-Expedition (R. Schlechter), 1899/1900. Berlin, 1900. Illus., maps.

AV 36. Zimmermann, Emil. Neu-Kamerun; Reiseerlebnisse und wirtschaftspolitische Untersuchungen. Berlin, 1913.

AV 37. Zimmermann, Oskar. Durch Busch und Steppe vom Campo bis zum Schari, 1892-1902; ein Beitrag zur Geschichte der Schutztruppe von Kamerun. Berlin, 1909.

The author was an official in the colonial army.

AV 38. Zintgraf, Eugen. Nord-Kamerun. Berlin, 1895.

AV 39. Zöller, Hugo. Forschungsreisen in der deutschen Colonie Kamerun. 3 v. Berlin, 1885-86.